Joachim Knape
Modern Rhetoric in Culture, Arts, and Media

Joachim Knape

Modern Rhetoric in Culture, Arts, and Media

—

13 Essays

DE GRUYTER

Translated by Alan L. Fortuna

ISBN 978-3-11-029245-9
e-ISBN 978-3-11-026250-3

Library of Congress Cataloging-in-Publication Data
A CIP catalog record for this book has been applied for at the Library of Congress.

Bibliographic information published by the Deutsche Nationalbibliothek
The Deutsche Nationalbibliothek lists this publication in the Deutsche Nationalbibliografie; detailed bibliographic data are available in the Internet at http://dnb.dnb.de.

© 2013 Walter de Gruyter GmbH, Berlin/Boston
Typesetting: Meta Systems GmbH, Wustermark
Printing: Hubert & Co. GmbH & Co. KG, Göttingen
♾ Printed on acid-free paper
Printed in Germany

www.degruyter.com

MIX
Papier aus verantwortungsvollen Quellen
FSC
www.fsc.org   FSC® C016439

Contents

Modern Rhetoric. An Introduction

In most European countries, the study of rhetoric as a formal subject disappeared from university curricula in the 18th and 19th centuries, replaced by the various branches of philology and other disciplines in the humanities. After this period, the analysis of language and literature became the focus of academic interest. The study of strategic communication from a 'production-theoretical' viewpoint, however, was largely displaced; it was not until the 20th century that such study was revived in the academic world. Today, rhetoric as a university subject must be rediscovered by many academics, despite the fact that its practical use has always been present in social discourse in one form or another. Modern democratic societies need rhetoric as a civilized method to affect socio-political decisions. Such decisions deal with questions of power that can only be negotiated openly and peacefully through constant communication. Accordingly, one of my definitions of *rhetoric* is that it is the communicative method by which a change (*metabole*) of opinion in a society or group can be peacefully achieved. To this definition I would add the following paradox: rhetoric is also the method of re-establishing order and connections (*systasis*) once such change has taken place.[1]

The topic of rhetoric in politics has been and continues to be the subject of countless publications by academics from a wide array of disciplines around the world.[2] In general, these works are based on a practical understanding of *rhetoric* that is oriented towards either common prejudices, on the myriad books that deal with practical everyday rhetoric, or on textbooks that deal with ancient rhetorical theory.[3] There is also a wide array of literary studies that sail under the flag of rhetoric. By contrast, there have been a dearth of studies that attempt to develop a modern and genuine theory of rhetoric and that take the idea of rhetoric as an independent scientific paradigm seriously, while fulfilling contemporary theoretical demands. The fact is that in the 20th century, only a very few thinkers devoted themselves to the question of a modern theory of rhetoric; Kenneth D. Burke (Berkley, USA) and Chaïm Perelman (Brussels, Belgium) represent two original and independent exceptions to this trend. The attempts of some German philosophers (Martin Heidegger,[4] Hans Georg Gadamer, Hans Blumenberg) have been unable to newly contour the theoretical understanding of the specifics of an independent discipline of rhetoric.

---

1 Knape 2000a, p. 34.
2 For a selection of titles on this subject see: Jasinski 2008 and Bergsdorf 2009.
3 The references to specific textbooks can be found in Chapter 2 of this book.
4 Knape/Schirren 2005b.

Other philosophers, such as Jürgen Habermas, have gone so far as to reject rhetoric altogether.[5] At the same time, American postmodern philosophers such as Richard Rorty, have had an ambiguous relationship with rhetoric (if they have really spoken of rhetoric at all and not some other conception of communication).[6] On the one hand, such philosophers have strengthened the pragmatic approach of modern rhetorical theory. On the other, they have practiced a deconstructive and fundamental criticism of the strategic basis of rhetoric as a whole.

The following book seeks to solve some of these discrepancies. It will discuss questions related to the fundamental anthropological, communicative and cultural foundations of a terminologically consistent understanding of rhetoric. At the same time, a series of case studies will be used to illustrate the presence of rhetoric in culture,[7] and to show its meaning and function in each individual case.

A theory of rhetoric is first and foremost a theory of communication. But because communication touches on every aspect of culture, rhetoric is also part of a social and cultural theory. Still, we must be careful: rhetorical theory does not claim to be a general or overarching theory of communication. It is instead very specialized. A scientific theory of rhetoric concentrates on specific questions and problems of communication involved in the persuasive action of humans, and focuses exclusively on these issues. Thus, another of my definitions of rhetoric can be formulated as follows:

> In practice, rhetoric is the mastery of success-oriented, strategic processes of communication. Rhetoric is the communicative possibility for man to assert the social validity of an issue that is important to him (his oratorical telos) and, in doing so, to free himself, at least in the moment of communicative success, from social determination. Rhetoric has, from the beginning, always been about the emergence of man from social voicelessness, and the rhetorical imperative is: perorare aude! Have the courage to use your expressive capabilities![8]

The disciplinary perspective of rhetorical study is thus quite specific, and it is discrete from other (social) areas of study. For this reason, Chapter 1 of this book deals with the seven main fallacies found in intercultural rhetorical research. Intercultural contrastive rhetoric is itself a new academic branch that seeks to apply the systematic rhetorical approach originally developed in Europe to other

---

5 Habermas 1981.
6 For more on Rorty's theoretical role in rhetoric see: Knape 2000a, pp. 43 ff.; and Knape 2007c, pp. 44–47.
7 Greene 2008.
8 Knape 2000a, p. 33.

non-European and non-American contexts.[9] The area of fundamental rhetoric provides the necessary analytical approach for such research, because it defines when a rhetorical case (that is, an instance of persuasion) occurs. Only then can such instances be interculturally analyzed with a rhetorical focus.

Another systematic area of rhetoric is the organon doctrine, which deals with the means (instruments) that an orator (a rhetorically acting person or institution) can utilize in cases of rhetorical communication. With respect to these rhetorical means and ways, studies in intercultural contrastive rhetoric have demonstrated that clear differentiations exist: *true rhetoric* only occurs when socially acceptable means and methods are used, and varying cultures around the world have different standards about what constitutes acceptable and appropriate means of persuasion.

Discussions within contrastive rhetoric begin with the question of whether the conception of rhetoric that originated in Greco-Roman antiquity (and continues to form the foundation of Western rhetoric) is appropriate and meaningful for analyses of other cultures such as those in Asia and Africa. The answer is yes: if rhetoric is systematically conceived and theoretically rigorous (as all other modern synchronic sciences), then its application is appropriate in such situations regardless of its historical origins.

This discussion leads us to a completely different question: to what extent are purely historical studies on the development of rhetoric (especially those that deal with antiquity) still useful today? Chapter 2 deals with exactly this issue. In it, I draw the conclusion that diachronic or historical research on rhetoric continues to be useful because ancient theories of rhetoric long ago gained insights into human communication that remain valid today. At the same time, the practical history of rhetoric provides us with a valuable collection of empirical cases that can be systematically and structurally evaluated in order to learn more about the communicative behavior of humans in certain social formations (for instance when in small groups, in the political sphere, or in the courtroom). Regardless of the number and type of laboratory studies it may run, synchronic rhetorical science could never hope to replicate the amount of knowledge contained in human history. In this way, historical research on rhetoric is just as valuable as intercultural contrastive rhetoric: both fields of research provide us with systematically useable knowledge about the social and psychological history of persuasion. And persuasion is the core of rhetorical theory.[10]

This disciplinary focus on persuasion was established in Greek and Roman antiquity, and our modern thinking follows their lead. Knowledge of human

---

9 Meyer 2009 and Hinkel 2009.
10 Knape 2003a; Price Dillard/Miraldi 2008; Seiter/Gass 2008; Hosman 2008.

communication and interaction was already highly developed in these societies, in some respects even more so than today. Thus, it makes sense to incorporate ancient rhetorical knowledge into our modern conception of rhetoric; it already proved itself useful and practical in antiquity and is thus in no way speculative. As a discipline, rhetoric has had the good fortune to have been studied by some of the greatest and most perceptive ancient philosophers (Plato, Aristotle, Cicero, etc.),[11] all of whom dealt with rhetorical communication. Later, and especially since the Renaissance, other great minds have interested themselves in questions of rhetoric. Such historical knowledge provides important interfaces for a modern theory of rhetoric. Still, it is important to rethink and restate ancient insight so that it can be integrated into modern approaches (such as in the field of media theory, as we will see in Chapter 13).

A summary of this ancient knowledge about rhetoric, the *Institutio oratoria*, was written by Quintilian around 100 years after the birth of Christ. Quintilian concentrated the theoretical focus of rhetoric on three aspects of communication, which were defined in his second book as: 1. *ars*: the theory, 2. *artifex*: the orator as producer of orations, as an actor and specialized practical communicator, 3. *opus*: the rhetorical instrument of communication in the form of a manufactured text.[12] In the following I will discuss these three fundamental categories, and begin with the rhetorical actor, the Archimedean point of rhetoric.

Orator

Because the theoretical system of rhetoric is based on the connection between actor, text, and communicative setting, the theory of rhetoric explicitly retains the abstract category of the *historical author*, even though some representatives of modern literary theory believe it no longer necessary to address the concept of the author at all. According to Quintilian, the *artifex* is a "specialist", the expert of rhetorical communication who has knowledge of the tenets of the *ars* (rhetorical theory) and whose communicative actions are guided by this theory. The other important Roman rhetorical theoretician, Cicero, focused his theories almost exclusively on this aspect of communication; the modern titles of his works reveal the central importance of the role of the actor: '*De oratore*', '*Orator*', '*Brutus*', etc. Still, like all other important systematic components of rhetorical theory, the concept of the orator opens an anthropological perspec-

---

11 Cf. Knape 2000b; Knape/Schirren 2005a.
12 Quintilian: Institutio oratoria, 2.14.5; 12.10.1.

tive,[13] and is based on high level abstractions. Within the framework of rhetorical theory, then, we can say that the orator, "is to be understood as an abstract entity, as a theoretical construct that is analytically derived from the study of myriad discourses and can be observed from different perspectives: as a cognitive calculation, as a social role of action, or as a factor of communication and text constructing entity."[14]

For general analyses of communication, all parts of the communicative event are important. The field of rhetoric, however, focuses solely on problems involved with the rhetorically active part. In this sense the central perspective of rhetoric is the strategically communicating orator, often referred to as the "Sender" on the left side of the classic linear model of communication. The channel (including medium and text) in the middle and the addressees on the right side constitute its other two components. These three theoretical units trace their roots to, among others, Karl Bühler's 1934 book 'Sprachtheorie', and were brought together in Shannon and Weaver's 1949 book 'The Mathematical Theory of Communication' to form today's well known model.[15]

The main question of rhetoric is not how communication functions in general, nor how the three units or entities of the above model interact with each other. These are questions for communications studies and linguistics, whose findings are only relevant to us through the lens of rhetoric's unique perspective. Rhetoric as a specialized theory of communication has only one main concern from which everything else is derived: How can the 'sender', which we name the 'orator', strategically and effectively communicate to meet life-world goals?[16] This fixed perspective gives all other theoretical considerations about communication a focused direction. We see communication *sub specie oratoris*, that is to say: completely from the perspective of the orator. Thus, in the model of communication mentioned above, we focus above all on the left side of the equation: on the sender and his communicative tools, the "medium" and the "text".

The entire field of investigation described above is called *extrinsic rhetoric*. It is a rhetoric that looks outward, whose focus moves from the orator to the external world.[17] From the perspective of extrinsic rhetoric, the classical definition of rhetoric as an *ars persuadendi*, an "art of persuasion" is appropriate. The orator wants to persuade others, and does so in an interactive social envi-

---

13 Oesterreich 2008.
14 Knape 2000a, p. 33.
15 Bühler 1934; Shannon/Weaver 1949.
16 For the term "life-world" see: Husserl 1954, §§ 33–34; Knape 2000a, p. 40.
17 What is here called extrinsic and intrinsic rhetoric George Kennedy calls "primary" and "secondary rhetoric". See: Kennedy 1999, pp. 2 ff.

ronment. The actors, their actions, the sphere of activity, and the prerequisites for such actions are of primary interest here. We call this the external 'communicative universe', the universe of discourse within which the orator operates. The addressees, his audience, are also a part of the external factors of the communicative context.

Concerning the orator in general, there are two questions of importance: 1. the teleological question and 2. the question of roles.

The teleological question: A person is considered an orator when he/she has a *goal* (a *telos*), which he believes to be justified and which he seeks to achieve through communication. At the theoretical level, the most important problems here are social and are connected to human intentions and human manipulation. Behind these concerns is always a question of power relations. Above all, questions surrounding the limits of communicative goals are important: what is an ethically acceptable goal? Which goals are politically or legally tolerated? Are there definable limits to rhetorical goals? To this we can add questions regarding the overall method of communication. The starting point for all discussions of this topic (the social acceptance of rhetorical action) must be Immanuel Kant's *political categorical imperative*, described in his, 'To Perpetual Peace'. I quote: "All actions relating to the right of other human beings are wrong if their maxim is incompatible with publicity."[18] This publicity postulate is important in order for rhetoric to be seen as fundamentally different from manipulation. Those who "manipulate", we can say, have secret goals, do not act openly, and communicate using tricks. Such communicative action must be excluded from real rhetoric, which is by definition always tied to socially acceptable means.

The question of roles: The *role* of the orator is also an important topic of study for rhetoric. How are we to evaluate the social role of a strategic communicator? In this sense, rhetorical theory seeks to further develop a general theory of communicative action.

There are a series of questions related to this domain: How does a society shape the roles of orators? Is the orator function bound to specific professions (pastor, teacher, government spokesperson)? How does one take on the role of an orator? Is everyone, everywhere, allowed to assume this role (and thereby to attempt to achieve their goals through communication)? How is competition among orators organized and regulated within society?

In a dictatorship, all speech is seen as potentially dangerous, and access to the role of the orator is strictly controlled. Throughout history, gender specific

---

18 Kant 1795, appendix 2, p. 37. See also: Knape 2000a, p. 80.

restrictions have kept women from gaining access to the orator role as well. In modern democracies, on the other hand, the fundamental human right of freedom of expression demands the guaranteed access to the orator role for all individuals. In practice, however, there continue to be restrictions regarding such access. An important example of this is the system of mass media (with the exception of the web): not just anyone is allowed to write for the press, appear on television, or broadcast their opinions on the radio. Especially in these later cases, the view of an orator as a singular individual must be extended to the consideration of higher, more complex rhetorical institutions. This begs the question: Who assumes the role of the strategic communicator (orator) in those communicative systems where individual roles are limited and defined? In such cases, is each individual merely an operational part of the larger system?

Chapter 3 focuses on the role and theoretical model of the *orator*[19]. The starting point of this discussion is the rhetorical category of *ethos* from Aristotle's 'The Art of Rhetoric'. For Aristotle, the self-fashioning of the orator, his publicly presented self (*ethos*), constituted an important element of rhetorical success. The orator must demonstrate knowledge about his subject, integrity or credibility, and empathy with his listeners. Chapter 3 combines this ancient doctrine with the modern academic categories of *image, prestige*, and *reputation*. These forms of self-portrayal are implemented either in punctual settings or through long term communicative processes.

These questions and considerations of a theory of orators lead us to another important focus of modern rhetoric: the theory of *rhetorical resistance*. From the perspective of the orator, communication that mirrors a modified stimulus-response model of classical behaviorism would be the best and most effective solution for achieving life-world goals. According to this model, I would undertake some specific communicative act that would immediately create the desired effect in my audience. Naturally, this orator's dream has little to do with reality. In truth, orators face many types of resistance that continually obstruct successful communication. Every element that an orator deals with in the communicative realm can become an obstacle that stands in the way of his success; a theory of rhetoric must address the issue of how an orator is to deal with such resistance.

There are two primary sources of such resistance: circumstantial resistance (that which arises from changing contextual situations) and structural resistance (that which arises from unchangeable structures of communication).[20] The rhetorical analysis of communicative resistance must use empirical

---

19 Cf. Knape 2000a, pp. 33–45; Klotz 2008.
20 Cf. Knape 2000a.

methods to examine the conditions under which strategic communication is successful or unsuccessful.[21] Such analysis leads to the determination of specific points that must be overcome for an orator to be successful. In the following, I will name a few obstacles whose influence on communication should be further explored, and whose existence raises a range of open questions for rhetorical investigation.

1. *Situative* resistance: The conditions of a concrete face to face communicative situation can at times be problematic. When giving a lecture, I may find myself speaking to a hostile audience, which might distract me from my communicative purpose. Or the time of day might be inappropriate for my topic, or the room in which I am speaking might not be suitable for my audience or my needs. Each of these factors of resistance are directly tied to the situation that I find myself communicating in.

2. *Medial* resistance: In *dimissive* communication (communication that is transmitted over distances) a speaker needs a technical medium to carry his text to his audience. Each medium, however, has a certain amount of structural determination. The traditional telephone, for instance, can only send acoustic types of text (no optical signals) to listeners, while the newspaper can only send optical types of text (no auditory signals), and the television can't broadcast smells. Thus, every change in medium involves the loss of information, and a speaker must take such factors into account. More will be said about medial resistance and the overall concept of medium in Chapter 12.

3. *Textual* resistance: When constructing a text, I must formulate my text according to a general model of my chosen text genre and fulfill other expectations of conventional form in order to successfully communicate. Only by fulfilling such expectations will my audience accept my text as a legitimate form of communication. This can, however, become an obstacle when I attempt to formulate my thoughts into an appropriate text. In some respects, the analysis of textual resistance in antiquity had positive and productive side effects: it led to the development of a myriad of linguistic structures and forms that were held to be particularly effective. These were classified, named and catalogued as the so called *rhetorical figures*.

4. *Linguistic* resistance: No speaker has a complete command over the language in which he communicates in. As soon as I utter a word in a language that I have not myself created, I am subjugated to the rules and structures of that language. We (as speakers) must use languages as we find them, and must accept their rules and structures if we are to be under-

---

21 See also: Knape/Becker/Böhme 2009.

stood by others. Nonetheless, there are many things that I feel and think which I would like to express in ways that the conventions of my language do not allow. How do I overcome this resistance? How can I individually express my conceptions and ideas and still successfully meet my communicative goals?

5. *Cognitive* resistance: The theory of *radical constructivism* teaches us to conceive of each person as a closed cognitive system, and that in reality, the exchange of information between us is extremely difficult, if not impossible. Over the last decade, this radical constructivism has been modified, and rhetorical theory demands that the opinions of others can, indeed, be influenced. Still, penetrating the closed cognitive system of another person is a formidable obstacle to successful communication. How can I achieve my desired effect on my audience's mental state? To overcome this point of resistance, an orator must have a *projective calculation* in relation to his audience: he must imagine himself in the psyche of his addressees and formulate a rhetorical strategy tailored to the expectations and needs of his audience members. Such calculations are always imprecise and can be risky for the speaker. Above all, such considerations must focus on the communicative instruments that are most appropriate and effective at influencing a given audience.[22]

Theory

According to Quintilian, the Latin term *ars*, like the Greek *téchnē*, refers to that which can be taught as a well-defined area of study (*disciplina*) to others. One could say that an *ars* is the theory of a subject in relation to its practical domain. As early as antiquity, the development of a theory involved collecting and abstracting the knowledge available about the given practical field. What does this method mean for us today? In other words, what is a theory in the humanities today? What is a theory of rhetoric? What kinds of characteristics must an acceptable theory have?[23]

A theory concentrates on a specific subject area, defines it or one of its parts, and establishes its position as a part of an overarching system of knowledge. A theory collects various propositions about this subject area and develops a field specific terminology. A theory systematizes and orders the various phenomena that fall within the area of the subject, determines regularities,

---

22 Cf. Knape 2000a.
23 See here: Knape 2000b, pp. 9–22.

and develops structural models of the subject area. Finally, a theory also provides explanations for these phenomena and regularities, and can predict the appearance of certain phenomena within the subject field (prognostic function). This last feature points to the need for the general components of theories in the humanities and social sciences to be consistently modified to match concrete circumstances. The overall efficacy of a prognosis varies from subject to subject. In some fields of the humanities, for instance, that which we normally call a *prognosis* must be limited to the analysis of repetitive structures found in specific contexts. Even when the theory of rhetoric is able to recommend specific communicative instruments for specific settings, such a recommendation cannot lead to a mechanical prediction of success or simple stimulus-response expectations. Between the rhetorical stimulus and the calculated effect lies a wide array of environmental factors, among which the most important variable is the autonomous, text-analytical, cognitive 'system' of the addressee. Still, rhetoric has the courage to recommend optimal communicative strategies and specifically calibrated means to be used in a given setting.

Modern rhetoric derives a theory of production from the field of real world rhetorical communication. This production-theoretical approach differentiates rhetoric from philology, which is satisfied with purely analytical textual analysis. By contrast, rhetoric is ultimately concerned with gaining understanding for use in future communicative action. This practical relevance has been a constitutive part of rhetoric since antiquity.

Chapters 1, 2 and 3 of this book deal with modern theoretical perspectives on the discipline of *general rhetoric* and its interculturality and historicity. In these chapters, theoretical questions are discussed alongside questions of methodology, for instance: how should meaningful historical or intercultural contrastive studies be constructed? Chapter 4 also deals with such considerations, but the literary form of the chapter itself is unusual. It is written in the manner of a fictional Renaissance dialog, in which both living and deceased scholars discuss the question of the difference between linguistic and rhetorical research, and detail which methodological approaches are valid in each field of study. The goal of the chapter is to clarify that while linguistics and rhetoric are associated with one another, each has its own unique areas of interest, theoretical approaches, and methodological perspectives.

Dialog

Still, we must be clear about the fact that the entirety of ancient rhetorical theory depended on two specific practical prerequisites. On the one hand, it depended on the basic setting of *situativity* (face to face communication). Modern rhetoric must expand this conception to incorporate the second basic setting of *dimissivity* (communication over a distance of space and time, for instance with the help of the printing press or the modern internet). On the other hand, ancient rhetoric focused exclusively on the communicative mode of the monologue; we can go so far as to say that classical rhetoric is the rhetoric of monologous speech (unidirectional, unilateral, and non-interactive).

A theory of conversation was left to the philosophers. To this day there is no developed or theoretically well founded modern theory of the rhetoric of conversations. Following the systematic demands of the rhetorical approach, such a theory would have to focus on the persuasive concern of a conversational participant as an orator.

Chapter 5 addresses this problem directly. It discusses the basic principles of a rhetoric of conversation and, in doing so, concentrates methodologically on the perspective of a strategically oriented and persuasively motivated conversational participant. This participant must deal with the complex situational conditions of conversation, including the potential loss of oratorical control and the interaction with other, competing orators. Thus, dialogic settings give rise to a special set of problems regarding the theory of the orator. The rhetorical calculation of intervention can only succeed when an orator overcomes seven different management tasks in a given conversation as discussed in Chapter 5.

Verbal Text

Quintilian's previously mentioned definition of *ars* recalls the classical division between the categories of *natura* and *ars*. *Natura* refers to the natural characteristics of man, which are inherent and remain unchangeable. These characteristics are the purview of the natural sciences, not of theoretical rhetoric. Rhetorical abstraction addresses only those aspects of human communication which can be technically implemented, can be learned through study, and which can be consciously incorporated into practical situations. In this vein, rhetoric deals exclusively with planned, conscious acts of communication. Uncontrollable contextual conditions are integrated into the rhetorical theory of communicative resistance. Modern scientific rhetoric must focus on successful communication: how an orator can effectively and systematically construct the instruments of communication (e.g. texts), and how these can be used to successfully meet communicative goals. In short: a theory of rhetoric systematizes the knowledge needed to use communicative 'instruments' to successfully meet practical goals. This leads us to a discussion of rhetorical *organon*-doctrine, which represents a systematization of the instruments of rhetorical communication.

That which we here have called a 'communicative instrument' is associated with Quintilian's third main category of rhetoric, the *opus*. The *opus* is an orator's output or product. To quote Quintilian, "the work (*opus*) is that which is created by the rhetorical specialist (*artifex*), a good piece of prose (*bona oratio*)."[24] Thus, an orator should create a "good text", a *bona oratio*. But what is good in this sense? Within the context of this quote, it is clear that a text is good when it has been constructed under the aegis of rhetorical theory. The second common definition of rhetoric in antiquity corresponded to this conception: rhetoric as *ars bene dicendi,* "the art of good speech". Good speech in this context is again that which has been formulated and conceived according to the rules and insights of the elocutionary doctrine, which demands that the text be appropriately constructed (*aptum*) and 'well-formed'.

The study of the rules and principles of text formulation belongs to the field of *intrinsic rhetoric*. Intrinsic rhetoric turns its gaze inward, exploring (in short) the communicative instruments available to an orator.[25] Historically speaking, intrinsic rhetoric has been the main focus of academic interest, and the field of rhetoric has continually been reduced to questions related to the intrinsic nature of communication in modern times as well. Over time, rhetoric has come to be seen more and more as purely a theory of text formulation (*elocutio*) combined with a set of stylistic devices and instructions for the construction of phrases (*compositio*).

This trend has led to a well-known stereotype: that rhetoric is nothing but empty wordplay. Today, rhetoricians take a nuanced position to this complex of problems. On the one hand, the modern theory of rhetoric takes seriously Aristotle's division between rhetoric and normal speech, found in the third book of the amazingly systematic philosopher's 'The Art of Rhetoric'. According to Aristotle, the entire systematized arsenal of figures (which was already highly developed in his time) associated the pragmatic prose of the orator too much with poetic texts, exemplified by the aesthetically heavily overcoded speeches of the Sophist Gorgias.[26] Accordingly, he insisted that rhetoric distance itself from such ornate forms of expression; the metaphor is the only exception to this rule.

---

24 Quintilian: Institutio oratoria, 2.14.5.
25 Thus we use the Greek term *organon* to describe this part of rhetorical theory; Kennedy 1999 (pp. 3 f.) calls intrinsic rhetoric "secondary rhetoric".
26 For overcoding, see: Eco 1976, pp. 133 ff.; and Nöth 1990, p. 212.

On the other hand (and also following Aristotle's lead), rhetoric has traditionally intensively cultivated the figural doctrines. Over the course of history, rhetoric has collected a well-stocked arsenal of linguistic-aesthetic variations of overcoding under the aegis of *elocutio* (the doctrine of formulation and figures). Still, and this must be clearly stated, these figural structures are only interesting for a modern, more strictly defined theory of rhetoric when they are activated (functionalized) in actual rhetorical cases; that is, when they are integrated into acts of persuasive communication. For centuries, figural rhetoric (which is in reality only a theoretical subcategory) dominated the schools and heavily influenced the understanding of rhetoric. At least since the 18th century, this limited conception has led the discipline of rhetoric into an epistemological abyss. Gérard Genette and Chaïm Perelman have called this pure eloquence rhetoric a, "restrained rhetoric" that leads away from the actual theoretical core of the subject.[27] In other words: for particular historical reasons, rhetoric has developed a linguistic-aesthetic system, which we today (under the conditions of modern academic systematics) understand as an intersection of poetics, aesthetics of language, and modern stylistics. For practical reasons, modern rhetorical research dedicates itself to studying these phenomena under historical, structural, and functional aspects, because these forms of expression can be persuasively activated and functionalized at any given moment. In the interest of theoretically sound positioning, however, modern rhetoric must be able to distinguish the linguistic-aesthetic case (someone has formulated their text well) from the rhetorical case (someone has used this well-formedness to influence others).

The theoretical core of intrinsic rhetoric is based on a model of text production that has existed since antiquity. This model divides the production of texts by an orator into five or six tasks of production (*officia oratoris*). These individual tasks are depicted in the middle column of Figure 1. The first task (generally referred to as the "zero" stage), *intellectio*, refers to the general preliminary considerations of strategy and the selection of communicative means. Then comes the concrete work on the *text*.[28] The result of the two stages after *intellectio* is a complete text. The *cognitive stage* of production focuses on planning and general preliminary considerations of topic selection and the development and the overall structure of the text.

This phase also deals with the considerations related to the use of specific "superstructures"[29] in a text, in short: when do I tell (*narrativity*), when do I

---

27 Genette 1972b, pp. 158 f.; Perelman 1977, p. 11.
28 Rolf 1993, p. 28.
29 For more on the concept of superstructures see: van Dijk 1978, p. 128.

use logical proofs (*argumentivity*), and when do I simply describe (*descriptivity*)? In the *semiotic stage*, the focus shifts to the characteristics of text formulation itself, for example, the incorporation of particular rhetorical figures (metaphors, etc.). Modern rhetorical theory does not assert that these stages are necessarily temporally distinct from one another: they often occur simultaneously and interact with each other during the process of text production.

The doctrine of the stages of production was a core element of the Roman rhetorical tradition, and we find examples of this doctrine in the writings of every important Roman rhetorician. Indeed, the quality, appropriateness and persuasive power of a text that can be developed with this model, as well as the quality of its later performance, are decisive conditions for rhetorical success.

But let us return to more fundamental considerations of rhetorical theory. Taken together, we can call the above mentioned stages of text production *textual rhetoric*. Textual rhetoric concerns itself with one main question: how do the communicative intentions of an orator become text? Relevant theories for this type of analysis include intentionality theory and speech act theory. The more complicated a text is to produce, however, the more difficult it becomes to describe the incorporation of speaker intention into its structure as direct transposition. This problem arises especially regarding artistic texts, which depend on extremely specialized communicative conditions.

This latter point raises the subject of specific frames of communication. Since antiquity, rhetoric has been classified as belonging to the standard (or normal) communicative *frame*. In every instance of communication, the *framework of interaction* and the knowledge of its meaning help establish relevant expectations and shape appropriate judgments for all participants. For the text theoretician Teun A. van Dijk, such *frames* are,

> certain forms of organization for the *conventionally established knowledge* that we possess based on the 'world'. Frames thus form a part of our semantic general memory; [...] Knowledge of the frame is required for the correct interpretation of different events, for the adequate participation in such events, and in general in order to give meaning to our behavior and that of others. For example, 'eating in a restaurant', 'travelling by train', and, 'going shopping' are frames that determine which actions we must take, and in which order and with what degree of necessity we must take them if we want to reach a specific social goal. This shows that these frames represent a form of mental organization – for complex, stereotypical actions and events.[30]

When Aristotle established the need for truth in the first book of his 'Art of Rhetoric', he did not mean that rhetoric had the same goal in the search for

---

30 van Dijk 1978, pp. 169 f.; see also: Genette 1974.

truth that philosophy has. That would go too far. What he meant is that rhetoric, by definition, is subject to the conditions of actuality, and takes place under a mutual assumption that *binding* cooperative acts occur with the help of pragmatically relevant prose texts. Cicero's conception of the orator as an *actor veritatis* is also to be understood within this context: he describes a person that deals with true issues and real matters, who acts with and within the framework of the true and real, i.e. under standard communicative conditions.[31]

Our cultural knowledge instills in us specific expectations in a variety of different settings. The influence of a silent 'contract of factuality' establishes the rules of normal communication, which demand a high degree of reliability and commitment.[32] This requires a framework of understanding in which the four *conversational maxims* defined by the British philosopher of communication Herbert P. Grice are active without restrictions: the maxims of Information (Be informative!), Truth (Be honest, say nothing that you believe to be false!), Relevance (Be relevant!), and Economy of Expression (Be clear!). According to Grice, these maxims can be derived from a more general principle of cooperation in communication.[33] Breaking the Griceian maxim of truthfulness, for instance, can lead to the harshest of life-world consequences (e.g. legal problems).

This seriousness of material or life-world communication does not exist in cases of licensed or *specialized communication* (in the de-pragmatized textures of the arts, in literature, theater, advertising, carnival, etc.). The frame of understanding that defines specialized communication is usually established by specific markers, sometimes pragmatically through the mere existence of an edition from a certain publishing house (which may indicate that a text is literature), or purely textually (through genre specifications such as 'novel').

This creates the need for a clear distinction between normal/standard and specialized modes of communication.[34] Does this mean that rhetoric, focused primarily on standard communication as it is, has nothing to do with situationally created art? In the beginning, ancient theory did not have a unique concept of that which we today call *literature*. Aristotle reminded his students of this by writing a separate theoretical work for this kind of text (his 'Poetics') in order to clearly distinguish it from rhetoric. This second work described his

---

31 See: Cicero: De Oratore, 3.214.
32 See also: Grice 1967 (ed. 1975), pp. 45 ff.; and Knape 2008a, pp. 898–906.
33 Grice 1967. See also: Knape 2008a, p. 899.
34 Knape 2008a, p. 900; for more on this topic see: Habermas 1985, pp. 185–210; on frames: Goffman 1974.

doctrine of poetic text construction and creation; it discusses mimetic, i.e. play-ful, simulative creation, "with words alone"[35] (that Plato had dismissed and questioned). Modern theories of fiction (for instance, that of French literary theorist Gérard Genette) are founded on Aristotle's ideas.[36]

Chapters 6, 7 and 8 use three case studies to put this classical division to the test. They analyze texts that could hardly be more different: one deals with medieval chronicles, while the others deal with a short story by the Austrian author Thomas Bernhard and a novel by the American novelist Katherine Anne Porter. In these cases of literary rhetoric,[37] the composer of the text plays with the boundary between fact and fiction, and thereby with the line between standard communicative and specialized communicative frames. This flirtation with boundaries was in all cases a conscious decision by the authors, even though the genre expectations of chronicles demand truth, and those of short stories or novels demand fiction. Despite these expectations, in the three cases something occurs that I call the *rhetorical factor*. Although neither historio-graphical nor literary genres envision rhetorical persuasion as a core character-istic, these authors brought components of cognitive influence into their works. According to the 19th chapter of Aristotle's 'Poetics', these components repre-sent the rhetorical factor, which also falls under the purvey of rhetoric even when found in literature.[38]

Aristotle's focus on the rhetorical factor consummated a systematic reori-entation that focused the concept of rhetoric on the question of influence in a way that no other communicative discipline had before. Against this back-ground, Chapter 9 revisits the approaches of *New Rhetoric* and *Deconstruction*. The modern systematic and terminological differentiation of phenomena makes it no longer possible to fundamentally define rhetoric solely around the so-called rhetorical figures. I have already briefly mentioned that the figural doctrine is – systematically seen – today more closely associated with aesthet-ics or structural stylistics than with rhetoric. In this respect, we can no longer say that the figural approach of postmodern literary analysis is *rhetorical* per se. Still, the results of such analyses can lead to insight into strategies for dealing with the rhetorical factor.[39]

We speak of the *rhetorical factor* in all cases where the text genre and communicative frame suggest the use of other production calculations and

---

35 Aristotle: Poetics, 1.1–2.
36 See: Genette 1991.
37 Cf. Deciu Ritivoi/Graff 2008.
38 Aristotle: Poetics, 19.
39 Cf. Knape 2008a.

expectations (e.g. aesthetic), but where rhetorical components (those concerned with life-world relevant influence of addressees) are present. The search for this rhetorical factor in non-rhetorical settings, contexts and texts is also the focus of the chapters in this book listed under the heading *Intersemiotic Rhetoric*. The starting point of all of these discussions is the question of whether rhetoric can exist outside of verbal language at all (e.g. in other acoustic and optical systems of signs).

In light of this question, Chapter 10 deals with the subject of a rhetoric of music. If persuasion is the central operation of rhetoric and consists of moving humans from a mental state A to a mental state B,[40] then the question arises of how such change is possible through music. Music is not based on a strong, discrete code (as verbal language is), but music can obviously trigger emotions. Can it also do more? It is quite possible that the rhetorical approach reaches its explanatory limit in posing such questions.

This may also be the case regarding images, and Chapter 11 addresses this question. While the issue of rhetoric in images is an intensive branch of research within the visual studies, these approaches still lack a convincing foundational theory.[41] This dearth stems from the fact that international research on images lacks unity on even a minimal definition of the image itself, much less a fully developed theory of images as images. Accordingly, we can little hope to find a clear concept of the rhetoric of images in this myriad of studies. Chapter 11 discusses how we can integrate the image as a means of rhetorical communication into an overarching theory of rhetoric. In particular, this chapter attempts to transfer important rhetorical categories (such as the doctrine of stages of production) to the strategic communication with images. The important questions to be asked in this regard have nothing to do with questions of art or aesthetics; they are exclusively concerned with the question of rhetoricity. This perspective is reflected in my definition of the rhetoric of images: "The 'rhetoric' of an image is defined as the strategic calculation used in its production and its potential for interaction (in relation to action theory) that is ingrained, structurally sedimented, and focused on a communicative effect."[42]

A film is a film, and not an image in the terminological sense. This fact must be explicitly stated in order to emphasize the complex semiotic character, the audiovisual complexity, and the moving and linearly sequential nature of film relative to images as "stills". The challenges of a *rhetoric of film* are accord-

---

40 Knape 2003a, col. 875.
41 Cf. Foss 2005 and p. 196 in this book.
42 Knape 2005e, p. 138; Knape 2007b, p. 17.

ingly complex as well; a unified theory of film rhetoric would have to limit itself to generalized statements about the rhetorical nature of film. Instead, well developed rhetorical theories of film must limit themselves to specific genres, among which the most important are documentary film, experimental film, and feature film. Chapter 12 focuses on the genre of feature film with a case study of the 1931 Fritz Lang classic "M". The focus of these considerations is the difference between aesthetic and rhetorical calculations of production. Films of the genre *feature film* are usually produced on the basis of aesthetic calculations. Nevertheless, the example of "M" demonstrates well that the *rhetorical factor* (the purposeful influence of the thought and will of the audience outside of mere generation of moods) can play an important role as well.

Medium

According to classical doctrine, there are two *performative stages* at the end of the process of text production (as illustrated in Figure 1) known in antiquity

Stages of Production	Tasks of Production (*officia oratoris*)	Results
Cognitive	0. Intellectio (Planning)	TEXT AND PERFORMANCE
Cognitive	1. Inventio (Invention) 2. Dispositio, Arrangement (Structure)	TEXT
Semiotic	3. Elocutio, Style (Text Formulation)	
Performative	4. Memoria, Memory (Saving) 5. Actio, Delivery (Performing)	MEDIALIZATION AND PERFORMANCE

Figure 1: Stages of Text Production.

as *memoria* and *actio*. In these phases, the prepared text is saved and performed. Are there related modern theories which rhetoric can use to describe these stages? The answer is yes, and they are found in modern media theory.[43] Still, the theory of rhetoric must find its own way, because media theory is in the process of sinking into terminological and systematic chaos at universities around the world.

Chapter 13 thus begins with an overview of the dominant confusion regarding a terminological definition of *medium*. The word *medium* has yet to be well defined as a *terminus technicus*. Instead, it is usually used as a colloquial or arbitrary plastic word. For it to be acceptable as a modern theoretical category, the expression *medium* must assume the character of a well formulated technical term that is categorically distinct from the concept of *text*. For this reason, we must also develop a specific modern *media rhetoric*.

A rhetorical theory of media explores issues related to what media achieve as media, which profiles of leistung (power or performance) of different media are appropriate for various communicative goals, and the relationship between an active orator and a medium as communicative instrument in combination with its text. An important part of the abstract rhetorical definition is that *media* both save and perform texts. With this approach, a rhetorician can develop theories that are capable of predicting the potential for communicative resistance and calculating the efficiency of various media for the fulfillment of specific communicative goals.

The most famous media theorist of the 20th century, Marshall McLuhan, once spoke metaphorically of the media as "massage".[44] A massage is normally defined as a "treatment through the mechanical manipulation of bodily tissue". This definition is useful for rhetoric in a figurative sense. In order to see how this metaphor applies to media, let us imagine an orator who wants to convey a given text. To get an even more concrete picture, let us imagine an advertising executive who wants to promote a product. To be successful, he must carefully consider which *medium* to utilize in order to most effectively transmit his advertising *text*. In order to select the appropriate medium for his purposes, the following sub-questions must be definitively answered: Which medium has the best chance of reaching his target audience? Which medium has the correct social value or highest appeal to suit his purposes (should he use a book or a plastic bag as his medium, or radio)? What does this selected medium do to the original advertising text? Which medium can strengthen the advertisement, and which might weaken it? Should he utilize the medium of a newspaper, or a flyer, or rather radio, television or cinema advertising?

---

43 Knape 2005c.
44 McLuhan/Fiore 1967; Knape 2005c, pp. 35–39.

If he chooses television, what time of the day should his ad run (in prime-time?)? What kind of format should it run with (that is, what kind of show should it be shown during? A crime drama?)? How often should it run and how long should the video-clip itself be? How should his video-clip be designed so that the peculiarities of the television medium do not negatively influence the advertising pitch, e.g. so that viewers do not simply change the channel? How can he assess and evaluate the issues of cost associated with this medium?

These examples from *media rhetoric* reveal some of the difficulties and tasks that modern theory formation in the humanities often has to overcome. A modern theoretical conception of rhetoric is no exception. It is often the case that scientific concepts and terms must first be liberated from their historical bonds and the bonds of everyday use; they must be more strictly systematized so that discrete analytical levels and concepts can be defined. The scientific principle of Ockham's razor[45] is also helpful in defining the scope of new and more distinct theoretical standpoints. In this way, even the common concept rhetoric can be freed of much historical ballast and transformed into a sleek and well systematized theory.

---

45 See: McCord Adams 1995.

General Rhetoric

1 Rhetorical Fallacies and the Foundations of Intercultural Contrastive Research in Rhetoric

In 2000 and 2001 an interesting controversy arose between two USA Anglicists, H. G. Ying from the University of Colorado at Denver and Paul Kei Matsuda from Durham.[1] The debate centered on the question of the origin of contrastive rhetoric in America. This controversy is interesting because it directly illustrates the misunderstanding (or even incomprehension) of modern scientific rhetoric that has led to the naïve handling of the topic in many academic disciplines. For this reason, I will devote the first part of this essay to discussing the widely used pre-academic conception of rhetoric, and to outlining the seven most common fallacies held about the discipline of rhetoric. This will allow me to then, in the second part of this essay, suggest a modern scientific conception of contrastive rhetoric that can be used across multiple disciplines.

1 Rhetorical Fallacies

The starting point of our discussion is the simple question: What is rhetoric? What is the research subject of general rhetoric as an academic discipline? The modern theory of rhetoric calls this the fundamental perspective of rhetoric. The field of fundamental rhetoric concentrates on the question of when a *rhetorical case* arises in the world that researchers can then investigate.

I will now take a look at seven different fallacies regarding the discipline of modern rhetoric that are widespread in the academic world.

1.1 Linguistic Fallacy

At first, the Ying-Matsuda controversy mentioned above focused on the role of the Sapir-Whorf hypothesis in the development of contrastive rhetoric.[2] The discussion hinged on the claim that, "the Sapir-Whorf hypothesis of linguistic relativity is basic to contrastive rhetoric because it suggests that different languages affect perception and thought in different ways."[3] Ying contrasted this with Robert B. Kaplan's conception,

---

1 See: Ying 2000; Matsuda 2001; Ying 2001.

2 Ying 2000, pp. 259–263.

3 Connor 1996, p. 10.

unlike Sapir-Whorf, who argue for a causal determination from linguistic patterning to cognition, Kaplan did not claim that *language or rhetoric* determines thinking. Rather, he argued that language and rhetoric are 'evolved out of a culture'. There is little doubt that Kaplan views culture as the matrix (a causal determination), and language and writing as the result.[4]

This debate hinges on linguistic problems that (according to modern scientific disciplinary differentiation) belong under the purview of linguistic theory and have nothing to do with the field of rhetoric. Based on this quote, it is clear that the English word *rhetoric* as used here is in no way a rigorous scientific terminus; it is an informal plastic word that can be used to designate just about anything that has to do with language or communication. For Kaplan, *rhetoric* was clearly a synonym for "language and writing". Should we rhetoricians in fact be considered linguists? The clear answer to this question is *no*.

1.2 Fallacy of Textuality or Composition

Let us continue our search for a well-defined technical definition of the term *rhetoric* by turning our attention to the common fallacy of textuality or composition. This type of fallacy brings us back to Kaplan's thought. In 1996 he wrote that, "contrastive rhetoric has its origins in notions of language structure, learning and use which are not strongly autonomous, and its goal is to describe ways in which written texts operate in larger cultural contexts."[5] In his contribution to the debate, Matsuda sought to differentiate Kaplan's concept from Whorf's, and represented this difference visually with the diagram of Figure 2.[6]

Whorf:	language → thought
Kaplan:	cultural patterns → language → thought (logic) → 'rhetoric'

Figure 2

Kaplan himself used data from more than six hundred texts from English as a Second Language courses to support his theory. His contamination of a concept of textuality with a concept of rhetoric is nothing out of the ordinary for American researchers. But as a rhetorician, I would suggest continuing to use the

---

4 Ying 2000, p. 262.
5 Grabe/Kaplan 1996, p. 179.
6 Matsuda 2001, p. 258.

term textuality or textualization or *composition* to refer to the concept discussed here. This is an independent and separate area of study in which the rhetorical case that we are looking for need not necessarily occur. One example of this would be composition according to purely informational or aesthetic strategies, which have nothing to do with the rhetorical approach.

1.3 Aesthetic Fallacy

This brings us to the third fallacy, which relates to aesthetics. In 2009 Hui Wu posed the question, "why do the Chinese relate rhetoric only to stylistic devices in writing?"[7] His answer, "western oratory was lost in translation in Japan, where Chinese students first made contact with western rhetoric," and, "western concepts (particularly the concept of rhetoric) were translated/transformed into a theory about prose studies in China."[8] Similarly, Asa-Bettina Wuthenow's article, 'Rhetoric in Japan' in the 2009 volume 'Rhetoric and Stylistics' focuses above all on Japanese poetics and stylistics.[9] In this context, it is little wonder that the American sinologist XiaoMing Li criticized her colleague Xing Lu's 1998 book 'Rhetoric in Ancient China' by saying that it focused too much on China's, "ancient political and philosophical treatise," and too little on its rich literary tradition. Further,

> I have found that the impact of China's literary tradition is far more palpable on their writing than the entire enterprise of philosophical treatise. For example, *sanwen*, one of the more popular genres in Chinese schools, a prose that resembles to some extent English free verse, is a direct offshoot of a tradition that regarded poetry as the supreme genre.[10]

This confusion of rhetoric with poetics or aesthetics also occurs widely in Europe, and not just in research on contrastive rhetoric (cf. pp. 186 f. in this volume). But even the great thinkers of antiquity, above all Aristotle, had a significantly clearer idea of the differentiation between these fields. For this reason, Aristotle even went so far as to deal with rhetoric and poetics (and the aesthetically motivated text structures) in separate theoretical works. The so-called 'rhetorical figures' (structural patterns that can be used in all kinds of texts) are, in fact, found in both poetry and in rhetorical prose. Poetics and

---

7 Wu 2009, p. 148.
8 Wu 2009, p. 149.
9 Wuthenow 2009.
10 Interview with XiaoMing Li in: Wang 2004, pp. 175 f.

rhetoric thus do intersect at the level of the rhetorical figures. Over the course of history, these aesthetically useful structural patterns were firmly assigned to the field of rhetoric. According to modern systematic premises, however, we must evaluate the situation differently and insist on discrete scientific differentiation. The fact is that an aesthetic case of communication is not necessarily identical to a rhetorical case of communication. Therefore, rhetoric cannot be reduced to aesthetically calculated structural phenomena. Unfortunately, many contrastive works have sought to establish figural universals as genuine "rhetorical" phenomena in their intercultural comparisons.[11]

There is an additional theoretical specification that must be made regarding rhetoric and communication. Rhetoric deals only with *standard* or *normal* communicative frames, in which the Gricean maxims hold without restrictions.[12] These maxims define the expectations among communicative partners that what is being communicated is both binding and honest. In contrast, artistic communication (especially literature and poetry) works with *special* communicative frames. Fictional poetry works with the *as if* of the pure game; nobody expects to see real speech acts in theater.[13] Thus, the communicative strategies underlying rhetoric and fiction are completely different. This is clear to all observers of such phenomena, even though (or perhaps due to the fact that) some writers of fiction work by consciously crossing the boundary between the two frames.[14] Observers do not actually expect someone to be beheaded when a judge in a theatrical play reads the grim verdict. In a real courtroom, the reaction would be much different. It is in this real world of communication that rhetoric is active. Aesthetic speech is subject to a separate, aesthetic theory of communication; it is therefore theoretically questionable to demand and utilize literature as a source for rhetorical research as XiaoMing Li has done.

1.4 General Communication Fallacy

In his well-known work on the establishment of communicative paradigms in ethnology, Dell H. Hymes utilized the term *rhetoric* in a variety of ways. One way he used the term identified rhetoric as an overarching general theory of

---

11 For one example see: Karickam 1999; see also an overview by Meyer 2009, pp. 1876–1880.
12 Cf. p. 15 in this volume and Grice 1967.
13 Both Austin and Searle commented on this in their works. See: Knape 2008a.
14 See chapter 7 on literary rhetoric and Thomas Bernhard in this volume for more on the distinction between fiction and reality.

communication: "it is not linguistics, but ethnography – not language, but communication – which must provide the frame of reference within which the place of language in culture and society is to be described."[15] This opinion corresponds to a widespread conception of rhetoric found in other disciplines, for example in visual communication. Thus it is not surprising when we read in an article by Sonja Foss, that, "rhetoric is an ancient term for what now typically is called *communication*."[16] This misunderstanding of rhetoric is connected to the common use of the English word. If we want to drag this word out of the colloquial and establish it as a legitimate academic term, then it must refer to something specific and not merely a birds-eye view of a general theory of communication. Rhetoric is not a general theory of communication: it is highly specialized. The general theory of communication deals with the entire two-way interactive event among actors according to the classical model of communication as conceived by Shannon and Weaver in 1949. The differences between a general theory of communication and rhetoric are illustrated in Figures 3 and 4 below:

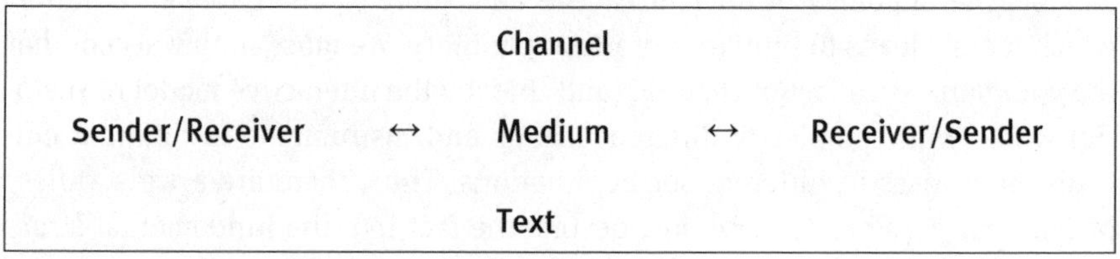

	Channel	
Sender/Receiver ↔	Medium	↔ Receiver/Sender
	Text	

Figure 3: General Model of Two-Way Communication.

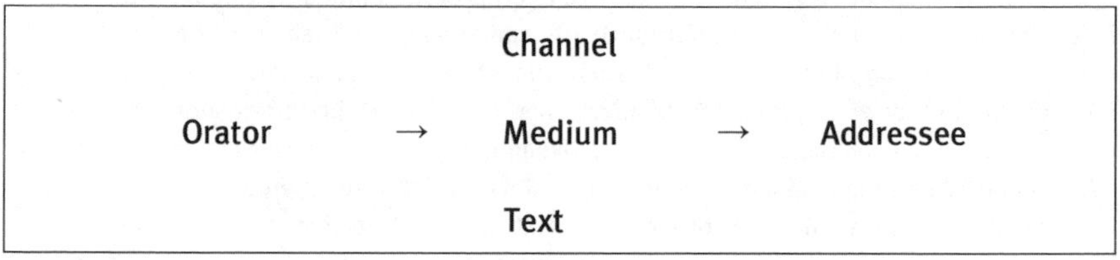

	Channel	
Orator →	Medium	→ Addressee
	Text	

Figure 4: Rhetorical Vector Model.

---

15 Hymes 1964, p. 3.
16 Foss 2005, p. 141.

The critical difference between these two models are the vectors or arrows: the theory of rhetoric is interested exclusively in communicative transfer of influence from the left to the right hand side of the model.[17]

1.5 Fallacy of Means

A further fallacy involves the confusion of the entire rhetorical model of inter-action with individual means, instruments, and processes of communication. The rhetorical case, the rhetorical event as such, cannot be reduced to the instruments that are used in the event itself. Such reduction regularly leads to a lack of theoretical clarity, in particular by those who doubt the universality of rhetorical phenomenon or the existence of 'rhetorical universals'.[18] The communicative instruments that are utilized in a given instance are only a part of the overall rhetorical event. If such instruments do not exist in certain cultures, for instance, this says nothing about the existence of the rhetorical model of interaction as such. Well known Western rhetoricians such as George Kennedy further abet the fallacy of means when they unscrupulously seek to apply the technical terminology of ancient Greece and Rome to other foreign cultures, which merely leads to problems of incompatibility. We must simply accept that the communicative fact of rhetoric (and thereby the interactive model of rhetoric) works with completely different means and instruments in different cultures, and arises in different social situations. Thus, there are a wide variety of different possible descriptions, despite the fact that the fundamental structure of rhetoric remains the same. Thus, when H. G. Ying says, "the basic prem-

---

17 The idea of influence can be both theoretically and methodically conceived in a variety of different ways. Compare with the chapter, "Kommunikation als Steuerung/Regulierung", that Werner Nothdurft felt needed to be provided in his work on intercultural research, "the manner of speaking of communication as regulation prevailed primarily through the influence of cybernetics on science in the 1950s and 1960s, and then spread to the everyday observation of communication. This conception of communication is similar in functionality to that of a thermostat. Similarly, one could call it the refrigerator theory of communication: communication is seen as a dynamic system that is self-regulating and seeks to maintain a homeostatic balance. In the foreground of this perspective is the dynamic and functional character of a communicative event or communicative system. The behavior of participants is seen primarily from the perspective of their contribution to stabilization or destabilization (escalation) of the system. This perspective was ground-breaking in the research of the so-called Palo Alto group around Gregory Bateson, in particular in the work *Pragmatics of Human Communication* by Watzlawick, Beavin and Jackson." Nothdurft 2007, p. 26.
18 Mao 2003, p. 401.

ise of contrastive rhetoric [is] that *rhetoric* varies from culture to culture,"[19] we need to be more precise, and reply that, "*rhetorical means* vary from culture to culture."

1.6 Script Fallacy

The script fallacy exists on the same theoretical level as the general communication fallacy. Some researchers have sought to label even highly conventionalized and script led communication as rhetoric, even though this model of interaction shows little to no relation to the rhetorical *differentia specifica* of influence. Research on socially determined communicative patterns is not derived from rhetorical theory. At most, script oriented communication (which does not require rhetorical effort because it is in some ways automated) can be seen as a sort of opposing model of impartiality and unintentionality to the theoretical system of rhetoric.

In this way, Hymes' conception of a culturally patterned rhetoric was not based on a serious systematic and theoretical rhetorical foundation, but rather continued to use the unscrupulous and colloquial meaning of the word *rhetoric*. H. G. Ying described Hymes' thought as follows,

> to Hymes, the ethnography of communication describes the patterned uses of language in a particular cultural group, including 'the particular patterns of cultural rhetoric' (1964a: 7). Essentially, his argument was that language has a patterning of its own, and this patterning is cultural in organization. Hymes further pointed out (1962: 26) that there are significant 'cross-cultural differences' in language use, including 'the presence or absence of writing'. Thus, in the context of the ethnography of communication, variations in the use of language are systematically related to the distinctive cultural patterns.[20]

This ethnological-communicative concept of a set interactive script implies that persuasive action is (largely) unnecessary, and virtually eliminates the possibility for such persuasion. Unfortunately, Hymes has inspired a series of other works that all utilize the same misleading conception of *rhetoric*. Some examples include Ethel M. Albert's 1964, 'Rhetoric, Logic, and Poetics in Burundi: Cultural Patterning of Speech Behavior,' and Robert T. Oliver's 1971, 'Communication and Culture in Ancient India and China' in which, "ancient ceremonies and etiquette," and, "different kinds of rituals and ritual actions," were areas of focus.[21]

---

19 Ying 2000, p. 263.
20 Ying 2000, p. 264.
21 See: Ying 2000, p. 264; and Mao 2003, p. 404; Albert 1964; Oliver 1971.

1.7 Natural (Biological) Fallacy

Philosophers ranging from Marcus Tullius Cicero to Hans Blumenberg have connected the discipline of rhetoric with linguisticality in general (as an anthropological constitution of mankind) through analyses of the original Greek term *rhesis* (speech activity). For Blumenberg, rhetoric is a social acquisition of all humans because it displaces the *agōn* (competition, even war and aggression) to the level of symbols, and thus contributes to our humanization.[22] In this way, rhetoric raises war to the level of communicative activity; it must be understood as a social practice and cultural phenomenon that allows for the peaceful balancing of interests in human society. Rhetoric indeed is a device for avoiding the need to resort to violence.[23]

Against this background, we must reject a biological derivation of rhetoric as conceived by the American researcher George Kennedy in his 1998 work 'Comparative Rhetoric'. There are at least two arguments against his position, one based on communication theory and the other on cultural theory. Kennedy sought to anchor rhetoric in natural laws, and saw rhetoric as, "a form of mental and emotional energy," found in every individual, "animal or human". For Kennedy, rhetoric even exists in the animal kingdom: it is, "a universal phenomenon, one found even among animals," and he claims to have observed that animals, "seek to persuade others."[24]

This is, of course, nonsense, since animals do not communicate the way that humans do. If we exclude primates (and even in primates the question is unclear), animals only know systems of signals that correspond to a direct stimulus-response (SR) model and which are almost entirely genetically anchored. Such communication is only marginally related to complex human communication, which takes place through the use of texts or symbols. The symbolic interaction among humans places a text- or symbol-processing instance between the stimulus and the response, namely, the human consciousness. Rhetorically seen, semantic transfer among humans takes place according to a three part model of Stimulus – Processing – Response (SPR). An animal does not really possess this stage of processing. On the other hand, the freedom of processing (and therefore interpretation) makes the "influencing of the soul (*psychagogy*)"[25] of rhetoric high risk; it is a steering with uncertain effects. Or, as Johnstone put it, "to argue is inherently to risk failure."[26]

---

22 Blumenberg 1981.
23 Cf., however, the skeptical position of Johnstone 1963, p. 36.
24 Kennedy 1998, p. 3; cf. Knape 2003a, col. 876 f.
25 Plato: Phaedrus, 261a.
26 Johnstone 1963, p. 30.

The premises of Kennedy's biological anchoring of rhetoric are questionable: the only thing he seems to have left out is postulating a rhetoric-gene.

We must also agree with LuMing Mao's cultural theoretical counterargument to this rhetorical fallacy. With noble restraint, Mao gave Kennedy's thesis a proper assessment,

> to be fair, Kennedy never states that he is promoting this kind of assumption. Nevertheless, one cannot help but associate his approach with the ideology of rhetorical Darwinism, because the semblance between the two is just too eerily strong to be ignored. A project that aims to develop a theory of rhetoric for all cultures simply cannot afford to promote such resemblance or even the semblance of it – his disclaimers notwithstanding.[27]

2 Fundamental Rhetoric (The Rhetorical Case)

Enough with the fallacies. But what remains of a positive definition of rhetoric? After all this, I still believe we have enough material for a solid definition of a modern scientific rhetoric. Before moving on, however, it must be noted that the knowledge gained by those academic disciplines mentioned in the discussion of rhetorical fallacies (linguistics, aesthetics, sociology, anthropology, etc.) is important, and the results of that knowledge should always be integrated into genuine rhetorical research. At the same time, it is important for rhetoric to clearly define itself separately from these fields.

Up till now I have defined the competencies and jurisdiction of rhetoric through a process of elimination and by disassociating the term from other, pre-scientific uses. I will now proceed with a positive description of the rhetorical approach organized into two sections: 1. Fundamental rhetoric, which focuses on questions surrounding the rhetorical case, and 2. Instrumental rhetoric, which asks questions of how and with which instruments and methods a communicative (rhetorical) concern can be technically aided and transported. From the perspective of rhetorical theory, the challenges of a contrastive rhetoric are focused on these two areas.

Some researchers (in particular, some from the field of anthropology) have claimed that rhetoric represents yet another case of Eurocentrism.[28] The debate revolves around the question of whether rhetoric is a purely European or white American product, merely because the Greeks were the first to scientifically describe it. I would answer such questions with a question of my own: Is

---

27 Mao 2003, p. 410.
28 See: Mao 2003, p. 410. For more on rhetoric in ethnological debates, see: Meyer 2009, pp. 1871 ff.

physics a European product, merely because the first scientific physicists were ancient Greeks? Is there such a thing as a German physics, as the Nazis claimed up until 1945? Is culture an American phenomenon that no other nation has? Does communication only take place in the Western world, but not in the Eastern regions of the world? Is there an economy in Frankfurt, but not in Singapore? Is there a German biology, or German mathematics, or German logic? Does rhetoric only exist in Western nations?

At first glance, the answer to these questions might be in doubt if we read Robert Kaplan. According to Kaplan,

> Logic (in the popular, rather than the logician's sense of the word), which is the basis of rhetoric, is evolved out of a culture; it is not universal. Rhetoric, then, is not universal, either, but varies from culture to culture and even from time to time within a given culture. It is affected by canons of taste within a given culture at a given time.[29]

As I showed earlier in this essay, we now know that Kaplan's *rhetoric* does not, in fact, refer to the rhetorical model of interaction, but rather to *textuality* or *composition*. And in this he is correct: single-language and cultural norms do play a role in the composition of texts. But what about the actual fundamental rhetorical perspective? For a theory of an inter-culturally contrastive rhetoric we need a theoretical model that provides us with a *tertium comparationis*, otherwise no comparisons are possible. In 2000, the American linguist LuMing Mao made a very good methodological suggestion. He alluded to the common linguistic differentiation between *emic* and *etic* perspectives on linguistic data. According to Mao, an *etic* characterization of a subject is based on an ahistorical categorization of abstract, theoretical content, while an *emic* characterization involves the concrete, experiential and phenomenological realization of the subject. According to Mao,

> to study non-Western rhetorical traditions, one surely must start somewhere – usually from where one *is* and with terms and concepts close to home. In other words, we may not have any other choice than to articulate other rhetorical traditions first by seeking out frames and terms found in our own tradition. But if our larger goal is to study these traditions on their own terms, we must move from the etic approach to the emic approach – so that attention can be directed toward material and conditions that are native to these traditions and so that appropriate frames and language can be developed to deal with differences as well as similarities between different traditions.[30]

While I certainly agree with this formulation, the question remains: how are we to arrive at the abstract scientific categories that make up the *tertium com-*

---

29 Kaplan 1966, p. 2.
30 Mao 2003, pp. 417 f.

parationis of rhetoric and which determine the disciplinary focus of rhetoric? And what are these categories?

We must first note that rhetorical theory excludes a wide array of communicative phenomena that do not meet the requirements of a rhetorical object of investigation. A category of rhetoric that is distinct from a more general conception of communication is only meaningful when it is not used arbitrarily: when it is only applied to a specific sub-set of communicative phenomena. Both anthropological and social-psychological universals play a role here as well, as they allow us to define a culturally independent fundamental structure of rhetoric as an abstractly formulated model of interaction. According to this model, the rhetorical case requires a mental asymmetry that results from an agonal interaction: from some sort of communicative contention in the form of competition and conflict. Scripted communication, as we saw earlier, takes place without this premise of dissonance; because it is in some ways conventionally ritualized, there is no need for rhetorical effort.[31] In keeping with the fundamental theory of rhetoric, and following Mao's suggested *etic* perspective, we can define modern scientific rhetoric along the following lines: rhetoric is to be understood as a social model of interaction in which human actors act in a particular way: they are persuasive. Thus, the *rhetorical case* comes into existence when one person seeks to persuade another person.

To persuade someone means to change either their *opinion* or their *attitude*: to cause a change from mental position A to a new mental position B through communication. This is the disciplinary perspective from which all other questions within a theory of rhetoric arise.[32] Rhetorical research thus focuses exclusively on one problem, namely: how can the rhetorical communicator (that is, the orator or group of orators[33]) successfully advance a concern that he believes to be legitimate? The fundamental methodological structure is persuasive (communicative) action that is based on strategic calculations and utilizes socially allowable communicative instruments.[34] These instru-

---

31 Rhetoric is not necessary when ordering a drink in a bar, for instance; this is an act of scripted communication. Rhetorical effort is only needed when your order is ignored by the bartender.

32 Knape 2003a.

33 For more on the concept of *orator* see: Knape 2000a, pp. 33–45. From the perspective of communications theory, the rhetorical category of *orator* must be considered an abstract and is not connected to the European concept of the individual. Knape 2000a, p. 46; see also: Mao 2003, p. 407; and Han/Shavitt 1994.

34 See: Knape/Becker/Böhme 2009. It is rare for practical guides to refer to explicit evidence of persuasion in the strategic patterns of the classical art of war (which has always been the basis for strategic theory). One example is found in the chapter on "Sun Tzu, the Art of War and Negotiation" by Patrick Kim Cheng Low in: Low 2010, pp. 55–61; the terms

ments can naturally vary widely from culture to culture. On the other hand, the conversational maxims coined by English philosopher of communication Herbert P. Grice must be valid in all rhetorical cases. If his maxims are not valid, then the communicative case at hand is not rhetorical; it is a case of manipulation, demagoguery, or deception, etc.

If there are human populations in which total mental harmony reigns, where no one person seeks to further a concern in the minds of other people (and therefore no persuasive action takes place), then these are cultures without rhetoric. The fields of ethnology and oriental studies have taken different positions as to whether such cultures exist.

Mao advised against such rash assertions under the section titled, "The Trap of the Deficiency Model,"

> There have even been attempts to address directly the lack in Asian rhetorics of Western rhetorical characteristics or attributes. In an essay titled 'The Absence of Rhetorical Tradition in Japanese Culture,' John Morrison claims that 'Japanese culture does not have the necessary institutional ingredients to nourish a rhetorical tradition' (90). He bases his claim on the hierarchical structure of the Japanese family, which values cohesion and harmony and which minimizes individualism and such a structure thus has little, if anything, to do with a rhetorical tradition (90–93). To substantiate his sweeping claim, Morrison examines the Japanese national character, which is characterized in one fell swoop as socially submissive, rhetorically non-argumentative, religiously meditative, and linguistically handicapped in following logical processes (95–100). All these characterizations naturally contribute to this lack of a rhetorical tradition in Japanese culture.[35]

Mao criticized Morrison's position by noting, "the fact that Japanese culture does not include the Western rhetorical tradition does not mean at all that it does not have a rhetorical tradition."[36] In general, the question of whether the rhetorical model of interaction exists in non-Western society must be distinguished from the question of how a given society uses and theoretically integrates this model into their episteme. As a result, one can ask the question of how the process by which rhetoric changes mental states reacts to opposing cultural postulates (values), such as those of stability and tradition in the Confucian world.[37] In order to clarify exactly this topic, Xing Lu researched the integration of the existing rhetorical approach into five philosophical traditions: Confucianism, Daoism, Mohism, Legalism and the school surrounding Ming.[38] In commenting on her results, Lu

---

persuasion, strategy, and rhetoric do not appear in the wide array of introductory works on intercultural communication that I have checked.

35 Mao 2003, pp. 406 f.
36 Mao 2003, p. 408.
37 Mao 2003, p. 405.
38 Lu 1998; cf. Mao 2003, p. 415.

insisted that, "it is important to be sensitive to the implicit, multifaceted, and sometimes paradoxical nature of rhetoric embedded in Chinese philosophical, literary, and religious texts."[39] According to Lu, instead of searching for equivalents to European categories, the phenomenology of Asian rhetoric should be described with its own independent terminology.

3 Instrumental Rhetoric (Rhetorical Methods)

The theoretical area of instrumental rhetoric is concerned with the culturally specific practices used in the application of the rhetorical model of interaction. To what extent can research in this area legitimately use European terms and concepts? Mao made his position clear:

> Kennedy certainly would tell us that the use of these terms for 'testing purposes' is not the same as the thoughtless imposition of them on target traditions. I concur. However, this kind of 'testing' can easily reduce comparison to some simple or forced identification of similarities and differences by relying on superficial congruencies or mismatches (Garrett, Review 432).[40]

In any case, it is important that the divergence among differing rhetorical instruments not lead to fallacies of the rhetorical approach itself: the phenomenology of the methods must not be confused with the entirety of the rhetorical model of communication as such.

In the context of intercultural contrastive rhetoric, even the core of the European rhetorical organon (i.e. instrumental) doctrine, classical argumentation based on logic, must be reconsidered. This central, cognitively and logically applicable rhetorical instrument appears in a variety of different forms in different cultures.[41] In a 2001 experimental study, for instance, Salwa A. Kamel clearly demonstrated that Arabic students in Cairo had significant difficulties with the European logical-syllogistic style of argumentation, even if their English skills were very good.[42] What conclusions can we draw from these findings? It seems to be the case that a different cognitive style is preferred in the Arab world, one that cannot be reduced to strict forms based on logical syllogistics. A similar phenomenon seems to exist in some Asian cultures as

---

39 Interview with Xing Lu in: Wang 2004, p. 174.
40 Mao 2003, p. 411.
41 See for example: Lloyd 2007.
42 Kamel 2000; for more on problems of argumentation see also: Bar-Lev 1986; and Dolinina/Cecchetto 1998.

well.[43] Still, Mao warns of, "the trap of deficiency," of exaggerated contrasting concepts: "one continues to hear that Eastern rhetorical traditions practice indirection (as opposed to directness), deprecate argumentation (as opposed to debating), and promote or value silence (as opposed to talking)."[44] For Mao, the mere existence of such contrasts and generalizations themselves stem from a Western style of thought.

It is now clear that the manifest intercultural differences in the methods of persuasion among humans are worth further study, and should be a central theme for contrastive rhetoric:

> To study non-Western rhetorical traditions on their own terms can lead to positive representations of these traditions rather than to conclusions involving ‚deficiency' that we have encountered in some of the studies discussed previously. This outcome is demonstrated in Jensen's 'Values and Practices in Asian Argumentation'. Rather than focused on the 'lack' of argumentation practices in Asian rhetorics, Jensen provides ample evidence to show that these practices do exist in Asian rhetorics, whether based on authority, analogy, or other methods of reasoning (158–162). There are only rhetorical differences, not absences versus presences, between East and West (164).[45]

In a 2004 interview, Mary Garrett advocated this kind of contrastive differentiation between cultural instances of rhetoric,

> how is rhetoric being conceived? As argumentation and disputation? As including epideictic? As symbolic inducement? The definition applied will determine, to what extent, what is seen and brought forward. I myself think that seeing rhetoric as argumentation and disputation is to narrow for both the Western and the Chinese situations; too many important and interesting phenomena are missed.[46]

The fact remains that the realm of communication is highly diversified. The rhetorical case of communication, however, must be precisely defined in order to demonstrate its difference from other phenomena. If the concept of rhetoric is to be stable and meaningful, if it is to be a *terminus technicus*, then it must refer to a discrete scientific concept. A program of contrastive rhetoric that is based on the fundamental asymmetry in the model of communicative interaction, and uses persuasion as the focus of its approach, was formulated well by LuMing Mao in 2003, "in fact, as long as there is communication, there is rhetoric – people using language in competing contexts to communicate, to discover, to build relationship, and to enhance communal values."[47]

---

43 See: Mao 2003, pp. 413 f.
44 Mao 2003, p. 417.
45 Mao 2003, p. 412.
46 Interview in: Wang 2004, p. 175.
47 Mao 2003, p. 408.

2 Rhetoric between Historicism and Modern Science

Books that seek to acquaint the modern reader with older theories of rhetoric, and with ancient rhetoric in particular, are published on a regular basis.[1] The existence of such books, and the fact that the 'International Society for the History of Rhetoric' holds a bi-annual congress, seem to demonstrate that historical research on rhetoric is both necessary and useful.

The truth is, however, that such activities only prove that research that deals with the history of rhetorical theory and practice is taking place; their existence does not answer the question of whether such backward-looking research makes sense from a theoretical point of view. When considered in isolation, research with a purely historical approach is a luxurious game. The social value of such work can be and is questionable as long as it involves conducting history merely for history's sake. The situation is, of course, different for disciplines which operate *purely* historically: their concern with rhetoric is narrowly focused and specialized. When conducting their research, philologists, historians, art historians, etc. encounter the problems of rhetoric and treat them as a kind of epiphenomenon. The fact is that the academic discipline of rhetoric needs such interdisciplinary exploration into its history because there are only a few full-time rhetoricians actively working in institutes around the world. This point was clearly demonstrated by the attendance list at the conference of the 'International Society for the History of Rhetoric' in Strasbourg in 2007 (to mention but one example).

What about the question of history within the discipline of rhetoric itself? Let's take a look at the University of Tübingen, the institutionalized center of rhetorical research, and the only institute authorized to confer degrees in rhetoric in Germany. As a natural result of this monopoly, our research and academic programs always include the historical side of the disciplinary knowledge of rhetoric. We consider this a necessary part of our work. Thus, for example, our department did not simply publish a rhetorical dictionary, but rather an *historical* dictionary of rhetoric. Does such an approach merely signify a traditional understanding of rhetoric, in which the classical attitude

---

1 I would like to mention only a few recent book-titles: Øivind Andersen's 'I Retorikkens Hage' (1995), published in German under the title 'Im Garten der Rhetorik' in 2001; James Fredal's 'Rhetorical Action in Ancient Athens' (2006); Wendy Olmsted's 'Rhetoric. An Historical Introduction' (2006); 'A Companion to Greek Rhetoric' (2007), edited by Ian Worthington; or the 'Oxford Readings in the Attic Orators,' edited by Edwin Carawan.

(prevalent in Europe and Western culture) of considering the Greek and Roman antiquity as the origin, or "cradle of civilization", is taken for granted?

If so, it begs the question of whether such an approach is justified and demanded by our discipline and its systematic approach. While the founders of the aforementioned historical lexicon (Historisches Wörterbuch der Rhetorik) took the historical perspective for granted, their approach is no longer a matter of course. Nowadays, disciplines focused exclusively on historical research are under fire. Up until the 19th century, historical deductions and proofs created legitimacy for social institutions such as nation states. But modern democratic and scientifically oriented systems hardly consider the question of 'how it used to be' relevant in justifying decisions or enunciating theories. Modern medicine does not need to know what Aristotle thought about the rumored black gall. Nowadays, state institutions prove their legitimacy via regular elections and plebiscites. Historical arguments are, at most, used for emotional propaganda; they are rarely used to make rational justifications.

Thus, thought and argumentation along historical lines of reasoning – accepted as normal in the bygone age of historicism – can no longer be taken for granted; the purely historical argument is, in fact, rarely valid anywhere today. If it aspires to be a scientific discipline, rhetoric has to adapt to the modern understanding of science that no longer focuses on diachrony, but rather on synchrony. Without such adjustments, rhetoric would quickly lose its justification as a university subject. Within this system, the standards are set by the empirical and experimental natural sciences. The modern behavioral and communication sciences, both neighboring disciplines of modern rhetoric, also take their cues from this paradigm. These disciplines frame questions using modern methodologies and theories that a scientifically formulated rhetoric must also take seriously. If we define modern rhetoric as a discipline that focuses on finding out how persuasive and effective communication works today, then the value of research on Aristotle and other ancient rhetoricians is called into question. Why should a modern society spend money and time dealing with such snows of yesteryear, with material from a bygone age?

In my opinion, one can only seriously justify research into the history of rhetoric, with all of its financial and infrastructural expenses, if such research yields results that have some sort of systematic utility in setting up rhetorical theories in the present and in the future. Thus, the main question of this essay: can *historical* research in rhetoric provide answers to questions that stem from, and are relevant to, current research? If so, what can such historical research teach us?

In the following pages, I will lay out some possible answers to this question. I will first approach this subject from an extrinsic perspective and state the above-mentioned main question more specifically: what can historical research in rhetoric, in particular the exploration of historical rhetorical practice, accomplish in the interdisciplinary context? Furthermore, what can historical research in rhetoric contribute to a discussion of the problems of modern society?

Here I would like to emphasize the complex of epistemology and research into the history and structure of ideas. In these areas, there is no such thing as spontaneous creation or ahistorical structure-building. Knowledge-systems, ideas and mentalities are, consciously or unconsciously, links in the chains of cultural tradition that break time and again, but that can also continually be repaired. Feeling and thinking never take place without preconditions, without history; they are always the result of cultural, and thus historical, developments. Historical research on rhetoric can, for example, help explain how the modern system of philology emerged from the old study of rhetoric through a process of selection and differentiation of subjects and disciplines. Nowadays, the modern system of philology is itself breaking apart, and is undergoing further differentiation into an array of cultural studies. In this way, it is possible that historical research can help determine a new place for rhetoric within the current panoply of subjects.[2] Regarding research into intellectual history (the history of ideas and mindsets), we are regularly confronted with prejudices, opinions, doctrines, dogmatisms and fixed ideas that have been developed, transformed, revised, transferred, and precipitated through long historical processes. Lothar Bornscheuer characterized these elements as the result of "social imagination" in his standard work on 'Topics'.[3] Rhetorical research on topoi cannot be done without looking backwards, that is, without an historical dimension. By looking backward we can gain insight into the cognitive and mental states of populations from a myriad of times and places. In doing so, we seek to explain which historical mechanisms of persuasion have led us to think the way we do now. We may even find that such mechanisms are antiquated or inadequate for modern thought.

I will illustrate this point with three examples from the history of rhetoric. The first example concerns the English Royal Society's campaign against the metaphor or any other rhetorical influence on scientific texts at the end of the 17th century. For the natural sciences, the Royal Society formulated the postulate that a "direct verbal access to the referential object demanded a plain style with perspicuity as its principle feature. The rejection of the artificiality of

---

2 For example, by providing a new awareness of the key qualifications for modern scientific theories.

3 Bornscheuer 1976.

rhetoric led to a kind of anti-rhetoric."[4] In 1690, John Locke, also a prominent representative of this view, stated in his 'Essay concerning Human Understanding',

> [...] all the Art of Rhetorick, besides Order and Clearness, all the artificial and figurative application of Words Eloquence hath invented, are for nothing else but to insinuate wrong *Ideas*, move the Passions, and thereby mislead the Judgment.[5]

Today, however, "a reversal of this attitude has taken place."[6] We know today, for instance, that modern physical theories cannot be explained without the use of metaphors and rhetorical schemes.[7] As the Danish scholar Søren Kjørup phrased it in his 1996 book 'Humanities',

> Scientific innovations often take place by means of new terms, and, as has been shown, these terms are often metaphors or other tropes. A very early example of this kind of analysis can be found in Mary Hesse' publication on analogy and metaphor in science; later in the work of Lakoff and Johnson, who showed that our everyday thinking is structured by metaphors.[8]

In this work, Kjørup summarized the current state of the discussion as follows,

> As the theorists of science took notice of rhetoric, their interest was directed initially at stylistics. It was soon revealed that even sober-looking scientific explanations applied tropes and schemes of persuasion, ornamentation, and other rhetorical instruments which were originally called 'literary' elements. One example of such research is Joseph Gusfield's survey on alcohol research titled 'The Literary Rhetoric of Science' (1976); another example is Hayden White's analyses of historical science texts such as 'The Historical Text as Literary Artifact' (1978). Such works have a rather banal punch line that actually reveals more about rhetoric than about science; strictly speaking, they merely prove that the terminological system of rhetoric is broad enough to cover scientific texts, too. But at the time, this confirmation was somewhat provocative, and it opened the eyes of those theorists that until then had seen a clear border between science and rhetoric, between factual conviction and language-aware persuasion.[9]

This "language of science" example lets us identify an historical difference between the conceptions of rhetoric in the Baroque period and today. By analyzing such differences we can also discern interesting developments, revisions, and errors. Surveying such different positions in the history of rhetoric

---

4 Plett 2004, p. 62.
5 Locke 1690, 3.10, § 34.
6 Plett 2004, p. 63.
7 Fahnestock 1999.
8 Kjørup 1996, p. 207.
9 Kjørup 1996, p. 206; Hesse 1963; Lakoff/Johnson 1980; Gusfield 1976; White 1978b.

can show us how science develops and which epistemic dynamic forces play a role. At the same time, we must recognize the constant danger of linguistic and intellectual obscurantism and note that it is worthwhile to continually scrutinize the relationship between linguistic encoding and reality.

Let us turn now to my second example. The conflict between Plato and the Sophists in ancient Greece played not only an important role in the history of rhetoric, but also intellectual history and epistemology in general. In historical terms, this conflict can be interpreted as a paradigm for future disputes about rhetoric. Steven Mailloux, for example, sees this very conflict at the core of American neo-pragmatism: "Contemporary neo-pragmatism can be viewed as a postmodernist reception of sophistic rhetoric, and it is as such that its advocates and opponents demonstrate the continuing relevance of the struggle between Platonism and sophistry."[10] Methodologically speaking, neo-pragmatism utilizes "rhetoric to practice theory by doing history."[11]

This *figure of thought* could also be stated another way: in order to better understand the contemporary practice of rhetoric, or to be able to understand it at all, one must look back at the past. The study of influential discussions and competing views on rhetoric throughout history creates a "space for conscious reflection" (*Denkraum der Besonnenheit* – Aby M. Warburg)[12], in which we are able to recognize the structures of the present more distinctly; structures within which we may normally be too ensconced to examine carefully. Thus, historical research allows and enables us to comment on the "rhetorical climate" of the present. Knowledge of such a "climate" is primarily interesting for modern rhetoric as the pragmatic context within which the successful communicative action of orators must take place.

The term "pragmatism" leads us to the third example of the advantages of an historical perspective in rhetoric, and also leads to a completely different problem area. Philosophical pragmatism, the roots of which lie in the Anglo-Saxon countries, particularly in America, is closely linked to the principles of modern democracy. Pragmatism proceeds from the assumption that the concepts and values of a society are not set in stone, but rather develop through communicative processes. Within such a system, rhetoric represents the, "dynamic factor of communication,"[13] because it plays, "a significant role in the constitution of social meaning."[14] Hence, rhetoric can also, "emphatically," be referred to, "as one of the great factors of cultural motion."[15]

---

10 Mailloux 1998, p. 22.
11 Mailloux 1998, p. ix.
12 Warburg 1920, p. 267; see also chapter 12 on the rhetoric of film in this volume.
13 Knape 2000a, p. 86.
14 Knape 2000a, p. 80.
15 Knape 2000a, p. 82.

Against this background, the rhetorical democracy thesis (the idea that democracy is dependent on rhetoric) becomes comprehensible. The origins of this thesis trace back to Tacitus' link between the existence of the republic and rhetoric. In his 'Dialogus de oratoribus' (1st–2nd century A.D.), Tacitus linked the flourishing of rhetoric with the existence of the Roman Republic before the Imperial Era. In 18th century Germany, Johann Gottfried Herder, voicing an opinion held by some at the time, represented this thesis as follows,

> But eloquence only lived where the republic was, where freedom reigned, where public deliberation was the driving force of all affairs [...]. Since we hardly have any opportunity for public speeches apart from the pulpit, where eloquence is surrounded by such cold air, and since Germany has always been the fatherland of the ceremony and a wooden servitude, it is indeed folly to look for rules of an art where art itself is missing.[16]

In 1965, Walter Jens, the founder of the Department of General Rhetoric in Tübingen, returned to the rhetorical democracy thesis, stating that the 18th century German thinkers realized, "that the destiny of rhetoric, as a daughter of the republic that could only develop in times of freedom, is inextricably linked with the destiny of democracy. When the people reign, speech reigns, when despotism reigns, the military drum roll reigns."[17]

This third example shows politics as a further constitutive field of social and rhetorical action. The orator not only operates in culturally encoded situations, but also always within a concrete political context that determines the structures of his actions. The history of rhetoric is full of examples in which politics has assigned rhetoric a certain status in society. The social status of rhetoric is decisive for the manner in which rhetoric is understood, taught and practiced at any given time or under any given form of government. The birth of rhetoric from the spirit of Attic democracy is the origin of the history of rhetoric. At the same time, the idea of birth in antiquity has also been a recurring topos in systematic rhetorical explanations. The significance of practical eloquence for decision making in political questions is indisputable. So too is its functional change in monarchic or totalitarian contexts. In this respect, the knowledge of historical variance is indispensable for the competent orator, since it can have a decisive influence on his chances of being successful. I shall return to the issue of variance as a part of oratorical competence at the end of this essay.

Let us now consider the history of rhetoric as a contribution to the present discussion on democracy. The authors of the 2003 book, 'A Synoptic History

---

16 Herder 1785, letter 42, pp. 194 f.
17 Jens 1965, pp. 24 f.

of Classical Rhetoric' took a similar view in their introductory sentence: "The purpose of history is to help us understand the present by seeing it in context and providing it with a sense of continuity."[18] In the American context, so the preface, their historical account indirectly illuminates America's role as "leader of a free world" and returns to the roots of democracy, in particular American democracy: "Representative democracy did not spring full-blown from the heavens."[19]

When we take a look at the history of rhetoric, we can also see that the rhetorical democracy-thesis is only valid under certain circumstances. A precondition of this thesis is that society has legally defined the, "access to the orator-role," as a fundamental civil right and liberty.[20] If, "access to the orator-role becomes a privilege of only those in power," then rhetoric is no longer a component in the history of democracy, but rather becomes an important component in the history of other forms of society and government. This is apparent if we take a look at Machiavelli's concept of rhetoric, or at the courtly eloquence of the Baroque period, or at fascist or other totalitarian regimes of the 20th century.[21] These examples show that there have been a variety of opinions on the power of words throughout history. Studying the interruptions and the continuities in the history of rhetoric can be useful for identifying the remnants of such opinions in our present conception of rhetoric. At a more general level, such work is useful for explaining the connection between political communicative order and society at large.

What about the intrinsic perspective? How is historical research actually justified within the field of rhetoric itself? Here, we can differentiate between two approaches to the history of rhetoric. On the one hand are those works in rhetoric that take the primacy of ancient theories as a given and seek to simply directly apply them to modern problems. On the other, we have those works that systematically classify theories of rhetoric within their historical contexts and modify them to better fit modern needs and questions. We could perhaps call the former approach traditionalist, and it is still represented by some in the disciplinary field: I would mention the American philologist Edward P. J. Corbett as representative of this approach. In his 1963 essay, 'The Usefulness of Classical Rhetoric', he set the utility of the classical rhetorical systematics against the arbitrariness of "modern" teaching methods like Creative Writing,

> but hasn't the cult of self-expression had a fair chance to prove itself in the classroom? How many creative writers have we produced? [...] But what most of our students need,

---

18 Murphy/Katula 2003, p. xi.
19 Murphy/Katula 2003, p. xi.
20 Knape 2000a, pp. 81 f.
21 See: Burke 1950, pp. 158–166; Knape 2006b; Braungart 1988; Burke 1939, pp. 191–220.

even the bright ones, is careful, systematized guidance at every step in the writing process. Classical rhetoric can provide that kind of positive guidance.[22]

In his 1965 textbook 'Classical Rhetoric for the Modern Student', Corbett declared the ubiquity of eloquence under the chapter heading, 'The Relevance and Importance of Rhetoric for Our Times.' Corbett's explanation here was similar, "if 'rhetoric' is such a pervasive activity in contemporary society, it behooves us to be aware of the basic strategies and principles of this ancient art."[23] In this way the traditionalist view of rhetoric accepts the ancient systematics as a foundation that can still serve as a model for the present-day teaching of eloquence or the critical reception of rhetorical activities.

But is such an approach specifically historical? Indeed, it makes reference to historically constituted forms of rhetoric, and to their historically developed curricular content. When one takes a closer look at the systematic textbooks and curricula that stem from this academic tradition, however, it becomes apparent that the ancient systematics is treated as a universal that is expected to have validity at all times and places throughout history.

With good reason, such viewpoints have aroused criticism. One variant of such criticism is aimed at the common, often didactically justified, simplification of ancient doctrines. Critics like Kathleen E. Welch demand a much more differentiated approach to ancient texts. In her contribution to the 1987 work 'The Contemporary Appropriation of Ancient Discourse', Welch asserted,

> If 'classical rhetoric' consists primarily of the familiar 'three kinds of speech, epideictic, judicial, and legislative,' or as 'the five canons of rhetoric, invention, arrangement, style, memory, and delivery,' or even exclusively as 'the faculty of discovering the available means of persuasion in the particular case' (Aristotle, *The Rhetoric* I), and if these concepts remain unconnected to Greek and/or Roman culture, speech, writing, and politics, then 'the forms of power and performance' (Eagleton 205) in classical rhetoric tend to disappear.[24]

Others have gone even further, and have attacked the self-reflexivity of such a treatment of ancient rhetorical theory. Such critics insist on the necessity for ancient knowledge to be updated and appropriately modified for modern applications. Here I point to Wendy Olmsted's 2006 book, in which she wrote,

> Many scholars have 'theorized' rhetoric by articulating specific principles that provide direction for inquiry to persuasion and communication. Yet such theories tend to remove

---

22 Corbett 1963, p. 164.
23 Corbett 1965, p. 25.
24 Welch 1987, p. 79.

themselves from historical contingencies and varied modes of representation [...]. But the art of rhetoric requires reasoning about particular circumstances in light of broad cultural understandings.[25]

Edward Schiappa and Jim Hamm recently described this more contextually based approach as fulfilling two separate goals,

> Scholarship on Greek rhetoric may be usefully described as motivated by two basic purposes: historical reconstruction and contemporary appropriation. Described most simply, historical reconstruction engages classical texts to describe the intellectual, aesthetic, economic, or political work that such texts performed in their own time or what such texts might have meant to those living in the classical era. Contemporary appropriation is typically motivated by a desire to draw inspiration from classical texts to meet current theoretical, political, or pedagogical needs.[26]

The previous discussion has, I believe, provided a first answer to one of the questions posed at the beginning of this essay, whether *historical* research in rhetoric can make any contribution at all.

My answer to this question is unequivocal: yes, it can. Diachronic research in rhetoric can make a methodologically fruitful and theoretically meaningful contribution, even to synchronous lines of investigation, because it refurbishes and systematizes certain kinds of knowledge that can be called on with great profit when setting up modern rhetorical theories. The question remains, however: what kind of knowledge are we dealing with, and why do we need historical heuristics? Couldn't such knowledge be generated simply through synchronous experiments or by observing the current behavior of people?

In order to ensure clarity in this discussion, we must briefly concern ourselves with the specifics of the disciplinary knowledge of rhetoric. The first duty for a scientific rhetoric is to glean knowledge about practices, techniques, and possibilities for successful communication and condense such insight into well-founded theories. The ultimate aim of such work is to be able to train competent orators. The knowledge gained by a scientific rhetoric refers to human actions that we can label with the term "cultural practices." The main focus of rhetoric, rhetorical success, is embedded in a mélange of culturally imparted practices of interaction. To the orator, these practices represent a complex context of conditions that continually change depending on the individual situation and occasion. This is an important difference to other fields of research. It would be great if we were dealing with natural laws in rhetoric that could be described with the construction of universally valid "classical"

---

25 Olmsted 2006, p. 1.
26 Schiappa/Hamm 2007, p. 3.

systematics. Indeed, it would be great if we in rhetoric were able to find any kind of "principles" or "laws" such as those that exist in the natural sciences. Instead, the diversity of variables in any specific instance of human interaction, and in communicative practice in particular, inevitably turn rhetorical calculations (the core of oratorical competence) into cases of strategic negotiation of contingencies. In such situations, the orator (as a historically concrete agent) has to recognize and examine that which is considered communicatively convincing, plausible, and persuasive in any given situation.[27] In order to accomplish this decisive analytical task, the orator has to acquire encompassing knowledge about communicative conditions and contexts. In the following I will take a moment to consider these contexts and conditions of communication.

Here, synchronous research can shed light on important aspects of the anthropological constants of man (if they exist at all). Modern experimental psychological studies, for example, can provide information on the emotional household of man, on the response potentials of anxiety, delight, and passion. Modern philosophical logic and cognitive science can tell us a great deal about logical and argument-based thinking. Psychology can also tell us about the cognitive preconditions of human creativity. Søren Kjørup describes how many modern, synchronously operating disciplines in the humanities are currently turning towards the field of rhetoric:

> Language researchers [...] have indicated a renewed interest in the use of language, in linguistic pragmatism. A somewhat odd example is Stuart Chase's 1938 book 'The Tyranny of Words'. Inspired by rhetoric, logicians were able to renew their theory of argumentation. The most important names [in this tradition] here being Stephen Toulmin with 'The Uses of Argument' from 1958 and especially Chaïm Perelman, who wrote a treatise on argumentation entitled 'La nouvelle Rhétorique' in the same year along with L. Olbrechts-Tyteca; the title of the work simultaneously indicates its theoretical direction.[28]

Scientists from the areas of anthropology, social psychology, and economics have all developed a new focus of research, based on pragmatics, in which rhetorical thinking has an important place. Each of those groups, according to Søren Kjørup, "calls its own thinking a 'Rhetoric of Inquiry,' that is, 'research rhetoric.' The previously mentioned 'New Rhetoric' (Perelman) is closely related to this."[29]

One thing that exclusively synchronous research cannot tell us is how we can use creativity and our knowledge of cultural rules to create concrete rhetor-

---

27 Aristotle called this element of communication the *pithanón*.
28 Kjørup 1996, p. 204.
29 Kjørup 1996, p. 209.

ical strategies within a given set of situational conditions. Incidentally, this problem is found in both synchronous research and exactly that school of thought which cultivates an ahistorical understanding of classical rhetorical systematics.

Based on this, I would assert that historical knowledge is indispensable. Again we must recognize the brilliance of the old teachers of rhetoric that recommended the didactic three-step of proceeding from the *praecepta* through the *exempla* to the *imitatio*. Knowledge of action-patterns and structural-patterns, of cultural-communicative regularities, and of rules forms the heart of oratorical competence. Historical studies are indispensable for acquiring such structural and rule based knowledge.

The ideal qualities of an orator, for example – a core topic of many rhetorical treatises and textbooks – get their contours from the intellectual-historical background of their respective epochs. Such ideals are also substantially influenced by the prevailing political system of the time and place. Thus, he who wants to communicate "well" or "successfully" is advised to analyze what has been considered "good" or "successful" throughout the course of history and to focus particularly on the reasons behind such value assessments. Scrutinizing historical cases sensitizes the individual orator and the rhetorical scholar to the variety of problem solving strategies that have existed under very specific contextual conditions. Additionally, the study of historical theories of rhetoric equips an orator with the knowledge to be able to systematize standard cases.

At this point, a radical contemporarist might argue that rhetorical knowledge of models, cases, problem solving strategies and rules of communication for modern orators can also be gathered merely on the basis of contemporary empirical studies. Such a position is partially justified: one can legitimately ask the question whether it would be a loss if Aristotle were left out of rhetoric entirely. To put it another way: is it still worthwhile to study theorists such as Aristotle today?

I will answer such criticism with the help of three arguments. The first is based on the economics of knowledge: it would be inefficient to ignore the numerous case-studies and results of former rhetorical theories and to attempt to replace them with extravagant contemporary studies. The insights into communication and text theory gained in antiquity weren't simply speculative; they were gathered empirically. Theories have had to prove themselves in political practice throughout history; to a certain extent, they retain their validity even today. It is not usually very wise to try and reinvent the wheel. By contrast, modern research that is based on the results of history seeks to both clarify open questions, and simultaneously to adapt existing insights to fit modern conditions. Antiquity did not, for example, develop a rhetorical theory of media or a noteworthy theory of dimission (i.e. rhetorical communication under conditions of spatial and temporal distance). In such cases, modern theory needs to fill in the gaps left by historical rhetoric.

The second argument for a historical perspective in modern rhetoric is epistemological. The theory of knowledge cannot ignore that the invention of writing and the invention of media external to the body (such as print media) have driven knowledge and the sciences to a new qualitative level. For over five thousand years, it has been possible to disseminate information in written form across time and space and across social barriers. Since then, theories have no longer had to be created over and over again; indeed, a developed culture can no longer afford to formulate theories redundantly. A culture that doesn't develop methods for storing and developing valuable insights in the cultural household loses its intellectual vigor. A culture, yes, mankind as a whole, has to keep the achievements of significant thinkers, scholars and scientists present in order to not have to reinvent the wheel every fifty years. This, of course, does not apply to *all* kinds of knowledge that have been passed down to us: we require knowledge that is adaptable to the present and not based on mere speculation or on esoteric ideas (Wahnsysteme).

Today, new generations of researchers must have the opportunity to concentrate on the genuinely new and yet have a stable footing on the shoulders of the greats of previous eras. The best method for the creation of new knowledge is when past knowledge that is still adaptable to the present is saved and kept accessible in society. Thus, it is important that the fields of philosophy and rhetoric (as a special school of communication and textual science) ensure that the results of important theorists such as Plato, Aristotle, and Cicero are not forgotten. Their contributions to rhetorical theory in particular are still valuable. On the one hand, their empirically based models of communication can be profitably used today. On the other, and this is much more important, their high philosophical and theoretical standards make their works worthwhile for new generations; they enable a deeper insight into the character of interpersonal communication and textual functionality. In other words: an intelligent modern reading of such works proves to be refreshing stimulation.

Nevertheless, if such great thinkers are to remain attractive, we must avoid attaching too much historical and philological meaning to them. Although we must make sure that ancient theories are adequately understood, we must also show the courage to interpret them in new contexts. In integrating ancient theories into modern systems of thinking we must accept individual and evaluative interpretations as well as misunderstandings and idiosyncratic interpretations. In this way, rhetoric is also partially involved in a programmatic divorce from historicism. Leopold Ranke, the famous German theorist of historicism, summarized this sort of approach thus, "history has had assigned to it the task of judging the past, of instructing the present for the benefit of ages to come. The present study does not assume such high office; it wants to show only what actually happened."[30] Ranke's reductionism, his retreat behind the question, "what actually happened?" is not enough for modern research in rhetoric. On the other hand, Ranke's quote implies an acceptable two-pronged approach to history that includes both evaluative and instructive components. We must not only examine "what actually happened" in Ranke's sense, but also return to his principles of "judging the past" and "instructing the present" for the benefit of those to come. Rhetorical theorists that follow such an approach are in good company.

The third and final argument for historicism in rhetoric is methodological, and touches on some of the points mentioned previously in this essay. Another argument against our hypothetical radical contemporarist is to simply point to the specific achievements of the historical approach in rhetoric. There are three purely historically anchored approaches that justify historical studies in rhetoric; all of them deal with meta-structural elements.

1 Knowledge of the variance of models and thinking that considers variance: Throughout the course of history, we can identify and systematize repetitive text types and communicative models of interaction. The problem of variance is a decisive factor in such systematization: we can only recognize patterns through comparisons with history. Comparisons always demand recourse to history because social developments and changes are only discernible by comparing the present with the past. Such comparisons may refer to a theory that is only twenty years old, but can just as easily reference a theory that is two thousand years old. In a more specific rhetorical sense, looking back at history we can focus on familiar rhetorical practices and their codification. Thus, we can articulate the following requirement as an essential element of oratorical competence: always be aware that you have to produce what the situation requires; use the variety of rhetorical instruments appropriately. Historical research can shed light on the variety of possible models that might be useful in certain situations, or at least impart sensitivity for the appropriate use of rhetorical models.

2 Knowledge of different situations and thinking that considers structural differences: An orator who only utilizes contemporary standard models will not be very successful. Studying historical cases can teach him the critical role

---

30 Ranke 1824, p. 4; translation according to: Krieger 1977, p. 4.

that recognizing the specific differences of each setting plays in calibrating the calculation of communicative success. This is the core of the strategic negotiation of contingencies, and requires oratorical creativity. Here, rhetorical prognostication means using observations of differences in the past to derive difference-calculations for future tasks.

3 Knowledge of dynamic forces and thinking that considers dynamic structures: Studying the history of rhetoric, especially its theoretical history, makes clear that there have been numerous continuities. It sometimes seems as if a lot of dead scholarly material has been dragged through history. We also see, however, that development, updating and differentiation has taken place. The number of formal rhetorical figures, for example, increased from the 65 figures found in *Auctor ad Herennium* to roughly 200 in the late Renaissance. In the Baroque period, a variety of new theories were constructed especially for certain specific communicative cases, for example for the art of making compliments, for the wedding speech, or for behavioral rhetoric (e.g. Knigge), etc.

Thus, change, development and adaptation are indispensable elements of a lively rhetoric. Exploring such historical elements is the *proprium* of specific historical research in rhetoric. These arguments, and the points made clear throughout this essay, demonstrate that historical research has a firm methodological and theoretical footing in a modern scientific rhetoric.[31]

---

31 This chapter is taken from a speech given on the 23rd of November 2007 in Oslo at the "Vitenskap og retorikk" conference held by the Norwegian Academy of Science to commemorate their 150th anniversary. This conference was one of seven held on a variety of topics. German version in: Knape 2008f.

3 Oratorical Image, Prestige, Reputation and *Ethos* in Aristotelian Rhetoric

1 The Orator as a Credible Source in Modern Research

Common conceptions of rhetoric concentrate their understanding of the rhetorical process of persuasion on the ability to skillfully argue. The modern scientific theory of rhetoric, however, takes a more complex view of the act of persuasion; one which was already suggested by the theoretical approaches of some ancient thinkers. We recognize these ancient approaches in one of the most important modern theoretical models of persuasion, known as the *Elaboration Likelihood Model* (ELM).[1] As its name suggests, this model deals with probabilities related to the amount of processing that communicators (for instance, in oral speeches) expect of their addressees (audience members). The basic model distinguishes between two routes to persuasion that must be taken into account by a speaker: the *central route* (primarily through rational argumentation) and the *peripheral route* (using other communicative measures and epiphenomena of the communicative event, including non-verbal modes of communication). According to many psychological studies (and contrary to its name), the central route of persuasion is not always the most important. Recent empirical research on the foundations of the ELM has further developed and refined the model's approach. Such development has highlighted three aspects of persuasion in particular: first, the "persuasive argument" and "argument quality"[2] as classical factors of the central route that are bound to the speaker's text; and second, "message framing,"[3] which deals with the entire complex of setting and peripheral areas of communicative interaction.[4] Finally, the third important factor is "source credibility"[5], which is also a part of the peripheral route of persuasion.

Research on "source factors" on the basis of "source credibility" with corresponding "source effects"[6] grant the source of communicative intervention the same status that it used to have in classical rhetorical theories of the orator

---

1 Petty/Cacioppo 1986; see also: Petty/Wegener 1999.
2 Sinclair/Mark/Clore 1994.
3 Kahneman/Tversky 1979.
4 The setting establishes the entire set of conditions for rhetorical intervention, in which the message is to be conveyed to the audience. For more on this topic see: Knape 2000a, p. 87.
5 Jones/Sinclair/Courneya 2003.
6 Jones/Sinclair/Courneya 2003, pp. 181 f.

(although rhetoric considers the orator to be the "Archimedean point" of the entire rhetorical system).[7] These recent studies have concluded that "greater persuasion" is to be expected from "expert sources", an unsurprising result for rhetoricians.[8] In other words, the rhetorical actor who (as the source of a statement) is considered to be an expert by his audience has a persuasive advantage.

2 Processuality in the Construction of Personal *Image, Prestige* and *Reputation*

Such considerations place the personality of rhetorical communicators in social contexts in the spotlight. One can ask the question of *why* a given orator's statements are attributed the qualities of expertise and credibility. An important dimension of such questions is the concept of development: in modern research, characteristics such as *esteem, image, prestige* or *reputation* are considered to be the result of procedural occurrences. In other words: when addressees attribute the categories of *image, prestige* or *reputation* (to stay with these three terms) they resort to conceptions that have been shaped by their own individual experiences.

Is it conceivable that such mentally charged imaginative complexes, variable between each individual, can be discretely defined using these three terms and that these three terms can be clearly differentiated from one another? There seems to be a consensus in research on the topic that these termini are related, but that they can, indeed, be differentiated using certain criteria. Firstly, it should be noted that *image*, as used in social psychology and communication science, is *descriptive*: it is oriented towards a relief-like modeling of the reference object (in this case, a rhetorically active human being), and thereby moves in the direction of some kind of object definition. The terms *prestige* and *reputation*, on the other hand, entail a positive *evaluative* judgment of the reference object. This difference can be used as the main characteristic of a terminological distinction. In general, one could say that *image* is (not entirely, but primarily) a descriptive term, while *prestige* and *reputation* are evaluative terms. Still, one can and should make further distinctions:[9]

Reference Object: The scientific term *image* is applied to a wide spectrum of socially relevant objects and subjects, to 'things' of all kinds (persons, insti-

---

7 Knape 2000a, p. 33.

8 Jones/Sinclair/Courneya 2003, p. 182, referring to: Heesacker/Petty/Cacioppo 1983.

9 For more on the following distinctions, see: Brenzikofer 2002, pp. 113–203; Eisenegger 2004, pp. 14–40; Rademacher 2006.

tutions, companies, technologies, cities, professions, animals, products, or goods). In contrast, one can say that the terms *prestige* and *reputation* are regularly restricted to "*actors*, to (*collective) subjects* that are equipped with a consciousness."[10] In this vein, Barbara Brenzikofer, in a 2002 study on the focus of behavioral and economic sciences, stated, "as the bearer of reputation, the individual actors are in the foreground of the theoretical approaches used here. This is not anything surprising for a scientific discipline in which observed events at the social level are reduced to the actions of individual persons under the terms of methodological individualism."[11] Since Max Weber, the concept of *prestige* as a sociologically identifiable reaction has been defined as an, "evaluation that other people make about an individual, a group, or a situation."[12]

Selection and extent of characterization: The construction of an image can incorporate all conceivable individual aspects of the perception of an object or subject in its image-making model. The resulting "image" will be of further interest later in this chapter. The stimulus or catalyst of *prestige*, on the other hand, is largely social success in a certain area ("arising from success"[13]) that is based on talents or competencies and is associated with a certain "glamour"[14] as a component of presentation. These elements create the social reaction of *admiration* and *esteem*.[15] *Reputation* is stimulated or catalyzed by performance, merit, achievement, possessing an advantage in qualification or competence, and talent (which also serve as criteria of judgment). These qualities (in an actor) attest to their ability and competence in a certain area or field and help others avoid uncertainty related to the area or field. Further features of *reputation* include reliability and performance-readiness, which both take the risk aversion of the counterpart into account. In relation to the reactions addressees, *prestige* and *reputation* are characterized equally by the attribution of high esteem and attractiveness. The definition of an actor's reputation is also particularly influenced by social (e.g. professional) influences (*consequence*).[16]

Value sign: In our context, the term *image* does not imply any special evaluative orientation relative to people or objects, and can be associated with any

---

10 Eisenegger 2004, p. 14.
11 Brenzikofer 2002, p. 133.
12 Brenzikofer 2002, p. 134.
13 Shenkar/Yuchtman-Yaar 1997, p. 1362.
14 Drever 1973, p. 221.
15 Becher/Kogan 1992, p. 111.
16 Becher/Kogan 1992, p. 111.

and all value orientations. Accordingly one can talk about both a positive image and a negative image, or about a damaged image. As scientific terms, *prestige* and *reputation*, in contrast, are partially defined by an important positive-evaluative semantic attribute.[17] In the context of social interaction, they are often associated with the reactions of recognition or "speaker attractiveness."[18]

Strength of validity and the foundation of order: Naturally, *image, prestige* and *reputation* can ultimately be traced back to individual impressions and judgments. Prestige and reputation, however, display their social effects through group manifestations. The creation of image, on the other hand, can be a very individual reaction on the part of the addressee. Clearly, the social power of images (for instance, in the form of situative group reactions during public speeches) is made effective by group consensus. If this leads to any kind of sociologically definable ordered structures, however, then these structures are highly instable. Therefore, *image, prestige* and *reputation* can, indeed, be used to denote differences. On the part of the speaker, *prestige* is manifested by, "signs and prestige symbols," and functions on the part of the addressees as a form of symbolic social differentiation. In this way, it constitutes, "a factor of social order."[19] The fact is that the social factor of *prestige* is exactly as fragile as that of *image*, while the order generating force of *reputation* is significantly stronger. Due to its, "*evaluative function*, the social resource of reputation is attributed a central role in the establishment and maintenance of social order," in a given field, since it allows for the formation of expert-hierarchies. "Reputation is an integral part of the social process by which individuals are assigned rank and place within society."[20]

Social areas of validity: The *image* of a person or thing that has been created by communicative processes can have very personal importance, but can also lead (through media) to a wider social tuning. Accordingly, the creation of an image covers a wide spectrum between mainstream and idiosyncratic beliefs. *Prestige* displays its importance only within groups and entire societies: the single opinion of an individual cannot constitute *prestige* as a social-psychological unit. Viewed psychologically, *prestige* is first, "a subjective variable. At

---

[17] This despite the fact that the common English usage of the word reputation can be either positive or negative.

[18] Voswinkel 2001, p. 23; and Hosman 2008, p. 1120. A contrasting view can be found in Brenzikofer 2002, p. 139, where the sociological concept of reputation is considered "neutral" (in contrast with "positive" prestige).

[19] Brenzikofer 2002, pp. 135 ff.

[20] Eisenegger 2004, p. 19.

the same time, however, sociology demands that it be valid as an objective metric of structure,"[21] that affects even the, "hierarchical social fabric."[22] *Reputation*, on the other hand, is normally, "conceived as a particular social good."[23] What does this mean? *Reputation* is usually created in more narrowly defined groups (e.g. professional groups) and in social networks where the judges (constituents) can be more clearly defined (e.g. customers or co-workers in business or expert peers in the sciences).

Communicative context: Today, social scientific and psychological research is largely unified in the sentiment that the expression of *prestige* and *reputation* is embedded in communicative *processes*, and is not created in isolated instances. This cannot be said so definitively for *image*, as I will detail later in this chapter. Here, we must again concede to the wide variation in the creation of *image* in addressees (for instance, in the context of a series of completely individual experiences). In contrast, modern research is ready to attach extremely restrictive conditions to communication dealing with *reputation*: "Public communication is the *conditio sine qua non* for the creation and maintenance of reputation. Thus, the term reputation is reserved for public communication, and particularly for communication transmitted by [technical] media."[24]

Temporal dimension: The dimension of time appears to be quite flexible in the creation, endurance and end of *images*. *Prestige* seems to be similar. At the same time, there are academic statements about the consistency and inconsistency of *prestige*, in particular when the attribution of prestige is directed at an individual. According to Brenzikofer, *prestige* is, "subject to relatively strong changes," because it is created, "by the continually renewed interaction between the bearer of prestige and the interpreter of prestige," and, "must be confirmed."[25] The dimension of time in *reputation* is formulated through periods of slow development and crisis-laden breaks: "A good reputation is driven by many, markedly difficult and tedious tasks. And, unfortunately, one other thing is clear: the hard earned reputation can be ruined in a heartbeat."[26] Having said that, we also see that *reputation* is an important factor of social sustainability through the consideration of *reputation* in areas such as personnel decisions in the business world. "Reputation is insofar an inter-temporal

---

21 Wegener 1985, p. 209.
22 Brenzikofer 2002, p. 137.
23 Eisenegger 2004, p. 16.
24 Eisenegger 2004, p. 41.
25 Brenzikofer 2002, p. 136.
26 Offenhäuser 2006, p. 95.

construct as decisions on optimization are made over multiple periods such that its utility is optimized over time."[27]

3 The Modern Concepts of *Image* and *Ethos* as Found in Aristotle

The rhetorical approach always clearly distinguishes between production-theoretical and reception-theoretical perspectives. Naturally, everything that we might know about possible addressee reactions can be useful for an orator's effective calculations. But the rhetorical perspective focuses on the orator's problems. Thus, rhetorical theory primarily asks the question of with which strategies, and on the basis of which calculations, an orator is able to integrate his own personality in communicative interventions. Such considerations can easily be joined with a long list of theoretical offerings from modern psychology and sociology. Almost all of the, "techniques for self-portrayal and impression-management found in the literature have the function of drawing a positive image of ones own person and transmitting this on some kind of audience."[28] A comprehensive survey of these impression-management techniques was given by Hans Dieter Mummendey in his 1995 book, 'The Psychology of Self-portrayal.'[29] Research has investigated the following components of self-portrayal: signaling high standards, highlighting titles (*entitlement*), emphasizing competence and expertise (*expertise*), portraying oneself as popular, attractive and exemplary (*exemplification*), enhancing one's own standing through acquaintances with celebrities or other contacts (*basking in reflected glory*) or using these to distinguish oneself from others positively (*boosting*). In situativity (face-to-face communication), elements such as body language and facial expression can play an important role. Occasionally, depending on the given concrete setting, even displaying an over abundant sense of self-worth (*self-enhancement*) or an overabundance of self-confidence (*overstatement*) can be appropriate. Here, research speaks of *self-promotion*, since the goal is to portray oneself in the best possible light to addressees. Rhetorically speaking, such tactics are not considered simple flattery or unserious ingratiation, but rather articulate those qualities that are expected by addressees in the communicative process: "status and prestige, reliability and credibility, candor and humanity."[30] Sociologist Erving Goffman said that in many social

---

27 Brenzikofer 2002, p. 133.
28 Mummendey 2000, p. 47.
29 Mummendey 1995; prior to this see also: Mummendey/Bolten 1985.
30 Mummendey 2000, p. 48.

situations, we have no choice but to assume certain role schemata or to fulfill certain role expectations. He spoke of a social 'face' (lat. *persona*) that we assume: "The term *face* may be defined as the positive social value a person effectively claims for himself by the line others assume he has taken during a particular contact."[31] Goffman's approach has been further developed by others such as Penelope Brown and Stephen Levinson. They distinguish between an internal self-image (positive face) and an external self-image (negative face) that is variable based on situation and thus represents a statement of free personal expression.[32]

Aristotle, a sharp observer of the social conditions of the Greek polis, clearly anticipated such considerations in his rhetorical theory of *ethos*. But before delving into his theoretical suggestions, another interface between ancient and modern doctrine must be examined more closely: the concept of the image. This concept, too, can easily be associated with Aristotle's thoughts on ethos. The previously mentioned scientific category of the *image* has been well developed in American research since the works of Burleigh B. Gardner and Lee Rainwater in 1955 and Kenneth E. Boulding in 1956. Such research has focused on that which we can tentatively call the rhetorical *image* of the orator in concrete communicative processes.[33] As I made clear in the previous section, the word image is also used today in social psychology, market research, and in other social sciences to denote a defined person, organization or thing.[34] Our concern, however, is whether, and to what extent, this term can be integrated into the cannon of rhetorical theory. From the perspective of a rhetorical theory of production, the image would have to be an offering (in the sense of the above mentioned impression-management) that the orator exhibits in communication, with the expectation that a certain reaction will take place in the addressees if they accept (or partially accept) it. An orator would then make an image calculation in light of these expectations.

In his periphrasis of the psychological concept of *image* from 1991, economic psychologist Reinhold Bergler explained what kinds of expected cognitive reactions can be evoked in addressees by a productive image-offering from a reception-theoretical perspective. We call these possible reactions the 'receptive image':

---

31 Goffman 1967, p. 5.
32 Brown/Levinson 1987, pp. 61–64.
33 Gardner/Rainwater 1955; Boulding 1956.
34 Faulstich 2000, p. 125. The multidisciplinary use of the term *image* has also lead to accusations its lack of "clarity" and therefore to its unacceptability as a terminus technicus: (Faulstich 2000, p. 124). Overviews of approaches to image research can also be found in: Holly 2001; and Borgstedt 2008, pp. 73–116.

A [receptive] image is a simplified, over clarified, and evaluative mental image, a quasi-judgment that knows no limits to its validity and is not sufficiently empirically secured. All objects that are accessible to human perception, experience and thought are always also simplified – as images – Landscapes, countries, technologies, cities, professions, sciences, people, animals, plants, climates. Images (judgments) are a universal phenomenon. They represent reality not in photographic detail, but rather draw their conclusions from key stimuli, exemplary performances, individual successes; but also from individual failures. As the psychology of first impressions makes clear, images are created rapidly on the basis of a minimum of information. The requisite psychological mechanisms function at high speed and largely automatically, without interference from thought. Skepticism and doubt are turned off, the ifs and buts are not tolerated, but for those subjectively plausible, apparently unambiguous judgments.[35]

Accordingly, there are four mechanisms that constitute the *receptive* creation of images on the part of addressees:
1. Simplification through classification in the sense of a reduction of complexity to a few core features.
2. Generalization from individual experience that are personally considered acceptable.
3. Over-clarification through the higher valuation of certain features to the detriment of others, much like the effects of a microscope.
4. Radical partisanship for a particular possible judgment in order to loosen the breaks on further action due to uncertainty.[36]

Rhetoricians, however, are above all interested in the complementary side of these considerations: the *produced* image. This involves observing a structure that has been released and can be observed in communicative processes. For Aristotle, this structure is primarily to be found in texts, is called *ethos*, and refers to the consciously presented character of the orator that can be found in situative speech texts.[37] In reference to this, Roland Barthes spoke of facial expressions and tones as "attributes" of the speaker, which he must produce, implement in text, and "show" the audience before their own receptive power of image creation can unfold.[38]

Why are such elements necessary? Is the power of logical argumentation not sufficient? Aristotle, too, posed such questions, and took a clear position in relation to other contemporary rhetoric teachers: "for it is not the case, as some writers of rhetorical treatises lay down in their 'Art,' that the worth (*epi-*

---

35 Bergler 1991, p. 47.
36 Compare to: Bentele 1992, p. 154.
37 Fortenbaugh 1992.
38 Barthes 1970, p. 74.

Handwritten note: ethos - most effective aspect of persuasion / rhetoric

eíkeia) of the orator in no way contributes to h
contrary, moral character (*ēthos*), so to say,
means of proof."[39] Aristotle left no doubt abou
cal components of self-portrayal, which we ha
within the concept of a produced image.[40]

Why is this so? Aristotle found the answe
rhetorical communication.[41] If a given interaction is to be considered a case of
rhetorical communication, then a mental difference (an asymmetrical condition) must be present among partners: something must be in dispute or there
must be contradictory judgments.[42] Rhetorical effort is only necessary in order
to elicit a decision one way or the other; in other words, to cause a change in
opinion, attitude or behavior. For this very reason, Aristotle began his apologia
on image construction at the beginning of the second book of his 'Art of Rhetoric' with the words,

> But since the object of Rhetoric is judgement (*krísis*) – for judgements are pronounced in
> deliberative rhetoric and judicial proceedings are a judgement – it is not only necessary
> to consider how to make the speech itself demonstrative and convincing, but also that
> the speaker should show himself to be of a certain character and should know how to
> put the judge into a certain frame of mind.[43]

Thus, in rhetorical situations the addressees should be primed in a certain
way, be furnished with something additional, be prepared for rational argumentation. It is obvious that rational argumentation alone cannot entirely suf-
fice in all situations, but often requires a communicative framework (a *framing*)
which builds an additional layer of meaning that helps create understanding.
In communication research, frames are understood as, "patterns of interpretation of mass media themes," which, as Urs Dahinden has somewhat roughly
stated, are, "not identical with these themes," but rather, "are transferrable to
other themes as generalized interpretation patterns."[44] In this sense, the positive or negative evaluation of an orator that is at least somewhat based on
his image can serve as a frame for an audience; as an orientation point for
understanding his rational arguments.

---

39 Aristotle: Rhetoric, 1.2.4.
40 Wörner 1981.
41 For more on the fundamental problem of defining rhetorical communication, see: Knape
2000a, p. 64.
42 Knape 2003a, col. 874 f.
43 Aristotle: Rhetoric, 2.1.2.
44 Dahinden 2006, p. 18; see also: Goffman 1974.

Why isn't it possible for purely rational argumentation to stand alone in rhetorical situations? Because the concrete communicative settings described by Aristotle in which rhetoric takes place (in people's assemblies and in the courtroom) do not normally deal with apodictic-syllogistic proofs, but rather with probabilistic proofs that are based on purely probabilistic premises. In such situations, consensus must first be built among communication partners. According to Aristotle (translated by Martin Heidegger), the theme of these communicative situations is that, "which [is] always already habitually an object of deliberation."[45] As Heidegger himself continued in his description of Aristotle's rhetoric,

> because of this, there is a definite concrete orientation toward that wich is the topic of conversation. Insofar as it concerns [...] *éndoxon* [opinion], insofar as there is discourse of general opinions in opposition to general views for the purpose of cultivating a definite view, this discoursing is not situated in the realm of *dialégesthai* [discussing scientifically].[46] In this discoursing, concerned as it is with such objects, the speaker and the one who is spoken to are fundamentally important. In *dialégesthai*, on the other hand, it is to a certain degree a matter of indifference to whom it is spoken, and a matter of indifference who I am, how I operate therein. In speaking in the previously mentioned sense, the *ēthos* of the speaker and the *páthos* of the one spoken to, are relevant. For both of these determinations ground the manner and mode in which *dóxa* [opinion] is possessed, the way in which he whom the view is to be imparted stands with respect to the view.[47]

Thus, it is about, "how the speaker and the addressee conduct themselves toward the *dóxa* of which there is speaking."[48] The importance of the *ethos*, that is, the construction of image, emerges from the unsure ground of mere opinion upon which rhetorical arguments in social life often stand. The image provides a special factor of security and judgment for the communicative event. Heidegger translates the relevant passage of Aristotle's 'The Art of Rhetoric' (1.2.4) as follows:

> If we have firm views, then, 'we trust all the more quickly, and to a greater extent, the decent human beings who make a good impression, *perì pántōn mèn haplōs*, and above all when the matter is controversial, where there can be arguments on this side and that side, where the matter remains unsettled. It is only settled by the manner and mode in which the speaker offers himself'.[49]

---

45 Heidegger: Basic Concepts, § 16 a), p. 109.
46 *dialégesthai*: That, "which is treated in scientific discussion", relies upon that kind of "speech" that, "has no further aim, which does not follow from the natural function of practical speaking." Heidegger: Basic Concepts, §15 e) β), p. 107.
47 Heidegger: Basic Concepts, § 16 a), p. 109.
48 Heidegger: Basic Concepts, § 16 a), p. 109.
49 Heidegger: Basic Concepts, § 14 b), pp. 82 f.

In the Freese's translation, this same passage reads:

> The orator persuades by moral character when his speech is delivered in such a manner as to render him worthy of confidence; for we feel confidence in a greater degree and more readily in persons of worth in regard to everything in general, but where there is no certainty and there is room for doubt, our confidence is absolute.

In the moment of the fleeting situative performance of an orator's text, the addressee needs extra indicators, extra information, and extra proofs (provided by the above mentioned frames) in order to accept the argumentation. The already present or provided image of the actor's personality, or that of the primary orator that stands behind them (the actual 'sender'), provides insight into the pragmatic status of the statement they make, whether it is competent in content and of urging importance and relevance to the addressees.[50] For Aristotle, this is clearly the case, "as proofs are established not only by demonstrative (*apodeiktikós*), but also by ethical (*ēthikós*) argument – since we have confidence in an orator who exhibits certain qualities, such as goodness, goodwill, or both".[51]

4 The Rhetorical Ethos in the Moment of Speech

Modern rhetoric clearly recognizes the processual character of rhetorical intervention.[52] In this respect, however, there is one clear difference with ancient

---

50 This is also clearly expressed in Heidegger's interpretation of the concept of ethos: "The *ēthos* of the speaker must be something altogether determinate with which he appears to the audience as one who, as a person, in fact speaks for the matter that he represents. The *ēthos* must satisfy the definitions of *aretē* [integrity], *phrónesis* [knowledge about the subject], and *eúnoia* [empathy, good will]. The *ēthos* is nothing other than the manner and mode in which is revealed what the speaker wants – willing in the sense of the *prohaíresis* [decisiveness] of something. In this way, Aristotle also determines the role of *ēthos* in the 'Poetics': *ēthos* 'makes manifest, at the moment, the being-resolved of the speaker.' [Poetics 1450b8]. There is no *ēthos* in the sort of discourse whose sense does not depend upon being resolved about something or bringing others to a definite resolve. Rather, such discourse depends on *diánoia* [thinking]: that which is necessary in order to be able to exhibit something with respect to its being-character. Setting down these conditions of discourse at each moment is not something that has been exhausted up to now, as one can ask to what extent, in scientific and philosophical accounts, *lógos* [the performed text] is to be taken simply as *deiknýnai* [showing], and to what extent there is *prohaireĩsthai* [deciding] in them. This is not the place to explain these connections more precisely. I am merely pointing out that is would perhaps be in order if philosophers were resolved to reckon what it actually means to speak to others." Heidegger: Basic Concepts, § 16 c), pp. 114 f.
51 Aristotle: Rhetoric, 1.8.6.
52 Knape 1998.

rhetorical theories: their concepts focused completely on settings with punctual, situative and oral speech events. The truth is that some theories of the 4th century B.C.E. went significantly farther, for instance as clearly seen in Plato's 'Phaedrus' or in Alcidamas' writings.[53] Both saw an oratorical product created in the moment of the event, and performed by *ex tempore dicere*, in the impromptu (the *autoschediasmós*), as the true and authentic operation of rhetoric. We can add to this Plato's well known theoretical exposition on the worthlessness of writing in 'Phaedrus'.[54] From the perspective of the history of communication and rhetoric, it is interesting that the originality of face-to-face situativity was so radically exalted. The structural conditions of the fundamental "situative" setting are characterized by all communicative partners being proxemic, that is, physically near each other in an interactive face-to-face context. This has a wide array of psychological, cognitive, textual and media-theoretical implications. For the Aristotelian concept of *ēthos*, for instance, the reference to situativity demands that an orator must prepare and offer his image stimulus in the moment. Aristotle is clear about the fact that the rhetorical efficiency calculation is made in relation to a punctual situative event in which all rhetorical effects must unfold. The well-known unity of time, place, and action found in Aristotle's poetic theory is also clearly valid here.[55] Here, the communicative action is naturally bound up with the concept of the orator, who was always treated as both a text producer and a text performer in ancient theory.[56] But Aristotle did not go so far as Alcidamas, who insisted that speech texts should never be written and prepared in advance. By allowing for the pre-construction of texts, Aristotle did not completely expose his orator to the contingency of the situation. He believed that rhetoric is indeed a *techné*, with codified knowledge that can be applied to concrete communicative situations. This knowledge is related somewhat vaguely to the technical arts, as we find later in Sophist and Roman theoreticians. In his work on rhetoric, Aristotle first identified and systematized the fundamental factors that, in his opinion, could be rhetorically relevant (in contexts of argument and persuasion). These factors are Logos, Ethos and Pathos.

Naturally, logos, the text of a speech intended to be orally presented, was assigned particular importance. Within the logos, structures must be created,

---

53 Alcidamas: On Sophists.

54 Plato: Phaedrus, 274b–277a.

55 From text generation to performance, everything is to be viewed as a single concentrated and cohesive event.

56 This despite that fact that even in ancient Greece, there were famous speech writers (*logographs*) as secondary orators whose speeches were then given performed by primary orators.

that take heed of the cognitive and perceptive limits of the listener. The 'ephemeral' (non-persistent), the rapid linearity in the performative 'time-flow', and the logical sequence of argumentation found in orally performed speech texts[57] demand the calibration of the logos to the momentary and real perceptive possibilities of the *listeners*, even when the text has been prepared beforehand. For this reason it sometimes suffices when argumentation based on the rhetorical sister of the syllogism, the enthymeme (which has been created especially for the given setting and contains only probabilistic premises), is plausible in the concrete speech event. Aristotle naturally also envisioned situational tuning in the use of the other argumentative instruments, ethos and pathos.[58]

Important for the concept of ethos, for starters, is that it is also considered a form of evidence in persuasive contexts. And like the others, it is also activated by the text of the speech itself, which means that it must be found within the logos. In the enumeration of the three forms of evidence, ethos is found at the very beginning of Aristotle's rhetorical work, and thus is given hierarchical prominence, "now the proofs (*písteis*) furnished by the speech (*lógos*) are of three kinds. The first depends upon the moral character of the speaker (*ēthos*), the second upon putting the hearer into a certain frame of mind [referring to *páthos*], the third upon the speech itself (*lógos*), in so far as it proves or seems to prove."[59]

Despite the primary position of ethos in the book, later references to this topic in Aristotle's second book are quite brief. For this reason, they are inviting subjects of further development and thought in modern times, in particular because they provide important fundamental insights that are easily incorporated into the modern theories of impression-management and image. In his 1970 work on 'The Old Rhetoric', French semiologist Roland Barthes summarized these considerations thus,

> *Ethè* are the attributes of the orator (and not those of the public, *pathè*): these are the character traits which the orator must *show* the public (his sincerity is of little account) in order to make a good impression: these are his "airs," his qualities, his expressions. Hence there is no question here of an expressive psychology; it is a psychology of the imaginary (in the psychoanalytic sense: of the imaginary as an image-repertoire): I must signify what I want to be *for the other*. This is why – in the perspective of this theatrical psychology – it is better to speak of *tones* than of characters: tone in the musical and ethical sense which the word had in Greek music. *Ethos* is, strictly speaking, a connotation: the orator gives a piece of information and *at the same time* says: I am this, I am not that.[60]

---

57 Knape 2008b.
58 Knape 2010a, p. 26.
59 Aristotle: Rhetoric, 1.2.3.
60 Barthes 1970, p. 74.

When the speaker takes the stage, multiple things must occur *simultaneously* in the moment of the performance of the text.

> We would like to subsume the observation of these phenomena in modern rhetorical theory under the concept of the rhetorical 'threefold saying' (triphasis), according to a trifold calculation of interaction. In situative settings we must presuppose the necessity of a multi-tracked interaction, or of multi-factorial, stimulating intervention on the part of the orator. Aristotle thereby considered the main instrument of the orator, his text, and clearly visualized three semantic layers within the logos: first, pure argumentation on the subject, which does not involve a pure exchange of *information*, but rather persuasively relevant proofs, which are primarily associated with the concept of enthymemes (logical level). Second, the simultaneous evocation of tuned emotional states (pathetic level) that are favorable for the acceptance of the argument (emotional level). Third, and also simultaneously, the construction of a particular *image* of the performing orator (*ēthos*), (anchored in the addressees as an association with characteristic features of the text creator and performer) that also creates favorable conditions for the orator's argumentation (source level).[61]

Each level represented its own *pístis* for Aristotle, its own method of persuasion, proof, or authentication.[62] These methods can be simultaneously activated in a text, even given different emphasis; they can make themselves independent. And when one seeks to give a special sort of speech that is directed at personal characteristics, a 'speech of self-representation' (an *ēthikòs lógos*) that focuses on the self-image of the orator, then it should not be over laden with rational proofs. According to Aristotle, "nor should you look for an enthymeme at the time when you wish to give the speech a personal character (*ēthikós*); for demonstration involves neither character (*ēthos*) nor inner resolution."[63]

5 Ethos as Rhetorical Signal of Cooperation

For Aristotle, the conditions of performance in normal speech are decisive for the support of rational argument with ethos and pathos (image and emotional components). In the rapid linear progression of the verbally performed text, the addressee cannot always clearly (or without help) get an overview, test, or understand every informational claim, or the degree of reality, facticity and binding statements contained within. Despite this, the addressee seeks to

---

61 Knape 2010a, p. 27.
62 For more on these topics see Christof Rapp's 2002 comments in his edition of Aristotle's Rhetoric (Aristoteles: Rhetorik, Zweiter Halbband [Commentary], pp. 980–983).
63 Aristotle: Rhetoric, 3.17.8; transl. Knape.

retain his trust and the assumption of credibility in the orator until proven otherwise. In doing so, he is attuned to the standard communicative *frame* in which Grice's maxims are valid; I will speak about these maxims more below.[64]

The German linguist Hans Jürgen Heringer accounted for this attunement on the part of the addressee (with reference to Herbert P. Grice's theory) with the fundamental, psychosocially anchored principle of cooperation that we all expect in normal communication. Communication is, "in general, a cooperative task," because,

> the speaker/writer wants the hearer/reader to understand him, and because these actually have the desire to understand him. The principle of cooperation is found in the fact that both must undertake coordinated actions in the fulfillment of this goal. This fundamental communication forms the most external frame of all communication. It is only within this framework that competition becomes possible. I can only effectively argue or verbally spar with someone that also understands me. Thus, I will generally act as if he understands me, and in this respect stick to the principle of cooperation. Even a liar holds himself to this principle. He too, says something that the one who is lied to understands; in fact, he will even adjust his speech to his victim, because he wants ensure that his lie appears plausible. Only then will it be believed. Communication is an interplay between cooperative and competitive goal setting. But the outer boundary is cooperation, and this comprised of shared conventions and shared knowledge.[65]

Because of the risk of lies (noted by Heringer above), and also because of mistakes, nonsense, and errors that can be inherent in every text, addressees must look for other indicators, external to the text or the argument, that at least provide the feeling of security (in the sense of cooperative expectations) with regard to the textual semantics and argumentation. The image is one such indicator. It is part of our method for establishing the credibility of a speaker (developed and refined over the course of our lives), which we automatically utilize when we find ourselves in dubious communicative situations and are unsure how the assumed principle of cooperation is to be construed.

"Maxims of human communication were discovered amazingly late. While the relevant insights are contained in the proverbs of many cultures, but – as it so often is with proverbs – one can also always find the opposite."[66] A systematic catalog of maxims was first provided by Grice in 1967.[67] "His functional perspective clarified the values of maxims in human communication. Grice began with the assumption that human communication is a rational and

---

64 For more on the difference between the expectations of standard or normal communicative frames and specialized frames, see: Knape 2008a and p. 15 in this volume.
65 Heringer 1990, p. 87.
66 Heringer 1990, p. 84.
67 Grice 1967.

cooperative undertaking, even though he also admitted that there may be other forms of communication."[68] For Grice, the principle of cooperation was fundamental: make your contribution to conversation such that it fits within the accepted goal or direction of the conversation.[69] From this core principle, Grice derived four maxims:

1. *Quantity*: Be informative! "Make your contribution as informative as is required", say no more or no less.
2. *Quality*: Be honest! "Do not say what you believe to be false" or that you have no reason for believing to be true.
3. *Relation*: Be relevant! Say only that which you truly believe is important for your partner.
4. *Manner*: Be perspicuous! Speak understandably and avoid vagaries, keep your statements as brief as possible and well ordered.

According to Heringer, "while the maxims 1 through 3 are directed at that which is said, the fourth addresses more the how."[70] Especially in light of the rhetorical, agonal-competitive starting position of persuasive processes, it might,

> be surprising that Grice selected the principle of cooperation for the foundation of his maxims, and even declared such cooperation to be rational. Is this not somewhat naïve? Isn't our communication full of conflict, guile and fraud, and thus full of competition? There are two factors here to consider:
>
> (i) Human cooperation has developed as an evolutionarily stable strategy, and we can prove that it is (in principle) superior to competition.
> (ii) a linguistic act, a conversation, must not be either cooperative or competitive. It can be both – though admittedly at different levels of judgment.[71]

Without mentioning it explicitly, Aristotle also assumed a connection between rhetorical competition and fundamental communicative cooperation. His theory of ethos must be viewed with this background. In his consideration of ethos, he identified three productive components of image, which if lacking could shake the expected principle of cooperation.[72] Heidegger explained the three components as follows: "1. *phrónesis*, 'looking around' – the speaker must appear to be someone who looks around in discourse itself; 2. *aretē*,

---

68 Heringer 1990, pp. 84 f.; Grice 1967 (ed. 1975), pp. 47 f.
69 Cf. Grice 1967 (ed. 1975), pp. 45 ff., and p. 15 in this volume.
70 Heringer 1990, pp. 84 f.
71 Heringer 1990, pp. 84 f.
72 As Aristotle wrote, "for speakers are wrong both in what they say and in the advice they give, because they lack either all three or one of them." Aristotle: Rhetoric, 2.1.5.

'seriousness', transcribed earlier with *spoudaîos* (earnest); 3. *eúnoia*, 'good attitude,' 'good will'."[73] The speaker that considers these components and is able to bring them to bear in speech will, "have real trust – he will himself be a *pístis* [proof, evidence] in his *lógos* [spoken text]."[74] These three components of image are also reflected in Grice's maxims. Using Heidegger's words, we can unify these maxims with Aristotle's concepts:

1. *Expert knowledge*: "In his discourse, the speaker can appear," as one who has, "*the right perspective on the matter* about which he speaks [...] The view that he conveys is [...] oriented toward what the matter genuinely is".[75] This aspect of image can be directly correlated with the first Gricean maxim of information. Its function is *to safeguard* the accuracy of the statements as coming from someone that is competent in the subject.

2. *Integrity, which is expressed by earnestness*: the speaker says everything that, according to his own best knowledge and conscience, "appears to him to be the case, about which he has this or that view." He does not screen his own position and view of the matter, holds nothing back, and makes clear that he is, "*serious*" about, "what he says to his audience."[76] This aspect of image can be correlated with Grice's second maxim of truthfulness. Its function is to *authenticate* potentially dubious claims about a topic by proving the seriousness of the source.

3. *Engagement and positive attitude towards the addressees*: "In the counsel he delivers," the speaker does not want to, "withhold the most decisive positive possibility that his *phrónesis* has entirely at his disposal."[77] He demonstrates good will for his communicative partner and hopes that both empathy and sympathy are given to him in return. He makes clear that people interest him, that he dedicates himself to them, and that he only wants to say and advise the best for them.[78] Here, we see Grice's third maxim of relevance. The benevolent orator signals that he will only say relevant and important things to his addresses. Accordingly, the function of this image aspect is to make the thematic information *acceptable* through an emotional appeal.

In light of these categories, the threefold strategic calculating and acting (the triphasis) that the orator must consider in the rhetorical event is clear. While

---

73 Heidegger: Basic Concepts, § 16 b), p. 111.

74 Heidegger: Basic Concepts, § 16 b), p. 113.

75 Heidegger: Basic Concepts, § 16 b), p. 112.

76 Heidegger: Basic Concepts, § 16 b), p. 112.

77 Heidegger: Basic Concepts, § 16 b), p. 112.

78 Heidegger: Basic Concepts, § 16 b), p. 112.

the persuasive text should articulate the competitive and help to evoke opinion change using all means possible, the construction of the image should highlight the cooperative, and thereby couch the argumentation in the desired contextual orientation. This is strengthened by pathos effects as well.

The argumentative level in the logos may indeed be militant and demanding, but its source – the orator – should be recognized as having a very specific sort of structure. This is consolidated in the addressee's concept of the orator's "image" as a source of the text. And in the middle of this concept stands the principle of cooperation. The image serves as a psychological support that indicates to the addressee: even if the content of the text or its argumentation is confrontational to you, and may even be unpleasant because it seeks to undo your trusted ideas and move you to change your mental position (and this is exactly the mechanism of persuasion), the framing created by the image can allay your fears because it signalizes that the orator wants to cooperate with you.[79]

---

79 German version of this chapter in: Knape 2012b.

4 Language or Rhetoric? A Dialog

The title of this chapter implies a dichotomy that does not, in reality, exist. Nevertheless, I chose this title to draw attention to an important distinction. Our scientific categories should refer to clearly defined terminology and well-defined areas of research. In the majority of cases, however, the terms "language" and "rhetoric" are not used precisely; the colloquial and scientific meanings of these terms are often confused with one another.

Imagine yourself participating in a unique and extraordinary expedition with a group of other scholars both living and deceased. A new island has been discovered and we are the first people permitted to pay a visit to the unique culture that exists there. It is the dream of every anthropologist! We are allowed to bring back a recording of this trip depicting life in the marketplace of this unknown island. We are to deliver a report on the island's culture to UNESCO solely on the basis of this video material. To ensure that the ecological and cultural system there can develop without outside influence, never again will anyone be allowed to set foot on this island.

What do we see and hear in this film? We can see the colorful hustle and bustle of the marketplace as the camera zooms in on different scenes. In the first scene, we see that the wind has blown over a stall full of wooden barrels. Many friendly bystanders are silently helping the salesman to rebuild his stand and to put the barrels back in place. The second scene shows us a group of women who seem to be noisily haggling over a piece of clothing. In the third, a tradesman is obviously talking up his melons; we also notice that people are buying his melons while ignoring his neighbors' product. The fourth scene focuses on a group of men sitting in a circle who seem to be engaged in conversation. Finally, in the fifth scene we see a man addressing passers-by. Some of them carry on walking, some stop. Some of the listeners nod approvingly, while others make signs of disapproval. The man waves his arms, then stands still, all the while continually uttering sounds. He sits down on the ground, crouching, folding his arms, and lowering his head. Then he gets up again and raises his hands to the sky. Not once does he stop making noises. He sits, he cries, his gestures become calmer and finally, he laughs. Throughout it all, he continues to utter, sometimes loudly, sometimes quietly, but without pause. Then, suddenly, he leaves the market. Many of the listeners follow him; we do not see what happens next.

The film shows other things as well, but let us concentrate on these five scenes. As time is running short, each participant in this imaginary expedition is only allowed to focus on one aspect of these scenes so that our report can be formulated as swiftly as possible. At first, we are at a bit of a loss; suddenly each of us is forced to select a single aspect from the wide range of possible observations. Every participant's final assessment depends on what he or she has chosen to focus on. Each observer must decide on a specific scene to observe, consider the theoretical focus of his investigation, and commit to an observational perspective. Before splitting up to do our research a conversation begins about the differing interests and perspectives among the participants in our expedition.

Claude Lévi-Strauss, the leader of our expedition, is the first to announce his aims, "I want to observe the men's behavior in the fourth scene and to consider whether there are some kind of ritual regularities in the process of conversation. To do this, I shall observe the people's gestures and their overall behavior."

Margaret Mead speaks up, "I want to observe the interaction of the men and women rebuilding the collapsed stand in the first scene. I want to find out if one can determine a hierarchy of the sexes solely by observing behavior."

Umberto Eco says that he will examine the fact that there seem to be no semiotic codes present in the marketplace that resemble any known written or pictorial representations. "At first sight," he says, "conventional codes seem to be missing completely". C. G. Jung and Aby M. Warburg have their doubts on this point. They want to scrutinize whether there may yet be some symbols present that we can recognize from other cultures, for instance the symbol of a snake.

Max Weber steps forward, "given that we are pressed for time, as a sociologist I merely want to examine whether the people's behavior and their interactions in the first scene can be interpreted as 'work'."

The conversation carries on like this for a while, then stops. A second group of participants in the expedition reluctantly begins to speak. Stephen Tyler is the first to speak up, "I would like to find out whether stories are being told in the fourth and fifth scene, how they are structured, and if formulaic patterns are used." Claude Lévi-Strauss and Clifford Geertz join him in this interest. Lévi-Strauss says, "to me, the particular contents of the stories are very important: are they myths and do they contain binary oppositions, similar to the contrast between the raw and the cooked?"[1]

Hans Küng also belongs to this group, "for my great project 'Global Ethics' it would be important to know whether interculturally comparable ethical principles play a role in the fourth and fifth scenes."

The interests expressed by this second group are met with general approval by the others. After a while Lévi-Strauss asks them, "why did you hold back your ideas and why were you reluctant to speak up?"

---

1 Lévi-Strauss 1964.

Stephen Tyler replies, "well, those of you who spoke first can observe the behavior, the environmental phenomena and the cultural symbols of the people in the marketplace. You can try to find classifications and explanations by comparing your observations to familiar civilizations in the known world. But our observations are necessarily limited. We have no gateway to our scientific objects, to the formulae, to the narrations, to the myths or the ethics of these people."

Confused, someone asks, "what do you mean by gateway?" to which Tyler replies, "The language! We can only 'observe' and analyze our scientific objects, which appear to us as texts, after we have first passed through the gates of language. But these gates are closed to us."

This causes a stir in the group. Somebody shouts, "but Jung and Warburg also want to survey the symbols through which these people interact! This is similar to communication with language!" "But it is not quite the same thing," Tyler explains. "Symbols such as the snake are what we call 'motivated': the signifier (or the form) of the snake-symbol is determined by the form of the signified object |snake|. That is why you can recognize, perhaps even understand, motivated pictorial symbols more easily across cultures. As soon as the snake-symbol becomes an element of a real 'language', as it is in Egyptian hieroglyphics for instance, everything changes. 'Languages', if they are actual languages, have 'arbitrary', conventional signs. This means that the perceivable form of the symbol has a meaning that is only known by those who speak the language. These signs are combined by rules that are also known only to members of the speech-community. All of this taken together is called the 'grammar' of this language. The arbitrariness leads to a kind of isolation that makes every 'language' a mystery to those foreign to it. That is the core of our problem. In the film we hear many utterances but we do not understand any of them."

Paul Feyerabend speaks up, "hold on, how do we know that the inhabitants of our island are actually using language at all?"

Noam Chomsky interrupts him, "that is the typical Feyerabend-scepticism! If these are indeed humans on this island – and this seems to be the case – then they also have a language, albeit their own. Their ability to use language is innate, as it is for every human being. They possess a genetically encoded, general linguistic competence."

Feyerabend shoots back, "now that's what I call the typical Chomskyan linguistic-biologism!"

"Please, let's not fight over this!" says another linguist, John Lyons, trying to mediate the dispute, "let us just sum up where our discussion about 'language' has led us: on the one hand we are describing the specific symbolic and expressive conventions of a group of speakers, on the other hand we are talking about the constitution of human biology. But let us return to our concrete task. In the film we hear a continual series of sounds produced by the people on the marketplace. Even though we can't understand a thing, it sounds like speech. It could well be speech. Only humans possess a truly perfect physical apparatus for speaking. Primates are not as well equipped, something that a phonetician would be able to explain more precisely. There are also animals that can produce a continuous sequence of sounds that have nothing to do with language, like birds for example. With this I want to make clear what we as linguists have to observe on this island: the audible, spoken sounds of these people."

"But are we really observing our islanders' 'language' when we examine the sounds they utter?" I ask. "This flow of audible utterances must already represent some kind of 'text'. Does 'language' in reality exist or is it instead 'texts' that we observe in discourse?"

Lyons replies, "language-systems cannot be equated with real 'natural' languages. They are theoretical constructs, postulated by the linguist in order to account for such regularities as he finds in the language-behavior of the members of particular language-communities – more precisely in the language-signals that are the products of their language-behavior. If we regard the sounds in our film as human speech and examine them systematically from the linguistic perspective, we will observe that everyone speaks differently in one way or the other. However, there is sufficient stability and homogeneity in the speech of those who would generally be considered to speak the same language for the linguist's postulation of a common underlying language-system to be useful and scientifically justifiable. I would like to refer to Wilhelm von Humboldt, who emphasized as early as 1836 that, 'In all investigations which are to penetrate into the living essentiality of language, *connected discourse* alone must in general always be thought of as the true and primary. The break-up into words and rules is only a dead makeshift of scientific analysis.'"[2]

"If we carry this point to its logical conclusion," I interrupt, "this means that the English 'language', for example, does not exist in real life at all, but consists merely of a group of oral utterances in a speech-community from which observers dissect the English 'language' as a 'system.' This then is the grammarians' view, held by our colleague Ferdinand de Saussure. If we take a look at modern linguistic textbooks we always find the same components of this 'system of language: thus we find 'sounds', 'words', 'sentences' in one

---

2 Lyons 1982, p. 59; von Humboldt 1836, p. 49.

textbook, 'sounds', 'words', 'sentences', 'meanings' in another, and 'morphology and syntax', 'semantics', 'phonetics and phonology' in yet a third."[3]

This moves Ferdinand de Saussure to speak, "yes this is true. Language (*la langue*) is not a function of the speaker (*sujet parlant*); it is a product that is passively assimilated by the individual. For the purpose of textbooks it can be constructed as a system. But some linguists also call it a *social institution*. Institutions are also always abstractly superordinate to the individuals."[4]

"Is that the reason why Roland Barthes calls language 'fascist?'"[5] I ask.

"Yes, indeed," replies Jürgen Trabant, "the reason for such a view is the famous theory of 'linguistic Relativism', represented by scientists like Benjamin Lee Whorf. His example of the Hopi Indians who think in a totally different way than speakers of Standard Average European (SAE)-languages has become famous. According to Whorf, the Hopi cannot imagine the concept of 'time', for instance, because they lack the appropriate linguistic tool to express 'time'. Whorf's view, therefore, is that thought not only differs from language to language, but is also totally enclosed within each language's specific peculiarities. The spirit that Leonard Bloomfield and linguistic Behaviorism had cast out of language (and of linguistics) is now imprisoned in the singular language. Aside from the fact that the linguistic findings about the Hopi were, at a second glance mistaken, the 'amateurism' of Whorf's concept of language can be found in his ideological exaggeration of the diversity of the human construction of language or linguistic relativity. It is not true that the semantic structures of single languages determine people's thinking like a one-way street, as if there were no such thing as thinking independent of single languages, and as if the languages were compulsory systems of the mind."[6]

"In that case, there is still hope that we will discover some kind of common ground with our completely unknown islanders," I say. "But first we must pass through the gates of their language. We have no choice. In order to be able to learn the 'language' of our islanders we have to describe its systematic structure. Only then can we observe the five scenes in terms of what kinds of texts are being constructed with this linguistic 'building material' and find out what they mean. Whoever wants to examine human language has to begin by observing an incomprehensible conglomeration of sounds. One of our great theoreticians of language experienced this phenomenon," I say, turning to Karl Bühler.

---

3 Crain/Lillo-Martin 1999; Weisler/Milekic 2000; Fromkin 2000.
4 de Saussure 1916, p. 14 and p. 10.
5 Barthes 1978, p. 14.
6 Trabant 2003, p. 276; see also: Whorf 1956; and Bloomfield 1933.

Bühler nods, "when we recently recorded children's first words in concrete life situations and tried to cope with these beginnings of human speaking according to the rules of linguistic analysis, my associates and I gained some idea of how the analytical grasp might have been when writing did not exist. It was not so much understanding or interpreting what was said, but rather the fact that the structures involved still had an uncertain and variable phonematic character or imprint that made the greatest demands on analysis."[7]

De Saussure raises his head abruptly, "when we first encounter what we call a 'language' it is always with the individual forms of speaking of 'la parole', i.e. with the practical-empirical utterances of individual speakers."

Bühler agrees and continues, "that is why we will probably be able to derive a 'language' from our islanders' utterances rather swiftly: we already have centuries of experience with grammatical abstractions. It is important to bear in mind that writing offers us a rather good notational system. Who knows if a respectable science of language would have emerged and made progress without the *previous analysis* that was available in the optical rendering and fixation of the structures of spoken language in writing? Our writing, which is able to transform the acoustic sounds into the visual, has enabled us to isolate the genuine 'sounds' and even separate the 'words' of a language from the flow of the spoken, indistinct sounds of countless people. And this is how we need to proceed in the case of our island, too. First, we must try to set up a transcript of the sounds we can hear in the film. For this we can use our Latin letters as a trial. After all, people once began to note the complete linguistic utterances of the Germanic languages in these foreign Latin characters. Moreover, in those days they also had problems because the Latin writing code could not record all of the speakers' actual sound phenomena. I am sure, that many more fundamental and indispensable insights are owed to ancient and modern language research that worked on the basis of language texts that had been previously analyzed by means of writing than many of our contemporaries would care to admit. By transcribing the sounds, the *flatus vocis*, the sound waves, we can hear in the film, we are taking the language researcher's logical first steps of induction. We start with *the concrete speech event* as we experience it with the speakers in the film. It is something unique, like each stroke of lightning and sound of thunder and Caesar's crossing the Rubicon, a happening here and now that has a certain place in geographical space and in the Gregorian calendar. The object of the language researcher's fundamental observations is concrete speech events; he fixes the results of these observations in the initial propositions of his science. The phonemes are the natural

---

7 Bühler 1934, p. 19.

features (or recognition markers) by which the semantically relevant units of the sound stream of speech are recognized and kept apart in the sound stream. These are the first acts of linguistic abstraction. Concerning our island, we are in the same situation as the first discoverers of modern phonology. European language researchers came along and had to make an inventory of the sounds of the Caucasian languages; they had to develop an ear for things, *get attuned to things*, that is, learn to grasp what is diacritically relevant in the foreign sound images. In much the same way, the lexicologist must *get an idea* of a foreign lexicon, and similarly the syntactician must get an idea of foreign symbolic fields. The fact that he is able to do this can be attributed to his training as a language researcher and ultimately to his general ability as a speaking person to participate in conventions such as the one made by our signaling partners above. Of all the recorded utterances the analyst only appoints as a component of the 'language' that which is of *abstractive relevance*. Therefore the pitch or peculiarities of speech shown by a particular speaker in our film are not integrated in the grammatical body of rules and regulations of our island's language, rather only that information which we need to know if we want to learn this 'foreign language'. Sometimes we will recognize regularities, repetitive structures, and groupings in the transcript of the spoken sounds. Maybe we will even be able to derive a first set of rules from which some kind of order can be made from the utterances. Perhaps we can even formulate the first rules of a grammar."[8]

Tyler raises his hand, "but I am nevertheless still far from being able to interpret any texts. Mere regularities of sounds and phonetic arrangements do not mean anything to me!"

"Absolutely right!" Bühler says. "The issue of meaning remains crucial."

Before he can continue, Bühler is interrupted by de Saussure, who announces loudly, "language, by which I mean *la langue*, is a system of signs in which the only essential thing is the union of meanings and sound-images."[9]

"For our purposes, this means that we have to, above all, examine how the people's interaction in the film corresponds to their utterances," adds Bühler. "By doing so, we will gain a first insight into the meaning of words. When we have reached this point, we can start to refer to our islanders' utterances as 'language.'"

"And we should begin with the meaning of individual words." Willard van Orman Quine, who until this point has remained silent, raises his head. Bühler

---

8 Bühler 1934, pp. 18 ff. and pp. 52 f.
9 de Saussure 1916, p. 15.

asks him if he has any suggestions for a method to solve the problem of meaning. "By all means," Quine continues, "the best method would of course be to conduct experiments of word meaning directly in the field. We would show our natives an object or an animal, for instance a rabbit, and wait to see what they called it. If all of them make the same utterances in reference to the rabbit, if they all say 'gavagi' for example, then we have discovered the first word in the dictionary of our new language: rabbit = gavagi.[10] Since we only have our film, however, we must observe various scenes in which the same utterances are used by multiple individuals to indicate the same object. In doing so, of course, we cannot be sure that these utterances only apply to one word with a single meaning and don't imply entire sentences, such as 'rabbits run quickly'."

"You are already discussing the 'level of words,'" interjects John Lyons, "but what about the analytical level below that? Just by observing the utterances of the natives we can identify internal – if only phonological – regularities, for instance how many and what kinds of sounds can be found on our island."

"Hold on a moment. Are you saying that we can only be sure in our assignment of meaning if we try to understand the singular word within the whole language system?" Chomsky wants to point to the difficulties in Quine's methodology and focus his priorities elsewhere. "To me, it only gets interesting when we analyze how they construct their sentences. I regard the syntactic rules and regulations as the real core of a 'language'."

"Of course you do! Yet again we see the restricted world view of the systemic linguist," interrupts Paul Feyerabend.

"Don't sneer at systemic linguistics," Marga Reis says in a soft voice. "This approach has allowed us to understand our own languages much better, and let us not forget: without systemic linguistics we wouldn't have had the great advances in the fields of artificial intelligence, computer linguistics and in language translation programs that we have experienced in recent years."

Lyons continues his thoughts, "all of your objections are valid. Every language must be studied and described as a closed, self-sustaining grammatical system at a wide array of analytical levels of observation. This closed, systemic nature of language is, however, also the reason that we can learn a new language at all, even at long distances and without physical contact to the inhabitants of the island."

For a moment, there is silence. Then Stephen Tyler speaks up, "Herr Bühler, please go on. I like how you approach the issue of 'language' from its very beginning."

---

10 Quine 1960, § 7.

At that, Bühler continues, "by now we have recognized that we encounter linguistic phenomena when we concretely observe the peoples' actions on the marketplace as *subject-related* phenomena. These stem directly from what Husserl calls the 'life-world' of real, historical people."[11]

"We have to isolate this as a separate theoretical level and can call it speech," interjects Ferdinand de Saussure suddenly.

Bühler carries on, "yes. Think back, for instance, to the story of Cato the Elder. At every meeting of the Roman Senate he repeated that Carthage had to be destroyed: 'Ceterum censeo, Carthaginem esse delendam' (By the way, I think that Carthage must be destroyed). In this example we can see what the general status of sayings in human life is: how they sometimes signify decisions, how they determine the fate of the speaker and others, how they honor diplomats and so on. Every familiar quotation and everything that has been said but is not quite so quotable can be considered a human *action*. For all concrete speech is in vital union with the rest of a person's meaningful behavior; it is *among* actions and is *itself* an action."[12]

At this point I allow myself to interject, "now we have reached the point to which my research interests apply."

"Oh yes," remarks Lévi-Strauss, "you haven't yet told us what *you* want to observe in the marketplace."

"I want to examine the rhetoric in the marketplace," I respond, "and this is partly embodied in the people's actions. I imagine that Herr Bühler is actually thinking of such matters in his reflections."

"Yes," Bühler says, "in a certain situation we see that a person goes at things with his hands and handles what is graspable, physical things, he manipulates them. Think of the first scene of our film, when the collapsed stand is being rebuilt. Another time we see that he opens his mouth and speaks. In both cases the event that we can observe proves to be directed towards a goal, towards something that is to be attained. That is exactly what a psychologist calls an action."[13]

"And that is exactly what the rhetorician terms the 'rhetorical factor' which occurs in all specific speech actions," I add.

"The ordinary German language has provided us with a term suitable for scientific use: '*Handlung*' (action)," Bühler continues. "We generalize even in everyday life, we do not only call the manipulations in which the hands actually play a part and are at work 'actions', cases of *hand*ling, but also other

---

11 Bühler 1934, p. 58; Husserl 1954, §§ 33–34.
12 Bühler 1934, pp. 59 ff.
13 Bühler 1934, p. 61.

doings, we call all goal-directed doings of the *entire* person actions (or handlings)."[14]

"The rhetorician observes exactly such actions," I say. "Speaking thereby becomes part of an intentionally oriented action complex."

"The integration of speaking into other meaningful behavior deserves a specific term," Bühler adds. "We can call linguistic utterances integrated into the varied human experience '*empractical* utterances'."[15]

Bühler has impressed his listeners and a general buzz of approval can be heard from the group. Brigitte Schlieben-Lange finds the opportunity to add a further incidental remark, "having touched upon the Greek lexical field for 'action', we might just as well mention the term 'pragmatics'. This term refers to the interrelation between linguistic and non-linguistic actions and the question of how the meaning of linguistic expressions can be determined by observing such connections."

"That is important," adds Eugenio Coseriu, "but as a rhetorician you should be much more interested in a different aspect of the matter at hand: where does the 'text' (as a linguistically complex but closed unit of speech) actually exist?"

"In the midst of life, of course, just like everything with and in language!" For the first time Ludwig Wittgenstein speaks up, "It is rather obvious that the *speaking* of language is part of an activity, or of a form of life. People living together and interacting within their languages as if playing a series of language-games. This ranges from giving orders and making up a story to asking, thanking, cursing, greeting, and praying."[16]

"Dear colleagues, you are of course aware of the fact that Herr Wittgenstein is talking about speech acts, i.e. of utterances which always also involve a counterpart. Asking, thanking and greeting at the same time always imply asking *someone*: thanking him, greeting him." With these words John Austin moves closer to Wittgenstein and continues, "communication is the reality of language. You don't just chatter aimlessly, but rather are always doing something in the world."

"Here we see the practical-thinking Anglo-Saxon," Andreas Gardt comments enthusiastically. "The title of your book 'How to do things with words', my dear Mr. Austin, contains the fundamental idea of all pragmatics."

"And since everyone communicates and acts differently, we might as well do without the precise analysis of language," Chomsky murmurs, nodding his head derisively.

---

14 Bühler 1934, p. 61.
15 Bühler 1934, p. 61.
16 Wittgenstein 1953, § 23 [11ᵉ f.].

"Young fellow!" Wittgenstein turns to Chomsky in a friendly manner, "my mind was also once full of idealizations. I had an ideal language in mind, perfectly precise, free from the inexactitudes of everyday speech. But what does inexact mean anyway, what does precise mean? Am I being inexact when I do not give our distance from the sun to the nearest foot, or tell a cabinet maker the width of a table to the nearest thousandth of an inch?"[17]

"Of course it is inexact," Chomsky replies defiantly.

"But that's not the point," Wittgenstein now insists, somewhat more severely. "It is not important whether a description is virtually correct 'in itself', because such an 'in itself' is not at all possible in the field of linguistic meanings. Whether something is a useful description or not, however, *is* a rather important question. The only thing that counts is the functioning of the words, the working of language." And with the remark, "explanations come to an end somewhere," he turns away from Chomsky.[18]

Suddenly there is an unpleasant tension in the air. But then Arnim von Stechow interjects. Up until this point he hadn't said a word, and seemed to be almost sleeping, but he had obviously been listening with his eyes shut: "your point of view is sensible and reveals your worldly wisdom. But is it also scientific? How do you intend to define words if you do not possess any precise method of description?"

Wittgenstein laughs, "it's rather simple. You just have to trust your eyes and your ears, because the meaning of a word is its use in the language."[19]

De Saussure frowns and is just about to raise an objection when Karl Bühler clears his throat. He wants to change the subject away from the unpleasantly strained situation, "may I interrupt you? We are drifting away from the actual question that was raised: the question of textuality!" He turns towards me, "what you call a 'text' I – primarily from a gestalt-psychological point of view – regard as a kind of closed whole. Here my wife Charlotte's insights in the field of child and developmental psychology become relevant. They can be combined in the Aristotelian terms *praxis* (action) and *poiesis* (production). In his play, the child between the ages of two and four practices before our eyes first praxis and then poiesis; the child advances slowly through various materials, step by step, until it produces, it advances to 'productive maturity' (*Werkreife*), as my wife Charlotte calls it. The child's first illusion games have the actions of adults as their topic; the producing games, which come later, take as their topic the production of what people make. There is

---

17 Wittgenstein 1953, § 88 [42^e].
18 Wittgenstein 1953, § 3 [3^e], § 5 [4^e], § 1 [3^e].
19 Wittgenstein 1953, § 43 [20^e].

a considerable, palpable difference between games of activity and games of production; for in the former what is actually *supposed* to happen with and to the material is only fleetingly and symbolically implied. But then the child makes headway and learns to regard the product of his activity as a work (and this is by no means a matter of course). The first hint that this will happen is when it stops after the fact to look at and admire and to get others to admire what has come to be from its manipulations. Later, the decisive phase follows, the phase in which the result of the activity is anticipated in a conception and thus begins to regulate the operation on the material prospectively and in which finally the activity does not come to rest before the work is completed. For all of us there are situations in which the problem of the moment, the task at hand is solved by speaking directly from within the life situation: *speech actions* (Sprachhandlungen). And there are other situations in which we work productively on the adequate formulation of a given stuff, and produce a *language work* (Sprachwerk). The *language work* as such must be capable of being regarded and must be regarded at a remove from its position in the individual life and experience of its author."[20]

"So then you actually want to distinguish between ephemeral and persistent, fleeting and durable, provisional and structurally-calculated texts?" I ask.

"You could put it that way", Bühler answers. "To bar any misunderstanding: a product always comes out when a person opens his mouth; a product emerges even in the child's purest game of activity. But let us look at these products more closely; as a rule it is scraps that fill the play-room as long as it is still praxis that is being played; it is not until poiesis is played that the products are 'buildings' and the like. This not only occurs in children's play-rooms, but also in the world of adults. At this point it is relevant to think of works of art and literature. Whether their material is an external event, an experience or something else, at any rate the view to the work in language attends to the *formulation* (*Fassung*) in all cases, and in many cases it attends minutely to the *uniquity* of the formulation and formation as such. But there must also be appropriate general categories for grasping the individual case; for every science is founded on general 'principles'."[21]

"Now we have reached an important point of transition," I remark. "As soon as we pay attention to 'principles', we step away from concrete reality and begin to make abstractions. Is this the point where we transcend from *la parole* to *la langue*, from speech to language?"

"Indeed, the phenomenon of *abstraction* is the key. I already mentioned the term 'abstractive relevance'," Bühler replies. "What does this mean? *Every*

---

20 Bühler 1934, pp. 62 f.
21 Bühler 1934, pp. 63 f.

grammarian knows that the 'dictum' (sentence) *Carthaginem esse delendam* was first spoken by Cato the Elder at a certain meeting of the Senate, and then repeated at certain further meetings of the Senate, but *no* grammar knows anything about this; it is of no interest to it, indeed a grammar has no business taking any interest in the fact. In this example, abstractive relevance means that on the level of la langue, i.e. at the structural level of the Latin language, the only matter that counts here is the form of expression which can be used again and again: the so-called AcI (accusativus cum infinitivo). And with regard to the Latin dictionary, it is important that this example includes words which can be used again and again: *esse* and *delere* (in the case at hand the grammatical variant *delendam*). Thus the term 'language' refers to a systematic reconstruction of phenomena *independent of a subject* (*subjektentbunden*), phenomena that have an intersubjective fixation. Accordingly, we can try to isolate structures from our islanders' repeated use of speech and words in order to formulate rules and to systematize a kind of grammar and a dictionary of the 'language' spoken on this foreign island."[22]

Stephen Tyler intervenes, "this means that you and the other linguists must first try to reconstruct the language on the island as an autonomous system so that we can learn it. Before you can do this, however, you must first manage to identify something like 'language structures' from the relatively alien sounds in the film."

Bühler agrees and continues, "no linguist has described the logical character of *language structures* (*Sprachgebilde*) as aptly as Saussure has done directly on the basis of his own successful research work."[23]

Being too absorbed in his own thoughts, de Saussure does not even react to this compliment. Bühler is thus able to continue without interruption, "Saussure lists the following details about the object of the *linguistique de la langue*. First, the recognition of the clear *separability* of the 'object' of the *linguistique de la langue* has methodological priority."[24]

The sound of French words finally makes de Saussure take notice, and he completes Bühler's remarks, "we can dispense with the other elements of speech; indeed, the science of language is possible only if the other elements are excluded."[25]

Bühler laughs, "you speak with the wisdom of a successful empirical researcher! Your second point is the application of the key proposition of the semiotic nature of language."[26]

---

22 Bühler 1934, pp. 58 f.
23 Bühler 1934, p. 67.
24 Bühler 1934, p. 67.
25 de Saussure 1916, p. 15.
26 Bühler 1934, p. 67.

De Saussure reminds his listeners that *la langue*, "is a system of signs in which the one essential is the union of meanings and sound-images."[27]

"Yes this is true. We can't emphasize enough that it is indeed *semantic relationships* that constitute the object 'language',” replies Bühler. "Third, dear Monsieur Saussure, you also insist on the consistent implementation of this regulative principle in all linguistic structures. Fourth, you have very clearly described the intersubjective character of linguistic structures and their *independence from the individual speaker*. On this point you may have even overstated your case somewhat."[28]

Ignoring Bühler's last remark, de Saussure again adds an appropriate definition, "*la langue* is not a function of the speaker. It exists outside the individual who can never create nor modify it himself; it exists only by virtue of a sort of contract signed by the members of a community."[29]

Tyler interrupts him, "but how can any innovations enter the language then? How can 'language' react at all when the world is changing?"

I try to find an explanation, "if I have this right, then it is not the language that reacts to changes in the world, but rather the speakers themselves (at the level of *la parole*). As a result the systematic reconstruction of a language can only exist for a certain point in time and in hindsight. After a few years, more or less dramatic changes can occur amongst the speakers of the language, which then consequently change the grammatical and lexical conditions of *la langue*."

"Yes, you could put it that way," Bühler says. "Our colleague de Saussure claims that the core of all linguistic structures is *separable* from the abundance of irrelevant details of the concrete speech events here and now, and no linguist would contradict him on this point. For example scholars of Greek and Latin are heard to say that it is really marginal to the scope of their interest how the languages in fact sounded when spoken by the Homeric Greeks or by Cicero. The true contents of the science of the Greek and the Latin language are not essentially distorted by the fact that they can only be read from written documents."[30]

Lyons objects, "there are differing opinions on that. At least where modern languages are concerned, practical phonetics and phonology are extraordinarily important. Badly articulated words negatively influence communication in oral discourse with non-native speaking contemporaries." Reis nods.

---

27 de Saussure 1916, p. 25.
28 Bühler 1934, pp. 67 f.
29 de Saussure 1916, p. 14.
30 Bühler 1934, p. 69.

Bühler carries on, "for me, something else is important regarding 'language.' In Platonic terms the structures of language are idea-like objects, in terms of modern logic they are classes of classes like numbers or the objects on a higher level of formalization of scientific thought. In this respect I have a different point of view than our honorable colleague de Saussure, who sees *la langue* as a kind of concrete object. To me this is a material fallacy which contradicts the concept of abstraction that I mentioned before."[31]

Bühler carefully looks over to de Saussure who says with a smile, "dear colleague, you must have misunderstood me. In my opinion, too, language only exists as a set of rules in the minds of the speakers. *La langue* is a psychological entity, while *la parole* constitutes a concrete physical (acoustic or visual) textual phenomenon. Our American colleague Whitney shares this opinion, saying that one could imagine that 'language' uses a totally different physical organ with each concrete speaker. Men might just as well have chosen gestures and used visual symbols instead of acoustical symbols. The question of the vocal apparatus obviously takes a secondary place in the problem of speech."[32]

"I am concerned with the connection between the concrete and the abstract," Bühler tries to explain. "The arithmeticians do not take notice of the fact that it was a pair of shoes and a pair of socks in one case or in another case a pair of eyes and a pair of ears on a certain person's head that 'so to speak' acted as and continue to act as a perceptual clue for the apprentice calculator in reaching the result four. For arithmetic is not a doctrine of eyes, ears, trees or abacus balls, but the science of numbers; its objects were hence defined with respect to the properties of *groups* of things as classes of classes, and not with respect to the properties of the things themselves. If we draw a parallel between numbers and linguistic structures we find that the determination 'classes of classes' can be transferred to the latter by analogy. Instead of the specific grammatical example, the *accusativus cum infinitivo*, we could just as well have discussed a lexical example. There are conceptual objects (or classes) everywhere, but the fact that numbers become important in physics, and linguistic structures are important in linguistics as classes of classes is a highly remarkable fact, one that refers back to the significative nature of language phenomena. At any rate, propositions about the concrete speech event no more have a place in pure phonology, morphology or syntax than do propositions about trees or apples in pure arithmetic."[33]

---

31 Bühler 1934, p. 70 and p. 68.
32 de Saussure 1916, p. 10; Whitney 1875.
33 Bühler 1934, p. 59.

Now Heinrich Lausberg rises, "classes of classes also occur on other levels of linguistic events: I mean in rhetoric. Rhetoric also seeks to show the *langue*, which is the conventional means of expression of the *parole*. Poets, for example, draw from the thesaurus of possible rhetorical expressions. This thesaurus consists of the positive social-historical tradition which makes up the rhetorical langue."[34]

Stephen Tyler agrees enthusiastically, "you are certainly referring to the rhetorical schemes and 'ready-mades' of discourse. These multilexical constructions which are also treated under the general rubric of 'idioms', or 'frozen expressions', are not mechanically predictable by part-part-summation. They are merely one kind of schematic ordering. They are of the type whose parts and their relations are fixed, such as: 'I mean ...,' 'gimme a break ...,' 'take a break ...,' 'break a leg ...,' 'stick 'em up ...,' 'get off my back ...,' 'he went 'n ...,' and so on. Some of these are relatively fixed, but most have optional expansions or transformations of one sort or another. Schemata are much closer to the form of inner speech and thought than are sentences and propositions. Oral discourse and thought too, are orders of schemata. But it is an order without the usual grammatical *constraint*. When in talk we come to a schema, the rocky road of discourse opens into a broad, smooth highway which we speed along with ease, and that is why most talk – and writing, too – is not novel, but consists of long stretches of freeway interspersed with construction detours. Easy idioms bridge the gaps and comfortable metaphors ease us through the traffic."[35]

Heinrich Lausberg remains silent for a while. He is obviously thinking over Tyler's point. Then he says, "the fixed idiomatic expressions you mentioned do not belong in my rhetorical thesaurus. They are partially complex – i.e. simply 'multilexical' – constructions, but they remain lexicalized expressions of single languages. You could call them formulas or idioms. Like words, they belong in the dictionaries of single languages or dictionaries for particular groups (lawyers, sportsmen, youth etc.). Rhetorical figures, on the other hand, are constructions which are not restricted to a single language. They follow universal rules of production which are at a minimum valid for the Indo-Germanic languages. The rhetorician distinguishes between three kinds of figures: 1. tropes, 2. schemes, and 3. figures of thought. Rhetorical figures like metaphor, anaphora and chiasmus can be created in every language, which is why one can also speak of a second, rhetorical grammar. But what should such a grammar look like? The production of rhetorical schemes (a) follows rules of

---

34 Lausberg 1960, p. xxviii and § 1246, p. 904.
35 Tyler 1987, pp. 105 ff.

construction and rhetorical schemes (b) can be recognized due to a fixed structure. For example, the rule of production for the figure 'chiasmus' in all languages is, 'construct two sentences in such a way that they are parallel in syntax, but reverse the order of the corresponding words, the pattern being a mirror inversion at a particular axis'. Its pattern can be represented as follows: abc|cba. Here a few examples:

'But many that are first shall be last, and the last shall be first'

or

'when the going gets tough, the tough get going'."

"The important thing is what we *do* with such rhetorical figures," Stephen Tyler says. "Rhetoric is the mark of the author's will, and all allusion, allegory, metaphor, simile, and ornaments of style are its instruments. They point to the author's character, creative skill, and intent, and proclaim the worth of subject."[36]

"I agree," I say, "but I must make a restriction. In his work on 'The Death of the Author', Roland Barthes says, 'it is language which speaks, not the author'. This comment lacks clarity, which corresponds and can be attributed to Barthes' inexact concept of language. When an 'author speaks' he formulates a text. But the text is the realm of communicative freedom. Texts allow a subject free reign to construct meaning. Whether this meaning leads to communicative success is another story entirely. Barthes is correct in saying that every speaker has to fall back upon the given system of language and is therefore constrained. But the special quality of texts is that they can work around the constraints of the language system. Texts work with language as a building material, but under favorable conditions the speaker can determine which textual house is actually built."[37]

"But let us return to an important point raised by Herr Lausberg," I continue. "He was talking about 'the language' (la langue) of rhetoric. Here it would be more than consistent to postulate a 'second grammar', because rules for figures do actually exist. I myself, however, would be rather careful with the terminology. If we wish to talk *clare et distincte* (clearly and distinctly) with each other, in the sense of the philosopher Descartes, we should use the term 'language' solely for the 'systems' of single languages derived from discourse. Everything else relates to the use of languages, not to language in and of itself."

Noam Chomsky obviously impatient, loudly exclaims, "if we want to pursue language research seriously, then we have to clearly define our object of

---

36 Tyler 1987, p. 8.
37 Barthes 1967, p. 143.

observation. From now on I will consider a *language* to be a set (finite or infinite) of sentences, each finite in length and constructed out of a finite set of elements."[38]

Chomsky looks out the window silently, and for a moment, the group falls still. Then John Lyons comments on this remark, "we should grant Mr. Chomsky his rather reductionist point of view. His definition says nothing about the communicative function of either natural or non-natural languages; it says nothing about the symbolic nature of the elements or sequences of them. Its purpose is to focus attention upon the purely structural properties of languages and to suggest that these properties can be investigated from a mathematically precise point of view. But indeed, linguistic units contain characteristics of their conditions of use, especially as far as the meaning of words and sentences goes. Many scholars would say that utterance-meaning falls outside the province of linguistic semantics, as such, and within that of what has come to be called pragmatics."[39]

"If I understand you correctly," I enquire, "linguistic semantics deals with the meaning of 'language' as a system, whereas pragmatics is concerned with meaning in the practice of speech (*le langage, la parole*)?"

Lyons replies, "Perhaps you could put it that way. But there are numerous further correlations to both of these fields. Chomskyan generativists tend to equate the distinction between sentences and utterances and the distinction between semantics and pragmatics with competence and performance."[40]

"'Competence' here refers to the linguistic body of rules and regulations which a speaker has, to a certain extent, internalized and which he can activate in practice as 'performance'," I add. "But for me, something else is important. As soon as we discuss issues concerning the concrete construction of texts, we have reached another level, namely that of the *use* of language. The rhetorician has to go one step further. He also has to take into account the wide range of communication. This includes all of the other conditions of symbolic interaction among people. Thus, we have to distinguish between the theoretical levels of language, text, and interaction (discourse and communication)."

My remarks are met with applause from Scott Jacobs, "the concepts of language and communication, although intimately related, have never really been happily married. Communication scholars will readily recognize that the use of language to formulate messages and to perform social actions is the paradigm case of communication. Almost all cases of communication that

---

38 Chomsky 1957, p. 13.
39 Lyons 1982, pp. 7 f. and p. 140.
40 Lyons 1982, p. 164.

interest communication researchers involve talk or writing in some way. Still, efforts to ground notions of 'message meaning' or 'symbolic action' in a detailed account of the organization of linguistic forms and functions has always seemed to be so technical and tedious a task that it has been generally bypassed in the process of building communication theory. Likewise, students of language have often been reluctant to integrate their theories of language structure with what is manifestly the paradigm function of language, that of communication. Knowing what language does has commonly been thought to be superfluous to knowing what language is. While this attitude has begun to fade, the term *language* has been so thoroughly appropriated by the technical structural interests of sentence grammarians that any effort to study the use of language or the structures of language beyond the sentence requires use of a whole new term: *discourse*. Discourse analysis is an effort to close the gap between conceptions of communication process and language structure and function."[41]

"And what role does rhetoric play in this context?" Lévi-Strauss asks, turning to me. "We still do not know what it is, specifically, that you want to examine in the marketplace of our islanders."

I answer, "first of all I want to watch the fifth scene, that is, the scene in which the man is standing in front of a group. This scene reminds me of a classical rhetorical speech-situation: an orator is trying to influence a group of people. As a result, his listeners carry out a certain action by following him away from the market. But the bartering women in the second scene (if they are really bartering), the competing melon-sellers in the third scene and the conversation in the fourth scene are interesting, too. In all of these instances an analysis might show that we are dealing with persuasion, i.e. that during the course of the communication, one or the other speaker is trying to impose his own point of view or his own intentions through the use of persuasive speech. In short, my observation focuses on the *rhetorical factor* in communication. This factor is the phenomena of persuasion, with all its implications. Thus, I am not simply interested in the question of how they communicate on the island in general: how their language is ordered, how it works, what kinds of texts are exchanged, what is narrated etc. On the contrary, I look at the matter from a very specific angle, namely: what are the conditions of successful communication on this island? That is the rhetorical question."

Lévi-Strauss isn't satisfied with this answer, "although this is a clearly directed question, the phenomena you want to analyze go far beyond what Herr Lausberg has just presented to us as 'rhetoric'."

---

41 Jacobs 2002, p. 213.

"You're right," I reply. "Herr Lausberg concentrates entirely on the internal set of rules and regulations that have been established over a period of two-and-a-half-thousand years for the composition of rhetorically overcoded texts. He represents a tradition which views rhetoric as an art of speaking well, an *ars bene dicendi*. These rhetoricians devote their attention to the linguistic and non-linguistic overcodes that have arisen over the course of history. They are regularities that join with the grammatical regularities in the construction of a text. The grammarian is interested in convenient and correct sentences. The *intrinsic* rhetorician is interested in overcodes, in forms like parallelism or chiasmus, which you can build on top of the grammatical foundation, and which promise some kind of specific effect. This intrinsic perspective is of course very limited, despite the fact that it stems from a long-standing tradition."

"That is why I called my book the 'Handbook of *Literary* Rhetoric'," Lausberg interjects.

"And we are very grateful for this extensive handbook of yours," I continue. "But we should not forget that rhetoric is a discipline that deals with successful communicative action, with the interaction of people. That is why *extrinsic* rhetoric is particularly important. The extrinsic perspective takes a look at the connection between the speaker's communicative means or instruments and the external circumstances of his action. In particular, extrinsic rhetoric asks about the resistance that an orator encounters: what hinders his communicative success? Which types of resistance must the speaker overcome? Which communicative, linguistic means are particularly suitable in a given situation? How must the body, voice and linguistic text be coordinated so that persuasion occurs? In this sense, rhetoric becomes an art of persuasion, an *ars persuadendi*, as they used to call it in ancient times.

In the fifth scene of our film, we could investigate everything the man does in order to convince part of the group to follow him. We could also certainly ask why part of the group does not follow him. But it is doubtful that the film contains enough information for this purpose. We still do not know enough about the island. If the linguists succeed in analyzing the islanders' language at the level of meaning, they also have to pay methodical attention to the correlation between the intrinsic and extrinsic perspective. Meanings of linguistic units only become apparent when you observe the connections of actions. As soon as this is done, we can set up a grammar and a dictionary: we can isolate a 'language'. It has always been the dream of rhetoricians to set up such a secondary grammar which assigns certain values of success to certain textual structures. This is what Herr Lausberg basically meant by *la langue* of rhetoric."

Stephen Tyler speaks up, "yes, but why shouldn't we be able to create such a rhetorical grammar?"

"I think that the term 'grammar' may lead us astray," I respond. "Unlike linguistic grammar, the rhetorical overcode (rhetorical figures, etc.) is not concerned with the connection between correctness and understanding. We need grammar in order to compose correct and convenient sentences and to understand them. But rhetoric wants more. Not only does it want to evoke understanding, but also approval and compliance. That is the core of persuasion. If someone speaks the sentence 'The world is bad', then grammar teaches me to understand this sentence. But it does not teach or motivate me to agree with this sentence. I can share a totally different opinion even if I have understood the meaning of the sentence. I might believe that we live in the best of all possible worlds. Understanding is not approval. That is the core of the rhetorical problem. Rhetoric has the task to make me *agree* with this sentence too. If I agree, I might also act (I might try to do good in order to improve the bad world). Opinion change might thus lead to behavior change."[42]

Scott Jacobs agrees, "any theory that equates message meaning with the literal meaning of what is said will miss how coherent and meaningful messages are produced and understood"[43] in communicative interaction.

I continue, "let's remain at the rhetorical level of the text. If a rhetorical overcode is working here, then it always has to be about the connection between appropriateness and mental change. Grammar teaches us what is always in a language to enable us to understand it. Rhetoric teaches us to examine the appropriate wording of a text in a particular communicative situation in order to cause a mental change in a communicative partner."[44]

Lévi-Strauss, "I've got the feeling that we should all watch our film again. It is likely that we will now see and hear things in an entirely different light. So, let's get started!"

---

42 Knape 2003a.
43 Jacobs 2002, p. 217.
44 Knape 2000a, p. 34.

Dialog

5 A Rhetoric of Conversation

1 Conversational Rhetoric

Is conversation an element of modern rhetorical theory? A connection between theories of conversation and rhetoric is not self-evident, as a short overview of the classical rhetorical tradition below will show. Conversation remains new territory for the theory of rhetoric in a strict sense, despite the fact that Cicero and other ancient practitioners demanded that a well-educated communicator should also deal with elements of conversation. Such concerns never went so far as to incorporate conversation into the cannon of rhetorical theory; "an actual rhetoric of conversation was never fully formulated. Ancient rhetoric never integrated the reply into its casuistic system."[1] Looking at the history of science, this exclusion of conversation from the field of rhetoric (in a strict sense) can be seen in the development of new research fields of dialog, discourse, and conversation in linguistics, psychology, sociology and philosophy. Such approaches have rarely been developed on the basis of rhetorical research or using the rhetorical perspective; they have been based on more general considerations of communication and linguistic perspectives. Only in the last few decades has this situation begun to change, as illustrated by trendsetting volumes by Bausch and Grosse (1985), Kallmeyer (1996), Weigand (2008) or Gansel (2009). Through these and other research activities, the rhetoric of conversation has become the object of linguistic reflection and, "has incorporated the linguistic research of conversation into the history of the reception of rhetoric."[2] The following discussion should outline this rhetorical perspective in a narrower sense; it will describe how rhetoric accesses and approaches conversation as a communicative activity. First, however, a few notes about the Greco-Roman tradition.

2 Oration and Conversation in Antiquity

Ancient Greek tradition made a clear distinction between rhetoric, the art of long, monologic oration, and dialectics, the art of dialogical conversation. This division is clearly displayed in Plato's 'Gorgias' from the 4th century B.C. In it, Socrates emphasizes the point that his partner in the dialog, Polus, "has had

---

1 Bauer 1969, p. 6.
2 Mönnich 2011, p. 112.

more practice in what is called rhetoric (*rhētorikē*) than in discussion (*dialé-gesthai*)."[3] Socrates also makes clear that he prefers the use of dialog in philosophy when he admonishes Gorgias to avoid the use of long speeches and to remain using the conversational form of speech, "then would you be willing, Gorgias, to continue this present way of discussion, by alternate question and answer, and defer to some other time that lengthy style of speech (*lógoi*) in which Polus made a beginning?"[4] Plato's student Aristotle, on the other hand, overcame the platonic primacy of dialectics as the way to ascertain the truth (and as a theory of conversational argumentation) both by writing the first rigorous work on a theory of rhetoric, and by beginning that work with the sentence, "Rhetoric (*rhētorikē*) is a counterpart of dialectic (*dialektikē*)".[5] This statement places Aristotle's theory in direct confrontation with Plato's by considering rhetoric equal to dialectics.

In Roman times, an orator was required to cultivate competence in both fields. Thus, Cicero, writing in the first century B.C., stated,

> The man of perfect eloquence should, then, in my opinion possess not only the faculty of fluent and copious speech which is his proper province, but should also acquire that neighbouring borderland science of logic (*dialecticorum scientia*); although a speech (*oratio*) is one thing and a debate (*disputatio*) another, and disputing (*loqui*) is not the same as speaking (*dicere*), and yet both are concerned with discourse – debate and dispute are the function of the logicians; the orator's function is to speak ornately.[6]

For Cicero, it was clear that an orator seeking the best possible education should learn both the art of conversation and the art of oration through the individual study of each field:

> I therefore expect this perfect orator of ours to be familiar with all the theory of disputation (*loquendi ratio*) which can be applied to speaking; this subject, as you well know from your training along this line, has been taught in two different ways.[7]

In general, however, comments on the topic of conversation are rare in ancient texts on rhetoric. Quintilian (1st century A.D.) is no exception. He introduces the topic of conversation only briefly in his description of the three cases of rhetorical oration (*genera causarum*) and functional oratorical genres. In his overview of relevant theoreticians he mentions Plato's 'Sophistes' (222c), in which he introduces the colloquial (*proshomiletic*) style of speech,

---

3 Plato: Gorgias, 448e.
4 Plato: Gorgias, 449b.
5 Aristotle: Rhetoric, 1.1.1.
6 Cicero: Orator, 113.
7 Cicero: Orator, 114.

Plato in his *Sophist* in addition to public and forensic oratory introduces a third kind which he styles προσομιλητική (*proshomilētikē*), which I will permit myself to translate by 'conversational' (*sermocinatrix*). This is distinct from forensic oratory and is adapted for private discussions, and we may regard it as identical with dialectic.[8]

3 Monologue, Dialog, Conversation

Cicero's mention of dual methods or of a twofold teaching program (*duplex docendi via*) at the end of the quote above illustrates the view that oration and conversation are two separate modes of communication, each of which requires different oratorical competencies that must be taught by separate courses of study. In his interpretation of Greek theoreticians, Cicero was admittedly unable to provide exact or discrete criteria that would allow us to differentiate between the two modes of communication. He wrote,

> Zeno, the founder of the Stoic school, used to give an object lesson of the difference between the two arts; clenching his fist he said logic (*dialectica*) was like that; relaxing and extending his hand, he said eloquence (*eloquentia*) was like the open palm. Still earlier Aristotle in the opening chapter of his *Art of Rhetoric* said that rhetoric is the counterpart of logic, the difference obviously being that rhetoric was broader and logic narrower.[9]

Cicero attempted to base his differentiation between the two forms on the types of text found in each, which he described with vague opposing pairs:

Short (conversation) vs. long (oration)
Clenched (conversation) vs. spread (oration)
Purely argumentative (conversation) vs. occasionally ornate (oration)

In these differentiations we find an idea (also cultivated in Plato's academy) that distinguished between philosophically rigorous and direct discussion and the longer, elaborated form of speech found on the Greek forum. It is augmented by the idea, alien to rhetoric, that conversation among philosophers involves the *purely rational* exchange of arguments leading ultimately to 'truth' (an idea whose influence is still found in Jürgen Habermas' 1981 and 1984 formulation of the possibility of a coercion-free discourse, in which the "forceless force" of the better argument should always win).[10] The tradition of philo-

---

8 Quintilian: Institutio Oratoria, 3.4.10.
9 Cicero: Orator, 113–114.
10 See: Knape 1998.

sophical dialog according to Plato's model is found today in the so-called "Socratic dialog" referred to by philosopher and pedagogue Leonard Nelson (1882–1927).[11]

From the perspective of modern rhetoric, the idea of goal oriented communication that is completely free of rhetoric is far too abstracted from reality.

Even the ancient division of the two types of communication is insufficient. The discrete characteristics of oration and conversation must be explicitly defined so that the specifically rhetorical aspects of each can be clearly demonstrated. Such definitions can be derived from the differences found in the rhetorical calculation that an orator makes in each situation. For the empirical rhetorician, the *differentia specifica* between the two types of communication are to be found in the definitional combination of at least three criteria: the empirical model of performance, the settings, and the characteristics of their respective texts.

The Oration

Using the three criteria named above, we can define the communicative mode of *an oration* according to rhetorical premises as follows:[12]

Model of Performance: Monologic form of action. Unilateral, unidirectional and performatively continual speech by an orator towards addressees who are not themselves orators in the given event.[13]

Setting: Communicative conditions, occasions, and social, ritual or situational guidelines[14] that do not require (or include) 'turn-taking' among different speakers during the performance of the spoken text. Here, the speech has a clearly defined place within the process of communication. A special case arises when the speech is a part of a macro-situational context, in which a series of speeches are given due to customs, rituals, or rules of procedure present in the communicative situation (during parliamentary debate for instance). It is often the case that a speech is combined with other types of

---

11 For more, see: Birnbacher/Krohn 2002.

12 See also: Knape 2003b; and Gutenberg 2000.

13 An orator in this context is an active communicator focused on persuasion. See also: Knape 2000a, pp. 33–45; Klotz 2008.

14 Situational guidelines are problematic in cases of unplanned, spontaneous oratorical events. The oratorical performance (when successful) is couched within a frame of acceptance created spontaneously by the audience based on common, ritualized models designed to prevent interruptions in the speech.

communication (e.g. a follow-up discussion) or allows monologic parallel actions on the part of the audience (e.g. interjections, paralinguistic or other types of reaction).[15]

Characteristics of Text: Characteristics of cohesion and coherence with reference to a singular (possibly collective) orator and his communicative strategies.

The Conversation

The *conversational* mode of communication is defined as follows:

Model of Performance: Dialogical form of interaction in which a minimum of two orators are present. They express themselves poly- or bilaterally, poly- or bidirectionally, and perform discontinuously (through 'turn-taking') with direct reference to the other orator(s). Other orators are neither passive nor relegated to the non-speaking role of addressee, rather they are active partners of communication; they are thus considered rhetorically active contra-orator(s).[16]

Setting: Communicative conditions, occasions, and social, ritual or situational guidelines that specifically enable or require turn-taking among the various speakers in the course of communicative interaction.[17]

Characteristics of Text: Characteristics of cohesion and coherence with reference to at least two orators. The discontinuities in the complete text created by turn-taking are particularly evident at the levels of semantics and stylistics (e.g. through a structurally defined principle of stichomythia, which enables sharp changes of semantic direction under certain circumstances). Pragmatically and (usually) with respect to the leading topic, however, the individual

---

15 In the latter case, the audience may be able to react within the oratorical situation (within the monologic context of those communicative events that involve the performance of the text genre "speech"), but their reactions (applause, discomfort, whistling, objections, etc.) have the status of parallel actions with parallel texts, which are distinctly separate from the orator's text itself and to which the orator must choose to react to.
16 The existence of multiple orators in such situations requires that orator related analyses of conversation first define which actor (speaker) is the focus of analysis.
17 Situativity (being face-to-face) is constitutive for "conversation". Conversational settings involving secondary medialization (such as video conferences) represent a special case with their own phenomenology. See: Knape 2005d, p. 135. There have also recently been a series of investigations into dimissive dialog as found in works such as Beißwenger 2003.

parts of a conversational text form one singular (overarching) text as a whole.[18] Failed conversations that lead to generally incoherent or only slightly coherent series of (ultimately monologic) expressions must be specified as deviations.

Modern research on conversation has differentiated itself into a diverse range of fields (such as dialog grammar, discourse analysis, conversational research, and conversational analysis) and generally approaches the topic using premises other than those used in rhetoric. Such research has defined a wide range of further distinctions and specifications related to the communicative mode of conversation.[19] The following will briefly discuss two concepts widely discussed in works on the topic: the existence of a dialogic universal and the connection between textuality and conversational types from the perspective of rhetoric.

First we have the problem of dialogicity, which some theoreticians conceive as a universal that influences every form of communication. The Czech literary theorist Jan Mukařovský (1891–1975) was not the first to conceive of monologic and dialogic components of communication as "simultaneous and indivisible" in the psychological processes upon which speech is based. Thus, monologue and dialog are not to be understood as, "two separate and step-like ordered forms," rather, they should be conceived of as two forces that, "continually fight for dominance," over the course of a conversation. Even the short form of a command, or a prayer to a non-present God, normally considered purely monologic texts, are to be understood as, "dialogs with extra-linguistic replicas."[20]

The assumption of a dialogic universal is obviously also common in the field of linguistic "dialog analysis" as represented by the remarkable research of Edda Weigand and Franz Hundsnurscher. Weigand differentiates between cases of "functional dialogical" and "formal dialogical" language use. "Monologues", are thus,

> Cases of language use that are not formally dialogically realized, that is, do not aim at specific reactions in a concrete communication partner. But even monologues are a manifestation of dialogical language use, because they are dialogically oriented at the functional level. They are directed at a communicative partner, who remains – in contrast

---

18 A *text* is here understood as an ordered and bounded sign-complex created with communicative intentions. The discontinuity found in conversational texts is therefore a function of the performative conditions, within which the expressions of multiple orators constitute an overarching text as a whole.

19 Some good examples can be found in the summary articles in the handbook: "Linguistics of Text and Conversation" by Brinker/Antos/Heinemann/Sager 2000–2001. See also: Hess-Lüttich 1994; Hess-Lüttich 1996; Heinrichs 1972; and Lorenz 1980.

20 Mukařovský 1948, p. 113, pp. 136 f. See also: Best 1985, pp. 90 f.

to letters – undefined; there is no concrete, specific partner but rather anybody, everybody.[21]

This postulated ubiquity of dialogicity stems from the assumption that every communicative act directed, "at a communicative partner," is, "functionally dialogical." Since every instance of communication (i.e. symbolic interaction) involves some form of a partner by definition, Weigand assumes that *all* communication is functionally dialogical. This led Jörg Kilian to remark in 2005 that, "against this backdrop it is questionable whether monologic acts of speaking, in a strict sense, even exist."[22]

This theoretical position of "dialog analysis" conceives of the dialogical as a universal. In fact, however, it is merely a semantic implicature. By contrast, rhetoric (with its focus on concrete pragmatics and theories of production and performance) begins with the assumption that, in practice, that (monologic) oration and (dialogic) conversation involve quite different calculations, strategies, and operations on the part of the orator. Such an approach also naturally has theoretical consequences as well: rhetoric insists, for instance, on the clear division between *monologic* and *dialogic performance* as described earlier in this chapter.[23] According to rhetorical theory, directionality alone does not make for dialogicity. This stems from the desire for discrete terminology; the connection between action and reaction, and what rhetoric calls the anticipatory addressee calculation cannot be simply subsumed under the term "dialogicity", even when it is only used metaphorically and improperly. In science, metaphors should only be used in two cases: when there is no other term available, or when difficult and complex topics are being explained. Reciprocal awareness of content and the mere existence of parallel reactions in participants in communicative situations (which may, for instance, be oriented towards the context of communication or the speaker himself) do not constitute dialog. A dialog requires mutually active work related to a guiding theme of conversation.[24] For rhetoricians, the so-called 'implicitly dialogical', or 'dialogicity' in monologic oration is simply directionality towards addressees.

---

21 Weigand 1986, p. 119. See also: Weigand 2008.
22 Kilian 2005, p. 2.
23 "Performance is that which a medium, as a textual platform, does with a text." Knape 2008b, p. 146.
24 Here, it helps to take a closer look at Jan Mukařovský's theory of "dialog". His theory connects the psychological aspect of dialog (which lies outside of the specific realm of a rhetorical orator-theory) with the mental conditions of a speaker, which express themselves in the "mutual demarcation of the subject of a dialog," in a given, "psychological situation." Such situations involve the regular use of the role polarity of "Me" and "You" among dialog partners, often through the use of specific linguistic devices that emphasize the difference between their opinions, feelings, and desires. At the same time, Mukařovský emphasizes the

Weigand's underlying definition of monologicity and the monologic is also debatable. The term "monologic," according to Weigand, refers to those cases where, "the use of language [...] is not formally dialogically realized," that is, "does not aim at specific reactions in a concrete communication partner." This limits the concept of monologicity to extremely special cases of language use in which there is no expectation of any sort of addressee reaction. Moreover, this restriction is limited to dimissive settings, cases of communication at a distance with the help of specific media that deny access to a "concrete communication partner."[25]

Rhetoric, on the other hand, holds that monologic speech also exists in situative settings.[26] In reference to the role that communicative basis settings play in communication, both Weigand and Kilian have postulated two, "existential forms of dialog": 1) Conversation (in situative settings) and 2) Written correspondence (in dimissive settings).[27] The conception of "dialog" thus designates any communicative actions in which at least two partners come into contact and work together on a conversational text or super-text (hypertext). Rhetorical theory can accept such a conception as long as it ensures that the term "conversation", strictly speaking, excludes cases of dimission. Whether the chosen term, "correspondence", is adequate for the myriad dialogical types of communication that can occur in a dimissive setting is up for debate. In such cases it may simpler to speak instead of dimissive dialogs.[28]

A brief note on sorting conversational texts into meaningful groups: Aristotle believed it was important to develop theoretically definable specifications of the various disciplines that deal with communication and language, and to divide text-types into their respective fields. This led to his separate works 'Poetics', 'Rhetoric' and 'Sophistical Refutations,' in which he differentiated between four separate forms of conversation: didactic, dialectic, peirastic (examination-arguments) and eristic (contentious arguments).[29] Since Aris-

---

coherence of the topic (in the sense of a macro or guiding theme) which (from a production theoretical view) draws on the psychological conditions of communication, and which requires that partners are prepared for dialectical "self-assertion" and "self-disengagement" in order to create a real dialog and not just two parallel monologues. Mukařovský 1948, p. 118. See also: Best 1985.

25 With respect to communication with mass media, such cases only occur when texts are embedded in certain forms of 'push-media'.

26 For more on situative and dimissive settings, see: Knape 2005c, pp. 30 f.

27 Kilian 2005, p. 4. See also: Kilian 2002, pp. 73 ff.; Weigand 2008, p. 121.

28 The complex communicative situation in conversations leads to particular difficulties in generating a typology of setting, medialization, and performance conditions. See: Adamzik 2001, p. 1479.

29 Aristotle: Sophistical Refutations, Sec. 105a-b.

totle, the system of classification for conversational texts has expanded dramatically.[30]

In the modern field of textual linguistics there has been resistance to assign "conversational types" the status of *text*,[31] because the term is usually consciously separated from, "verbal communicative texts, especially conversations,"

> For a long time they were seen only as complex units and – if only due to the lack of common intentions between the partners and other functional and situational specifica – as a discrete class. For the detailed classification of textual phenomena at a low level of abstraction found in recent work, the analogous term 'conversational type' is often used.[32]

This requires that, "conversation taken as a whole, however complex it appears upon analytical approach, ultimately represents a phenomenon that is functionally unified insofar as it can be described as a unit using specific taxonomic-typological criteria."[33] From the rhetorical perspective, one could say that conversations can indeed be rudimentarily sorted using only the concept of *text*: conversations must be assigned to the relevant operational level of "conversational text" within a theory of production, despite the fact that such categorization is insufficient for the construction of a typology.

Meanwhile, a fundamental distinction that has been developed in the field of conversational analysis regarding the prototypical concept of "conversation" is particularly interesting for rhetoric:

> There are conversations that, to a certain extent, depict the dialogical counterpart as a part of intentional, goal-oriented monologic oration and others in which there is no consistent intention, in which no specific goal of communication [*télos*] can be identified that is valid for all participants from the start. This fundamental differentiation is found in various attempts to create a typology of one form or another [...] and can be roughly described as the difference between goal oriented and non-goal oriented conversation. Especially (older) approaches that fall within the hermeneutic tradition consider non-goal oriented conversations as a core area of interest, as 'conversation' in the strict or proper sense. In contrast, (newer) conceptions that have been heavily influenced by communications theory and linguistic pragmatics find their prototype of conversation in forms that can be described as parts of intentional actions.[34]

---

30 See: Geißner 1996, col. 957 f.
31 Rolf 1993, p. 29.
32 Heinemann 2000, pp. 514 f. See also: Hundsnurscher 1994; an overview of conversational types in business also in: Brünner 2000.
33 Sager 2001, p. 1464.
34 Adamzik 2001, p. 1474. See also: Hundsnurscher 1994.

4 The Case of Conversational Rhetoric

The mention of "intentional action" in the previous quote leads directly to the *proprium* of conversational rhetoric. Rhetorical action consists of strategic, goal oriented, and (where possible) planned and calculated acting and reacting under conditions of resistance. As mentioned previously, conversational research assumes a number of different types of conversation, each with a specific goal (e.g. sales conversation, advisory conversation, courtship conversation, etc.). Additionally there are other forms of conversation that lack a specifically defined goal (*telos*) but still serve some sort of social or individual purpose. In all of these forms of conversation, the rhetorical case occurs when *agonality* and persuasiveness (the basic conditions of rhetoric) enter the equation.

Aristotle saw the core of rhetorical-analytical competence in the ability to recognize the belief causing or persuasive aspect in every situation (and by extension, in all forms of conversation).[35] Persuasion is only required under mentally asymmetric conditions: when there is a mental difference among conversational partners regarding the subject and one of the participants (the orator as a communicator with rhetorical aims) seeks to change others from position A to B. Without this asymmetry, the rhetorical effort is unnecessary.[36] Thus, the rhetorical event in conversation occurs in the moment that someone seeks to defend or win recognition (*agonality*) for a concern under conditions of resistance (*antistasis*). In conversation, this automatically means that each participant can assume the role of orator. If the potential for conflict or dirigistic methods are utilized, Kallmeyer and Schmitt describe the conversation as "forced" or having an "aggravated pace".[37]

Kallmeyer correctly insists that conversational research distinguish itself from an understanding of rhetoric that focuses on eloquence rhetoric. Such reductionism may lead to a restricted view of the complex conditions involved in conversational interactions, and give researchers motivation to merely, "identify the known rhetorical figures in conversation and to describe the participants' act of formulation."[38] Instead, we must insist on using the proper rhetorical approach based on a theory of persuasion. With this as a precondition, Kallmeyer sketches the following cogent research program,

---

35 Aristotle: Rhetoric, 1.2.1
36 See: Knape 2003a.
37 Kallmeyer/Schmitt 1996. See also: Schwitalla 2008.
38 Kallmeyer 1996b, pp. 9 f. See also: Morel 1983.

Conversational rhetoric thus concentrates on the practical rhetorical problems of linguistic action under interactive conditions. Even if the participants in the interaction have no occasion to give a long speech, they still shape their contributions rhetorically. This aspect is most obviously recognizable in complex utterances, but is independent from the length of the contribution. Reduced to a simple formula, it's about 'rhetorical procedures in interactive processes'. The particular moves of individual action in interactions entail both opportunities and dangers for the assertion of interests and the further development of interaction. Rhetorical analysis takes these elements into account by describing the rhetorical potential of linguistic procedures under certain contextual conditions. This rhetorical potential illustrates the chances and risks of action and demonstrates alternatives for action. The description of chances and risks does not involve normative claims; conversational rhetoric is descriptive.[39]

5 The Core of the Conversational Rhetorical Approach

From the perspective of rhetorical theory, research must methodically focus on problems surrounding the successful communication by an orator under conversational circumstances. In doing so, all questions must be approached from the perspective of the orator. This is a contrast to traditional linguistic research, which is normally concerned with describing the complex interactional character of conversation from a bird's eye point of view. Such research has certainly been successful, and rhetorical approaches can thankfully fall back on some of its results.

For rhetoricians, however, the central concern is the perspective of an orator who strategically considers his communicative goals and integrates premises of steering from action theory into his acts of communication. This focus within the rhetorical approach dates back to ancient theorists such as Plato, who described rhetoric as psychagogy, as the, "influencing of the soul," in his 'Phaedrus'.[40] Modern linguistic research on conversation has also begun to accept this perspective, as demonstrated in an article by Liisa Tiittula that begins with a discussion of the concepts of, "steering, dominance and asymmetry," and thereby clearly references the rhetorical perspective.[41]

Under such auspices, rhetoric concentrates on problems of communicative efficiency and success. From the perspective of action theory, the strategies and calculations of persuasion take a central role.[42] If we envision the network of interactions that take place in a conversation, it raises the question of who's

---

39 Kallmeyer 1996b, pp.10 f. (introduction to Kallmeyer 1996a).
40 Plato: Phaedrus, 261a; see also: Knape 2000a, p. 9.
41 Tiittula 2001.
42 Knape/Becker/Böhme 2009. See also: Knape 2003a; Hess-Lüttich 1991.

goals are under consideration. Conversations can, of course, have collective goals (for instance, to bring about peace among all participants). In such cases, the isolation of goals and the judgment of their success becomes a matter of interest for all participants in the conversation, even though each is to be considered a separate orator (with his own individual strategies, etc.) from the perspective of rhetoric.[43] This differentiation is based on the experience that it is never possible to perfectly tune sub-goals, strategies, emotions, or communicative operations in a group setting.

Rhetoric does, however, expect that over the course of a conversation individual participants will have or gain (at least temporarily) a lead in comparison with other participants. The Greeks used the term *protérhēma* to describe such leads, the first place in front of another person or the advantage that one has over others. From the rhetorical perspective, such advantages are in many conversational settings for participants that seek to realize individual global- and sub-goals through the use of appropriate conversational strategies.

The subject of 'proterhematic' positioning is also the core topic of rhetorical training as an element of multifaceted courses designed to train communicative skills.[44] Rhetorically focused training focuses on teaching and improving the analytical and proactive communicative competences that can help potential orators to gain a proterhema, regardless of communicative situation. In this respect, courses designed to improve conversational skills should focus on the improvement of rhetorical "dialog competence" for the here and now, based on the rapid analysis of conversational conditions, the positive implementation of individual concepts within the dialog, and how to deal with aspects of communicative resistance.[45]

A critical analysis of rhetorical guides by Regina Bergmann clearly shows that the proprietary elements of conversation are still little understood, and that such works instead propagate the traditional rhetorical perspective focused on monologic oration.[46] In an analysis of the dominant doctrines of communication training, Reinhard Fiehler comes to the conclusion that an "instrumentalist" and orator-centric perspective is prevalent. He summarizes thus,

> Language is a tool in the mouth of an individual with which, through the use of specific *techniques*, the opponent should be 'machined' as adeptly as possible. The specifics of

---

43 Whether the oratorical goals of participants are discussed openly and honestly is a question of opportunity and social responsibility that is subject to general rules of ethics. Such considerations do not belong to the field of rhetoric.

44 Fiehler 2001b; Fiehler/Schmitt 2011.

45 Kilian 2005. See also: Becker-Mrotzek/Brünner 2009.

46 Bergmann 1999, pp. 231f.

this conception become clear when comparing it with an interactional model that conceives of conversation as a *collective* creation that may not correspond with the intention of an individual participant in either its *course* or its *result*.[47]

As previously mentioned, the, "analytical approach to conversation founded in a theory of interaction," noted in this quote has indeed become the standard in modern linguistic research on conversation.[48] Such an approach is, in some ways, methodologically valid. A rhetorician can accept it as long as he expands his conception of the problem of conversation to include the specifically rhetorical point of view as well. For practical reasons, the rhetorical concerns of the orator must remain the core focus of the theory of rhetoric, even when this approach is sometimes met with misunderstanding.[49] Fiehler does not deny this as found in the reality of business communication. His, "understanding of communication," not only underlies training in this field, it is,

> also persistently newly *constituted* in light of training practices and thus continually updated. Such a conception of communication is especially functional and manifest for the business world, which is organized to a large degree through division of labor and marked by instrumental relationships. Nonetheless, this conception is in no way limited to this field alone.[50]

Just as the subjective camera establishes a specific viewpoint or a special perspective on a problem in film, so too can the rhetorical orator-perspective be used both in practical training and as the focus for academic research and knowledge. Research by Nuri Ortak, for instance, has demonstrated that such approaches can lead to interesting results.[51] Certainly, one must admit that the rhetorical perspective poses a particular methodical challenge for traditional research. At the very least, such challenges arise in instances where research results from various fields are not only interpreted from the perspective of the orator, but when the empirical research itself is planned based on this perspective.

6 The Tasks of a Conversational Orator and the Rhetorical Concept of Conversation Management

Conversational rhetoric focuses on the possibilities of successful communicative action by a communicator under conditions of permanent interactive pres-

---

47 Fiehler 1999, p. 29.
48 Kallmeyer 1996b, p. 9.
49 For instance as found in: Schmitz 2000, pp. 317 f.
50 Fiehler 1999, p. 29.
51 Ortak 2004.

sure in multi-oratorical constellations of participants and the structural contingency and low event predictability that arises from such ephemeral instances of communication. In other words: conversational rhetoric studies how an individual or collective orator can secure his own communicative success (how he can defend or even establish his concern) in situative, and thus fleeting, communicative events in which multiple orators with differing goals actively participate, leading to a complex and highly contingent situational patchwork.

The conversational orator, as a rhetorically active and oriented collocutor, requires three types of competencies for the preparation and performance of a conversation, all of which a developed doctrine of rhetorical conversation must define in a useful way: conversational planning, conversational analysis, and conversational management. In light of the previously mentioned structural conditions found in conversational settings, it is clear that an orator must develop an instantaneous ability to overcome situational difficulties that he may find himself in. Due to the situative nature of conversation, this must include the ability for rapid analysis, decision making, planning and action.

In this context there are six primary tasks that can be defined for rhetorical collocutors (conversational orators). These rhetorical *officia collocutoris* define analytical levels and thus should not be understood as temporally successive procedural steps:

- Intellection;
- Invention;
- Process observation;
- Process interpretation;
- Action calculations;
- Intervention.

6.1 Strategic Calculations Prior to the Conversation

For the trained rhetorician, the communicative procedure does not begin with the moment of performance or in practical situative interaction. The perfected orator always makes plans in advance that deliberately attempt to consider all possible contextual conditions.[52] One could go so far as to say that the decisive cognitive advantage (the proterhema) that a rhetorically trained orator has over other participants stems from his careful and thorough preparation prior to the communicative situation. The central point of such preparation is always

---

[52] For more on this, see: Knape 2000a, pp. 87 ff.

a strategic anticipatory addressee calculation.[53] The concept of strategy is central to rhetorical thought. But what do we mean by strategy in this context? As I have written elsewhere:

> a rhetorical strategy consists of the calculation of success and effectiveness that an orator makes in light of a complex communicative situation, which focuses primarily on the analysis of relevant goal-resistance-means-relations. This rhetorical strategic calculation is anticipatory. Viewed analytically, this calculation is found at the level of planning and thus is not a part of the actual act of communication.[54]

6.1.1 Intellection

In rhetoric, the purely cognitive calculations and preparatory actions that an orator must take prior to conversation are generally grouped under the term *intellection*. All of the various setting conditions, especially those that involve expected areas of resistance, must be considered here under the auspices of an anticipatory addressee and instrumental calculation. The chances and risks involved in each genre of conversation (be it a job interview, a sales pitch, mediation talks, etc.) must be weighed against each other, knowledge of a genre's possible phase steps or standard sequences must be incorporated into anticipatory action plans, and information about the other participants must be expanded and integrated into strategic considerations.[55] In particular, thought must be given to strategies that cope with expected points of crisis in the conversation and with expected reactions based on the personalities of individual participants.[56] The calculation of media selection also plays a role at this stage of planning.[57] An orator must prepare both possible general strategies (conflict, reconciliation, insistence, indifference, etc.) as well as a set of possible tactics for interaction (for instance, stalling, a radical turn-around, avoidance maneuvers, but also emotional tactics such as complimenting, showing empathy or sympathy, intimacy or humor, dispassionate practicality, provocation, distancing or confrontation) all of which must be calibrated to

---

53 Rhetoric sees its production-theoretical approach as complementary to the reception-theoretical research of other disciplines. This relationship is made clear in Walter Schmitz's essay from 2000.

54 Knape/Becker/Böhme 2009.

55 For more on each of these aspects see: Sacks/Schegloff/Jefferson 1974; Rath 2001; and Spiegel/Spranz-Fogasy 2001.

56 Wagner 1978; Watzlawick/Beavin/Jackson 1967.

57 See: Knape 2007d, pp. 54–57.

his concrete conversational partner according to the rhetorical postulate of appropriateness (*aptum*).

6.1.2 Invention

In rhetoric, the stage of invention is traditionally seen as the first task that deals with the concrete text itself. Here, an orator must gather all of the material that he wants to use later in his performed text: dates, figures, names, quotes, aphorisms, striking formulations and leading concepts. Additionally, this stage involves preparing creatively formulated key definitions, forms of expression that stimulate the imagination, and variations on the thematic focus. One's own arguments, as well as possible objections and counter-arguments, must also be assembled.

6.2 Observation and Tactical Calculations in Conversations

After entering into a conversation, the orator finds himself in a practical test. The strategic calculations made prior to the conversation itself are heavily endangered due to the loss of total oratorical control in the situation; the often rapid turn-taking mode of conversation requires swift reactions in responding to the moves of the 'rival' orator (in the form of the conversational partner). The goal here is to make the appropriate mental adjustments at every 'turn' of the conversation in order to find the most fitting tactic and thus adjust to the ever changing conversational situation.[58] This requires the two previously mentioned analytically essential steps: the continual observation and interpretation of the conversation, and the subsequent step of proactively planning time sensitive intervention. These steps must be based on a familiarity with the patterns and rules found in a wide range of different kinds of conversation.

6.2.1 Process Observation

The successful observation of conversational processes depends on good analytical training based on both the linguistic and psychological elements of conversation. Such training must enable orators to recognize and systematize the structure of conversational progression, crisis phases, and the actions and reactions of conversational partners. The highest priority in such analysis is to achieve one's own *proterhema* by maintaining consistent cognitive distance

---

58 For more on the term 'tactics', see: Knape/Becker/Böhme 2009, col. 154.

from the situation; the degree of mental and emotional loss of control due to individual participation must be reduced through continual analytical activity. Of particular importance is self-monitoring: keeping distance from one's own emotions and from the event with the help of self-observational techniques.

6.2.2 Process Interpretation

Learning the observational techniques that take the rapid pace of conversation into account is a pre-requisite to oratorical point-analysis, as is the ability to make time sensitive interpretations of the conversational process. Well-trained event diagnostics go hand in hand with rapid tactical reflection. This is true even when well trained analytical competence and experience based expertise leads to extremely rapid automated reactions that are often considered signs of "natural talent" or "intuition" in layman's terms.

6.2.3 Action Calculations

The rhetorical systematization and interpretation of the conversational situation is almost simultaneously, and often seamlessly, accompanied by new oratorical tactical calculations, partial plans and new calculations of intervention. Important for such processes is an accelerated situative creativity, which has often been connoted by terms such as "presence of mind", "quick-wittedness" or, again, "intuition".[59] From the rhetorical perspective, such creativity is (for the most part) the result of focused training. As always with rhetorical competencies, this depends on the successful acquisition of knowledge about the spectrum of possible interactions (cognitive advantage) and a well-trained ability to optimally prepare for conversation (preparatory advantage). Without a doubt, an experiential advantage in conversational situations also plays an important role. Those who continually find themselves in certain kinds of conversations (such as certain types of sales pitches) can often much more easily maintain their protherematic position over partners that have less experience with such conversational types. Under such conditions, situative rhetorical creativity involves the rapid transfer of patterns or models to concrete situations, the recognition of applied rules, behavioral conventions or idiosyncrasies of personality, the swift assessment of recurring phenomena and finally, the derivation of time-sensitive options for action.[60]

---

59 See: Pawlowski 2004.
60 The cognitive result of this extremely rapid process can also be called intuition.

6.3 Taking Action in Conversation

What remains is the important analytical level of action by an orator in conversation. Seen systematically, such action is the result of the previous strategic and event induced analysis based on interaction with communication partners. At the same time, however, we must take into account that the orator may also act spontaneously and uncritically in the heat of conversation. Under the strict premises of rhetoric, such outbursts are signs of a loss of oratorical control; they are neither strategically nor tactically planned. In such cases, the continual conversational observation and interpretation should help an orator to intervene in order to "repair" or compensate for such loss of control. Situations in which an orator fails to recognize or compensate for these factors are considered (rhetorically) unsuccessful.

6.3.1 Intervention

At this point it is clear that the highly contingent conditions of conversations pose particular challenges for the rhetorical competencies of an orator as a participant. In such situations we are justified in describing rhetoric as "communicative contingency management."[61] This means that rhetorical, persuasion oriented conversation (including success oriented strategies of text formulation) leads to a reduction of contingency through communicative actions that seek to selectively narrow the wide array of possible reactions and comprehension that may occur in conversational interaction. Such actions should lead to the establishment of oratorically induced order in both the thoughts and feelings of addressees. The decisive problem for the orator is to avoid ostentatiously violating the regulatory principle of cooperation in communication as formulated by the philosopher of communication H.P. Grice. Many communicative settings designed for monologic text types make it easier for an orator to temporarily or even permanently establish and hold his own mental order (for instance, by allowing for longer argumentation without interruption).

In most conversational settings, on the other hand, such oratorical control is much more difficult, because many types of conversation depend on proaction and reaction, on steering and counter-steering, on strategic forecasting and tactical adjustment. Often, entire strategies must be revised on the fly in order for an orator to reach his communicative goal. The term *management* is meant to take this special challenge caused by conversational turn-taking into account. In the tumult of most conversations, an orator must proactively mod-

---

61 Knape 2006a, p. 12.

erate the interaction while at the same time reacting cooperatively to contradictory intervention by his conversational partner. An orator must compensate for his own loss of control, accept the preset structures of the conversational genre, and never lose sight of his concerns or strategy despite unforeseeable circumstances. In this sense he must provoke positive reactions from his partner (evocation) and generally ensure that his main evocation leads all conversational participants to work together towards the oratorical project; he must lead his conversation partners to participate in a consensual endeavor or have a particular point of view.[62]

6.3.1.1 Oratorical Conversation Management

The rhetorical event takes place when an orator takes part in a conversation with the intention of incorporating his concern and using the conversation to help advance his goals. In such cases, the oratorical job of management deals with moderating (steering) the conversation in a way that is appropriate to set goals while still following Grice's postulate of, "cooperation under competitive conditions."[63] Rhetorical theory assumes that influence using socially acceptable means is also possible in conversation, that a "moderation-evocation nexus" exists and that the orator can formulate his calculation of interaction with the expectation that certain 'steering-activities' can evoke specific reactions in conversational partners.[64] This conclusion admittedly says nothing about the required situational context or questions of accuracy, appropriateness, and sustainability of intended effects. Still, rhetorical theory dating as far back as Aristotle recognized that an orator can purposefully intervene in a monologue in four different ways: relationship management, rationality management (argumentation), image management, and emotion management. In conversation (in a dialog or polylogue), these management activities take place on different but related levels. The following will name only the most prominent and important aspects.

Relationship Management

Regardless of the role that a participant in a conversation plays (be it as a partisan participant in a discussion, an unspecifically positioned part of an

---

62 In this sense, Kallmeyer also sees a connection between the "success orientation" of conversations and mutual "work of participants" in conversation. Kallmeyer 1996b, p. 10.
63 See: Wagner/Petersen 1993, p. 271.
64 For more on the "moderation-evocation nexus" see: Knape 2008a, pp. 916–924.

informal discussion group, the leader of discussion in a debate, a moderator in a mediation, or part of a conversational dyad, e.g. as an applicant in a job interview), if he sees himself as an orator (or is considered such) he must pay special attention to maintaining relationships within the group. While the idea of *image management* focuses specifically on self-referential calculations, the perspective of *relationship management* focuses on cooperation among partners within the structural limitations of turn-taking found in conversations. Research in this area often has good reasons for treating these two types of management together, but the fact remains that the specific oratorical task of maintaining relationships should be considered systematically separate from oratorical image management.[65] This separation is necessary because it can be problematic should an orator (acting consciously as an actor in the process) neglect the group constellation, the role expectations, the general group dynamics, and all other principles of cooperation demanded by the conversational situation in favor of his own interactional presence or even dominance. Additionally, the systemic character of conversation[66] suggests its characterization as a network of relationships. Oratorical intervention should be arranged accordingly, for instance, it should be evaluated whether there are reasons for focusing attention on one single conversational partner or whether attention should be paid to multiple or all partners involved.

Initially, an orator must clearly determine the kind of relationships that exist with his various conversational partners. A relationship constitutes a connection between two or more people. Such relationships directly impact these interaction calculations, his actions, and especially his courtesy towards other participants. The relationship with any given partner may be influenced by life-world experience or may emerge from the conversational situation alone. Thus, the interpretation of relationships relies on the awareness of group cohesion. Such understanding forms the foundation of strategic oratorical planning. The type of connection, and thus the type of relationship, is determined by elements that regulate the connection between participants and what is allowed by the context that they consider themselves a part of. In practice, such elements are derived from the set of rules, rights, duties, and practices of interaction that participants recognize and accept (or must accept) under the given interactional conditions.

In order for an orator to derive insight, a first step might be to classify relationships according to the dichotomous positions defined by Judee K.

---

65 For examples of works that treat both types of management together, see: Holly 1979; Holly 2001; Schwitalla 1996; and Kallmeyer 2007.
66 See: Hausendorf 1992.

Burgoon and Jerold L. Hale in 1984: dominance vs. submission, intimacy, affection/hostility, integration/segregation, depth/superficiality, intensity of involvement/trust, emotional arousal/composure, similarity/dissimilarity, formality/informality, and specific task roles/a more general social orientation.[67] With their interdisciplinary "taxonomy of dimensions", Burgoon and Hale expanded on the psychological triad of Watzlawick, Beavin and Jackson (1967), which restricted itself to dichotomies of dominance/subordination, antipathy/ sympathy and distance/proximity.[68] Ideally, all of these dimensions of interpretation would be analytically isolable through, "relationship intensive linguistic forms of expression," found at the level of speech acts.[69] An orator could use such structures as a starting point for his own linguistic intervention.

In positive cases, relational structures that are thus or similarly constructed give an orator a chance to intervene; in negative cases of conflict they create obligations to intervene. In all cases, maintaining relationships within the context of group dynamics is one of the most important tasks of an orator, and begins with forms of politeness such as greeting rituals.[70] Normally, such maintenance involves avoiding conflicts and confrontations, preserving the images of partners, maintaining cooperative balance (by avoiding dominant behavior or inconsiderateness in personal speaking style), not undermining trust (for instance, with awkward imaging)[71], and by avoiding any and all kinds of psychological interference in conversational partners.[72] Access to the role of orator can become problematic within the turn-taking dynamic of conversation when there is a lack of needed sensibility for partners (for instance, when the orator interrupts or attempts to dominate the conversation).[73] Contemporary research on conversational styles has clearly demonstrated that the art of rhetoric must be firmly grounded in the deft combination of conventionality and individual speaker behavior.[74]

---

67 Burgoon/Hale 1984; Burgoon/Humpherys/Moffitt 2008.
68 Watzlawick/Beavin/Jackson 1967.
69 Holly 2001, p. 1389. See also: Sager 1981, p. 171; Adamzik 1984; and Schwitalla 1996.
70 Hoppmann 2008.
71 See: Wolf 1999.
72 See: Sager 1981; Goffman 1967, pp. 16 f.; also: Adamzik 1994; Schank/Schwitalla 1987; Deppermann 1997; Schwitalla 2001. For more on conflicts of interaction and sources of misunderstanding from the perspective of oratorical steering see: Tiittula 2001, pp. 1370–1373; on misunderstandings in conversation in general see: Hinnenkamp 1998.
73 For more on problems dealing with access to the role of orator, see: Knape 2000a, p. 82. See also: Tiittula 2001 for more on the process of steering in "conversational organization".
74 Schwitalla 2008.

Image Management

The rhetorically important conditions of trust, credibility, approval and acceptance are heavily influenced by the way that participants in a conversation view the orator as a "partner".[75] This insight played an important role in Aristotle's theory, which used the term *ēthos* at the beginning of the second book on rhetoric to describe the emergent characterization of a speaker: his image. Accordingly, both an orator's prior reputation and the image that he establishes within a conversation are especially important for rhetorical success.[76]

In Erving Goffman's classic work on image research, we find the following definition, "the term *face* may be defined as the positive social value a person effectively claims for himself by the line others assume he has taken during a particular contact. Face is an image of self-delineated in terms of approved social attributes."[77] Important in this definition is that Goffman recommends strategic behavior by a speaker (that which someone, "effectively claims for himself") that leads to an evaluation by those around him of his constructed "image of self." Thus, an orator's goal (*télos*) must be to convince as many of his communicative partners to view him as having positive characteristics so that he can embody the positive image necessary to reach desired conversational results. An orator must continually work on the construction, care, and maintenance of his image in conversation and be prepared to regenerate it in cases of conversational crisis where his image might be threatened.[78]

Conversational linguist Werner Holly has drawn conclusions from Goffman's approach based on linguistic usage and posed the question of how personal images are established in conversation through specific patterns of linguistic activity.[79] Such establishment takes place through the use of image-

---

[75] "One aspect of the persuasion process that is important is the judgments made of persuaders and their messages. Researchers have identified several impressions that are salient. One is speaker credibility. Numerous studies (Perloff 2002) have linked persuasion to speaker credibility: speaker competence, speaker trustworthiness, and speaker dynamism [...]. A second is speaker attractiveness. This could refer to physical attractiveness, but usually it means that others would find the speaker likeable, friendly, or approachable. A third impression is speaker similarity. Studies (Perloff 2002) indicate that similarity between a speaker and receiver can be persuasive in two ways: One is belief of attitudinal similarity, the second component is communication similarity." Hosman 2008, p. 1120. For more on the category of "confidence/trust" ("a cornerstone in the development of close interpersonal relationship") see: Millar/Rogers 1976, p. 90; and Deppermann 1998, pp. 100 ff. For more on "approaches in credibility research", see: Deppermann 1997, pp. 25–48.

[76] Wörner 1984.

[77] Goffman 1967, p. 5.

[78] Goffman 1967, pp. 19 f.

[79] Holly 1979 and 2001.

making, image-strengthening, and image-validating conversational units. Initially, such structures include expressions of interest and sympathy (through the use of questions or compliments), polite offers, invitations, introductions, or greetings, and further, certain forms of affirmation, such as ratifications (all types of approval) or further acts of politeness. Like Goffman, Holly has also researched threatening incidents (impoliteness, disrespect, insults, etc.) that can damage a speaker's image and may require corrective measures on the part of the orator. Such corrective measures can include apologies, justifications, admissions of guilt, polite entreaties, or denial. These considerations have been further developed and differentiated within the field of conversational linguistics by other researchers as well.[80]

Rationality Management

For Aristotle's cognitive rhetorical approach, *diánoia* (thought processes) were central to rhetorical activities because people are often convinced of something for rational reasons (*rationes*). Thus, modern theoreticians such as exponents of the Elaboration-Likelihood-Model (ELM) have spoken of rationality as the "central route" of mental influence.[81] Behind such reasoning is the undeniable assumption that logic and rationality function similarly in all people; only then does the level of rationality present good persuasive possibilities.

With its origins in argumentation theory, modern pragma-dialectics (and its model of *critical discussion*) follows this assumption by establishing formalized regularities and a system of speech acts designed to solve differences of opinion in discussions.[82] Related to this is the concept of *strategic maneuvering*, which systematically integrates the rhetorical perspective.[83] Important here is a methodical analysis of argumentative strategies based on four parameters:

1. Which results can be achieved in which phases of discussion?
2. Which dialectic profile and which steps in discussion lead to which results?[84]
3. Which institutional restrictions play a role in the given communicative situation?

---

80 See: Schwitalla 1996; and Wolf 1999.
81 Petty/Cacioppo 1986. For more on the concept of *diánoia* in Aristotle's writings see: Knape 2000a, pp. 126 f.
82 van Eemeren/Grootendorst 2004.
83 van Eemeren/Houtlosser 2006.
84 For more on the ideal of a dialectic profile see: van Eemeren/Houtlosser/Snoeck Henkemans 2007.

4. Which common duties and starting points are defined by the argumentative situation?[85]

Research has only recently begun to focus on the very specific, concrete conditions in which argumentation in conversations takes place. These conditions include contingency of interaction, the ephemeral nature of the event, turn-taking, psychological pressure due to the immediate presence of partners, and additional non-verbal factors. In this area, the work of sociolinguist Arnulf Deppermann is of particular interest. He has called for a new empirical approach to argumentation, especially as found in everyday conversations (types of conversation that are not subject to strict rituals). In this regard, he has formulated six desiderata which are in need of further development.[86] An important criticism can be leveled at the underlying normative approach of traditional theories of argumentation, whose defenders at times see no problem in basing conversational analysis on the transformation of ideal structures that do not actually appear as such in conversational processes.[87] Examples include the elimination of redundant information, a change in the order of

---

85 van Eemeren/Houtlosser/Snoeck Henkemans 2007, pp. 375–380.

86 These desiderata can be summarized by the following six questions: 1. What can be counted as an argument in conversation (question of the subject)? 2. What kinds of linguistic indicators denote argumentation? 3. How well do normative conceptions of argumentation describe "argumentation" as found in everyday conversation? 4. How do the logical structures of arguments behave within the argumentative processes of conversation, which are often neither logical nor coherent? 5. What conception of argumentation could allow for the pragmatic incorporation of rational speech in everyday contexts (does such a conception always deal with problem solving processes)? 6. How are we to conceive a typology of argumentative processes in real world conversations? See: Deppermann 2003.

87 The implied opposition is here inadequately defined by the terms "normativity" and "descriptivity". In reality it is a relationship that is best expressed in the sense of Saussure's difference between *langue* (abstracted systematics) and *parole* (concrete text). Using a structuralist approach, it is certainly possible to derive regularities, patterns, and ideal models (as a sort of *langue* of argumentation) from existing (real-world) texts (*parole*). The reception of such abstractions can also be recognized even though they are rarely found in their pure form, but rather as logical structures. Such structural condensation also gave rise to Schopenhauer's concept of *eristics*, which deals with fallacies, the pseudo-proofs and logically inconsistent conclusions often found in conversations. On this topic, Schopenhauer wrote, "the tricks, dodges, and chicanery, to which they [people] resort, in order to be right in the end, are so numerous and manifold and yet recur so regularly, that some years ago I made them the subject of my own reflection [...]. This led me at the time to the idea of clearly separating the merely formal part of these tricks and dodges from the material and of displaying it, so to speak, as a neat anatomical specimen." Schopenhauer 1851, pp. 25 f.

statements, or the assumption of certain implications simply due to a lack of explicitness.[88]

What conclusions can the rhetorician draw from this? The most important is that rational strategies can and must be maintained under conversational conditions (especially regarding time pressure, which hinders calm reflection, and the uncontrolled change of speaker). The measure for such strategies is the standard of plausibility that exists in the given situation, whereby some types of arguments are especially rhetorically effective because they appear to be useful in a variety of situations.[89] The practical events of conversation often involve breaks in both the cohesion and coherency of arguments, which leads to the need for lively tactical turns or makeshift considerations by the orator. Since rhetoric is always concerned with the assertion of one's own concerns in real world situations, it cannot require, "an ideal conversational situation that is simplified to eliminate disruptive factors (especially those that deal with psychological reality) and which postulate a model of communicative conditions in which a consensus can be reached in the determination of truth and rightness."[90] Provisional and makeshift thought, fragmented logic, and biased judgment must therefore be permanent considerations.

Through all of this, an orator can set argumentative processes (discussions on the basis of logical structures) in motion, can keep them alive despite resistance (deviations or breaks in the conversation) using strategies of insistence or persistence, can stay on task, and can attempt to reach a conclusion through permanent argumentational input.[91] Left unsaid is the problem of cognitive fitness, which considers the mental equipment and preparation necessary in order to parry intervention by opposing orators in the exchange of argumentative blows.

Emotion Management

Emotional tuning among conversational partners, often generally referred to with terms such as 'mood' and 'atmosphere' or described in reference to specific feelings towards certain topics, plays an important role in the success of conversations.[92] Aristotle also expected an orator to proactively and stimulatingly intervene emotionally in conversations. Theoretician Reinhold Schmitt

---

88 See also: van Eemeren/Grootendorst 2004, pp. 95 ff.
89 Pragmatic arguments are one example of this. See: Guhr 2008, p. 38.
90 Knape 1998, p. 55.
91 Spranz-Fogasy 2003.
92 For details on the concept of mood-management see: Langelier 2001a and 2001b.

has even spoken of a, "staging of emotional participation."[93] The strategic sub-goal of such staging is to generate emotional affinity or aversion towards a topic or person in conversational partners. An emotion is a psychic state of excitement that involves subjective qualities of experience beyond pure-rationality and measurable attendant physiological symptoms that influence the affinity or aversion of the subject towards certain phenomena in the world.

With his behavior, an orator can, "influence emotions, his own as well as others, and conversely, his emotions can affect and change his own and others' communicative behavior."[94] Operationally, the reciprocal processes of influence are reflected in the, "manifestation of emotions," (e.g. physiologically through shaking, turning pale, etc. or phonetically, through laughing, etc.) in the, "interpretation of emotions," and the, "interactive processing of emotions," (e.g. through acceptance, scrutiny, challenging, or ignoring as processing strategies).[95] An orator can also use,

> formal aspects of communicative behavior [... such as] conventionalized linguistic devices whose communicative function is to trigger emotions, or those that are thought to have such a function. The latter, considered emotionalized stylistic devices and strategies are important objects of stylistic and rhetorical theory. These are linguistic means, which conventionally seek to create feelings of interest, sorrow, festivity, elation, awe, and other such emotions. They do not only play a role in oral communication, but exactly in those moments of emotional triggering in written texts.[96]

Fiehler distinguished four rules meant to help regulate the emotional events in communication:
1. an emotional rule of situation, which determines which emotions are considered appropriate in various situations;
2. a rule of manifestation that regulates which emotions are allowed or required to be shown in certain situations;
3. a rule of correspondence, which determines the allowable emotions of conversational partners in various phases of conversation; and
4. a rule of coding, which establishes the normal behavioral repertoire in relation to certain emotions.[97]

In a given conversation, an orator can act in a way that either confirms or violates (through methods of deviation, shock, or surprise) these rules.

---

93 Schmitt 2003.
94 Fiehler 2008, pp. 757 f.
95 Fiehler 2008, pp. 760 f.
96 Fiehler 2008, p. 771. See also: Schwarz-Friesel 2007.
97 See: Fiehler 2001a; and Fiehler 1990, pp. 78 f.

Topic Management

The generally more technical types of management to follow are integral parts of all previously named areas of management; they are described separately purely for systematic clarity. One such technical area is topic- or theme-management, to which Liisa Tiittula devoted particular attention from the perspective of conversational steering in 2001.[98]

Rhetorically seen, a theme is a cognitive construct that the orator seeks to introduce into communication using signs (in the form of a text) and whose development or conclusion occasionally requires active participation or stimulation on the part of an orator in the process of communication. At the level of text and sentence, a theme is the object about which something is being said: "the theme is the communicatively constituted object or issue that is the continual subject of a text/text passage or discourse/part of a discourse."[99] In conversation, a theme is the temporary or continual object of the communicative event, which Gerd Schank has also called, "the intentional object in the focus of centered interaction." It is, "explicitly verbalized" by participants within the conversational text because, "they feel it is relevant."[100] This is based on the fact that every person can, "intuitively classify an expression in a conversation as belonging to a theme or not based on his communicative experience."[101] Additionally:

> A theme in a conversation is constituted on the one hand by the procedures and mechanisms that delimit themes, such as theme change, theme initiation and theme ending, on the other, it is realized by the development of thematic processes that are produced within these thematic borders.[102]

Theme management is one to the most important oratorical tasks because thematic focusing binds the cognition, emotion, and fantasy (or imagination) of conversational partners either temporarily or for a longer period of time. Theme determination and theme control are two of the most important tools that an orator has in steering a conversational interaction. Theme steering allows an orator to sustain his own concerns in the conversation and convey them through articulation. The introduction of themes can also be heuristically motivated and serve to gain information about little-known conversational partners through their handling of the theme.

---

98 Tiittula 2001.
99 Hoffmann 2000, p. 350.
100 Schank 1981, p. 22.
101 Hoffmann 1996, p. 74.
102 Hinnenkamp 1998, p. 53.

During his anticipatory calculation, an orator must ask himself the question, "which topics am I going to bring up and why?" Themes can be related to specific issues, or geared towards specific addressees, settings, or groups. From a rhetorical perspective, themes always require, "specific markets of communication," and they should always serve to support an orator's concern (at the level of factual issues, image, or emotions).[103] Risk laden themes are generally to be avoided and must occasionally be actively suppressed during conversation.

In setting his theme, an orator must always think about the rhetorical *topic*.[104] According to Aristotle, the *topic* offers, "a method by which we shall be able to reason from generally accepted opinions about any problem set before us."[105] In his 'Art of Rhetoric', he describes topoi as general propositions that can be effectively integrated into argumentation.[106] Because there are discourse specific topics ("group themes and group specific stereotypes," according to Schank[107]), a well-trained orator can arrange an appropriate repertoire of topical themes for any type of conversation that can then be introduced into the conversation at will.[108] On the other hand, topical themes can also be spontaneously introduced into conversation when necessary. "Successful communication in social situations depends on the mastery of such thematic repertoires."[109]

Management skills are not only necessary for the introduction of themes into conversation, but also in the further development of themes, where splitting, association, subsumption, or composition of themes can occur.[110] For an orator, all of this is a question of strategy: whether it best serves his purposes to implement one guiding theme throughout the entire conversation, or to allow a random series of themes to arise without intervention. An orator must thus consider which themes can be useful in various situations (theme-tactics) both before and during a conversation. If we look at the general phases of conversation (the introduction, the main phase, and the conclusion), it is clear that not all themes are appropriate for every phase. Themes with a high degree of intimacy would conventionally be highly risky at the beginning of an initial

---

[103] Schank 1981, p. 35.
[104] Bornscheuer 1976; and Graff 2008.
[105] Aristotle: Topica, 1.1.1.
[106] Aristotle: Rhetoric, 1.2.21.
[107] Schank 1981, p. 35.
[108] It is important to note that not every theme is also a common *topos*. See: Knape 2000c.
[109] Schank 1981, p. 35.
[110] See: Hoffmann 2000, pp. 353 f.

conversation, whereas so-called small talk themes are uncontroversial in the opening phases of conversation.

Particular skill is required for an orator to be able to effectively introduce a theme that is important to him into a conversation. An orator must have a feel for the art of association; the art of intelligent linking and thematic bridge-building. Conversational research has underscored the role of questioning and meta-communication in integrating a theme into a conversation.[111] The arsenal of so-called rhetorical figures of thought also present possibilities in this light (comparison, allusion, quotation, generalized sentences, etc.). Additionally, the narrative treatment of themes can also further oratorical concerns (through the use of apt examples, significant anecdotes, touching stories, etc.).

Formulation Management

Traditionally, rhetoric devotes separate systematic considerations to the reflective verbalization and the art of text formulation, for instance in the doctrine of rhetorical figures and the art of expression.[112] Newer studies on this topic have also given particular attention to questions of, "lexical diversity", "language intensity", or the, "power of speech style components."[113] It is thus appropriate for an orator to display care with the possibilities of expression under the special conditions of text production in conversation.[114] Such consideration is not merely about bringing up a theme in conversation; rather, an orator must be able to transition from linguistic self-management to considerations and actions that may influence the linguistic behavior of his conversational partners. The overall relevance of the connection between language and the relationships of participants does not need to be specifically emphasized here.[115] It is thus not only important for an orator to control his own formulations (for instance, to always carefully consider his formulation, to use the appropriate level of language, to be creative with central concepts, and to adjust his linguistic complexity to fit the group context), it is also important for him to influence the overarching style of the group.

From the perspective of the orator, the term 'style' originated in reference to strategies of textualization that define unifying principles underlying the work on a text. In the meantime, however, researchers have recognized the

---

111 See: Tiittula 2001, p. 1370.
112 Knape 1994a and 1996.
113 Hosman 2008.
114 Sornig 1986.
115 Sager 1981.

"integrative power" of style more generally as an important factor in communication.[116] To work together in a group on a common style of expression thus also means to work on the question of consistence with respect to both semantics and group-dynamics:

> Apart from suggesting interpretative frames such as formality or informality, different degrees of involvement, and so on, styles may be deployed as potentially culturally and subculturally specific resources of interaction that signal identity (or prompt ascriptions of identity) and allegiance to specific groups (cf. Gumperz 1982; Tannen 1984). In talk-in-interaction, we need to differentiate between speech styles on the one hand and conversational styles on the other (cf. Sandig/Selting 1997, 5): 'Speech style(s)' refers to the way(s) of speaking in talk-in-interaction, for instance the interactionally meaningful ways of combining lexico-semantic, syntactic, morpho-phonemic, phonetic and prosodic cues with the rhetorical structuring of talk in the wider sense (ibid.). In contrast, 'conversational style(s)' refers to the recurrent way(s) in which participants organize conversations in situations, including the use and alter(n)ation of speech styles as well as, for example, different ways of organizing turn-taking (complex) activities/actions, topics and modalities in conversation (ibid.; and cf. also Tannen 1984).[117]

Performance Management

The final important remaining area of management is that of performance.[118] In the general theory of rhetoric, this concept refers to all the components of communication that deal with the presentation, "showing", and staging of texts.[119] Here the idea of self-management again takes center stage, but it is not the only consideration: performance also refers to the entire medial framework, in particular the non-verbal aspects of communication such as gestures, facial expressions, and voice patterns. These elements include,

> (1) *affect displays* (displays of emotion), (2) *regulators* (gestures that manage the flow of conversation), (3) *illustrators* (gestures that accompany and complement or modify the meaning of a spoken utterance), (4) *emblems* (symbolic gestures that can substitute for words), and (5) *adaptors* (actions like scratching, rubbing, sniffling, and burping that are usually performed in private to alleviate psychological or physical discomfort)[120]

By managing these various instruments, an orator can influence active argumentation (e.g. through nonverbal expressions of approval or disapproval), the construction of his own image (e.g. by displaying restraint of dominance) and

---

116 See: Püschel 2008.
117 Selting 2008, p. 1039.
118 For more on the rhetorical term "performance", see: Knape 2008b and 2008c.
119 See also: Schmitt 2003.
120 Burgoon/Humpherys/Moffitt 2008, p. 790.

the general emotional conditions of the conversation (for instance, improving the mood by smiling and turning towards his conversational partner).[121]

---

[121] German version of this chapter in: Knape 2009.

Rhetoric of Verbal Texts

6 Historiography as Rhetoric in Medieval Times

Historiographical texts are tied to facts. For this reason, Aristotle said that such texts represent a lower philosophical achievement than poetry in chapter 9 of his 'Poetics'. Historiography is constrained to standard communicative frames of understanding, which is why Cicero listed the construction of historiographical texts as a task for the rhetorician. At the same time, Cicero's designation made it clear that he had no doubts about the "partisanship" or "bias" found in even factual *historia*. In the life-world, texts always have a function, and the author always to some extent gives their text an orientation; rhetoricians call these elements together the *message*. While historiography is bound to real world facts, over time the information available about these facts becomes vague, fragmentary, and in need of interpretation. In the moment of interpretation, the chronicler becomes a rhetorical orator. Similarly, he also acts as a rhetorician when deciding on a particular form of presenting.[1] In doing so he chooses one form of writing over another and gives his text a particular orientation.

1 Chronicles Memorialize the Traces of the Past

The past is something that is always already over when we talk about it. Living beings can only observe the past by reading traces that remain from historical events. These traces of past events are always merely shadow images of reality. Nevertheless, they are our only sources of knowledge about past events. Historical research involves interpreting these traces, which we can divide into two groups: 1) authentic and direct traces (i.e. cultural remains, monuments, documents etc., all of which we conceive as platforms of raw data); 2) memorialized traces. As rhetoricians, this latter form of historical material interests us the most. Memorialized traces are traces of the past that have already been interpreted by previous generations and which have been processed in texts (and thereby encoded). Historiographical works, that is, all works that explicitly aim to reconstruct past facts as facts of the past, belong in this group. Whenever we interpret such works today, we interpret traces that have already been culturally interpreted.

The oldest explicit theory of historiography is included in the second book of Cicero's *De oratore*. Until the eighteenth century, theoretical reflections on

---

1 Cf. White 1978a.

the *historia* (i.e. historiography) were the business of rhetoric.[2] Cicero wrote that the text of a *historia* is the actual life-form of social memory, and that an orator's rhetorical task is to create this specific, textual life-form ("historia est ...; vita memoriae").[3] Thus, Cicero phrased the concept of historiography as one of data storage. In the course of his work, Cicero made clear that there are quite different textual procedures when dealing with the traces of the past in texts – traces that we nowadays call historical data.[4] In doing so, Cicero addressed the principle of freedom of encoding: that the historiographer is allowed to independently arrange historical events in a literary way (e.g. by using stylized speeches or descriptions etc.) in order to create *evidentia*, vividness.

Historiography deals with the semiotic representation of the past. All past *events* are today only manifest as signs. We reconstruct complex structures of the past first by drawing conclusions from reduced traces, and second by creating new texts from these traces that generate a virtual reality in our minds. This virtual reality is a reconstruction of an actual and complex reality of the past. Cicero thus also wrote in *De oratore* that the text of a *historia* is the messenger of past times ("historia est ...; nuntia vetustatis").[5]

2 Three Modes of Historical Observation

When we observe older historiographical works today, we can see how traces were observed in the past by reconstructing the past as a text with the help of other, source texts. In such cases we are dealing with second-degree observations. Whenever we talk about our contemporary observation of the specific methods of prior observation, or talk about the specific way that traces were dealt with in the Middle Ages (i.e. historiography), we begin to approach the question of rhetoric. First, however, we must make an important distinction. When Cicero named the "light of truth" ("historia est ...; lux veritatis") as a further criterion in the definition of *historia*, he meant the principle of data-validity – a principle that historians of all times have felt obliged to.[6] In reality this principle used to refer only to a principle of 'source-validity' (*Quellentreue*), because there were not any *critical* methods of validating data available

---

2 Rüsen 1982, p. 15; Knape 1997a, p. 134; Knape 2000d.
3 Cicero: De Oratore, 2.36.
4 Cicero: De Oratore, 2.51–58.
5 Cicero: De Oratore, 2.36.
6 Cicero: De Oratore, 2.36.

at the time. This principle of source validity describes one specific task of historiographers: they look for secure data or information, which they conceive as the encoding of an extra-semiotic reality that they can then include in new texts. For historians, such data represents an infallible reconstruction of past reality. With regard to the theory of language, historiographers therefore concentrate completely on the representational function of language (*Abbildungsfunktion*); for them, texts reflect images of reality. Nowadays, skeptical historians admit that (at least as far as memorialized traces found in historiographical works are concerned) we are instead dealing with textually-reduced images of already textually-reduced images of reality. These historians admit that the final reference to an extra-semiotic and complex reality, to a past world outside of the text, can never be fully successful. With regard to questions of the past we have to stay within the world of discourse. Still, modern historians work with a wide array of highly complex methods (for instance, archaeological) in their quest to find historical traces that can better support their theories of the past.

In reconstructing the past, we are forced to move in a world of different texts. Nevertheless, the status of these texts varies at times. We speak of factuality in texts and we grant them data-validity even if they incorporate a high degree of freedom in their encoding, as is the case with medieval historiography. In contrast, when we speak of fictionality in texts (such as in poetry) not only do we grant a freedom of encoding, but also complete freedom from data validity.[7] The modern practice of methodical textual criticism helps us determine whether a given text is to be seen as factual or fictional. Such criticism involves the mutual examination of sources: all factual data must be able to be integrated into a systematic network of authentic (archeological, diplomatic sources) or memorialized traces (historiographical sources) without contradiction. The ultimate aim is usually an interpretive first-degree observation which we could also call a 'reconstruction' of facts. Through such observations we assume that the historical data enable us (the living) to reconstruct an event x (for instance, the assassination of Julius Caesar) which took place at the time t_1 (March 17th, 44 B.C.). Additionally, memorialized traces allow us to make an interpretive observation of the second-degree, which we call the observation of encoding. In the case of Caesar in particular, we want to see what specific textual structure the event x, which took place at the time t_1, was given at the later time t_2 (1143 in Otto's von Freising *Chronica*).[8]

With regard to the theory of language, such second-degree observations always deal with the representational function of language. Chronicles are read

---

7 Knape 1997b.
8 Otto von Freising.

as constative speech acts that make factual statements. If we advance further to a third-degree observation (which we may call the observation of message), we arrive at a completely different, rhetorical, perspective. Such observations focus on a third kind of trace, namely with the specific traces of text-production. From its very beginnings, rhetoric has been primarily oriented towards a theory of production: it focuses on how texts are produced and why they are produced as they are. With regard to rhetorical research in the field of history this means questioning the concrete conditions of text production in every individual case.

3 Analytical Rhetoric Examines Communicative Actions

Analytical rhetoric does not interpret texts per se, but rather interprets acts or processes of communication that originate from an author (or orator) with a specific strategic intention. The focus of rhetorical research is thus the communicative strategic function of texts. The rhetorician does not regard historiographical texts as works in which somebody makes statements about the past, but rather as works with which somebody acts communicatively. Thus, rhetoric does not pose the question of what *historiographical statements* Otto von Freising made about the event x at the time t_2. Instead, rhetoric asks what *strategic-communicative action* Otto von Freising carried out with his historiographical statements about the event x at the time t_2.

In order to explain the theoretical background, I would first like to quote from John Austin's pioneering work on speech act theory, *'How to Do Things with Words'*. The title of the book can be taken as a program for exactly the kind of textual rhetoric at issue here. Austin wrote:

> It was for too long the assumption of philosophers that the business of a 'statement' can only be to 'describe' some state of affairs, or to 'state some fact', which it must do either truly or falsely. Grammarians, indeed, have regularly pointed out that not all 'sentences' are (used in making) statements: there are [...] also questions and exclamations, and sentences expressing commands or wishes or concessions. [...] It has come to be commonly held that many utterances which look like statements are either not intended at all, or only intended in part, to record or impart straightforward information about the facts: for example, 'ethical propositions' are perhaps intended, solely or partly, to evince emotion or to prescribe conduct or to influence it in special ways.[9]

What Austin postulated here as a pragmatic turn in the philosophy of language has gone without saying for rhetoricians for two-and-a-half thousand years:

---

9 Austin 1962, pp. 1 ff.

language does not merely represent facts, but rather always acts as well. Still, rhetorical theory demands that we modify this statement: there is always *someone* who makes language speak, who acts communicatively with language. Similarly, communication never involves language in and of itself; it depends on the construction of texts which are made out of language. Texts are exponents of specific acts of communication. Thus, we can say that a communicator does not merely describe something with texts (knowledge function); he *acts* with them at the same time (pragmatic function).[10] The specific rhetorical perspective always focuses on a communicator strategically instrumentalizing a text in communication. In doing so, the communicator always deals with at least two elements: a matter (information) and a communicative concern (message). Moreover, in order to communicate, the author must establish his own specific way of dealing with the semiotic conditions of textuality and encoding. The rhetorical factor of a text determines whether the intended mode of communication succeeds or fails.

Taking all this into account, we still have to distinguish between the theoretical areas of textuality and communication. We can read every written text that has been handed down to us as a virtual world of its own. However, we know that texts do not write themselves. Therefore it is rational to presume a situative-communicative world in which the author spoke. Normally, such phenomena are not problematic for historians, even literary historians, who work on the basis of a naïve semiotic realism. It *is* a problem, however, for text-theorists whose attention is often confined to the primary text only. Rhetoric must insist on a theoretical connection between textuality and communication. It has to correlate the productive action of the *auctor* (as a communicator) with his text. In the process, the communicator can be theoretically broken down into three *hypostases* (we call them communicator-functions), generating three textual levels of meaning in one and the same process of production. These different functions are illustrated in Figure 5.[11]

4 The Three Rhetorical Gestures of the Text (Otto's von Freising *Chronica* and the *Chronicle of the Emperors*)

Inevitably, analytical rhetoric has to deal with an individual and distinct text in order to subsequently connect it to the overall communicative setting of the respective historical situation in a way that makes sense. The historiographer

---

10 Cf. Knape 2000a, p. 118.
11 For further explanation of this chart see: Knape 2000a, pp. 112–116.

Author	Text		
Communicator-Functions	*Bühler / Jakobson* *Functions of Language*	*Morris* *Semiotic Text-Levels*	*Dimensions of Text-Meaning*
Informer	Representation / Referential, Emotive	Semantics	Information (Grammatic or Systematic Meaning of Language)
Elocutor	Expression/ Poetic, Metalingual	Syntax	Structural Values (Aesthetic Meaning)
Orator	Appeal/ Conative, Phatic	Pragmatics	Message (Rhetorical Meaning)

Figure 5: Correlating Functions and Levels of Communicational-Theoretical and Textual-Semiotic Models.

encodes data and therefore information in his text, he gives this text a certain structure, and he has a message which he embeds in the text. This last aspect is decisive for rhetorical analysis, because the communicative function and the rhetorical action of texts are expressed in the messages they contain.

That which speech-act theory postulates with regard to single sentences, rhetoric has to apply to texts as a whole or parts of texts.[12] Analogously, one could speak of text-acts. However, I prefer the term *gesture of the text*. Texts always have messages woven into them, which result from the rhetorical gesture of the text or text section. The term *gestus* is a technical term used in the traditional rhetorical theory of performance often referred to as *actio*. This theory deals with how the orator should translate his textual concept into action during his lecture. In our context, gesture therefore means something analogous to what we may call an 'aspect of orientation'[13], or, perhaps, what speech-act theory calls the *illocutionary mode*. There are three main rhetorical *basic gestures* found in texts: 1. instruction, 2. construction of claims to valid-

---

12 An earlier attempt at developing speech act theory according to the lines of textual theory can be found in: Pratt 1977.
13 Knape 2008a, pp. 916–924.

ity, 3. evaluation. These three rhetorical gestures represent the basic rhetorical motions found in texts. These gestures must also always be in some way correlated with communicative conditions that exist external to the text.[14]

In constructing the text of a *historia*, the orator can develop these rhetorical gestures at all narratological levels. According to Gérard Genette, these levels include the 'story' or plot (*histoire*), textuality (*discours narratif*) and communication (*narration*: the "productive narrative act", being either internal or external to the text).[15] To illustrate this point, we will now examine and compare the various rhetorical structures found in Caesar's-story in Otto's Latin *Chronica sive historia de duabus civitatibus* (written between 1143 and 1146) and the German *Chronicle of the Emperors* (*Kaiserchronik*, ca. 1147–1172).[16]

1 Instruction: There are two possible variations of instructive gestures. The first is the instruction of matter (*Sachinstruktion*) in which the author constructs the *suchness* (*Derartigkeit*) of a case based on a specific determination of the facts. The author presents this version of events as the only possible way to interpret the case, and asserts that his description is inevitable. A confession of doubt (by admitting that the facts might be different than those presented) represents a special case. When dealing with this kind of instruction, rhetoric is interested in the specific techniques used by historiographers in the instruction of matter. The second mode is the instruction to act (*Handlungsinstruktion*), i.e. a demand for action ('you should act') in accordance with the text ('this is the way you should act and it is the only way').

In our example, the instruction of matter deals with Julius Caesar and the situation of the Roman Empire at Caesar's time (1st century BCE). Essentially, a chronicler achieves his specific instruction of matter at the level of the *histoire* via two procedures. First, he selects what he views as relevant personal data or facts. Out of the numerous sources available, Otto von Freising selected those facts that characterized Caesar as *vir bonus* and – in contrast – those that showed other Romans as being corrupt. He also selected facts concerning the conditions of civil war in Italy and facts accentuating Caesar's close connections to the Teutons. By contrast, the author of the *Chronicle of the Emperors* selected those pieces of information that gave the impression that all of Caesar's decisive actions had taken place in Germany or with the help of the Germans. The text even explicitly states that Caesar came from Germany.[17] The

---

14 Knape 2000a, pp. 120 f.
15 Genette 1972a, pp. 65–282.
16 Otto von Freising, II.48–51; Chronicle of the Emperors, lines 247–602.
17 For a detailed discussion of sources concerning our chapter see: Massmann 1854, pp. 460–547.

second procedure of instruction consists of 'unfolding' the implicature: the individual pieces of information that have been extracted from different sources and newly combined are surveyed with regard to their implications. These historical implications can then be independently arranged and developed. When Otto von Freising succinctly wrote that Caesar defeated even the Germans, the most belligerent of all peoples, it represented a source information for the author of the *Chronicle of the Emperors* that implicitly referred to the four main German tribes: the Swabians, the Bavarians, the Saxons and the Franconians ("Caesar's old relations").[18] As a result, the *Chronicle of the Emperors* introduces each of these tribes in long excursuses. With the help of these two procedures, each author succeeded in providing a specific instruction of matter with regard to Caesar's world.

The art of strategically constructing a text as desired was taught by grammarians in the Trivium. A good example of this is provided by the most famous medieval poeto-rhetoric: Geoffrey's of Vinsauf *Poetria nova*, dated around 1200, which established a rhetorical theory of discourse. By presenting different models of textual selection, the grammarian Geoffrey demonstrated the possible construction of different textual versions of one and the same topic.

The instruction to act (that may be present in a text) is directed at the listener or reader of the chronicle. Such instruction can take various forms. One possibility is that the chronicler directly formulates explicit imperatives (at level of the *text*) or derives rules of action out of the *story*. If such pragmatic implications are missing, we have to ask which instructions of action the chronicle (as a genre) can supply in general. Do chronicles represent a set of instructions for rulers? A chronicle such as the *Chronicle of the Emperors*, which follows the lives of rulers, could be read as a 'Fürstenspiegel', i.e. as a didactic work for the education of princes. In this case, the representation of Caesar's life may be perfectly used for learning by emulation of the model.

2 Construction of claims to validity: In constructing claims of validity, the author seeks to confirm that a case is socially valid or that a way of conduct is justified. Medieval chronicles can always be understood as a form of juridical instruction as well. The origin and nature of power- and legal-structures is represented at the level of the *histoire* in a particular and definite way ('this is the way things are and *there is no other way*'). At the zenith of his life, Caesar became the sole ruler of the world and thus became the archetype of a Roman emperor of the German nation. Does this position, this archetype, have any validity? Both chronicles assert that this is indeed the case: they claim that

---

18 Chronicle of the Emperors, line 344.

Caesar had outstanding virtues which he demonstrated both in battle as well as in politics, virtues which were ultimately rewarded by his rise to emperor. As soon as Caesar forgot the importance of virtue, the *defectus* of the heathen was revealed and he was murdered. Caesar also rewarded the Germans with gifts: only with the help of the loyal Teutons was Caesar able to seize power in corrupt Rome (according to the *Chronicle of the Emperors*, his army consisted of both Germans and Romans). Thus, right from the start, the power of the Roman emperor rested on German shoulders; in the literary world of Caesar, he and the Germans earned their share of the emperorship well.

Through methods of narration, an *historia* can make evident claims to validity regarding certain models. Further, the author may use other, explicit means to make claims of validity at the textual level. In the Caesar-story, consciously-placed commentaries skillfully connect the narrative and the argumentative superstructures of the text. The *Chronicle of the Emperors* recounts how at the peak of his power, "the young man," Caesar, "was happy that he had won all empires for himself."[19] As a result, the Romans introduced the *pluralis maiestatis* (*Ihrzen* in German, *vobisare* in Latin) as a way of addressing his majesty and gave up the more colloquial singular form of address (*Duzen* in German, *tuitare* in Latin) even in Germany, "because now he alone possessed all the power that had formerly been divided in manifold ways."[20] At this point the tale is interrupted and digresses into a long excurse, including an allegory of the biblical dream of Daniel. The story explains that the four animals of Daniel's dream symbolize four empires, and that the boar, the third animal, "represents the dear Julius Caesar."[21] The boar is allegorically interpreted in great detail. Afterwards, and by contrast, Caesar's murder is reported in only a few words.

Otto von Freising proceeded in a similar fashion. He too closed the Caesar-story with an argumentative passage in which he develops his theory of the wave-like movements that the *civitas mundi* (with its four empires) was subjected to.[22] Ultimately he connects these considerations with the announcement of Christ's birth which would soon follow. Just a few sentences prior to this, Otto quotes Cicero saying that he saw Caesar, "as being similar to a god;" later he points to the coming Christ as the true prince of peace, using a quote from the Apostle Paul.[23] This argumentative linking of Caesar's rule with that

---

19 Chronicle of the Emperors, line 515.
20 Chronicle of the Emperors, line 520.
21 Chronicle of the Emperors, line 572.
22 Otto von Freising, II.51.
23 Otto von Freising, II.50–51.

of Christ was consciously constructed: as in the *Chronicle of the Emperors*, Otto linked a secular *historia* with the Bible, the *historia salutis*. The reasons for this link lie in Otto's typological *figura*-thought, according to which the German Roman emperors referred their predecessors in order to place themselves in an analogous relationship that helped to legitimize their claims to the throne.[24] The claim of validity of a secular 'model Caesar' is supported by referencing to the Bible's indisputable authority, thereby summoning the hand of God.

This appeal to higher authority is especially evident in the boar-analogy in the *Chronicle of the Emperors (Kaiserchronik)*: Caesar's actions and the position of the empire he created are reflected in the body parts of the biblical animal figure, and are thus legitimized in a special way:

Daz dritte ain fraislich eber was,	The third was a terrible boar
den tiurlîchen Juljum bezaichnenet daz.	Which signifies the noble Julius
der ebir zehin horn truoc,	The boar had ten horns
mit ten er sîne vîande alle nidir sluoc.	with which he defeated all of his enemies.
er zebrach al daz er ane quam	Whatever came close to him, he broke
unde zetrat iz undir sîne klâwen.	and crushed underneath his claws.
Jûlius betwanc alle lant.	Julius conquered all countries,
sie dienden alle sînre hant.	all served his hand.
wol bezeichenet uns daz waltswîn	Well describes us the boar,
daz daz rîche zuo Rôme sol immir vrî sîn.	that the Roman empire shall be free forever.
	('Chronicle of the Emperors', lines 571–578)

In both chronicles, the claim of validity is not restricted to Caesar's reign alone, but rather is also constructed for the texts of the chronicles themselves. Again, the reference to authorities plays a crucial role. At two separate points in his *historia*, Otto von Freising introduced argumentative passages into the narrative of the Caesar-story that comment on his true sources, Josephus, Lucan, and Sallust.[25]

3 Evaluation: The mode of the evaluative gestures ascribes a value to facts or actions. This is done through the generation of rational value judgments (it is good/it is bad) or affects (love it/hate it). Again, the author can work at all three levels of the text. The plot of the *histoire*-level can become the basis of moral value-judgments, such as when Otto von Freising divided the good and the bad deeds among two groups of people. On the one hand, Caesar does only good deeds (with but one exception, which leads to his murder). The Roman antagonists Pompeius and Crassus, on the other hand, show only socio-ethically damnable conduct (e.g. out of pure greed, Crassus steals the

---

24 With regard to figuration see also: Otto von Freising, introduction, pp. LVIff.
25 Otto von Freising, II.48–50

treasures of the Temple of Jerusalem). Otto generated a positive affect regarding Caesar's humanity by letting him weep when presented with Pompeius' severed head. This follows the rules of rhetoric; even Quintilian wrote that the orator himself must cry if he is to move others to tears.[26] Rhetorical knowledge of this kind was widespread throughout Middle Ages.[27]

At the level of textuality, these judgments can be further emphasized. The most important means of emphasis are all kinds of attributions. An example for this kind of procedure can be found in the well-known rhetoric of discourse by Matthew of Vendôme (before 1175) and his theory of the eleven *attributa personae* and the nine *attributa negotii*.[28] In his *Chronica*, for example, Otto rates Caesar's gifts out of the national treasury as "extremely generous or very magnanimous (*magnificentissime*)," a positive and quite common attribute given to emperors. By contrast, Crassus' series of robberies are characterized with a term taken from the doctrine of vice (avarice / *avaritia*).[29]

Otto von Freising also inserted skillful evaluations at the third, communicative level of his text. Close to the end of the Caesar-story, he relates how Caesar had reconciled himself with Cicero, the greatest Roman philosopher and rhetorician. He comments on this deed of supreme magnanimity with a longer quotation from Cicero, taken from the speech 'Pro Marcello', which is full of praise for Caesar. In other words, Otto integrated another communicative act in his text (the speech of a famous authority) in order to give a positive evaluation of his subject (Caesar) by means of clever reflection.

5 The Message

Both Otto von Freising and the Chronicler of the Emperors made informative statements through a textual reconstruction of Caesar's world. They created an image of the decline of the Roman Empire, its subsequent rise on the basis of Caesar's magnanimous deeds as emperor, his close relation to the Germans and eventually the establishment of a universal emperorship (he conquered all other empires of the world: "die rîche alle").[30] The author's literary achieve-

---

26 The peak of the reception of Quintilian during the Middle Ages can be dated to around the twelfth century in the schools of Chartres and Bec. See: Mollard 1934 and 1934/1935. See also: Boskoff 1952 and Murphy 1974.
27 Cf. Buttenwieser 1930; Quadlbauer 1962; Ward 1972; Bliese 1974; Murphy 1974; Klopsch 1980; Copeland 1991.
28 Matthew of Vendôme, sec. 1.77 and 1.93.
29 Otto von Freising, II.48–49.
30 Chronicle of the Emperors, line 516.

ment, in the sense of the Aristotelian *poiesis* and *mimesis* (i.e. the creation of a literary simulation of reality), lies in the creation of this image. At the same time, both chroniclers acted rhetorically. With regard to textual analysis, the rhetorical question focuses on the messages they convey through the construction of their texts in order to regulate the attitudes of the recipients and eventually trigger actions. Let us recall another element of Cicero's definition of *historia*: a historiographical work "gives guidance to human existence" ("historia est ...; magistra vitae").[31] Some of the many messages found in the Caesar-story are as follows: 1) the Roman empire was inevitable and positive at its core, 2) Caesar's actions fit into the course of events intended by God and it was good, and 3) that Caesar was the legitimate founder of the institution of the Roman emperorship.[32]

The question remains as to what role the Caesar-story plays in the texts as a whole. In both cases it fits into the overall general concept. Caesar's rule begins the fourth world empire which then passes into the Christian empire. As Otto von Freising emphasized, Jesus wanted to be born as a citizen of the fourth and last empire, the Roman monarchy.[33] According to this conception, the one God should be worshipped in one empire under one ruler; Caesar created the prerequisites for this chain of events.

Yet another question still to be answered is what role the Caesar-story played in the contemporary debates of the twelfth century. This topic is large enough that it would require an essay of its own. One thing that is certain is that Otto von Freising clearly declared his position regarding the discussions of his time with his work. His theory of the fundamental conflict between the spiritual and secular empires surely referred to the tense relationship between the pope and the emperor, the struggle between *sacerdotium* and *imperium* in the late 12th century. If we look at the Caesar-story in isolation, the emphasis of the role of the emperor and his connection to the Germans could also imply a challenge aimed by Otto von Freising at his half-brother, the German king Konrad III, to embark on the necessary journey to Rome and bring the crown of the emperor to Germany at last, as German kings had been obliged to do for centuries.

---

31 Cicero: De Oratore, 2.36; cf. Knape 2000b, p. 116.
32 Cf. Otto von Freising, III, Prologus.
33 Otto von Freising, III.6.

7 On the Problems of Literary Rhetoric

> Do not suffocate the Philosophical in us
> given
> that such a Philosophical
> as even hidden inside of us
> It is a game of hide and seek
> (Bernhard: Der Weltverbesserer. 1979)

Somebody speaks; another sees judicial relevance because the communicative act contained in the utterance might be considered an act of violence in the form of an insult. A conflicted social situation is created; somebody claims to have a special communicative status. A court must now decide which status the various communicative acts that have taken place should have. Where is rhetoric in situations of conflict such as this? The answer to this question must begin with a clarification: in the case of the Austrian writer Thomas Bernhard, we are not talking about real speech in the sense of referring to a performance that is relevant to an oratorical situation. In this regard, there are only a few notable exceptions; Bernhard rarely spoke in public. Instead, he generally noted what he would have "said", and then wrote it down. At times he wrote amazing letters that, like many of his literary works, challenged the demarcation between standard 'life-world' communication and specialized communication. His words have been printed and widely distributed by well-known publishers. Occasionally they have even been re-medialized in theaters and finally brought to word by actors on a stage. All of this activity has become a part of modern public life. Rhetorical research is only interested in literature insofar as it represents a *communicative fact*. In this respect, the case of Thomas Bernhard is particularly illuminating.

In 1978 a volume of small pieces of prose by Bernhard was published without any further specification of genre (such as *tales, short stories*, or *anecdotes* in the subtitle) but rather with the singular title of 'Der Stimmenimitator' (The Voice Imitator).[1] The book was read with wide attention in and around Salzburg, Austria, including by a Mrs. Annelore Lucan-Stood, whose maiden name was Zamponi. In the 1970's, Thomas Bernhard was considered particularly scandalous in Salzburg due to certain references to the city that he had made in previous works. Thus, it wasn't long until the newspaper *Salzburger Nachrichten* published a story on the 20th of January, 1979 announcing, "Private suit against author Bernhard" on the basis of a legal charge of defamation. As the nephew of the former Salzburg state attorney and president of the

---

1 Bernhard 1978.

higher regional court in Linz, (Dr. Reinulf Zamponi) reported, "In the story 'Example' that Bernhard depicts in his new book 'The Voice Imitator', Annelore Lucan-Stood saw an affront to her father, who had in no way shot himself, and thus, had not left this world in an 'unchristian' manner."[2]

This piece of prose, which has generally been considered a "narration", is integrated into a wide collection of similar pieces in the published volume. The pieces are reminiscent in both subject matter and linguistic structure of the anecdotes and short prose published by Heinrich von Kleist in his 1810/1811 journal *Berliner Abendblätter*, which existed for only a few months. In the German version, Bernhard's entire text was only 5 sentences long; in the English translation, it is six sentences:

> *Example*
> The courtroom correspondent is the closest of all to human misery and its absurdity and, in the nature of things, can endure the experience for only a short time, and certainly not for his whole life, without going crazy. The probable, the improbable, even the unbelievable, the most unbelievable are paraded before him every day in the courtroom, and because he has to earn his daily bread by reporting on actual or alleged but in any case, in the nature of things, shameful crimes, he is soon no longer surprised by anything at all. I will, however, tell you about a single incident that still seems to me the most remarkable event of my whole career as a courtroom correspondent. Zamponi, a judge on the Provincial Court of Appeals in Salzburg, for years the dominant figure in the Salzburg Provincial Court – from which, as I said, I reported on everything conceivable – after pronouncing a sentence of twelve years' imprisonment and a fine of eight million schillings on, as he put it in his summation, a vile blackmailer, who was – I remember exactly – a beef exporter from Murau, stood up again and said that he would now set an example. After this unusual announcement, he put his hand under his gown and into his coat pocket as quick as lightning, pulled out a pistol on which the safety catch had already been released, and shot himself – to the horror of all those present in the courtroom – in the left temple. He died instantly.[3]

This text demonstrates a literary ductus very similar to Kleist's; indeed it shows an almost Kleistian narrative vehemence. This too is typical of Bernhard's writing. Of course, none of this concerned the plaintiff in the suit, Mrs. Lucan-Stood. Her focus was on the putative historical connections that could be found in the text: 1. The fact that the narrator reveals himself to be a court journalist, which could have been a reference to Bernhard's work in that profession in the 1950's; 2. The appearance of a judge named Zamponi, a possible allusion to the plaintiff's father; 3. The characterization of Zamponi as, "a judge on the

---

2 *Salzburger Nachrichten*, 20.1.1979. See also: Dittmar 1993, p. 86. For more on the problem of insult from the perspective of rhetoric, see: Knape 2006c.
3 Bernhard 1978, p. 13.

Provincial Court of Appeals," and as, "the dominant figure in the Salzburg Provincial Court", which fit the actual historical description of the judge and his duties in real life. The *Salzburger Nachrichten* also took a factual view of the tale, writing on the 8th of February, 1979, "The author claims to have witnessed how Dr. Reinulf Zamponi shot himself in a hearing room in the Salzburg courthouse after a court proceeding. This depiction does not fit the facts, since, as has been mentioned, Dr. Zamponi died a natural death."

Bernhard's reaction to the charge of libel was itself strangely contradictory and leads us to one of the main features of his writing: at times, he insisted that it should not be considered *fiction*. He often insisted that he wasn't a writer, but rather merely a person who wrote.[4] As we will see in the Zamponi case, however, Bernhard claimed to have the status of a writer of fiction.

We can see a sort of communicative dual strategy in Bernhard's actions. He silently claimed artistic autonomy, while at the same time his literary process repeatedly resembled heteronymous communication: he repeatedly used allusion to factual events and wove non-fiction into his literary works. In doing so, he made them subject to the pragmatic sanctions of standard or normal communicative expectations.[5] In the case above, Bernhard wrote two letters that help clarify the uniqueness of his writing. For our purposes we can summarize his literary method with the term *poetic facticity paradox*. We see this in the case at hand: Bernhard wanted to claim, on the one hand, the right to describe facts, real world situations, objects and people, but at the same time reserve the right to create fantasy according to his imagination. The results are hybrid-fictions that require a high level of tolerance from a public that is often affected by the inclusion of factual content and its mixture with fiction in his writing. In this respect, perhaps the "writer" from the third act of Bernhard's play "Hunting Party" would describe his writing as an, "artistic natural catastrophe," and would add, "And besides, everything only exists in our imagination [...] when we speak of it / we speak about it / as if / what we are talking about / is not real."[6]

In a letter to his accuser Mrs. Lucan-Stood, Bernhard spoke first about the factual nature of his work, "In writing my book, I was reminded of the extraordinary qualities that your father had as a jurist, and this led me to write the story *Example*."[7] Here, Bernhard has formulated the speech act of *praise*,

---

4 See: Dittmar 1993, p. 67.
5 For more on the difference between standard and specialized communication and the *frame*-expectations that arise in their communicative contexts, see: Knape 2008a, pp. 898–906; see also: Bauer/Knape/Koch/Winkler 2010, p. 9; and the introduction to this book.
6 Bernhard 1974.
7 Open letter from 20.1.1979, published in: *Oberösterreichische Nachrichten*, 22.1.1979.

which can only take place in real-world communicative situations where it is used pragmatically and is authentically relevant.[8] Bernhard emphasizes his use of praise in reference to the actual historical person Zamponi: in the "piece of prose, *Example* [...] is clearly written," that, "your father was 'for years the dominant figure in the Salzburg Provincial Court', which is high praise that can hardly be extended any further." After such praise, Bernhard could,

> hardly believe that you are unable to see *Example* for what it is, which is philosophical fiction in homage of your father. Since I remember the high qualities of your father quite well, even today, I am sure that *Example*, as a parable in which his name is used with the highest respect, would have caused him at least a little bit of joy.[9]

Here, Bernhard made it very clear that his story was about Mrs. Lucan-Stood's father, but at the same time called it "philosophical fiction" in the form of a "parable". He emphasized the poetic character of the piece of prose even more clearly in a second letter, written on the 8th of February, 1979, addressed personally to the prosecuting attorney and Zamponi's nephew, Harry, "I have thus never claimed that chief justice Zamponi actually killed himself. In fact, I have never claimed anything about him as a real, legal person or personality because I was writing fiction." Bernhard claimed that his book 'The Voice Imitator' was merely the publication of, "one hundred and four free associations and thought-inventions."[10]

In his previously published play 'Hunting Party' from 1974, the figure of the "Author" expressed an opinion on this very topic in the third act:

> That which is described gentlemen / is something different / just as that which is observed is something different / everything is different / possibly a philosophy / the General would say / If a one armed General appeared in my piece / then it is a different one / and perhaps, madam, it is told / that I myself am in my theater / but it is another.[11]

The Zamponi plaintiffs were unsatisfied by Bernhard's explanation on the basis of the *poetic facticity paradox*: they could not accept Bernhard's claim that his work deserved the special status of fiction. In the name of a real-world person, who was guaranteed protection of his personal privacy by the legal system, they demanded that the protagonist in the story remain unnamed. They did not want Bernhard to be able play with facts in his literary *possible*

---

8 I thus use the term speech act following both Austin and Searle's theory. For more on the impossibility of real speech acts in fiction, see: Knape 2008a, pp. 899 f.
9 *Oberösterreichische Nachrichten*, 22.1.1979; see also: Dittmar 1993, pp. 87 f.
10 *Oberösterreichische Nachrichten*, 22.1.1979; also published in: *Salzburger Nachrichten*, 8.2.1979.
11 Bernhard 1974.

world that had the potential to harm a person in the *actual world* who may have been a figure in the story (at least, according to the assessment of the affected relatives). In the eyes of the 'life-world' legal system, two objects of legal protection were in conflict: the protection of privacy and the artistic freedom of expression.

Bernhard accepted his accusers' request, and assured them in the open letter that, "the name Zamponi would be replaced alternatively by the names Ferrari or Machiavelli in future prints of the book."[12] In response, the case was dropped by the family. This result mirrored that of a similar defamation lawsuit that had been brought against Bernhard after the publication of his autobiography 'Die Ursache' (The Cause) in 1977. In that case, Salzburg's town parish, Franz Wesenauer, brought charges against Bernhard for his depiction as "Uncle Franz". Bernhard had characterized him as a man who, behind a "pink peasant's face", was actually a "disgusting individual."[13]

We have now reached the point where we can turn to the question of rhetoric. Before fully delving into this particular situation, I must first devote a few words to the theoretical cornerstones of the rhetorical approach to literature. Rhetoricians are less concerned with the systematic question of "what is literature?" that is so important to literary scholars.[14] Rather, rhetoricians are much more concerned with questions of where and how rhetoric appears in all kinds of communication found in the world, and which conclusions can be drawn from these instances for future rhetorical action. Texts that have been tagged as literature can also be observed under the aegis of rhetoric insofar as they can be seen as communicative facts.

If the Zamponi case had gone to trial, the question would have necessarily been posed whether the statements of the legal person Bernhard about a certain Zamponi, particularly those that claimed he had shot himself, were "true": whether or not the statements were based on facts or reported factual events. Ultimately, this case deals with the question of whether we can assign Bernhard's text to either a *standard* or to a *specialized* communicative frame.

Let us pause for a moment. Someone writes a "piece of prose", which is published with other similar pieces in a book by the Suhrkamp publishing house in Frankfurt. This is a publisher that has already published many other books from the same source, the same author. In reference to *this* piece of prose,

---

12 *Oberösterreichische Nachrichten*, 22.1.1979; see also: Dittmar 1993, p. 87.
13 Bernhard 1975, p. 119. See also: Huber 1987, pp. 62–67; and Dittmar 1993, p. 61.
14 This topic has recently been well discussed by Winko, Jannidis and Lauer in their new collection 'Grenzen der Literatur' published in 2009.

however, legal action regarding libel is begun. The same author or source, who goes by the name of Thomas Bernhard, then writes a letter that is published in the newspaper the *Salzburger Nachrichten* and because of the content of that letter, the legal suit is dropped. From the standpoint of the allegedly affected plaintiff, the daughter of a judge named Zamponi, the entire legal proceeding can be seen this way.

Thomas Bernhard, on the other hand, saw the situation much differently. He was unaware of the "fact of the crime" of "libel", and, as he wrote to his accuser, could not, "follow either your thoughts or your sentiments, and I ask with all courtesy and naturally with the utmost respect that you read the piece *Example* carefully and study it attentively," again under other leading signs.[15] According to Bernhard, if she would only do that she would find that he had, "composed a long lasting and permanent, if only poetic, monument," to judge Zamponi.[16]

What I have here called *leading sign* is, for Bernhard, a decisive condition of understanding his text. This 'leading sign of understanding' introduces a point of differentiation into the equation that emphasizes the claims to validity in human communication as a decisive criterion of division. For the plaintiff Lucan-Stood, all expressions of the speaker Bernhard had one and the same status of liability found in and influenced by standard communication in the actual world. As demonstrated by his letters, Bernhard wanted to differentiate between his standard communicative expressions (e.g. those that deal with legal issues) and his specialized communicative expressions found in specifically marked literary texts.

Admittedly, Bernhard took this position only in relation to the legally relevant meta-discourse involved in the specific work in question. In addition to classical artistic markers, which define the horizon of the *frame of understanding*, there are also the previously mentioned markers of text type and genre. The frame of understanding allows a text to be interpreted as a situationally liberated and historically undefined work. Definitions of genre imply a set of reading instructions. While some authors provide fiction indicating signals (e.g. through the use of subtitles on their covers), Thomas Bernhard often included other terms such as, "A Hint", "An Excitement" or, "A Friendship" which left the question of genre open. Most of the time, he provided no signal at all.[17] Classical literary genre markers such as "novel" or "comedy" (as in

---

15 *Oberösterreichische Nachrichten*, 22.1.1979; see also: Dittmar 1993, p. 88.
16 *Oberösterreichische Nachrichten*, 22.1.1979; see also: Dittmar 1993, p. 87.
17 Bernhard himself discusses the inherent problem behind all conventional expectations of genre in the conversation on literature in the third act of 'The Hunting Party' when the "General" says to the "Author": "As you were here the last time / you were writing a comedy / or better said something / that you described as a comedy / I myself do not

Bernhard's 'Immanuel Kant' from 1978) were even rarer. The tale we have analyzed here also lacks any sort of genre markers. In his meta-discourse, Bernhard named it merely a "piece of prose", which in turn, leaves everything open. When placed in the context of his decades of work, this piece becomes just one element of an obvious strategy of *frame-breaking*: Bernhard provides neither clear *frames* to his works, nor does he cash in on clear expectations. In this point we see another parallel with Kleist: the anecdotes and short stories from his *Berliner Abendblätter* (and still to be found in Kleist's collected works) also had an ambivalent authenticity when they were published, because readers were often unable to discern whether they were fanciful stories from the publisher Kleist or 'journalistic' contributions.[18]

My considerations are only concerned with clarifying the extent to which questions of rhetoric apply to literary communication. This question is particularly relevant for texts that have been explicitly created under the premises of fictional aesthetics. One could say that these texts lie outside of rhetoric's jurisdiction because they are subject to specialized communicative *frames* that generate corresponding expectations, one of which is that they are no longer subject to *actual world* judgments but rather create only *possible worlds* for the imagination. In short: the texts are de-pragmatized, and thus make no claim of veracity in their communication. Must rhetoric leave such texts to the field of poetics, aesthetics, and literary studies?

Such questions lead me back to our original 'Zamponi' case. Just as all other forms of art, literature can claim to have the status of specialized communication, and has done so since time immemorial. Normally, participants in such aesthetically marked communication act silently and willingly under the artistic or fictional contract; they expect that Grice's maxims for instance are either modified or suspended (for instance, the maxim of truth in fiction or in literary art, where redundancy, confusion and other such devices go against the maxim of economy). Participants in artistic communication normally also accept the specific cultural settings for "art".[19] On the one hand, the standard communicative and pragmatic frame of judicial communication demands the highest degree of validity from all participants under threat of sanctions. On the other,

---

consider a comedy / that which you call a comedy / A comedy is a fully established concept / that has nothing to do with what you are writing / What you are writing has nothing to do with comedy / I understand something different by comedy / but also by drama / You say a comedy / and the whole thing has nothing to do with a comedy / But one should not discuss definitions / with an author." Bernhard 1974.
18 See: Weber 1993, pp. 75–97.
19 Knape 2008a, p. 905; cf. p. 15 in this book.

the conditions of the aesthetic game allow the addressee, the reader or listener, to determine for himself whether the conceptual offering of the work, a fictional court case, is relevant to their material world or not.[20]

Thomas Bernhard described the story *Example* expressly as "fiction" and thus made a clear determination, which for him was relatively rare. Based on my previous comments, one might come to the conclusion that questions of rhetoric do not apply here. The history of persecution and discrimination of authors and artists of all types shows that even clearly marked artistic works are time and again subject to a sort of re-pragmatization pressure, and are time and again drawn back into the conceptual context of authenticity by addressees. The art of poetry (fiction) should be understood as de-pragmatized and situationally liberated. In reality, however, instead of being understood playfully literary works are continually ascribed a high level of life-world liability. This does not only apply to authors such as Bernhard, who, as we have seen, all but systematically work with the phenomena of frame breaking and thus consciously provoke such misunderstandings.

The reaction of addressees has something to do with the cognitive mechanisms of integration in the process of reception that remain present even in texts that are clearly purely fictional. Many poets take these mechanisms into account in composing their works. To put it another way, it is often the case that even purely fictional texts are composed using calculations of production other than pure aesthetics. Authors often seek to convey a specific idea, a worldview, or a philosophical or political concept to their addressees (audience) through their work.[21] In his 'Poetics' (Ch. 19), Aristotle identified this cognitive, knowledge based layer of fiction (poetry) as the rhetorical layer. According to Aristotle, those elements of a fictional text that deal with the cognitive faculty or "train of thought" (as a translation for *diánoia*) fall within the realm of rhetoric. Here we see a connection between the *possible* and the *actual world*. I will call those elements of fiction that can lead to insight in the life-world the *rhetorical factor* of literature.[22]

From the perspective of a theory of production, rhetoric thus demands that a rhetorical calculation be added alongside traditional fictional-aesthetic and linguistic-artistic calculations; one that can even utilize elements of two latter calculations for its own purposes. Addressees often both expect and look for

---

20 For more on the character of the game, see: Knape 2008a, p. 899.
21 Cf. Booth 1961; and the chapters "Language, Truth, and Idea" as well as "An Imperfect Medium: Using Language to Make Meaning" in: Carroll III 2011, pp. 181–197.
22 For more on the 'rhetorical factor' in texts, see also: Knape 2000a, p. 121 and the chapter on the theory of rhetoric in feature films in this work. For more on the material world consequences of fictional worlds, see: Appel 2005.

such a calculation; they often infer messages and draw their own conclusions, even when an author had no conscious intent that such inferences be made. This means that addressees often expect a rhetorical calculation, a calculation of production that seeks to impart insight and knowledge that is relevant to the life-world. This search for messages is often successful, even without explicit steering from the author.[23] The semantic universe of language in every addressee allows for a wide range of possible interpretations to those who are intent on going their own interpretive ways and drawing their own conclusions. In light of this phenomenon, rhetoricians must come to the conclusion that only those authors who also have something 'rhetorical' to say are considered significant as social communicators. In fact, only then does the discipline of rhetoric interest itself for the communicative roles of 'writer' or 'poet'.

In the Zamponi story, however, readers do not need to utilize this interpretive freedom, need not look for the existence of messages on their own. In the previously mentioned meta discourse about this story in particular (and it is clear that it is a story in the narratological sense, regardless of whether it refers to the real person Zamponi or not), Bernhard has already clearly stated that it is a "philosophical fiction", a "piece of prose that is not without philosophy," that is not without the rhetorical factor.[24] In fact, he goes above and beyond this by assigning it to the specific text genre of "parable". This explicitly impels a reader to deduce a rhetorically relevant message: according to one modern definition, a parable is, "a short, fictional narration in verse or prose that uses signals of transference to challenge a reader to find another meaning than that which is literally written, one that is in some way meaningful to real life."[25]

As I have already pointed out, many readers nave no need for a "signal of transference" in order to find a "meaningful" message in fiction. They simply assume that literature always contains the rhetorical factor, that it contains messages with which it seeks to influence the consciousness of people. This sets processes of inference and abduction in motion, because many readers are not content with the imaginative experience of a literary *possible world* alone. In the case at hand, however, Thomas Bernhard did, in fact, provide a signal of transference with the title *Example*. Every well-read reader knows that an example must always contain, either explicitly or implicitly, a thesis or design; it must contain a moralization (*moralisatio*) that is intended to pro-

---

23 The connection between steering (moderation) and evocation in literary texts, including seven potential aspects of orientation that can be controlled by an author, are discussed in: Knape 2008a, pp. 916–924.

24 *Oberösterreichische Nachrichten*, 22.01.1979.

25 Auerochs 2007, pp. 567 f.

vide us with relevant meaning in the life-world and demonstrate it through the example itself. The text at hand is divided into two parts, according to the rules of the genre (parable): it begins with a *promythion*, a pre-stated moral (*moralisatio*).[26] The actual example comes at the end. This automatically brings the words of the Bernhardian do-gooder to mind, "It is, on the one hand, not a piece of art / because it deals with philosophy / on the other hand is it the most artistic [...] it should be music / on the one hand / but music gives philosophy the nakedness of spirit."[27]

The actual example is thus found in the conclusion, and is formed by three artistically combined sentences whose Kleist-Bernhardian structure I will not discuss further here.[28] The core of the example lays in the story itself: it merely describes how judge Zamponi convicts a criminal, stands up after reading the verdict and says that he will now set an example, and does so by pulling out a pistol and shooting himself. That is the hard plot. We learn nothing of his motives, nor about background conditions or other contextual elements. At the center of this series of actions we have the judge's statement directly after the verdict has been read, where he says he will, "set an example." Breaking with all conventional expectations, and in a paradoxical reversal of the assumed situation, it is not the criminal that is shot (who would, under normal circumstances, be the one made an example of) but rather the ostensibly innocent judge, who even shoots himself. This scene presents a real challenge to a readers' ability to abduce the situation.[29] The nearest interpretation is that the events represent an obvious radical reversal of normal conditions. An example is made an exponent of the legal system, as opposed to an exponent of the other side, of guilt and criminality. The judge judges himself. Might he be guilty as well? Bernhard gives us a somewhat wider possible interpretation in the *promythion*. For him, the text has, as he says, a "philosophical" dimension. This indicates a dimension of meaning that the author offers us, one which is to have relevance in the life-world. Bernhard certainly saw himself as a sort of poet-philosopher, at the very least at a philosophical thinker, although not in any sort of scholarly way. Perhaps he sees himself as the perfect audience for the words of the General to the Author in the third act of 'Hunting Party', "Am I right that / what you are writing / is something entirely philosophical / Even though you call it comedy / Or am I right / when I say / that what you are writing is comedy / while you yourself claim / it to be about philosophy"?

---

26 More common is the *epimythion*, where the moral is attached to the end of the text.

27 Bernhard 1974.

28 Others have seen parallels to Stifter's syntax in Bernhard's prose. See: Eyckeler 1995, pp. 123–131.

29 On the problem of abduction, see: Eco 1987, pp. 31–60; and Eco 1983.

One of the unique aspects of artistic communication is that the literary addressee has already learned how to deal with such playful offerings (which retain the condition of poetic vagueness). Under this premise, a rhetorician can attempt to find an author's chosen literary strategy of influence through textual analysis. In the case at hand, we find this strategy in the form of an induction proof recommended by Aristotle himself. To a certain extent, the *promythion* puts forward a thesis for which the example should serve as inductive evidence. A veteran court reporter shines light a court chamber like a spotlight on a stage, upon which we see the "human misery" of the world in the institutional association of justice and injustice or guilt and atonement among judges and defendants in all its "absurdity". It is only natural that nobody can tolerate such a situation, "for his whole life, without going crazy." Our minds are automatically drawn to Kleist's 'Michael Kohlhaas' or his anecdote 'Current Event' ('Tages-Ereignis') from his *Abendblätter* (from November 7th, 1810). Bernhard goes further: "every day in the courtroom," an observer is shown "the probable, the improbable, even the unbelievable, the most unbelievable," crimes, whether they are "actual" or "alleged". And when judge Zamponi makes an example of something, then it is an example of this absurdity.

Bernhard is 'speaking' with us by writing, thereby allowing us to participate in his thinking. On the one hand, what he says may have the character of a rhetorical statement. On the other, it may represent an artistic possible world. In the process a fiction is created, but also judgments about the world, about concrete people, about countries, and about anything else that one might be able to interpret. What to him feels like the normal flow of words is presented to society by media, in the form of books, journals, magazines and newspapers, etc., each with certain genre specific expectations. In each individual case, the question of specialized communicative status is raised anew. Which of his subsequently reconstructible, public statements actually follow special literary rules? Thomas Bernhard doubtless saw himself in a special communicative role, the role of an artist. While he may have understood this role in a particularly unique way, he did not seem to have any particular persuasive intent: "You can write down impressions that you have," he said in a 1986 interview with Krista Fleischmann about his poetic intent, "There are visions of the future there, people like me have them too." He said very little, however, about that which interests academics, namely the status of the historical allusions and their connection to fiction in his texts. Instead, he emphasized that what he sought to convey to others through his literary works should, "radiate" from the works themselves. And that is all.[30]

---

30 A longer German version of this chapter in: Knape 2011.

8 Paratexts and the Rhetorical Factor in Literature

Sebastian Brant and Katherine Anne Porter

In the year 1497, print editions of Jakob Locher's Latin version of Sebastian Brant's *Narrenschiff* (Ship of Fools) appeared in Basel and three other German cities. This Latin version was the basis of the international success of Brant's work. Around 10 years later, in 1509, the first English translation was published by Alexander Barclay. All of these instances, however, represent later levels of reception. The original print of Brant's Ship of Fools had already been printed in Basel 1494, in German, by the publisher Johann Bergmann.[1] In this first edition the central text of the *Narrenschiff* is framed by a total of five paratexts:

1. Two title pages with woodcuts and their inscriptions (the second woodcut was also used by Katherine Anne Porter in 1962, see Figures 6 and 7).
2. Brant's preface (see Figure 8).
3. Brant's afterword: "End des Narrenschiffs" (The end of the Ship of Fools).
4. A colophon with the date "1494", the publisher's motto "Nüt on vrsach" (nihil sine causa/nothing without a reason), and the publisher's name "Johann Bergmann von Olpe".

In the year 1962, Katherine Anne Porter's *Ship of Fools* appeared in Boston and Toronto. This edition includes 13 paratexts:

1. Flap text on the dust cover.
2. The spine of the book, with title and a decorative trim taken from the *Narrenschiff*, which doesn't appear in Brant's book until chapter 5 (see Figures 10 and 11).
3. The author's handwritten signature on the front cover.
4. A brief title page on the flyleaf inside the book
5. A separate page showing Porter's other publications.
6. The actual title page, including woodcut (see Figure 7).
7. The imprint page, including the genre designation "this novel".
8. A dedication to the American publisher Barbara Wescott
9. On the same page, a brief biography of Porter's life between 1932 and 1962, the years in which the novel was written.
10. A preface by the author (see Figure 9).
11. A table of contents

---

1 Brant: Narrenschiff, ed. Knape 2005.

Figure 6: Second title page of Brant's *Narrenschiff* (Basel 1494).

Katherine Anne Porter

SHIP OF FOOLS

An Atlantic Monthly Press Book
Little, Brown and Company • Boston • Toronto

Figure 7: Title page of Porter's *Ship of Fools* (1962).

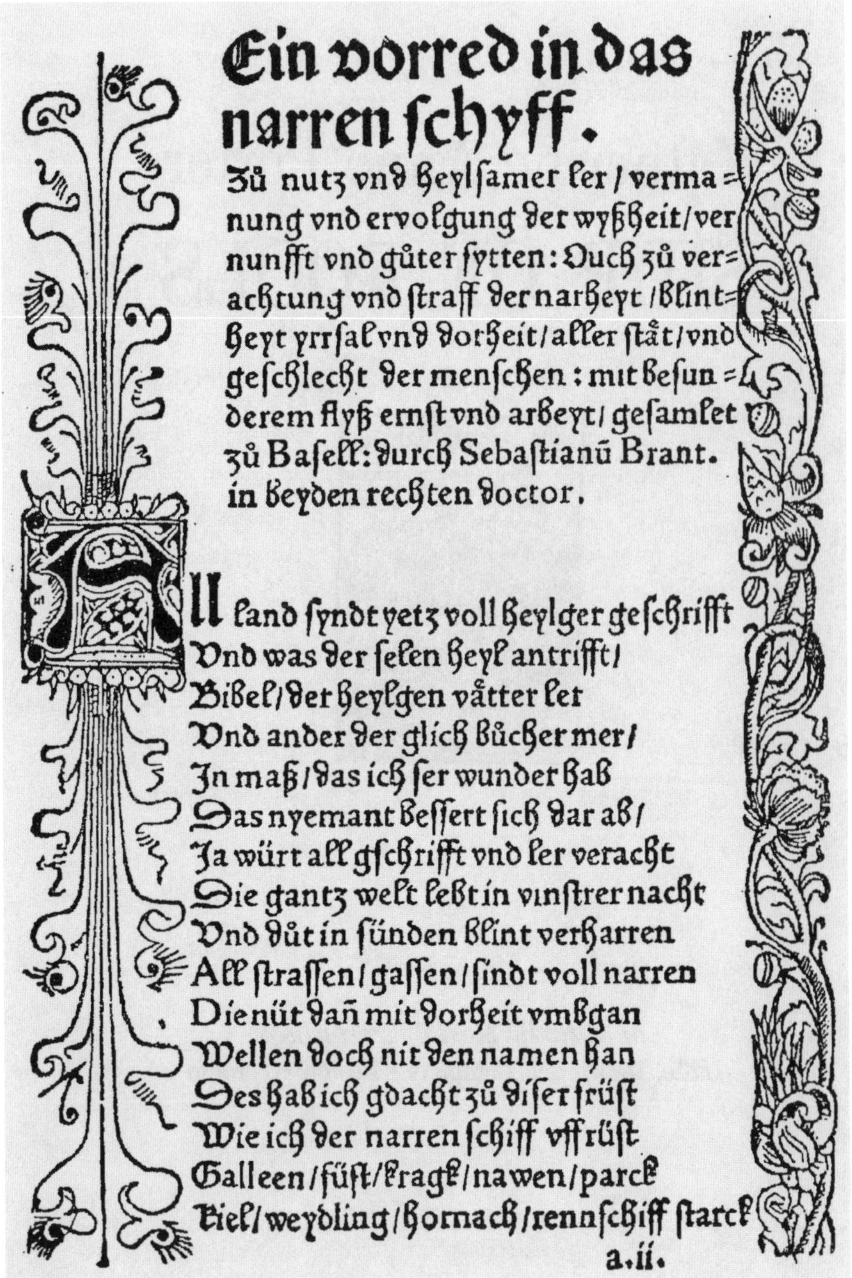

Ein vorred in das narren ſchyff.

Zů nutz vnd heylſamer ler / vermanung vnd ervolgung der wyßheit / vernunfft vnd gůter ſytten: Ouch zů verachtung vnd ſtraff der narheyt / blintheyt yrrſal vnd dorheit / aller ſtåt / vnd geſchlecht der menſchen: mit beſunderem flyß ernſt vnd arbeyt / geſamlet zů Baſell: durch Sebaſtianū Brant. in beyden rechten doctor.

All land ſyndt yetz voll heylger geſchrifft
Vnd was der ſelen heyl antrifft /
Bibel / der heylgen våtter ler
Vnd ander der glich bůcher mer /
In maß / das ich ſer wunder hab
Das nyemant beſſert ſich dar ab /
Ja würt all gſchrifft vnd ler veracht
Die gantz welt lebt in vinſtrer nacht
Vnd dût in ſünden blint verharren
All ſtraſſen / gaſſen / ſindt voll narren
Die nüt dan̄ mit dorheit vmbgan
Wellen doch nit den namen han
Des hab ich gdacht zů diſer früſt
Wie ich der narren ſchiff vffrüſt
Galleen / füſt / kragk / nawen / parck
Kiel / weydling / hornach / rennſchiff ſtarck

a.ii.

Figure 8: Brant's *Narrenschiff* preface (Basel 1494).

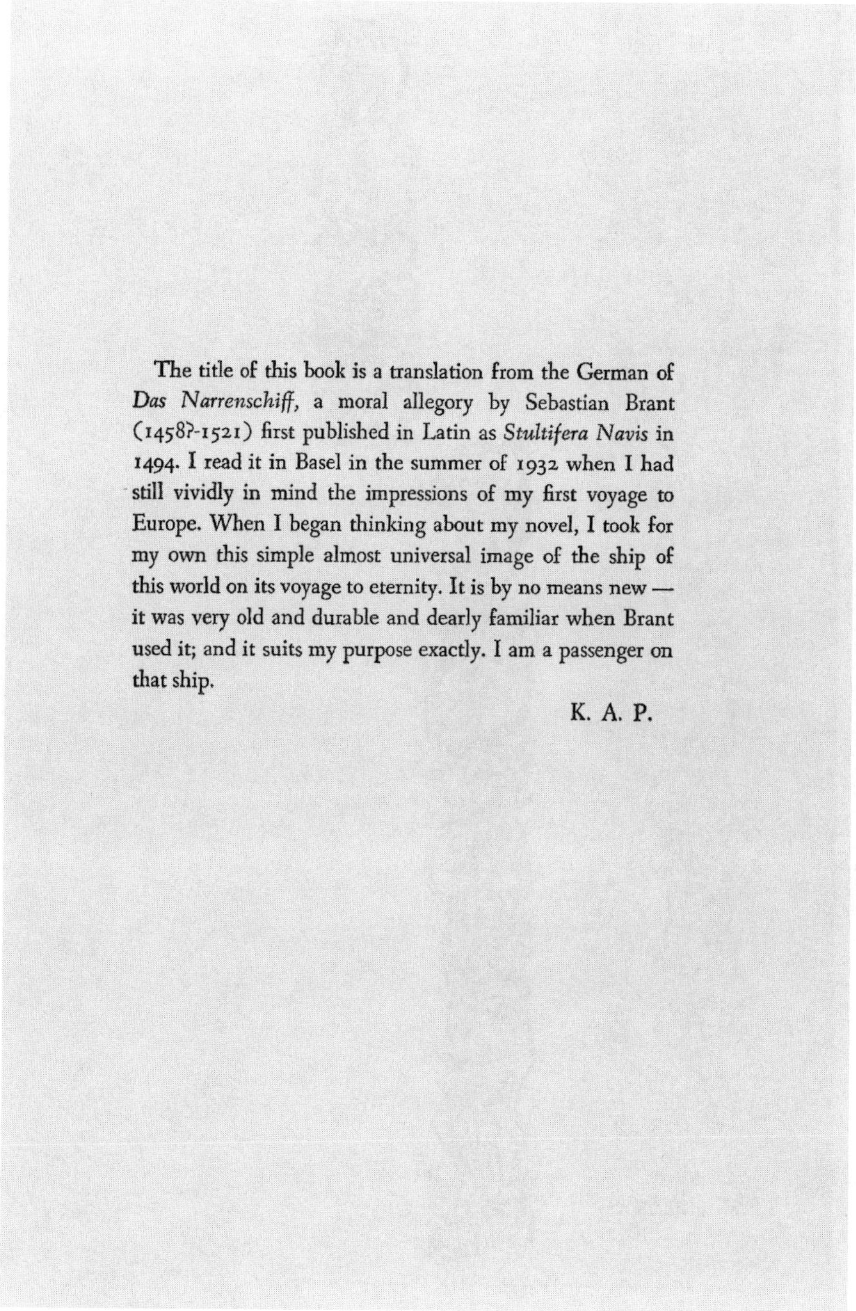

The title of this book is a translation from the German of *Das Narrenschiff*, a moral allegory by Sebastian Brant (1458?-1521) first published in Latin as *Stultifera Navis* in 1494. I read it in Basel in the summer of 1932 when I had still vividly in mind the impressions of my first voyage to Europe. When I began thinking about my novel, I took for my own this simple almost universal image of the ship of this world on its voyage to eternity. It is by no means new — it was very old and durable and dearly familiar when Brant used it; and it suits my purpose exactly. I am a passenger on that ship.

K. A. P.

Figure 9: Preface of Porter's *Ship of Fools* (1962).

Figure 10: Spine of Porter's *Ship of Fools* (1962) and sidebar of Brant's *Narrenschiff* chapter 5 (Basel 1494).

Figure 11: First page of Brant's *Narrenschiff* chapter 5 (Basel 1494).

12. An index of characters, such as in a play script or screenplay, or possibly as if in a passenger manifest. The characters are grouped by nationality "German", "Swiss", "Spanish"; etc. Like some other elements of the paratexts, these national identities were not given in the German translation published in 1963.
13. At the end of the central text, the two dates: *"Yaddo, August, 1941"* and *"Pigeon Cove, August, 1961"* on page 497.

The paratexts at the front of the book are clearly marked as separate: each page is given a Roman numeral instead of the Arabic numerals used in the main text.

Why am I speaking at such length about paratexts? Because these elements are a part of the rhetorical side of the communicative act and represent a part of the rhetorical factor in a literary event; while the novel itself primarily – not entirely – represents the aesthetic-poetic side of communication.

In his 1987 work on the accessory parts of the book, French literary theorist Gérard Genette defined paratexts as,

> what enables a text to become a book and to be offered as such to its readers and, more generally, to the public. More than a boundary or a sealed border, the paratext is rather a *threshold*[2] or – a word Borges used apropos of a preface – a 'vestibule' that offers the world at large the possibility of either stepping inside or turning back. It is an 'undefined zone' between the inside and the outside, a zone without any hard and fast boundary on either the inward side (turned toward the [central-]text) or the outward side (turned toward the world's discourse about the [central-]text), an edge, or, as Philippe Lejeune put it, 'a fringe on of the printed text which in reality controls one's whole reading of the [central-]text'.

Genette assigned a clear rhetorical function to these elements. For him, the symbiosis between the printed central text and its paratext,

> constitutes a zone between [central-]text and off-text, a zone not only of transition but also of *transaction*: a privileged space of a pragmatics and a strategy, of an influence on the public, an influence that – whether well or poorly understood and achieved – is at the service of a better reception for the [central-]text and a more pertinent reading of it (more pertinent, of course, in the eyes of the author and his allies).[3]

Our topic deals with an inside and an outside, with the virtual world of the novel and the actual world of the author and his readers, with the intrinsic

---

2 The French title of the book is *Seuils*, which means "thresholds."
3 Genette 1987, pp. 1 f.

and extrinsic perspectives: the aesthetic-poetic viewpoint on the one hand and the pragmatic-rhetorical viewpoint on the other.

Let us take a look at the most important paratextual element for Porter's main text, her foreword, in which she positions her work for us (see Figure 9). In this paratextual preamble, designed to steer our reception of the main text, Porter makes a total of seven statements that I will discuss in a different order in which they appear.

Her first statement is, "The title of this book is a translation of the German of 'Das Narrenschiff' [...] first published in Latin as 'Stultifera navis' in 1494." This statement is false. The woodcut that Porter selected for the title page of her book is, in fact, from the original 1494 edition, but this edition was published in German in Basel.[4] The decorative border used on the spine of Porter's 1962 edition is also taken from the 1494 German edition (see Figure 10).

Now her second statement: "I read it in Basel in the summer of 1932 when I had still vividly in mind the impressions of my first voyage to Europe." In other words: Porter connected Brant's series of fools with the experiences she had had with Europeans. We may be able to assume that she read Barclay's English translation of the work.[5] On the other hand, she may have read the inexpensive New High German translation by Junghans, which had been published continually since 1877 (one edition of which appeared in 1930).[6] She may have even known of the 1912 facsimile copy of the Basel first edition, which also contained all of the image and graphic elements of the original.[7]

By explicitly referencing Brant's work, and by borrowing his title, Porter sought to create a clear intertextual relationship between her work and Brant's *Narrenschiff*. This relationship is the intertextual nexus between *Narrenschiff* as the famous, early printing of the first large work of modern German literature[8] and at the same time, the most important poetic German contribution to European moral thought in the Renaissance.

Porter's third statement in the foreword is that the idea of a ship full of fools, "is by no means new – it was very old and durable and dearly familiar when Brant used it; and it suits my purpose exactly." In other words: Porter sought to incorporate a very old model as the root idea of her work, one that also just happened to have been used by Brant.

---

4 This error may be due to the fact that the second title page of the 1494 first edition (see Figure 6) contains Latin engravings and psalm verses. This may have led to the impression that the rest of the book was also written in the Latin language.
5 Barclay: Ship of Fools, ed. Jamieson 1874.
6 Brant: Narrenschiff, transl. Junghans 1877.
7 Brant: Narrenschiff, facs. ed. Schultz 1912.
8 Knape 2006a, pp. 105–168.

Let's take a look at Figure 10. The 112 German *Spruchgedichte* (lyrics) of the *Narrenschiff* are a part of the medieval tradition of *Sangspruchdichtung* (i.e. didactic, gnomic, religious, or political songs) which traces its roots to wisdom poetry. The owl-woodcut border sidebar of the *Narrenschiff* (see Figures 10 and 11),[9] illustrates the core principle of the work: the contrast between *sapiens* and *insipiens*, wisdom and foolishness. We see the tree of life, and we see at the bottom and in the middle two fools with fools' caps, symbolizing foolishness, trying to climb the tree. They represent the 109 dumb, foolish, and unreasonable personality types that Brant called "fools/*stulti*" (after his role model, the Roman poet Horace). They clamber up the tree of life in order to ultimately achieve insight, knowledge, or even wisdom. This goal is represented by the owl at the top of the tree, the symbolic animal of the goddess of knowledge and wisdom, Pallas Athena. In the *Narrenschiff*, the final chapters 107 to 112 in particular thematize the postulate of wisdom symbolized by the owl.

The panopticum of foolishness in the *Narrenschiff* is a mirror – ultimately one that reflects vice, deficiency, weakness, stupidity and sin[10] in a way that should be personally recognizable to all readers, so that each can find their way to a new understanding. In many areas of life, Brant saw foolish people that had problems dealing with norms and finding their right way through life.[11] Among the "problem areas" that Brant observed were: education, friendship, challenging the wrath of God, the correct evaluation of a given situation, the handling of overpowering physical temptation, the balance between the worldly sphere and the divine sphere, the relationship between wisdom and wealth, an affection for the world and the improvement of man, marriage and the relationship between a husband and his wife, fear in the social realm, the stubbornness of men, attitudes towards the religious, work ethic, the relationship between subordinates and their superiors, the deadly sins, politics and law, gratification and the gifts of God and the world, human self-care and human self-awareness, the relationship between men and women, belief in untruths, self-awareness and an awareness of others, rudeness, false priesthood, a happy social life, behavior in social roles, wealth, the betterment of man, attitudes towards God's judgment, attitudes towards the worldly and religious ideas of salvation, greed, and everyday hustle and bustle.[12] In Brant's time, which lacked psychology as a discipline, all of these themes were coded moralistically. Porter's work also deals with these same themes, but her version handles them differently.

---

9 One of the recurring decorative elements found as borders on each page.

10 Brant: Narrenschiff, ed. Knape 2005, Preamble (verses 29–44).

11 See also Knape 2006a, p. 152.

12 Gaier 1966, pp. 110–188.

For Brant, life was a search for and pursuit of self-awareness; elsewhere he once wrote, "Know thyself!" after the famous engraving on the temple of Apollo in Delphi.[13] In an adjunct to the 1497 Latin version of his work, Brant wrote, "Up, Up! Look in the mirror in which you seek to know the way of life, and the terrible end, of men."[14]

On the spine of the first edition of Porter's 'Ship of Fools' (see Figure 10), all that remain are the two climbing fools. The top part of the decorative illustration is cut off. Where Brant had placed the owl at the top of the tree of life, the spine of the 1962 book has the name,

Katherine
Anne
Porter.

Is *her name* supposed to stand for the *new owl of wisdom*? And what would a discussion of wisdom and awareness in her book look like?

This leads us to a series of poetological and aesthetic questions that are addressed by Porter's fourth statement in her foreword. According to her assessment, Brant's *Narrenschiff* is a "moral allegory."[15] According to Quintilian's classical textbook on rhetoric, an allegory is an utterance that "either presents one thing in words and another in meaning, or else something absolutely opposed to the meaning of the words," and is, "generally produced by a series of metaphors," such as a work by Horace, "in which Horace represents the state under the semblance of a ship (*navis pro re publica*)."[16] This definition also raises Brant's most important source of inspiration, namely Horace, who wrote in his ode to the 'Ship of State',

You haven't a single sail that's still intact now,
no gods, that people call to when they're in trouble (1.14.9 f.)

and

You must beware of being
merely a plaything of the winds (1.14.15 f.; transl. by A. S. Kline 2003).

As we can see, even Horace's ship allegory contains the melancholic and critical, not necessarily pessimistic but certainly not cheerful fundamental tone

---

13 Knape 2006a, p. 158.
14 In: Locher: Stultifera Navis, ed. Hartl 2001, pp. 34 f.
15 Porter may have even found a version of this completely acceptable interpretation in: Pompen 1925, pp. 295–299.
16 Quintilian: Institutio oratoria, 8.6.44.

that we later see in both Brant's and Porter's works. This is just how ships of fools work; they are not places of happiness, but rather places of squalidness and mental weakness. Michel Foucault misinterpreted this literary fiction, and in his 1961 book 'Folie et Déraison' even falsely believed that in the Middle Ages, mentally handicapped people were sent to live on ships of fools that floated up and down river.[17]

Let us move on to Porter's fifth paratextual statement. It can be found in the half-sentence, "when I began thinking about my novel." Here, Porter is speaking about her decision to write a novel, and about the conceptual phase of the work. Such considerations remain firmly within the field of poetics, because Porter's statement is also a declaration of the genre of her work. It should be a modern novel, one that has clear structural differences from the series of the 112 *Spruchgedichte* on individual types of foolishness found in Brant's image of a ship full of fools. This is a significant difference, and it speaks to the aesthetic core of the difference between the new and old ship of fools.

Brant dealt with the 109 different types of fools in individual chapters, each with (1) a motto, (2) an image, and (3) a didactic poem (*Spruchgedicht*). The poems dealing with each of the negative behavioral deviations are argumentative in nature, and only occasionally contain rhetorically functionalized narrative or descriptive elements. The fictional is provided by the framework of the ship allegory and the sketches of individual types of fools in the text. In Porter's novel, this dynamic is turned on its head. Porter's fictional virtual world is built through narrative, and only occasionally does she integrate argumentative and descriptive elements. In short: Brant's priority is arguing, while Porter's is telling.

In her modern novel, Porter tells the story of at least 30 people or groups of people (families, couples, twins, etc.). We encounter some of these people as real characters, as opposed to the woodcut-like sketches, the more abstract types of sinners found in Brant. Still, Porter's series of figures, which are all presented as equals in the work, demonstrate clear structural similarities with Brant's 109 fools. But while every one of Brant's figures gets its profile exclusively from an abstract discussion of negative morality, Porter's figures get their profiles primarily psychologically through their actions and through the mental processes that the author gives us a glimpse of. Components of an ethical discourse occur only secondarily (for instance, when protagonists reflect on the morality or amorality of the small children Ric and Rac). Thus, Porter presents us with a psychologically interpreted moral universe. Porter tells the common story of a common voyage of figures across the Atlantic. In doing so,

---

17 Foucault 1961, chapter I; cf. Kasten 1992.

her narrative utilizes a principal of film montage known as shot and cut, with alternating sequential syntagma; she thus incorporates a non-linear narrative flow. All of these partial episodes are presented – and this is important, and in the same way that each figure is presented with their idiosyncrasies – on equal footing. This fragmentation of character portraits throughout the work forces the reader to use their imagination to construct a holistic synthesis of each character.

On Deck A there is no main, or even secondary plot. This is a part of an important contrast to Brant's ethically individualist conception of fools; this is the reason why he handles each fool separately. In addition to profiling her individual characters, Porter modeled a social and socio-ethical context of interaction through her depiction of the overall ship. This is missing from Brant's work. Porter's readers can imagine a two-tier *Vera*-world, in which the exploited and non-privileged are penned up "in steerage" in the third class ("the oppressed and intimidated")[18]; where revolutionary potential rears its head. Above deck, in the first and second classes that we get a glimpse of, we see a world of delusion, of ideology and vapidly romanticized belief. Seen psychologically, readers are confronted with unhappiness, worry, and fear, with misunderstanding and neuroses. It is significant that the "bride and groom" on board (who represent existence of human happiness in the world) play no role in the narrative; their existence is only briefly mentioned. We experience how the Jew Löwenthal and Freytag, who has been branded as a Jew, also spin within the whirlpool of resentment due to their inner bondage; they are unable to free themselves. Not even the pair of American artists are able to free their minds. It is a world in which moral considerations, dominant in Brant's work, are psychologized as nothing more than subjective prejudices or learned group egos. It is a world of mutual racism, social discrimination, of boundaries and structural violence. And simultaneously, this entire upper class is largely and only provisionally held together through their mutual class-disdain of those in steerage.

Thus, in Porter's work we experience a world of ancient European thought that cannot rid itself of authoritarian structures. It is an image of prestabilized order and ever recurring sameness, as the not coincidentally pious Catholic Dr. Schumann articulates it in the story.[19] This train of thought and action is most clearly demonstrated by the captain of the ship, who represents an authoritarian-fascist social model as a substitute for the lost monarchy. He understands the fundamental model of an authoritarian system of privilege

---

18 Porter 1962, p. 365.
19 Porter 1962, p. 197.

and hierarchically ordered social relationships as a part of God's order.[20] Against the background of this world image (which, at the narrated time 1931, was beginning to decline), a pessimistic outlook on the world develops, as expressed in quotes such as, "There is no such thing as freedom," (Mr. Graf)[21], or, "Well, what do you expect of this world?" (Mrs. Lutz).[22] The Spanish students and the shady dancers of the Spanish Zarzuela troupe break into this model of social order as antagonists. Someone has paid for their passage on the upper deck. In contrast to the Germans and Swiss, they represent the opposing model of deviation and chaos. This is most clearly seen from the perspective of the devilish kobolds, Ric and Rac.

In reading the novel, what we imagine is the virtual world, the virtual cosmos of the ship *Vera*, whose name, not coincidentally, contains a programmatic statement of realism: "vera" in Latin = the truth, the real. The sum of the characters and the sum of the events constitute the basis for the virtual *Vera*-world in the novel.

In her sixth paratextual declaration, Porter provides an interpretation of this world in stating, "I took for my own this simple almost universal image of the ship of this world on its voyage to eternity." Sebastian Brant also established an important level of coherence in his work through the ever-recurring thematic image of the ship. For Porter, the ship becomes a strictly bordered, concrete space for interaction that the characters cannot escape. In the quotation from the foreword at the top of this paragraph, Porter uses two important terms: "world" and "image". She creates a fictional world in the virtual imaginative space of the novel, a *possible world* in the sense of Saul A. Kripke's *Possible World Theory*.[23] The world of the *Vera* is *potentially factual*; it is an indirect reflection, an "image" as Porter puts it. But what is it a reflection of? Doubtless, it is a segment of the real world in 1931/1932 as found in the memory and interpretation of the author. This image is neither photographic, nor is it an image that reflects real facts. It is a constructed simile, a *Verisimile*, a truth analogon: something *similar to the truth* whose concrete referents (the text-external referent people in the real world) are unknown to us. As readers, however, we *could* connect the characters to historical figures if we were to believe that Porter's work was not a 'novel' but rather a 'historical travelogue'. The genre declaration of "novel" seems to give us some clarity on this issue. As the term "novel" usually indicates, the work follows a specific Western-

---

20 Porter 1962, pp. 174, 248, 424–430.
21 Porter 1962, p. 442.
22 Porter 1962, p. 393.
23 According to the theory, the world would have to be contrafactual. Kripke 1980.

European aesthetic tradition, namely the tradition of the aesthetics of fiction, as Genette called it.[24]

What seems to be clarity provided by the declaration of the work's genre is called into question by Porter's seventh and last paratextual statement. The last sentence of the foreword states, "I am a passenger on that ship." What is this supposed to mean? It is clear that no real historical person can stand on the fictional ship of a novel. It is also clear, however, that this is not a reference to an actual historical voyage ("my voyage," it says in the second sentence of the foreword) taken by the real-world author Katherine Porter in 1931/32. A more appropriate interpretation might be that it is a recourse to Brant's paratext, in which he also claimed to be sitting in his own ship of fools. Even he belonged to the order of fools, as Brant states in the 'Apology of the Poet',[25] and thus would have to find his own place on the ship of fools.[26]

With such comments, both Brant and Porter consciously disturb the ontological levels between the virtual and the real world, and between fictionality and factuality. They suggest that we use our imaginations, our capacity for emotional sympathy, or our abstract thought to establish a connection between the levels of fictionality and factuality. Brant and Porter are telling us that even in the moment of immersion or illusion, we can fantasize ourselves into this poetic world. In this moment of imaginative participation, poetry creates in us every conceivable form of experience. That is the poetic communicative performance of fictional-aesthetic literature.

In contrast to the expectations of postmodern literary theory, we can also assume that both Brant and Porter acted rhetorically, that is, they wanted to express some sort of message to their readers. I refer here to Porter's sixth statement, in which she states that her 'Ship of Fools' is, "the ship of this world on its voyage to eternity." This is a commitment to an allegory, something quite surprising for a modern author. Thus, it is a commitment to a rhetorical figure, with whose help we can decode the poetically encrypted references relating to, for instance, philosophical viewpoints. Paratexts are a part of the rhetorical strategy of an author to make his poetic construct relevant to the real world. In this respect, the clear commitment to an allegory in Porter's work is important. In an allegory, the aesthetic-poetic and rhetorical-real world levels of communication work together. The allegory invites us to interpret a second statement from that which is first said in the text, to see a second something behind the concrete fiction, and, if we choose, to transfer this something into

---

24 Genette 1991.
25 Brant: Narrenschiff, ed. Knape 2005, chapter 111.
26 In: Locher: Stultifera Navis, ed. Hartl 2001, p. 34 f.

the facticity of the *life-world*, as Edmund Husserl called it.[27] Katherine Porter gives us a hint: the concrete ship *Vera* sails in the virtual world from Veracruz, Mexico, to Bremerhaven, Germany. This is the first level of understanding. At the same time, however, the ship represents the world, as Porter says in her paratext, a world which is on its course to eternity. This broaches a second level of understanding. We can understand this process of understanding as a progression from the concrete to the abstract. In doing so, we transform the semantics (denotations and connotations) of an aestheticized text so that we can integrate them into our lives. In other words, we take something out of our internal experiences of a fictional world and apply them to the real world. That is the rhetorical performance of literature.

What, then, can we say is the rhetorical message in Porter's case? To this final question there are two general and one concrete answer:

1. Every reader can, if he so chooses, make an individual and idiosyncratic inference or abduction. Everyone can derive a message that is meaningful only to him- or herself.
2. A professional interpreter can seek to utilize hermeneutic literary critical methods to derive an historically justified message.
3. Or, we can leave the authors to speak for themselves, by interpreting the paratexts and epitexts (i.e. other historical sources related to the central text) they provide us.[28] If there are no epitexts provided, then options 1 and 2 above are our only recourse.

In all of these cases, we must always take into account the historically dominant understanding of the roles of authors in society. The law professor Sebastian Brant understood himself as a teacher around the year 1500, and integrated explicit theorems and supporting arguments into his *Narrenschiff* that leave little room for variable interpretations. His work stands on the border between standard communication in the life-world and the exclusive specialized communication of art.[29] Katherine Porter takes the role of the modern writer, for whom the status of a 'novel' is quite clear. This type of author often understands himself or herself as nothing more than an analyst, a seismograph and recorder of the course of the world. Therefore, and in contrast to Brant, Porter does not give us any explicit directive. But if we are to take her conception of the *Vera*-world seriously, then we can only consider certain specific – rather unpleasant – *insights* into the world as her rhetorical message. And these insights were also, I think, important to Porter.

---

27 Husserl 1954, §§ 33–34.
28 For "epitext" see: Genette 1987, pp. 344–403.
29 Knape 2008a, p. 900.

9 New Rhetoric and the Rhetoric of Deconstruction

In general theories of communication, the complex world of communication is usually based on the three tiered model of the "sender – channel – receiver" for methodological reasons. Those who study texts often construe these three tiers as "author – text – recipient." With good reason, they often tend to approach the situation unilaterally, that is they focus on one side of the model as opposed to its two-sided entirety. The field of general rhetoric, for instance, focuses primarily on the left side of the model; its interest lies in a theory of production for the "author – text" complex. Many branches of the "interpretive" study of literature, on the other hand, fix their gaze on the right side of the model, concentrating their theoretical analyses on the "text – recipient" complex. Other research traditions, such as structuralistic fields, try to narrow their perspectives even further, formulating their models exclusively on the basis of the text, eliminating both communicator and subject from consideration as if they were researching a sort of freestanding geological formation. It goes without saying that each of these methodologically founded perspectives bears their own type of academic fruit. I have begun my discussion with these more general comments so that I can better locate the different ways that both Kenneth Burke and Paul de Man, the subjects of this article, understood rhetoric along this continuum. As we will see, Burke's understanding of rhetoric reflected the left side of this model; de Man's the right side. Since I have just claimed the left side of this model for rhetoric, it may seem that there is a certain amount of tension arising from an implicit contradiction. In light of both its historical genesis and its general characteristics, this tension cannot be viewed any other way. On the one hand, Paul de Man certainly accepted and incorporated suggestions from Burke, Richards, and others, while on the other hand anchoring his theory on the right side of the model according to the principle of negation that Burke emphasized. This also does not change the fact that de Man theoretically denied the dichotomy between production and reception in his later works. In the end, we will have to ask how far these two theories can be conciliated with each other.

Kenneth D. Burke, born in Pittsburgh in 1897, is often counted as a representative of the *New Criticism* movement that Paul de Man dealt with. The sheer variety of Burke's work, however, makes it difficult to clearly define his thought in one way or the other. Daniel Fogarty, writing in 1959, counted him along with Ivor A. Richards and other exponents of general semantics as one of the founders of the American *New Rhetoric*, a school that sought to combine classical rhetorical doctrines with modern scientific approaches, particularly those of linguistics and communication sciences. Burke's wide array of interests has led his works to be appreciated as standard reference books not only in American speech departments, but by theorists around the globe. Paul de Man was certainly as aware of Burke's work as he was of European theoreticians whose influence on him has already been well documented. In the following, I will only be able to make a few of the many theoretical connections between Burke and de Man regarding both their similarities and differences.

1 Dance and Drama

One of de Man's main concepts from his 'Allegories of Reading' can be found in his quote of Yeats' verse, "How can we know the dancer from the dance?"[1] The verse itself is significant for an understanding of de Man's theoretical position for multiple reasons. If we identify the "dance" as a text, how does that change its meaning and referentiality? De Man must admit that the functions of reference and message are normally considered the main functions of language (according to Jakobson); this is why de Man talked about the, "authority of meaning." But the fact that we can read Yeats' verse as both a rhetorical figure and as a real question (with all of the consequences this would have for the overall interpretation of the text) leads us first to the hermeneutic *aporia*, and then to a necessary tension of interpretation:

> The two readings have to engage each other in direct confrontation, for the one reading is precisely the error denounced by the other and hast to be undone by it. Nor can we in any way make a valid decision as to which of the readings can be given priority over the other; none can exist in the other's absence. There can be no dance without a dancer, no sign without a referent. On the other hand, the authority of the meaning engendered by the grammatical structure is fully obscured by the duplicity of a figure that cried out for the differentiation that it conceals.[2]

A consistent focus on the right side of the traditional model of communication creates a necessary interpretive tension (for both linguistic and text-theoretical reasons) caused by the implied solitude of a reader with the literary text. Some see this as the hermeneutic crux or interpretive misery, others as the gate to the realm of freedom.

The metaphor of dance also played a special role in the theoretical formulations of the New Rhetoric, although it was used in a completely different

---

1 de Man 1979, p. 11.
2 de Man 1979, p. 12.

way. In following with the overall tradition of general rhetoric, Kenneth Burke's perspective viewed the model of communication primarily from the left side. Thus, his fundamental considerations began with the individual as a catalyst, as an initiator and author of communicative acts that is connected with the second element of the communicative model (the channel or text, etc. understood by Burke rhetorically as an instrument of the author). Burke's second theoretical preliminary decision, to view questions of communication as elements of action theory, also fit within the rhetorical tradition. For Burke, this perspective took on an anthropological character. In his 1966 book, 'Language as Symbolic Action,' he attempted to summarize this conception in the following definition,

> Man is the symbol-using (symbol-making, symbol-misusing) animal, inventor of the negative (or moralized by the negative), separated from his natural condition by instruments of his own making, goaded by the spirit of hierarchy (or moved by the sense of order), and rotten with perfection.[3]

In light of this background, Burke viewed fictional (poetic) communication as symbolic action by an author. This is not the place to further detail Burke's theoretical conception of the symbol as an instrument of action and symbolization as an action in itself. In general, we can say that Burke generally distinguished between real and symbolic actions and between semantic and poetic naming in the generation of meaning. In 'Allegories of Reading', de Man expressly separated the textual levels of grammar and rhetoric from one another. Burke's theory indeed provided clues for de Man, as he indicated in his book:

> Kenneth Burke mentions *deflection* (which he compares structurally to Freudian displacement), defined as, 'any slight bias or even unintended error,' as the rhetorical basis of language, and deflection is then conceived as the dialectical subversion of the consistent link between sign and meaning that operates within grammatical patterns; hence Burke's well-known insistence on the distinction between grammar and rhetoric.[4]

We can equate these two levels with Burke's two types of naming, and at the same time connect them with the distinction between *denotation* and *connotation*. In 'The Philosophy of Literary Form' (originally published in 1941), Burke interpreted both as deictic actions. While the construction of "semantic meaning" (denotation), refers to an object outside of the level of the sign, the con-

---

3 Burke 1966, p. 16.
4 de Man 1979, p. 8.

struction of "poetic" meaning refers not to an object, but to the author himself, particularly to his "attitudes":

> Semantic meaning would be a way of pointing to a chair. It would say, 'That thing is a chair.' And to a carpenter it would imply, in keeping with his organized technique, 'By doing such and such, I can produce this thing, a chair.' Poetic pointing, on the other hand, might take many courses, roughly summed up in these three sentences: "Faugh! a 'chair!', 'Ho, ho! A chair!', 'Might I call your attention to a chair?'

The sentences, "Faugh! a chair!," and, "Ho, ho! A chair!" are, "weighted with emotional values, with *attitudes* [...] *Meaning* there would unquestionably be, since an attitude contains an implicit program of action."[5] Paul de Man, on the other hand, shifted the distinction between potential semantic and poetic meaning in a text to the side of the recipient, and used the terms "signification" and "symbolization" to refer to them. "Any reading always involves a choice between signification and symbolization, and this choice can be made only if one postulates the possibility of distinguishing the literal from the figural."[6] For Burke, those authors that seek to generate meaning at a purely semantic level (for instance the logical positivists) attempt to achieve a high degree of indifference and thereby, "eliminate the *attitudinal* ingredient from its vocabulary". The "poetic ideal", on the other hand, is constituted by dramatism. It is a process that tries to, "derive its vision from the maximum *heaping up* of [...] emotional factors." Therefore, "the semantic ideal envisions a vocabulary that *avoids* drama. The poetic ideal envisions a vocabulary that *goes through* drama."[7]

The extent of Burke's rhetorical thought is demonstrated by his belief that symbolization is a form of the expression of an author. The category of "dance", however, leads in a direction that forgoes a traditional conception of the rhetorical calculation in the composition of verse-texts in order to develop a (psychologically based) conception of automatic encoding. In this sense, the author unconsciously inscribes himself into his text and generates uncalculated structures:

> The symbolic act is the *dancing of an attitude* (a point that Richards has brought out, though I should want to revise his position to the extent of noting that in Richard's doctrines the attitude is pictured as too sparse in realistic content). In this attitudinizing of the poem, the whole body may finally become involved, in ways suggested by the doctrines of behaviorism.[8]

---

5 Burke 1941, p. 143.
6 de Man 1979, p. 201.
7 Burke 1941, pp. 148 ff.
8 Burke 1941, p. 9.

Thus, in reading Coleridge's poetry, we catch a "glimpse" of his "labyrinthine mind [...], the *puzzle* in its pace, 'danced' in the act of walking."[9] Burke did not leave his discussion with an author's *individual* psychologically oriented considerations of writing automatism. Rather, he also considered other (for instance, socially contingent) unconscious influences on writing that set limits on the rhetorical postulate of the conscious construction of texts, "and though he be perfectly conscious of the act of writing, conscious of selecting a certain kind of imagery to reinforce a certain kind of mood etc., he cannot possibly be conscious of the interrelationships among all these equations."[10]

Thus, even the process of writing a text cannot be totally consciously controlled. The author has plans and purposes (in such situations we speak of intention) but the calculation of production has its limits. The author is always exposed to a poetic loss of control. Paul De Man described it as the author being, "blinded", and that the "critical reader" is obliged to, "make the unseen visible," at a later level of reception.[11] Burke referred to Lucretius, who he saw as an example for how deconstruction can be implemented in the process of production and how the intended construction of meaning can be performatively called into question,

> Wedded, as a materialist ('philosophical scientist'), to the aim of analgesia [understood here as an explicit denial of poetic naming], Lucretius nonetheless builds up extremely emotional moments. For example, in trying to make us feel the great relief that would come to us from the abolition of the gods, Lucretius exposes himself to the full rigors of religious awe. He must make us realize *awe* [...]. So he becomes somewhat an advocate against his own thesis. For in trying to build up a full realization of the awe, in order to build up a full realization of the freedom that would come of banishing this awe, he leaves us with an unforgettable image of the awe itself.[12]

2 Tropes and Figures

In his essay 'Aesthetic Formalization: Kleist's *Über das Marionettentheater*', Paul de Man refused to shift his views to Burke's methodological and model-left-sided camp by ironically commenting on a question of Kleist's autobiographical intent that had been posed by some researchers,

> To decide whether or not Kleist knew his text to be autobiographical or pure fiction is like deciding whether or not Kleist's destiny, as a person and as a writer, was sealed by

---

9 Burke 1941, p. 10.
10 Burke 1941, p. 20.
11 de Man 1971, p. 141.
12 Burke 1941, p. 152.

the fact that a certain doctor of philosophy happened to bear the ridiculous name of Krug. A story that has so many K's in it (Kant, Kleist, Krug, Kierkegaard, Kafka, K) is bound to be suspicious no matter how one interprets it. Not even Kleist could have dominated such randomly overdetermined confusion. The only place where infallible bears like this one can exist is in stories written by Heinrich von Kleist.[13]

Although de Man refuses to accept Burke's research perspective, his arguments in 'Marionettentheater' are surprisingly coincident with the important categories of interpretation of *drama – dance – trope* found in Burke's writing. De Man invokes these dramatic categories when he speaks of the, "theatricality of the text"[14], which, "abounds in stage business"[15] and is composed "as a succession of three separate narratives encased in the dialogical frame of a staged scene,"[16] or when he asks, "is not the point of aesthetic form [...] to substitute the spectacle of pain for the pain itself?"[17] In the same way, it can be shown that Paul de Man was obsessed with the idea of the dance. Is this only because of his chosen topic of the marionette theater? In this situation it made perfect sense to reference Burke's categories; even when concentrating on various research done on Kleist's text the dance metaphor made an appearance, "the dance performed by the commentators offers only chaos,"[18] and, "the entire hermeneutic ballet is a display of waste."[19] When describing the story of the young man, he also spoke of how meaning, "is transposed in the sign-system of dancelike gestures."[20]

In explaining the puppet show, de Man was concerned with transferring the dance model to the textual level.[21] The tropes and figures of general rhetoric represent analogous elements. Thus, the most important "textual model" in the *Marionettentheater* is, "that of the text as a system of turns and deviations, as a system of tropes."[22] The search for figural structures becomes an important "interpretive" procedure. Paul de Man only vaguely concerned himself with the differentiation of figures: for him, the traditional figures of ellipse and parable could be considered tropes, and the stand-alone tropus,

---

13 de Man 1984, pp. 284 f.
14 de Man 1984, p. 271.
15 de Man 1984, p. 269.
16 de Man 1984, p. 268.
17 de Man 1984, p. 280.
18 de Man 1984, p. 272.
19 de Man 1984, p. 282.
20 de Man 1984, p. 281.
21 Cf. Knape 2008d.
22 de Man 1984, p. 285.

"synecdoche," was, "the most seductive of metaphors."[23] De Man's conception of the figures was too schematic for Jürgen Fohrmann,

> such as the differentiation between metaphor and metonymy, symbol and allegory, whose relationship can only reproduce the binary values of open and closed, etc. Or should it be about new functions, but not at all about a new theory of figures, rather a continuation of that which has been called 'rhetoric' since ancient times (and which also, as de Man himself discusses, had a diagnostic way of differentiating figures – for instance in the definition of allegory)?[24]

Paul de Man was obviously only concerned with a loose association with the traditional taxonomic systems of rhetorical figures. Rather, his interest was focused explicitly on figuration as a principle of text. This interest was grounded in the desire to reveal the specifics of the aesthetic level of texts.

> The aesthetic power is located neither in the puppet nor in the puppeteer but in the text that spins itself between them. This text is the transformational system, the anamorphosis of the line as it twists and turns into the tropes of ellipses, parabola, and hyperbole. Tropes are quantified systems of motion. The indeterminations of imitation and of hermeneutics have at last been formalized into a mathematics that no longer depends on role models or on semantic intentions.[25]

De Man was thus focused on excluding the semantic dimension of meaning in order to expose the level of aesthetic structures. Poetic naming then becomes a recourse to formal principles. For de Man, the term *drama* that we find in Burke was based too heavily on the author and his conscious or unconscious concerns (described by the concept of 'desire'). The realm of the aesthetic, however, begins outside of this level or dimension of the text.

> Unlike drama, the dance is truly aesthetic because it is not expressive: the laws of its motion are not determined by desire but by numerical and geometric laws or topoi that never threaten the balance of grace. For the dancing puppets, there is no risk of affectation (*Ziererei*), of letting the aesthetic effect be determined by the dynamics of the represented passion or emotion rather than the formal laws of tropes. No two art forms are in this respect more radically opposed than drama and dance.[26]

De Man's concentration on the aesthetic level of text (in which semantic naming has been eliminated) lead tropes and figures to be counted as the most important textual structures.

---

23 de Man 1979, p. 11.
24 Fohrmann 1993, p. 92.
25 de Man 1984, pp. 285 f.
26 de Man 1984, p. 286.

> Balanced motion compellingly leads to the privileged metaphor of center of gravity; from the moment we have, as the aesthetic implies, a measure of phenomenality, the metaphor of gravity is as unavoidable, in the sequential art forms such as narration or dance, as is the metaphor of light in the synchronic arts such as, presumably, painting or lyric poetry.

The motion of the puppets, "exists only for the sake of the trope."[27] De Man returned again to the auctorial perspective and more specifically defined the idiosyncrasies in the construction of figures:

> As we know from another narrative text of Kleist ['On the gradual development of thoughts in the process of speaking'], the memorable tropes that have the most success (*Beifall*) occur as mere random improvisation (*Einfall*) at the moment when the author has completely relinquished any control over his meaning and has relapsed (*Zurückfall*) into the extreme formalization, the mechanical predictability of grammatical declinations (*Fälle*).[28]

At the beginning of his '*Marionettentheater*' essay, de Man mentions the connection, "between trope and epistemology." This opens a much broader dimension of tropology that is no longer constrained to the structure of the text, but can also be conceived as something cognitive, as thinking in figurative structures.[29] This concept was well known by the *New Rhetoric*. De Man did not, however, speak in terms of "truth", which Burke often set in quotes when used in reference to questions of aesthetics. Burke devoted an entire chapter of his 1945 book, *A Grammar of Motives* to the "Four Master Tropes" of metaphor, metonymy, synecdoche and irony. In it, he sought to move away from the traditional, "'literal' or 'realistic' applications of the four tropes."[30] Instead, he conceived them as figures of thought, "with their role in the discovery and description of 'the truth'."[31] It is important to note, however, that Burke's conception included a special sort of "aesthetic truth", in which, "a kind of metaphorical truth," unfolds, as he wrote in his 1931 book 'Counter-Statement'.[32] Burke's epistemological approach to figures conceives of the metaphor as a methodical operation of *perspective*, of metonymy as *reduction*, synecdoche as *representation* and irony as *dialectic*. With respect to his connection with Paul de Man, Burke's transfer of figural analysis to the interpretation of literature is important because it shifted his perspective, however briefly, to the right side of the model. Synecdoche in particular fascinated Burke:

---

27 de Man 1984, p. 286.
28 de Man 1984, p. 290.
29 de Man 1984, p. 266.
30 Burke 1945, p. 503.
31 Burke 1945, p. 503.
32 Burke 1931, p. 168.

The more I examine both the structure of poetry and the structure of human relations outside of poetry, the more I become convinced that this [synecdoche] is the 'basic' figure of speech, and that it occurs in many modes besides that of the formal trope. I feel it to be no mere accident of language that we use the same word for sensory, artistic, and political representation.[33]

And,

The synecdochic function may also be revealed in the form of a poem. If event 2, for instance, follows from event 1 and leads into event 3, each of these events may synecdochially represent the others (the interwovenness often being revealed objectively in such processes as 'foreshadowing'). If the Albatross is put there to be killed [in 'The Rime of the Ancient Mariner' by Coleridge], it could be said to 'participate in the crime' in the sense that the savage, after a successful hunt, thanks the quarry for its cooperation in the enterprise. In being placed there as a 'motivation' of the mariner's guilt, its function as something-to-be-murdered is synonymous with its function as incitement-to-murder (recall that among the functions of synecdoche is the substitution of cause for effect and effect for cause).[34]

It is clear that Paul de Man learned much from Burke's point of view.

3 Negativity

Like Paul de Man, Kenneth Burke also knew Friedrich Nietzsche's fundamental position and his linguistic-philosophical examination of the rhetorical category of "figure". It is no coincidence that Burke places his two above mentioned processes of naming under a sub-section titled, "Beyond good and evil".[35] Nietzsche's renunciation of realism in language focused on the set of problems that we now refer to with the linguistic categories of arbitrariness, conventionality and the referentiality of linguistic signs. In his essay, 'On Truth and Lies in a Nonmoral Sense', Nietzsche asked, "and besides, what about these linguistic conventions themselves? Are they perhaps products of knowledge, that is, of the sense of truth? Are designations congruent with things? Is language the adequate expression of all realities?"[36] The theory of meaning in *New Rhetoric* searched for answers to these questions. Unlike Nietzsche, Burke's interest was not only in being philosophically and linguistically skeptical about figuration as an illustrative model of the semiotic detachment from the world, including

---

33 Burke 1941, p. 26.
34 Burke 1941, p. 28.
35 Burke 1941, p. 149.
36 Nietzsche 1872, p. 116.

the irreducibility of signs. His rhetorical postulate that individuals can intentionally act with language took priority. Burke's differentiation between the semantic and poetic dimensions of meaning is important insofar as it enables us to better classify the variety of tropes (such as the synecdoche). They belong at the theoretical level of text, not at the level of signs. Theoretical investigations of signs are fundamentally concerned with the question of referentiality posed by Nietzsche, about the connections between language, the world, and cognition. Rhetoric and poetics, on the other hand, leave fundamental problems of language substantialism and realism behind. In the moment of concrete text production, decisions regarding practical communicative action have already been made; the sender and receiver have generally pragmatically agreed on using a common grammatical code. The second (or even third) dimension of meaning created in concrete texts by tropes, as discussed by Burke and de Man, is of a different kind altogether than that at the grammatical level.

The principle of negativity that Burke postulated in all humans plays an important role in these procedures. It is also structurally formative in figuration. First, however, individuals must learn how to wield this negativity; they must learn that changes in meaning can be generated at the textual level through operations of negation:

> There is an implied sense of negativity in the ability to use words at all. For to use them properly, we must know that they are *not* the things they stand for. Next, since language is extended by metaphor which gradually becomes the kind of dead metaphor we call abstraction, we must know that metaphor is not literal. Further, we cannot use language maturely until we are spontaneously at home in irony. (That is, if the weather is bad, and someone says, 'What a beautiful day!' we spontaneously know that he does *not* mean what the words say on their face. Children, before reaching the 'age of reason', usually find this twist quite disturbing, and are likely to object that it is *not* a good day. Dramatic irony, of course, carries such a principle of negativity to its most complicated perfection).[37]

Burke's thoughts on negativity were based on the fact that it is exclusively an element of symbolic systems and that it does not appear in natural phenomena. Burke was inspired by Bergson, as he explicitly stated, but he believed Bergson's accentuation of the epistemological side of negativity to be problematic. The following quote makes this clear; he suggests that we solve Bergson's theoretical difficulties by taking a new approach founded on the communicative and strictly action theoretical *dramatism*:

---

37 Burke 1966, p. 12.

I would make one change of emphasis with regard to Bergson's fertile chapter. His stress is a bit too 'Scientisic' for specifically 'Dramatistic' purposes. Thus, in keeping with the stress upon matters of knowledge, he stresses the propositional negative, 'It *is* not.' Dramatistically, the stress should be upon the hortatory negative, 'Thou *shalt* not'. The negative begins not as a resource of definition or information, but as a command, as 'Don't'. Its more 'Scientistic' potentialities develop later. And whereas Bergson is right in observing that we can't have an 'idea of nothing' (that we must imagine a black spot, or something being annihilated, or an abyss, or some such), I submit that we *can* have an 'idea of No', an 'idea of don't'. The Existentialists may amuse themselves and bewilder us with paradoxes about le Néant, by the sheer linguistic trick of treating no-thing as an abstruse kind of something. It's good showmanship. But there's no paradox about the idea of 'don't', and a child can learn its meaning early.[38]

In this way, negativity is primarily understood as a principle of action, with consequences for the actions of those that seek to interpret texts. In antithetical expression, "what are often called 'polar' terms," one need not decide whether the positive or negative part should be considered dominant: the two are mutually dependent. Burke spoke of a Hegelian dialectic in this context. Despite this, when pressed to make a decision, Burke asserted the priority of the negative meaning in such expressions, "for this reason: (1) Yes and No imply each other; (2) in their role as opposites, they *limit* each other; (3) but limitation itself is the 'negation of part of divisible quantum'. (I am quoting from the article on Fichte in the *Encyclopedia Britannica*, eleventh edition.)"[39]

4 Rhetoric

When Burke spoke of the, "implied sense of negativity," in words and tropes as the foundation of their use, it is only consistent that the interpreter of a text recognize the principle of negativity as an instruction for action. There is no doubt that this was the case for Paul de Man, as his key example of the "question" in Yeats' verse made clear. This position is also valid in the famous 'Archie Bunker scene':

A perfectly clear syntactical paradigm (the question) engenders a sentence that has at least two meanings, on which one asserts and the other denies its own illocutionary mode. It is not so that there are simply two meanings, one literal and the other figural, and that we have to decide which one of these meanings is the right one in this particular situation.[40]

---

38 Burke 1966, p. 10.
39 Burke 1966, p. 12.
40 de Man 1979, p. 10.

A clear decision can only be made if we bring the whole model of communication into play, when we allow, "the intervention of extra-textual intention," when we include both the sender and the communicative situation in our considerations and do not leave the reader isolated with the text. De Man's model right-sided perspective of the communicative model, however, did not allow for this, "nor is this intervention really a part of the mini-text constituted by the figure which holds our attention only as long as it remains suspended and unresolved." Paul de Man sought to remain purely in the model right-sided world of literary "reading" (as envisioned by Roland Barthes' postulate that, "the reader is the space on which all the quotations that make up a writing are inscribed").[41] In this "world of reading", the figural structures of texts become riddles, and this world contains a special sort of literary rhetoric:

> I follow the usage of common speech in calling this semiological enigma 'rhetorical'. The grammatical model of the question becomes rhetorical not when we have, on the one hand, a literal meaning, but when it is impossible [for the reader at the level of the central text] to decide by grammatical and other linguistic devices which of the two meanings (that can be entirely incompatible) prevails. Rhetoric radically suspends logic and opens up vertiginous possibilities of referential aberration. And although it would perhaps be somewhat more remote from common usage, I would not hesitate to equate the rhetorical, figural potentiality of language with literature itself.[42]

General rhetoric traditionally focuses its perspective on the author and is thus always considered a field of strategic communication. How does this fit with Paul de Man's conception of literary figural rhetoric? Prior to de Man's writing, Ivor Richards' theory of meaning generation had clearly denied substantialist conceptions of language.[43] For him, language is, in all aspects, a fundamentally pragmatic phenomenon. Burke also proceeded from the fact that meaning is first generated in communicative interaction. The resulting instability of sign meaning in texts, however, makes language a problematic form of communication. Nietzsche clearly expressed this sentiment as well. The rhetorician Burke indeed believed in the constructive power of language in textual use, yet he was also well aware that it always seeks to gain independence, always calls the communicative power of man into question: "Do we simply use words, or do they not also use us?"[44] For Richards, it was evident that a theory of meaning must methodically deal with misunderstandings, and that scientific rheto-

---

41 Barthes 1967, p. 148.
42 de Man 1979, p. 10.
43 Richards 1936, pp. 11 f.
44 Burke 1966, p. 6.

ric is, "a study of misunderstanding and its remedies."[45] Ultimately this conception is optimistic and it focuses on the possibility that barriers of misunderstanding can be overcome. Paul de Man's category of "misreading" may have been inspired by Richards' "misunderstanding", but the two concepts are separated by an unbridgeable gap. Intermediary interaction between the left and right sides of the communication model, considered by newer constructivist theories to be necessary for the exchange of information, is not considered in de Man's theory. Factors of intervention outside of the text are, as stated, explicitly excluded from his theory. For de Man, the text remains an unsolvable riddle; he goes so far as to insist that only this kind literary texts are interesting at all ("draw attention to themselves").

From the historical perspective of general rhetoric, de Man's conception represents a form of *restrained rhetoric* that Gérard Genette deplored in a theoretically self-critical essay titled, 'La rhétorique restreinte,' and which Chaïm Perelman aggressively attacked in his 1977 work 'L'empire rhétorique'.[46] De Man himself admitted as much in discussing the dominant form of *elocutio*-rhetoric found in modern literary studies of Romanian and Anglo-Saxon literary criticism. He emphasized that tropes and figures not be grouped with "grammar", that they are defined by rhetoric, "not in the derived sense of comment or of eloquence or persuasion."[47] How can this perspective be harmonized with the much broader conception of general rhetoric? The central point is that de Man's theory focuses only on a particular kind of text, namely, those that work heavily with figural structures and are aesthetically marked. These are first and foremost (if not exclusively) literary, fictional and poetic texts. This has consequences for the constitution of such texts, which I will here only briefly address. From a left-sided perspective of the model of communication that focuses on a theory of production, the rhetorical postulate of "strategic" communication takes on a specific. Texts are the structural place where linguistic signs are arranged according to contextual processes of determination in such a way that people can meaningfully interact with them. In the case of the literary genres, the author steers his constructive attention towards other, aesthetic strategies of production based on the genre he has chosen, towards "poetic naming" (Burke), towards the "poetic function of language" (Jakobson). He goes above and beyond the general informational function of language, builds structures in his literary texts that are in principle independent of grammar, and gives aesthetic self-referentiality free reign. Strategies of

---

45 Richards 1936, p. 3.
46 Genette 1972b; Perelman 1977, p. 11.
47 de Man 1979, p. 6.

"semantic" overdetermination must be set aside in the production of the text, or the author must accept that extra-poetic messages might slip into the mix of his liberated literary language game. Additionally, this game opens a much wider door for further formations that generate subconscious meaning than in other text genres. Newer constructivist theories of communication point out that the means of communication (such as texts) as such do not have informational content. When applied to people, information does not travel between the left and right sides of the communicative model in the form of technical messages. Every cognitive system involved in communication initially generates messages based on its own individual capacities and abilities. Texts can only be communicatively functional by virtue of social interaction, through learning processes and experience with conventionalization. In literary communication, the sender and receiver must have both learned about its specific peculiarities, such as those found in literary fiction or poetic figuration. He who reads Günter Grass's 'The Flounder' as only a cookbook is missing out on an important dimension of the text. Because the complete reciprocal adjustment between sender and receiver is impossible, because language can only be repressed in the construction of texts to a certain degree, because the author can never win complete control over his text, and because literary texts seek to open "space" (and often have to do so in order to be accepted as literary), the recipient can and must engage with figural structures. In doing so, he sets his deconstruction against the construction of the author.[48]

---

48 German version of this chapter in: Knape 2000f.

Intersemiotic Rhetoric

10 The Rhetoric of Music

In the first act of the opera 'Don Giovanni', first performed in 1787, it quickly becomes clear just how much of a sex-addicted neurotic the main character is; he is certainly a perfect example for what is now often simply called "Don Juanism". In the eighth and ninth scenes of the opera, Wolfgang Amadeus Mozart and his librettist Lorenzo da Ponte show us the seducer engaged in a mini-drama yet again. This time, we get to see his approach course of action from beginning to end. The action begins with Giovanni coming across a choir of merry young country people, who he immediately identifies as a wedding party. Instantly, he "smells" a sexually receptive woman (as he puts it in a different scene of the libretto). In the first recitative, which can be seen as an introductory conversation among strangers within the framework of a theory of communication, Don Giovanni probes his chances of success as a seducer. His chances prove to be good, as the young bride approaches him on her own (both practical experience and modern behavioral research on flirting suggests that this indicates that she finds him to be attractive as a sexual partner). Don Giovanni reacts by demonstrating the necessary willingness to invest as a sexual partner by inviting the entire wedding party to a lavish meal. He presents himself in every way as a more attractive sexual partner and shows no hesitation to utilize the superiority of his person and status, as well as the arrogance of a noble, over the naïve and helpless groom Maseto. For his part, Maseto eventually backs down, but not without petulant resistance and a grim and lamenting aria of frustration. The erotic attraction of new partners is, in some ways, a classic setting of rhetorical persuasion.

Mozart and da Ponte depict such persuasion in a case study on the stage, and proceed to demonstrate a rhetorically skillful attempt at seduction in particular. In a second recitative, Don Giovanni, now alone with Zerlina, begins his argumentation with the sorts of conversation which are commonly deemed necessary in securing an erotic partner. Typical speech acts such as compliments and flattery make an appearance. The accompanying harpsichord reflects his style of easy and alluring parlando. The nobleman Don Giovanni clearly declares his fitness as a sexual partner over a simple farmer. He even goes so far as to offer a promise of marriage, which in Mozart's era was considered a particularly notorious trick offered by nobles in their attempt to seduce women. With this, he almost succeeds in winning Zerlina's attentions. In the famous final duettino:

Là ci darem la mano
là mi dirai di sì

he strikes the final blow. The dialog then transitions to a briefer, more emotional stichomythia, where the singers being to interrupt each other with ever more rapid and rash expressions as they find a way to go from flirting to consummation. Don Giovanni presses more and more, as demanded by the role of seducer, while Zerlina hesitates less and less as a reluctant but willing young woman. The sexual tension continually rises until Zerlina relents, leading to the tension breaking, "Andiamo! (Let's go!)." Both partners begin to sing their happy duet together, "Andiam, andiam!"

What happens next is well known. The expected consummation of Don Giovanni's efforts is interrupted by the sudden appearance of Donna Elvira, in the guise of a vengeful furie, who promptly thwarts his one night stand.

Using his theoretical-communicative perspective, a rhetorician can study this and other similar dramatic musical scenes in a certain way. In doing so, he seeks to answer the question of which rhetorical processes are simulatively performed through the interaction of the *dramatis personae* that appear in the opera. In effect, this intrinsic perspective (which turns inward to focus on the text itself) is cultivated both in older music theory and in countless modern works in musicology that concentrate on the question of rhetoric in music. According to such works, rhetoricity is also found in purely musical texts that lack further elements of discourse (linguistic semantization through a libretto, lyrics or theatrical staging) which might give them meaning.

In a particularly good survey article on the topic, 'Rhetoric and Stylistics in Musicology' the Viennese musicologist Hartmut Krones systematically describes the development in the way that older music theory and newer musicology have used the concept of rhetoric.[1] From a diachronic perspective, a rhetorician quickly notices the clear historical errors and confusion in the music theoretical adoption of the concept of 'rhetoric'. Seen synchronically (that is, from a modern, purely systematic point of view) categorical and theoretical vagueness in the approach to the question of rhetoric is also easy to find. The theory of music is certainly not alone in this respect; this theoretical insecurity can just as easily be found in the fields of art and literature, as well as other disciplines that try to incorporate the question of rhetoric into their fields.[2]

Historically speaking, rhetoric has continually developed more and more well formulated theories of production (*téchnai*, lat. *artes*) since Aristotle in the 4th century B.C. Since the Middle Ages, these theories have increasingly been borrowed by musical theorists for their own purposes. Such rhetorical

---

1 Krones 2009; see also: Wilson/Buelow/Hoyt 2001.
2 See: Knape 2008a.

theories of production have been considered paradigmatic due to specific assumptions that have been made concerning the relationship between rhetoric and music. One such assumption is that musical texts, like linguistic texts, serve as form of communication and thus that music is a communicative fact. While this point can be debated, rhetoricians are only concerned with music insofar as it represents exactly this sort of fact.

The historical integration of elements of rhetorical theory into other artistic disciplines was deemed appropriate because rhetoricians had already systematized a wide array of elements that were useful for the production of texts in other semiotic fields. In this respect, we can speak of semiotic universals that older theories of rhetoric systematized, to some extent for use in other artistic disciplines as well.[3] In particular, the doctrine of the five stages of production has been widely integrated into other fields. Thus, we also find invention (*inventio*) as the first stage of production in musical theory, and a model of disposition, in which the parts of the musical text are composed and arranged as the second. Thereafter, we find a stage not unlike the third rhetorical office of *elocutio*, in which the musical text is smoothed and polished. Finally, both the stages of *memoria* (a theory of saving the text) and of *actio* (as a doctrine of performance) can easily be incorporated to describe elements of the theory of music.

Upon closer observation we find that the problems of finding analogous structures between rhetoric and music first arise at the lower level of transfer that deals with concrete structures. The questions must be asked whether there really are such things as musical topoi or musical metaphors that mirror those elements found in verbal language, and how the entire arsenal of rhetorical verbal linguistic figures can be transferred to music theory.[4] Krones's article showed that although there are still some who are legitimately skeptical of drawing analogies between levels of rhetoric and music, the numbers of those that have proposed a systematic transfer of rhetoric to the structure of music production has grown. At the same time, it is clear that borrowing elements from the verbal-linguistic field of rhetoric (due a lack of terminological alternatives in the field of music) almost always involves the dubious practice of metaphorical, improper, and vague use of rhetorical terminology. The determination of musical or musically relevant structures through the use of rhetorical termini can lead to ambiguity: without the necessary critical approach, this transfer proves to be problematic at best. I would to express my personal skepticism of such approaches even more radically, and pose the question of

---

3 See: Knape 1994b.
4 Vickers 1984.

whether many of these supposed cases involve rhetoric at all. In doing so, I must leave the diachronic aspects behind and focus exclusively on a synchronic scientific perspective, that is, on a theoretically grounded and systematic point of view.

In Krones's article we find the following quote, "Goldschmidt (1971) proved that Beethoven's instrumental melodies often had the basic pattern of verse and stanza, and Niemöller (1980) provided an overview which, in addition to its historical elements, described newer theories of the linguistic character of music."[5] In the case of this article, such comments are acceptable because the handbook 'Rhetoric and Stylistics' also deals with the concept of stylistics in music in general. If this article were found in a work exclusively concerned with the question of rhetoric, however, it would have to be criticized because it perpetuates two of the most common categorical mistakes that arise out of a fundamental misunderstanding of rhetorical theory: the misidentification of aesthetics with rhetoric and the confusion of linguisticality with rhetoricity (cf. pp. 23–26 in this volume). Those who seek to analyze Beethoven according to patterns found in poetry, verse and stanza systematically borrow from an *aesthetic* theory of production, namely, that of poetics, which has been a separate and parallel theoretical tradition to rhetoric since antiquity. Similarly, the question of the "linguistic character" of music does not deal directly with rhetorical concerns. Instead it draws from the related field of linguistics, which addresses issues of "linguisticality" and grammaticality in verbal languages, including legitimate questions of how such structures can be analogously applied (with necessary modifications) to music.[6]

Naturally, the question can also be posed how, *sub specie artis rhetoricae*, we should deal with the analogies in light of the so-called rhetorical figures and the linguisticality of music. I will give only a brief answer here so that I can focus on my core question about the rhetoric of music. The question of "linguisticality", or better the linguistic analogy of music, is relevant for rhetoricians insofar as it asks whether music is based on intersubjective, conventional, and semiotic foundations that can be understood and interpreted by addressees in a listening community. If so, this would allow us to define music as a communicative fact. If this is indeed the case, then music is interesting for rhetoric. In seeking to determine whether music has a linguistic form or at least a communicative *sui generis*, we would need to work with what was called *causa necessitatis* in treaties from the Middle Ages: the need to determine the rules in a semiotic system (here, a linguistic system or system of expression) according to a correct/incorrect criterion (grammaticality).

---

5 Krones 2009, p. 1940.
6 Hörr 2009, pp. 93–115.

The rhetorical figures are called *rhetorical* figures merely because they were primarily codified within the framework of rhetorical theory. In reality, however, the countless figural doctrines describe only structures of expression that belong to an overcode outside of the grammatical and linguistic codes. Thus, they cannot be used in processes of overcoding according to the grammatical criterion of 'correct/incorrect'. In classical theories of rhetoric, all figures are placed under the rubric *ornatus* (ornament or embellishment). This term should make us sit up and take notice, because it points in the direction of structural aesthetics. As structural phenomena, both tropes and figures are in fact multifunctional and in no way confined to rhetorical functionalization. In practice (depending on the theory of production being used) they are integrated according to the 'aesthetic' criterion of 'beautiful/ugly' or according to the 'rhetorical' criterion of 'communicatively appropriate/inappropriate'. This formulation makes clear that tropes and figures are forms of expression that are functionally neutral in regards to theories of production. They are defined purely structurally according to rules of generation and are only assigned functional criteria with reference to the theory used in their production (whether it is the 'poetics' of aesthetics and/or 'rhetoric'). In other words: tropes and figures are used more like the semiotic universals described above and, from a systematic perspective, are not in and of themselves rhetorical merely because they have historically been grouped together under the framework of rhetorical theory. In looking at history itself, such elements have formed a core part of poetic theories at least since the Middle Ages, and they represent the most important theoretical intersection between 'poetics' and 'rhetoric'. Poetics, however, is based on a theory of production that focuses on aesthetic criteria. Over the course of the history of rhetoric, rhetoric and poetics have certainly often been unsystematically cross-contaminated. Additionally, the figural doctrines have again and again developed a life of their own under the label 'rhetoric', which has led to a reductionist or, as a modern French theorist has called it, a "restricted" conception of rhetoric.[7] As early as antiquity, this resulted in a school definition (literally a "school" definition) that describes rhetoric as an *ars bene dicendi*, as the art of speaking well, and postulates a sort of rhetorical "second grammar" for school lessons. In regards to music, we would thus have to speak of an *ars bene sonandi* or *vocandi*.[8]

Theoreticians in the Middle Ages were already aware of this set of problems. The most widely used textbook on figures from the 13th to the 15th centuries, with its distinction between *ornatus facilis* and *difficilis* (light and heavy

---

[7] Genette 1972b.
[8] Hörr 2009, p. 93.

figural ornament), was described by its author, Geoffrey of Vinsauf at the beginning of the 13th century not as an '*ars rhetorica*' but as a '*Poetria nova*', with Poetria used to mean the personification of poetry. Taken as a whole, the poetic-rhetoricians of the 12th and 13th centuries are a striking testimony to the cross-contamination between poetic and rhetorical theories of figures. Until the 17th and 18th centuries, rhetoric was used to designate both the trivium as well as a generic term for sub-theories such as poetics. Only in the disciplinary taxonomies of the early modern period was poetics conceived of as systematically independent. From a disciplinary perspective, aesthetics emerged first with Baumgarten's 1750 work 'aesthetica'.

Modern rhetorical theory is not the only perspective to consider the definition of rhetoric as the art of good formulation as under complex or underspecified. Sharp criticism of this definition and the normal approach to rhetoric taught by school grammarians can be found as early as antiquity in Ps. Longinus's work, 'On the Sublime', where the divinatory sudden inspiration is seen as the decisive factor of production. And the three holy pillars of ancient rhetorical theory, Aristotle, Cicero and Quintilian were in the end all in agreement, that the better definition for rhetoric was as an *ars persuadendi*, the art of persuasion. Under this definition, rhetoric occurs in cases of persuasive action, where a *causa persuasionis* exists. Plato defined rhetoric similarly as psychagogy, as a steering of the soul. From an academic standpoint, this persuasion-theoretical approach has to this day been considered to be the proper and more comprehensive definition of rhetoric.

I would now like to reformulate the question of rhetoric in music based on this position. First, however, we must change our viewpoint. The fundamental question of rhetoric in music is extrinsic; it focuses its gaze on the connections between music and its addressees or the world, and is primarily concerned with whether and how music functions in rhetorically devised interactional and communicative settings. The question of what goes on *within* a musical text, whether one incorporates some sort of musical figures for instance, (however they are to be defined) is dependent on the intended function of the text in interaction. A *causa persuasionis* would require us to judge the use of the so-called rhetorical figures according to the criterion of 'communicatively functional/dysfunctional'.

To return now to our original example, the question is thus: did Mozart and his librettist da Ponte write Don Giovanni with rhetorical goals? That is, did they seek to influence their audiences or to persuade their audiences of something? It goes without saying that such a rhetorical orientation of libretto and music would have to have repercussions on the calculations of production and the resulting structures in the musical text. And it is here that the case gets theoretically interesting.

In order to better understand the core question of rhetoricity in music, let us try and put ourselves in the place of a composer with a rhetorical concern. We approach the question in this way because rhetoric is fundamentally oriented towards a theory of production, and equally considers both the producer with his rhetorical concern and the communicative instrument that he produces, his musical text. The question of what can constitute a rhetorical concern will be addressed later.

Let us begin first with the production of the text. If our composer were to ask me for a rhetorical measure for his work, then as a representative of the neo-Aristotelian form of rhetoric found in Tübingen I would first point him towards Aristotle himself. In his book on rhetoric, we find the following: "Rhetoric then may be defined as the faculty of discovering the possible means of persuasion (*pithanón*) in reference to any subject whatever,"[9] in our case music. Interpreting this as a guideline for a composer leads to a series of possible calculations of production. These are *pithanón* calculations, working strategies that concentrate on the question of which elements in the given musical text are persuasive in relation to the rhetorical concern.

Under the condition that music is a communicative fact in social interactions, and without having theoretically determined all of its specific dimensions, the composer must deal, either consciously or intuitively, with the entire communicative context in his calculations of production. Only then can he fulfill the rhetorical expectation of introducing something persuasive into symbolic interaction through communication. The rhetorician would here speak of a strategy, of a, "forward-looking, reflective planning of actions and formulations," based on consideration of the, "relationship between goal, resistance, and means."[10] The goal of persuasive interaction is clear when generally formulated: the musician seeks to use communicative means to gain success in interactions, with the degree of success determined by social indexes of value such as prestige or money. In considering the possible types of resistance that might occur, the musician must primarily deal with the mental resistances present in his addressees, such as their skepticism regarding the quality of the work. If such types of resistance were not present there would be no need for any kind of rhetorically persuasive effort. The musical methods of persuasion must be tuned to the appropriate forms of resistance in order to successfully effect a change in the mental state of addressees. So far, so good: in principle, this is how rhetorical intervention through music would have to function. In concrete situations, of course, the problem of rhetoric is much more complex and complicated.

---

9 Aristotle: Rhetoric, 1.2.1.
10 Knape/Becker/Böhme 2009, col. 153.

In using the verb "effect" above, I have opened the door to the category of effects, and it is here that the difficulties begin. The desire for mental effects can namely also be found in purely aesthetic calculations. Aristotle's book 'Poetics', which he wrote as a kind of counter-point or analogue to his 'Rhetoric', deals with such aesthetic issues. Aristotle had specific systematic reasons for the clear division of these two theoretical areas, among which he counted the difference between the categories of *poiēsis* (creation) and *práxis* (acting in social settings).

The term "work" has not fared well in the recent history of theory in the humanities. Still, rhetoricians need the term as a category of difference in order to be able to distinguish between the communicative status of certain kinds of texts. Rhetoric uses the abstract term *work* (*opus*)[11] to describe those texts that have been released into communication as artifacts or that can be communicated though they have been de-pragmatized and deprived of their heteronomic designations.[12] A *work* is thus a "text"[13] that has been given autonomy, that has been "made" according to an aesthetic program, which can and should be introduced into communication as an independent entity, and is not or no longer dependent on a special situation or occasion (de-pragmatization). The "artistic question" in a stricter sense does not necessarily play a role in this definition. Aristotle gave this sort of text the status of a *poiēma*: something that has been made according to rules of production or an artistically created artifact.

Since the beginning of the art period (Kunst-Periode) of the 18th century, if one speaks of a "work" by this or that creator as a freed communicative artifact (such as a piece of music), this automatically also expresses certain expectations. These expectations are based on the assumption that the creators of these works use especially sophisticated intrinsic calculations in "producing" or "making" their textures. In certain forms of music, the general understanding of the concept of work is suggested both by the special conditions of medialization as well as the particular textual release from the usual structures of discourse found in direct everyday communication. This definition has nothing do to with postmodern thoughts on the deconstruction of the work unit, which, for their part, also follow a particular aesthetic work-calculation.

---

11 Knape 2008a, pp. 896 f.

12 At least after its first use in a pragmatic setting.

13 A bounded, ordered symbolic complex with communicative intentions. In modern poetic and film theory, the boundaries of a text are defined by a certain "closure": "The notion of closure is connected to the sense of finality with which a piece of music, a poem, a story, or a typical movie concludes. It is the impression that exactly the point where the work does end is just the *right* point." Carroll 2008, p. 134.

The calculations behind the production of a work must not necessarily be rhetorically motivated in any way, and this brings us to the critical point of this chapter. Since the rise of an emphatic conception of art in the art period, all kinds of pragmatic calculations have been stigmatized in favor of purely aesthetic calculations according to an idea (or should I say, ideology?) of "l'art pour l'art", art for art's sake. As a rhetorician, I have no problem with this trend. Artistic settings are arranged accordingly. For musical performances, for instance, special rooms (buildings) are built, the musical events are autonomous, and the corresponding group of artistic communicators is an insider's circle of connoisseurs with specialized competencies that allow them to better appreciate the aesthetic calculations and make them more receptive to the aesthetically evoked effects of the work. What exactly *are* these effects in the case of artistic music? We can characterize them with a few preliminary concepts: feelings, moods, affects (emotions, joy or fear), pleasure (in the sense of a direct stimulus-response reaction), or spontaneous acceptance, inclination, goodwill, or mental aversion. Aristotle mentioned these and other similar aesthetically evoked effects in his 'Poetics'. Still, such considerations remain completely within the context of aesthetic calculations. Naturally, this leads us to ask: is that it? Where does that leave rhetoric?

I would like to begin my comments by reminding the reader that at the moment we are considering a very specific communicative setting, namely that of modern artistic communication under specifically defined conditions. We can thus designate artistic communication as taking place under conditions of specialized communication. These conditions include specific media (for instance, specially prepared performance spaces), specific genres (opera, symphony, sonata, etc., each presenting their own textual challenges), and specific interactive partners (composers, orchestra members, chamber musicians, connoisseurs of classical music, etc., each with their own expectations and competencies). A composer interested in communicative success must deal with all of these elements in his calculations. These calculations may well be purely aesthetically motivated, and seek the effects that I have just mentioned above. In such cases, we would be dealing with what treatises from the Middle Ages called *causa pulchritudinis*, question of beauty, which is judged by the criterion "beautiful/ugly" (attractive/unattractive).

Aristotle made a similar assessment when he used the theater and tragedies of the Greek polis as the starting point for his poetic theory. In the 19th chapter of the 'Poetics', however, he mentions a category that opens the door for rhetoric. Within the framework of what we call artistic communication (social interaction through the use of de-pragmatized texts, such as theatrical performances of works), we can sometimes find a rhetorical factor in an Aristotelian sense. In other words, even those structures that have been integrated into a text according to aesthetic calculations can intentionally or unintentionally lead to a specific rhetorical effect.

What exactly is the rhetorical factor? Aristotle defined it, according to his cognitive approach to rhetoric, as the reorientation of human knowledge, thought and rational understanding. He uses the Greek term *diánoia* in this context, which can be translated into English as "train of thought" or "reasoning". Aristotle defined these cognitive components in 'Poetics' on the one hand as the textual offering of a de-pragmatized *work*, on the other as a systematic category of rhetoric, which designated the rhetorical factor in poetry. He wrote, "all that concerns Thought (*diánoia*) may be left to the treatise on Rhetoric, for the subject is more proper to that inquiry."[14] This rhetorical factor consists of generating a cognitive change from opinion A to opinion B. We also use the term *persuasion* to describe this change.[15]

Other than the above mentioned emotional effects, do we find any other rhetorical factors in purely artistic music, in non-verbal *musique pure, independent music* or *absolute music* (*absolute Musik*), however we choose to name it? Can the awareness evoked by music of this sort ever be more than the self-reflective recognition of inner-musical structures? Can such music even lead to philosophical insight, even though it contains no abstract or specific terms?[16] If the answer to these questions is yes, then there must be a sort of history of ideas in music. If the answer is no, on the other hand, then there cannot be an actual rhetorical factor in these purely musical texts.

Such considerations are naturally different in semanticized music that includes linguistic or behavioral correlations such as a libretto. Johann Sebastian Bach's cantatas were, in his time, neither de-pragmatized nor autonomous, but rather defined heteronomically and defined semantically by religion. Admittedly, the usual performance chamber of the church had by then already become an aesthetically specialized space that regularly licensed and even demanded highly aestheticized, independent structures in order to reflect the godly sublime in the art. Bach thus had no inhibitions to carry his aesthetic calculations quite far indeed. Essentially, today's music arises from a mixture of calculations associated with the pragmatic-public realm. In a new foundational work on rhetoric and music, my student Sara Hörr has recently shown

---

14 Aristotle: Poetics, 19.2.
15 Knape 2003a, esp. col. 875.
16 This question would focus on whether "absolute music" has included other types of conventionalized communication in various epochs in the history of music or whether abductive processes (in the sense of inference based on real world events according to Peirce) can be made possible through musical experiences.

how specific aesthetic calculations regarding the formulation of melodies correspond with rhetorical calculations in modern pop-culture.[17] Since her work adequately deals with the most important questions in this context, I can keep my comments in this area brief.

Since its creation, opera has been a further prime example of this type of mutually oriented calculation of production. Mozart's contemporaries expected an opera to have a clear rhetorical factor. Accordingly, the story of Don Giovanni was easily integrated into the contemporary discourse on morality, which was also by all means colored by religion. The belief that there is evil in the world and that God punishes the wicked was palpable for Mozart's audiences at that time. Lorenzo da Ponte sought to speak to such expectations with his original title of the work: 'Il dissoluto punìto o sia Il Don Giovanni' ('The punished sinner, or Don Giovanni').

The foundation of modern psychology has also provided us a variety of other categories that help us understand dramatic processes. In my introductory interpretation of the Zerlina mini-drama I was able to demonstrate how applied epistemic contexts expand the possibilities of insight: I psychologically interpreted Don Giovanni as a psychodrama focused on the clinical image of a sex addict. His rhetorical interventions thus result from this psychological addiction. Peter Schaffer, on the other hand, interpreted the creation of 'Don Giovanni' from a psychoanalytical perspective in his successful work 'Amadeus', which he also adapted to a screenplay for Miloš Forman's well known film of the same name. According to his interpretation, Mozart's conflict with his father was a decisive factor in the creation of the work, in which the murder of the commander represents patricide, and the commander's revenge is the symbolization of a type of self-inflicted punishment by Mozart based on his own feelings of guilt.

I mention Schaffer's fanciful Mozart-drama towards the end of my thoughts on this issue for a specific reason. Schaffer's poetic freedom allowed him to concentrate on a single rhetorically relevant constellation present throughout the story that I have not yet mentioned; namely, the artistic *agōn*. The Greek word *agōn* refers to the rivalry or competition among artists. In Schaffer's work, such competition led Mozart's colleague and successful Viennese composer Antonio Salieri to view Mozart as an existential threat, and led him to try and kill his competitor. At the very least, it is an historical fact that Mozart and Salieri were in competition with one another in Vienna at the time. From the perspective of a rhetorical orator theory, such facts are interesting because they allow us to assign recognizable strategies of artistic persuasion

---

17 Hörr 2009; cf. Lehmann/Kopiez 2011.

to both composers. He who wished to win in the Viennese agon of the time was obliged through his works to convince the connoisseurs of the city (I do want to speak here of an undifferentiated public) to become patrons, to give theatrical or concert commissions, or to donate money. Thus, the composer is an orator (a rhetorically persuasive actor) insofar as he seeks to convince his addressees of the qualitative superiority of his music.[18] In Schaffer's piece, this process of persuasion is demonstrated by a public rivalry between the virtuosi Mozart and Salieri that takes place at a dinner party scene (in which Salieri is naturally subject to the personal dishonor of being disgraced).

My comments on this subject have sought to categorically clarify the difference between aesthetic and rhetorical calculations of effect and production. I have also described how aesthetic structures can be used for rhetorical purposes. In other words: aesthetically motivated structures can indeed be functionalized in a *work* in order to create a rhetorical factor. I have left open the question of how rhetoric should approach absolute music. In normal communicative processes outside of artistic communication, musical persuasion takes on a more conspicuous character because rituals and verbal language take priority. In such situations, music often occurs as an additive or supplemental component with the function of amplifying the resonance of the performance.[19]

Finally, I also spoke directly about the musician himself, whether he be a mere composer or a virtuoso of performance. Pragmatic theories of music that interest themselves for rhetoric must also take such considerations into account. When a musician performs as an artist and considers himself to be an artist (in my opinion, not every musician needs to consider himself an "artist" in the emphatic way used in the art-period), then he necessarily takes part the artistic agon. In such cases, the musician must design the entirety of his artistic work such that his addressees assess his work to be superior and thus take socially relevant action that leads to an advantage for the musician himself (be it in the form of prizes, a higher reputation, or the disbursement of money).

---

18 Knape 2008a.
19 See: Hörr 2009.

11 A Rhetoric of Images

Although academic rhetoric has already accepted the image as a legitimate object of research, a rhetorical theory of images is still in its infancy. General rhetoric is able to integrate this new area of research into the framework of a "rhetoric of images" by approaching it from two theoretical angles: that of text production theory and that of action theory. As a texture, the image is a stimulus that is woven into communicative processes of interaction with the objective of helping the communicator's or – rhetorically spoken – the orator's aim to succeed. Thus, rhetorical theory focuses on those problems which arise when an orator strategically produces and employs images in communication.

1 The Status of Images within the Theory of Rhetoric

As early as antiquity, work on the theory of rhetoric continually pointed to the pictorial arts as a paradigm in order to explain its doctrines through the use of analogies. This comparison stemmed from the fact that the terminological and production-theoretical approach of rhetoric was developed based on the models and theoretical works (gr. *téchnai*) of the fine arts in ancient Greece. Linguisticality and iconicity were both considered part of the same semiotic context. Since then, rhetoric has been understood as a theory that focuses on the practice of success oriented communicators (orators). The *organon* theory of rhetoric focuses (for the most part) on the conditions of the production of communicative instruments, particularly linguistic texts that seek effective stimulation in the interest of effective communication. The image has its systematic place in rhetorical theory within this context. Since Aristotle, the discipline of rhetoric has taught orators to recognize the rhetorical factor in each and every form of communication, to systematize such knowledge, and to utilize it in the production of stimulating text components. Thus, rhetoric deals with operations, methods, and structures that are focused on effectively achieving specific communicative goals, in particular persuasion. In the interest of clear categorization, the normatively loaded concept of "manipulation" is to be held strictly separate from rhetoric; manipulation occurs when the (normative) maxim of honesty is violated and a communicator is insincere in his goal-setting, or his use of communicative processes and methods.

Since its inception in 1992, the Historical Dictionary of Rhetoric (Historisches Wörterbuch der Rhetorik) has included a series of articles devoted to a wide array of topics that have to do with images and the fine arts. In the first six volumes, for example, the following entries all deal with visuality and imagery: "Arabesque", "Architecture", "Baroque (Painting)", "Image/ Imagery", "Book Art", "Monument Rhetoric", "Iconology/Iconography", "Caricature", "Fine Art", "Art History", "Painting", "Photographic Rhetoric" and "Poster". Unfortunately, most of these entries do little more than bear witness to the meager state of the rhetorical theory of images. It is often the case that these articles offer nothing more than a collection of the shreds of ancient rhetorical theory that are then connected to the respective visual-artistic topic at hand. The most a reader can hope for is to be able to collect individual tessera from a wide historical puzzle; few of the authors ever approach the theoretical core of the problem. Telling is the following quote from a 2003 article, which admittedly deals more with sculpture than images per se:

> The connection between rhetoric and sculpture in the theory of art history is expressed through the, usually implicit, use of rhetorical categories such as, 'composition', 'proportion', 'perspective' (intended effect), the 'match' (das 'Zusammenstimmende'), 'contrapositive positioning' or 'mimesis'.[1]

There are two criticisms to be leveled at this viewpoint: first, these termini do not actually stem from the rhetorical tradition at all, rather they come from other theoretical schools and second, they refer to phenomena of aesthetic 'over-coding' that do not in and of themselves have anything to do with rhetoric. The continuation of the quote, in which classical rhetorical theories that deal with linguistic textures are referenced without explanation, demonstrates the overall lack of a clear theoretical conception. Other connections between rhetoric and sculpture are to be found, "... in the description of the aesthetic and rhetorical effects, the *delectare, movere, docere*, that have found their way into art curricula through the works of Cicero and Quintilian. The internal dependence between form and effect is demonstrated through the application of these rhetorical levels of style (*genera dicendi*), through which the emotions of recipients are guided and evoked in the viewer of a sculpted work."[2] This is a typical testimonial to the widespread intellectual helplessness in dealing with the rhetorical question as it relates to images.

2 Image Textuality

The theory of rhetoric deals with the question of images insofar as images are used for communicative tasks, that is, when an image is used to convey or

---

1 Bressa 2003, col. 1240.
2 Bressa 2003, col. 1240.

support a message.[3] We may begin the discussion of the definition of *image* with an everyday example. Let us assume that an art director at an advertising agency goes to his graphic artist and gives him the task to sketch three images for an advertising campaign. Each image should contain an ashtray and a cigarette. After three days, the drawings are finished, and the art director is pleased to find that all three images depict scenes containing ashtrays and cigarettes. How is this possible?

First, we must isolate the relevant theoretical problems from this little story. Take a look at the entire sequence once again: at the beginning, the graphic artist has no mental representation of a concrete image in his imagination or on his sheet of paper. Then, a verbal act of communication takes place, namely the art director's instructions. The end results (the sketches) are proof that the art director was able to count on his graphic artist having a specific cognitive endowment: the artist was obviously able to connect the verbal expressions (in the form of the verbal-linguistic signs | ashtray | and | cigarette |) with their corresponding image-signs 🖾 and 🖎. He was also clearly able to isolate and call up these images from his mind. This sequence leads to two necessary conclusions:

1. Both the graphic artist and his boss must have a pool of image-signs in their cognitive equipment that contains the conventionalized signs of 🖾 and 🖎 as types to be realized as tokens. We call this pool of signs the *code*. We speak of an *image-code* when this code is made up of signs that are motivated, that is, when their gestalt or expressive part is similar to optically perceivable forms in the physical world. As with every code, children must learn the meanings of these 'signs' early on in order to later be able to understandably note images. And just as with written codes, it takes time before children are able to note image-signs with skill.

2. The graphic artist is able to understand the individual elements of his boss' verbal-linguistic code (which we normally call simply *language*), namely | ashtray | and | cigarette |. And he is also able to translate these individual elements into 🖾 and 🖎, that is, into elements of another code (the image-code). This is only made possible by the cognitive ability of the human mind to make connections between different codes that are present in the brain.

Let us return again to the story of the art director and the graphic artist. At the end of the story, there are three images lying on the desk that the art director has never seen before, but which he is easily able to decode ('under-

---

3 Cf. Knape 2007b.

stand'). They are not considered images merely because they have the signs ⬭ and ⬕, but rather because these two signs are somehow connected to each other and are a part of a more highly organized association with other image-signs. This association can be created because the graphic artist has mentally saved a wide array of other image-signs (iconic types) that he is easily able to combine with the signs ⬭ and ⬕ as requested by his art director. Taken as a whole, the signs in the newly created image (combinations of signs that the art director is also able to understand) constitute exactly the kind of higher order semantics that define an 'image' in the terminological (not metaphorical) sense. The meaning of an image is not merely the sum of its individually identifiable signs. In other words: the sign for ashtray (⬭) is not, in itself, an image, but rather only one building block with which images can be made. The step from mere building material to an entire house is the step from a code (with its singular and conventional image-signs) to an *image-texture* (lat. *textum* or *textura* = engl. *texture* or *tissue*).

Here, *text* is understood as a bounded, ordered complex of signs arranged with communicative intention according to the expanded conception of text found in the semiotic theory of textuality.[4] The image-sign-*code* is conventional: the meanings of image-signs are learned and social phenomena, and they are not arbitrarily interchangeable. The code imposes its own meaning and rules on its user,[5] but the text opens the door to the realm of freedom. It is first at the level of text that the game of infinite combinatory possibilities begins in which a higher order semantic is produced according to the communicative needs of the creator. Every code (every language in a general sense) subjects us to the terror of grammaticality (that is, the *correct/incorrect* constraint).[6] But every text enables us to overcome this constraint through the free play of combinatory powers that are subject to new and additional rules of communication. These rules are aesthetic or rhetorical, and work according to the criterion of *appropriate/inappropriate*.[7]

An image-text is thus something that is created within the communicative reality of human culture, because it is meant to communicate something in relation to a current real-world state of affairs. For this reason, rhetoricians consider images to be communicative facts. The code provides the semiotic

---

4 Stöckl 2001; Bittner 2003, p. 24; Knape 2007b, p. 12; Knape 2010b, pp. 82 f.

5 For cultural codes see: Knape 2000e.

6 Cf. on "benchmarks of correctness"/"Korrektheitsmaßstäbe": Sachs-Hombach/Masuch 2007, pp. 55 f.; cf. also "Man, Some Mistakes Found in Children's Drawings"/"Der Mensch, fehlerhafte Kinderzeichnungen" in a book for teachers by Arno Gürtler 1948, part of plate 44.

7 Knape 2006a, p. 48.

potential for the image-maker (Chomsky would speak here of *image-competence*). The image-text, on the other hand, is a product of communication that is newly created and occasional; it does not exist prior to its creation. An image-text is something that emerges from the black box of human thought through notation.[8] This notation alone represents the image-text, which is culturally manifest and thus interesting for rhetoric (notwithstanding the fact that there was a prior mental representation in the mind of the image-maker).

The conception of the image-code as a cultural convention hints at another problem as well, namely that of combinatory rules that allow meaningful combinations of image-signs within an image-text so that others (image-interpreters) are able to understand it as a meaningful arrangement. Our art director is only able to immediately understand the new image containing his desired signs (⊖ and ◢) because both he and his graphic artist (as well as the intended audience) have command of a common set of rules for the combination of individual image-signs. If this was not the case, then the art director wouldn't be able to accept the sketches for his advertising campaign.

The theorem of linguistic analogy gives us a cue for the further consideration of this problem. If it is to make the creation of image-texts possible (and this seems to be the case), then the image-code must function similarly (not identically) to verbal language. The image-code must be a sort of language and exists in the mind (as a product of learning) before the creation of any text. According to Karl Bühler,

> a system of the type language is not based on one, but on (at least) two classes of positings (or conventions), and accordingly contains two classes of language structure. A system of the type language constructs every complete representation (that can be removed from the situation) [in texts] in two steps that should be abstractively distinguished; for the sake of brevity, we can put it as follows, though it is imprecise and subject to misunderstanding: it construes each situation through the choice of words and through the sentence pattern. There is a first class of linguistic structures and corresponding positings that work as if the world were to be cut up into rags or to be divided into classes of things, processes, or to be resolved into abstract factors, and as if a sign were to be assigned to each, whereas the second is intent on providing the significative resources for a consistent *construction* of the same world (what is to be represented) according to relations. From the point of view of the theory of representation, these are two different steps and ways of proceeding and must be clearly distinguished. This point must be made perfectly clear, and no one should be misled by the psychological fact that these two classes of language structures are used in smooth and frictionless cooperation.[9]

---

8 *Notation* is every type of construction of a text that emerges from the human body and is released into the interpersonal communicative world (Knape 2008a, p. 896; Knape 2008e, p. 134; Knape 2010b, p. 83). Thus, the term *Notation* is used here in conscious differentiation to Nelson Goodman's conception (Goodman 1969, pp. 127–173).
9 Bühler 1934, p. 85.

If the image-code is to be considered analogous to language, it too must be based on two conventions: on the overall pool of signs and on the rules for ordering signs. The image-code is special because of the fundamental motivation of the expressive part of the sign. What does this mean? With respect to both aspects (the form of the signs and their combinatory order), the image-code is determined by the collective learning history of people within a cultural realm, and this history applies to the optically perceivable forms of the physical world. It is important to note that the *motivation* of individual signs relates only to their expressive part. The content part of an image-sign is socially and culturally defined. This goes for the image-code as well. The meaning, however, is the deciding factor in whether communication with an image is successful. Wittgenstein said in his 'Tractatus' that "a picture is a model of reality."[10] In order to explain the rise of the image-code (i.e. the motivation of signs and the syntagmatic rules in images) we can reverse this sentence: "reality is the model for the picture." This explains why we are often irritated or puzzled by most of René Magritte's images for instance: Magritte regularly worked with the distortion of our learned image-grammar, which forces us to reassess our image-grammatical judgment of *correct/incorrect*. Since we assign his images the status of *art*, we accept his game and begin to apply Herbert P. Grice's conversational implicatures to the images in a certain kind of way.[11] On the other hand, if a child were to apply his image-notation in the same way as Magritte, his parents would most likely correct him with, "this is how you draw it *right*."[12]

3 Image Narrativity

Images are *stills* (and not *movies*)[13] that are only able to *show* without the help of verbal language (according to the *deixis* postulate of images).[14] The theory of narrativity in images must also deal with this problem. This brings us to a new theoretical level. One of the most important attempts to solve the difficult

---

10 Wittgenstein 1921, § 2.12, p. 15.
11 Grice 1967.
12 Cf. footnote 6.
13 Cf. chapter 12 in this book.
14 See: Knape 2007b, p. 16 and p. 12, n. 8. The mixture of codes (the use of multiple visual codes at the same time, e.g. writing and image-signs) is seen as a special case in the theory of images.

problem of narrativity in images was made by Marianne Wünsch in 1999.[15] Her convincing theoretical approach starts with the fully justified, strict precondition that a communicative utterance (e.g. a verbal text or a film texture) only has a narrative structure if it possesses the required components of an actor and action along a temporal axis: (1) "two states of the same human or non-human entity" and (2) "an operation that changes the state, a transformation."[16] In an image (as a still), however, these two components do not occur. An image, as such, does not contain a linear-temporal dimension; one cannot measure time in an image. In solving the narrativity problem, we assume that images are ordered complexes of signs that are arranged according to certain rules in order to construct a higher order semantic. This approach mirrors that of rhetoric, even though Wünsch's formulation is somewhat different. Some of these possibilities of arrangement indirectly contain something like a "*temporal* component": they must, "have the type of characteristic such that, based on our cultural knowledge, we can conclude that the condition represented in the image was something different before, or will be something different after."[17] This condition is necessary, but not sufficient. In addition to the question of time, we must also deal with the question of action in images. An image "cannot *represent*" an action, "rather it can only *indicate* by selecting a characteristic moment from the successive individual steps and time of an action, on the basis of which we can and must infer what came before this point in time and/or what will come after."[18] Thus (in the case of images), on the one hand we have a texture that only shows something unmoving, while on the other we have an act of perception by addressees and the cognitive processing of information.

Let us say that one of the images that the graphic artist from our original example shows the art director is a scene with two people sitting at a sidewalk café (and which also contains the signs ☕ and 🍴). Marianne Wünsch analyzed a similar scene taken from an advertisement. She described how the viewer of an image interprets what he sees:

> The style of clothing signalizes that there is some sort of social occasion taking place that more than only these two people are taking part in. Based on their characteristics it is

---

15 In reading her work, one notes that Wünsch, with her background in literary studies, has a well-founded theory of narrativity. On the other hand, her handling of the rhetorical figures, in particular her thoughts on "tropes" in images are not theoretically convincing. See: Wünsch 1999.

16 Wünsch 1999, p. 328.

17 Wünsch 1999, p. 331.

18 Wünsch 1999, p. 334.

not immediately intuitively clear what kind of social relationship the two people have to one another: foreignness and disinterest seem just as unlikely as familiarity and interest. The social situation between the two people is thus such that it demands an explanation. The hypothetical formulation of such an explanation, however, is equivalent with the construction of a possible story, that is, the assumption of a narrative structure from which the image has taken a single cutout." – "Insofar as the shown situation thus creates a *need for explanation* in normal addressees, it suggests the construction of a back-story whose result and final situation corresponds to the situation in the image. Insofar as the shown situation is temporary and unstable and cannot remain the same, it suggests the construction of a further story whose beginning the image represents. A scene is considered *requiring of explanation* when it does not correlate to a culturally standardized type of situation that we perceive as 'normal' and is saved in our mind. It is considered *requiring of a solution* because the displayed situation is perceived to be instable and unsatisfactory within our framework of cultural knowledge, as something which is, culturally speaking, not an acceptable final or permanent condition."[19]

Taking a look at an image narrative of a 'story telling' image, most observers can certainly formulate hypotheses about the "before" and "after", but few will be able to clearly reconstruct the fundamental plot behind the image: "No image that presupposes a narrative structure allows for only *one* possible pre- and/or post-story, but rather defines *a bundle of many possible stories* that shares the same abstract structure."[20] Narrativity in images is thus the result of abduction, or of inference (Wünsch calls it, somewhat clumsily, "presupposition") according to very specific deictic offerings in the image that are seldom clear.[21] Also: not every image tells a story.

4 Discipline-Specific Questions about Images

In light of such difficulties, the formulation of a more strongly defined conception of the rhetoric of images requires a series of definitional stipulations that make a rhetoric of images consistent with and relatable to the fundamentals of broader rhetorical theory. A rhetorical theory of images must be formulated as part of an overall theory of communication. In this context, an image is a fact of communication, despite that it is defined differently in other theoretical contexts. From the rhetorical perspective, image-maker must be seen as an orator, that is, as a communicator with a goal in mind (perhaps in the service of a client) who seeks to reach that goal through the strategic use of a commu-

---

19 Wünsch 1999, pp. 336 f.
20 Wünsch 1999, pp. 340 and 342.
21 For more on abduction, see: Eco 1976, pp. 131 ff.; and chapter 12, pp. 233–236, in this book.

nicative instrument (in this case, the image). Within the rhetorical *organon*, the overall body of rhetorical instruments, either the entire image or individual elements within the image are considered communicative stimuli. Thus, a rhetorical theory of images must also be regarded as part of a more general theory of textuality. The image is seen as a text that seeks to activate reactions of perception and understanding in the viewer through consciously arranged perceptive and conceptual offerings. In this way, the theoretical status of the image is identical to all other types of texts or textures. Accordingly, a rhetorical theory of images must deal with the problems of image production from the perspective of creating stimuli. This production-theoretical viewpoint must focus on consciously constructed messages (Botschaften). Rhetoric thus studies the image creator's attempt to determine the interpretation of their work by viewers with the way that they construct their image. Such an approach is valid for the normal instance of pragmatic pictorial communication that utilizes an image in the service of heteronomic goals.

Highly aestheticized imagery, in which such "determination" can exist despite an author's conscious disregard for particular perceptive and conceptual determination poses a special case.[22] Such examples raise the question of the 'artistic' character of images. From a systematic viewpoint, however, such considerations must be dealt with by other theoretical areas. The core questions of a rhetoric of 'images' must be clearly separated from the concerns of rhetorical theories that deal with specific forms of art and not exclusively with imagery such as painting, photography or sculpture.[23]

According to Aristotle, rhetorical competence consists of the ability of a communicator (here: image-maker) to determine what is persuasive or thought provoking in a given communicative setting. This raises the topic of the *rhetorical factor* in images. This factor must be implemented as a structural offering in order for the desired effects, the least of which being acceptance, to be activated in the audience. That which is considered persuasive in any given image depends on the communicative setting, in particular on the tuning of both interaction partners. In this way, an image-maker must reflect on which instruments he wants to use to best influence his given communication partner; whether to use photographs for a family or paintings for an art connoisseur. Such reflections are the focus of the rhetorical, projective calculation of the addressee and calculation of the means. One of the core concerns of the rhetorical approach to images is that the rhetorical factor is realized through

---

22 Such cases include an increased polyvalence and consider the image itself as an autonomous goal of the efforts of production.
23 Knape 2012c.

decisions made during the production of the image; the structures that function as stimuli must be elaborated. This much must be made clear: the selection and textual combination of design elements demands creativity, enthusiasm, playfulness and intuition on the part of the image maker, whereby intuition is understood as an experience based and rapid mental calculations.

A further focus of a rhetorical theory of images is the role that pictorial texts have in the processes of rhetorical communicative interaction for which the image-orator (the image maker or 'user') must develop strategies. The 'rhetoric' of an image is defined as the strategic calculation (focused on a communicative effect) used in its production. Its potential for interaction (in relation to action theory) is ingrained and structurally sedimented in the pictorial texture. While the controlled use of surprising, deviant, and unconventional means of representation can be considered 'rhetorical', involuntary factors, the effects of uncontrollable semioses and other such elements are not considered rhetorical because they are contingent on a variety of factors, due to uncontrolled processes.

5 Specific Problems of the Image in the Theory of Rhetoric

The description of a rhetoric of images constitutes an expansion of rhetorical theory insofar as the origin of the discipline concerned itself exclusively with verbal language (*rhesis*). In this context, foundational problems of a rhetoric of images may arise from the language-analogy theorem, which holds that all semiotic systems function structurally as verbal language does. I will assume here that this theorem is valid and that problems of analogy at the level of a 'grammar of images' have largely been resolved.[24] The world of rhetoric begins beyond the sphere of grammar, the *ortho*-systems of languages, which rhetoricians take as given. The following discussion thus focuses on a second system of codes, on the rhetorically relevant overcodes, and the theoretical level of the "text".

5.1 Coded Forms of Expression

The intrinsic theory of rhetoric deals with the repertoire of expression and body of rules that have been codified throughout the history of rhetoric and which are available to orators in the production of texts. In its most restrained

---

24 See my cornerstones of image theory in: Knape 2007b, pp. 12 ff.

point of view, the tradition of eloquence rhetoric concentrates on the expectation that such codes are optimally utilized in texts.[25] The actual rhetorical viewpoint, which focuses on communicative efficacy, is suspended in the historical dregs of the once broader theory of persuasive rhetoric. One could also speak here of a kallistic approach (from gr. *kalón*/beauty) which retreats to the rule-based construction of "beautiful" texts. Due to the modern differentiation of theoretical fields, such a de-pragmatized treatment of semiotic topics must be consigned to the theories of poetics or aesthetics. In the wider understanding of rhetoric that is used here, eloquence rhetoric can be juxtaposed with persuasion rhetoric (*ars persuadendi*/the art of persuasion). This form of rhetoric considers the rhetorical factor discussed above to be the single legitimate measure of rhetoriticity. We can speak here of a peithistic approach (from gr. *peithō*/persuasion).

In any case, intrinsic rhetoric deals with a set of rules for production that can be strategically used by an orator and are based on a series of semiotic and textual conventions found in specific (and definable) historical or contemporary communicative groups. The chapters of classical rhetoric that deal with such issues focus on designs for the organization of whole texts. First are the *patterns of genre* (*Gattungsschemata*), which are discussed in chapters on the parts of a speech or the textual modules trained by the progymnasmata. Such works propose ideal tectonic characteristics and standardized content-related elements of textures. Second are the *levels of style*, which recommend the levels of style integrated into texts as the result of a unified and systematically organized selection and combination of characters. Finally, we find chapters on the local phenomena of text production: *coded content* (topics which can take multiple forms and be triggered at certain places in a text) and *structurally defined methods of composition* (doctrine of figures and sentence composition), which recognizably modify and reinforce the texture.

With regard to the linguisticality of images (iconics), we must ask the question whether an analogous chapter of a future, more specific rhetoric of images can be written. The answer is yes, with the qualification that any theoretical-foundational work must be done with attention to detail. First and foremost, we must be clear that there is no ahistorical, universal image-rhetorical over-code. All rhetorical codification (the attribution of forms of expression to expected sensory and cognitive effects) is era specific, despite the fact that many such conventions are passed down from era to era. For an intrinsic rhetoric of images, the dominant conventions of each age must be dug up to deduce

---

25 According to this tradition, rhetoric is considered merely an *ars bene dicendi*, that is, the art of good speaking.

potential rules of production with the goal of constructing an intention-oriented semantics.

Every era has its own *scheme of image genres* (*Bild-Gattungsschemata*), the knowledge of which places the image-orator in a position to select his means according to the specific genre that will best serve relevant viewer expectations or, in the interest of achieving certain effects and according to a maxim of deviance, effectively break such expectations. Nota bene: such consideration must place the rules that apply to the entire image-text in the foreground. Analogous to the classical rhetorical doctrine of the parts of speech, we could refer here to the aesthetic tenants of image composition. The question of the *level of style* in images has been answered differently throughout history. Up until the early modern period, this status was often divided images into the three levels (low, middle, high) found in classical rhetorical theories. An example of this is the *rota Virgilii* scheme, which assigns specific themes, subject matter, and motives to each level respectively. In contrast to this vertical hierarchy stands the more horizontal concept of *stylistic movements* (*Stilrichtungen*), which an orator can factor into his production calculation and which demand entirely different selection criteria (e.g. aesthetics) in choosing the means of expression. So called *individual styles* are only considered rhetorical phenomena when the conventions of the communicative group demand that an image maker display his own individual repertoire of selection in order for his image to be accepted. Because such selection criteria cannot be more generally codified without losing their individual character they do not belong under the purvey of the intrinsic theory of image-rhetoric.

Let us now turn to the local phenomena of texture composition. Different periods have attempted to produce rules and standards for *coded forms of content* in the sense of *topoi* (Topics). The codified handbooks on drawing of the Baroque period, such as those by Gerard de Lairesse (1641–1711), are but one example. Coded forms of expression, such as the *Figura serpentinata* (a snake-like figure coiled upwards to represent strong emotions), also belong within this context. The 20th century saw the rise of Aby Warburg's concept of the "pathos formula", which tries to describe a repertoire of traditional iconographic forms of emotional expression that have remained stable and constant over thousands of years.[26] Indeed, we can identify a pool of coded, appellative visual *formulas of expression* that have been used throughout history.

Such formulas are often derived from specific physical gestures, for instance the 20th century's deictic "you-"appeal exemplified by Uncle Sam's call to arms from 1917 (see Figure 12).

---

26 Knape 2008e.

Figure 12: James Montgomery Flagg: I want YOU for U.S. Army (1917). Poster, Imperial War Museum London. In: Clark 1997, p. 106.

The author of this image, James Flagg, uses this image to underline the meaning of the caption, "I want YOU for U.S. Army"; even without the written caption a viewer can interpret the meaning of "this means you!"

As for the *structurally defined methods of composition*, there have been several attempts to conceive of iconographic rhetorical figures. These attempts have proven theoretically and methodologically disappointing, despite the fact that the transfer approach that they use is warranted in principle. We can demonstrate its legitimacy using the queen of the tropes, the metaphor. If we take the picture of an average hospital room with standard furnishings as the ortho-syntagma "hospital room", then seeing a car laying in the bed would be an 'absolute metaphor' because we see a semantically incompatible element placed within a known syntagma. Since tropes are always based on operations of production that involve local substitution of elements within syntagmata and thus involve a disruption of their semantic compatibility, it can be legitimately postulated that they can be found in images as well. More difficult, however, will be applying the linguistic-text-analogy to rhetorical figures in a narrower sense. Such difficulties arise because such figures are based on the surface operations of the linear processes of speech. Such linearity is not found in images, so that rhetorical figures based on linear positioning (for instance, repetition) can only be analogously construed with difficulty. What would an anaphor, for example, look like in an image?[27] In a consistent application of the linguistic analogy, it would have to be the exactly placed repetition of the same "image-word" within a larger image-syntagma, whereby the location of the beginning of repetitive "image-phrases" (one must avoid applying the term "sentence" in relation to images) would still have to be defined. The difficulties that such an approach would create for any theory of images are immediately clear.

What remains is the chapter of classical rhetorical theory that deals with *sentence composition*. At the verbal-linguistic level, this theory deals with patterns of organized word combinations such as rhyme, meter, etc. For images, we would have to find *formal* (!) criteria according to which image elements can be related to one another. One possibility could be a codified, local scheme of composition such as the *Figura piramidale*.[28]

---

27 Anaphor: Repetition of the same word or group of words at the beginning of successive clauses.

28 The integration of pyramidal triangle patterns within an image (through the arrangement of individual elements for instance) as an expression of harmonious combination and balance.

5.2 Rhetorical Image Interaction

The extrinsic theory of rhetoric primarily concerns itself with communicative *adpragmatization*, the integration of the produced instrument (the image) in communicative processes of interaction by the image-orator (image-maker or -user). The extrinsic perspective of rhetoric is peithistic and investigates the connections between communicative goals (towards which the text as a stimulus is constructed and calibrated) and the conditions of communication. Such investigation must account for the influences of setting (the occasion, addressee, place, time, media, etc.) that have an effect on the successful performance of the text. With this in mind, classical rhetoric developed the concept of the three types of oratorical cases (*genera causarum*): deliberative oratory (politics), judicial oratory (justice) and demonstrative oratory (acts of community). Each of these settings demands that the text be adjusted to fit the conditions of communication. The projective calculation that an orator makes with respect to his setting, the addressees, and the instruments is subject to the fundamental rule of practical rhetoric: the postulate of appropriateness (*aptum*).[29]

For the strategic communicative interaction with images, an analogous system would involve a taxonomy of the typical settings of pictorial communication and their conditional components. The number and character of such settings have changed over the centuries; private settings in particular have become more prominent since the advent of (digital) photography. In general, we can make a variety of distinctions including private/public (a family photo vs. an advertisement) and pragmatic/artistic (journalistic contexts vs. museum contexts). In all of these settings, different perceptions, interpretations, and expectations play an important role. As a stimulus, an image should be calibrated to fit such circumstances. The orator's calculation of interaction must also include an analysis of the circumstances of the rhetorical *agōn*.[30]

6 Methodical Procedures

The preceding discussion has, I believe, made clear that rhetoric does not see itself as a purely hermeneutic discipline, does not exhaust itself in the analyti-

---

29 To put it another way, an orator must attempt to predict how his addressee will react and which stimuli he can use to most effectively meet his goals. He must also calibrate all of the available factors of communication to match the concrete setting.
30 Namely, what other images must I compete with in the same communicative space and how should I react to such competition to meet my goals?

cal as philology and art history normally do. Historical analyses of the production of texts, the communicative actions of image-orators, and their identifiable effects have only heuristic significance for the theoretic approach to production and interaction in rhetoric (which is always focused on these perspectives). This heuristic must remain constant, however, because the type of contextual conditions we are discussing and their respective rules change continually over time within the fields of behavioral science.

Classical rhetoric developed a formal methodical approach to production and interaction that divided the work of an orator into a six-stage model. This model has proven both practical and efficient over the last few thousand years and focuses, as always in rhetoric, on the problems that an orator deals with in the production of his stimulus and its adpragmatization (integration into communicative interactions). These six oratorical tasks (*officia*) are not limited to the field of rhetoric; they are universal insofar as they are factors of any given production and use of textures (be they musical, linguistic, or pictorial). Naturally, these tasks can be entirely rhetorically conceptualized if we consciously focus on the aspects of each stage that are concerned with the *rhetorical factor*. In this case, the central question of each stage of production is identifying that which best serves the orator's purposes; that which best creates the rhetorical effect. It is important to note here that the rhetorical effect is not understood as a mere exchange of information or exchange of data (a man with a hat is pointing at the viewer, see Figure 12). Instead, it lies in the action oriented side of expression which is, in a certain sense, analogous to the concept of action found in speech act theory (a demand should be made of viewers). The rhetorically central element of persuasion isn't based on neutral observations of the world or pure information exchange, on purely quantitative changes in cognition (addition, subtraction, regrouping of knowledge, etc.). Persuasion only occurs where there is a change of judgment, valuation, opinion or attitude according to one of the following seven aspects of orientation:[31]

Instructive:	something is x and not y
Verificitive:	it is true/false, probable/improbable
Evaluative:	it is good/bad, beautiful/ugly, etc.
Axiomative:	it is valid or invalid
Emotive:	it should be loved/hated
Voluntative:	it should be done/not done
Direct-Stimulative:	it evokes spontaneous reactions

---

31 Knape 2008a, pp. 920–923.

These orientations are directed at distinctions and internal decisions. Rhetoric calls the effects of these aspects of orientation the *persuasive factor* of communication. This factor, when successful, leads to a certain mental state, which we call *zertum (certainty)*. In the short term this is manifested as a change of opinion, in the long term as a change of attitude. The *zertum* that arises from orientation change can, but need not, lead to behavior change on the part of the addressee. What follows is an outline of the six stages of production as applied to the rhetoric of images. Although they are laid out numerically, they need not necessarily occur in a strict chronological order.

0 Intellection: This stage deals with the specialized planning and thought that goes into conceptualizing the entire work in relation to an overall goal before production begins. Notably, an image-maker must consider his communicative goals (to trigger memories of a vacation or to the creation of church decorations) and possible points of resistance (constraints, guidelines, or consumer expectations) that might arise from their given communicative setting.

1 Invention: The stage of invention represents the first step in concrete work on the image-text and involves the practices of discovery and invention. Such thought considers contents, intellectual concepts, and above all strategies of persuasion that serve an overarching communicative goal and which guide the production of the work. We call this the calculation of content and concept. The main concern here is to identify thematic elements (including *topoi*) that are conducive to the pre-set goal and what should be "brought up" (more specifically: "put on display") with the image.

2 Disposition: The disposition considers perceivable order and structures within the whole image (as opposed to parts of the image). Relevant here is the 'architecture' of the image as a text, which suggests coded syntagmata that may serve the goals of production. The most well-known recommendation is the "golden section" (*sectio aurea*), in which a spatial syntagma is divided unevenly into two parts such that the ratio of the length of the entire work to the larger area is the same as the ratio of the larger area to the smaller one (A is to B as B is to C). This pattern can then be repeated *ad infinitum* within the smaller area of the image. In general, principles of composition deal with geometrically comprehensible models of symmetry and order, such as axiality, centering, and diagonality. These models are only rhetorically interesting insofar as they are anchored in a communicative community as perceptual and cognitive conventions (based, perhaps, on little more than viewing habits). Only then can an image-orator integrate such elements into his image calculation (often with the intention of breaking expectations through the use of deviant representation). In modern times, this entire complex has been associated with the larger themes of perspective and perspectivation, including the framing and angle of the camera in photography, as important mechanisms of selection in the production of images.

3 Elocution: As it concerns verbal language, this stage deals with textualization. It addresses the question of how one can arrange particular formulations into discrete textual units. What kinds of solutions can I find for problems that may arise in the design of individual segments of my image? Which elements of which overcodes (e.g. tropes, figures, or ornaments) should I include? To this calculation of "formulation" we must also add the recurring question of the semiotic mix, which can compensate for the structural deficits of particular symbolic systems. In an image, for instance, it is often contemplated how to make up for the fact that pictorial signs and image-texts (by definition 'stills') cannot display time, cannot show abstracta or collectiva in the linguistic sense.[32] Often this deficit is offset through combination with other, usually linguistic symbolic systems (realized in writing). The "Uncle Sam's Army" advertisement (see Figure 12) is a prime example: the message is made clear (and thus discrete) only through the written text.

4 Memoria: This stage of production deals with saving the text. In the ancient age of oral histories, the rhetorical mnemonic was entirely focused on the corporeal medium (the body as memory) within which verbal texts were generally to be saved. Accordingly, a range of memory techniques were developed to help train orators to remember their texts. Since that time, a multitude of body-externalized technical media have been developed to save texts. A precondition here is a categorical differentiation between the levels of text and medium (and medial system).[33] For the rhetoric of images, this means the following: according to a rigorous definition of a medium, media (book, magazine, drawing paper, painting, world wide web, etc.) are understood as the platform upon which image-textures are placed. Viewed through the lens of text theory, media theory is a theory of platforms. In relation to the *memoria* stage of production, the part of rhetoric that deals with media demands that a media calculation take place that examines which media (as platforms for image-texts) seem to have the highest prospects for success. Should an image of a battle best be presented on a postcard or as a painting? In the interest of its rhetorical efficacy, is the Uncle Sam image-text above best disseminated on television, on leaflets, or as a billboard poster? The complex relationship

---

32 This does not include symbols that incorporate elements of the image code!
33 Cf. chapter 13 in this volume.

between image-text and medium yields a series of interesting theoretical and practical questions for a rhetorical theory of images.[34]

5 Action: The final stage of production in classical theory deals with the performance of the text in a rhetorically relevant contexts of interaction. For our purposes, this stage involves the presentation of the medialized image-text; the text is set free to interact with the perception and understanding of the addressee(s). The performance of the pictorial text in communicative interactions (be it a slide show for the family, placards in a demonstration, presentation in a museum, a vernissage in an art gallery, or an advertising pillar on a busy street corner) is, in and of itself, a rhetorically relevant topic. In classical rhetoric, the theoretical chapter on *actio* focuses almost exclusively on forms of expression using the body as a medium (considerations of body language, mimic, gestures and intonation that a speaker should utilize in the performance of his text). Analogous here would be a rhetoric of image medialization. This field would concentrate on the question of which characteristic forms of expression of image carrying media play a role in rhetorical interactions (such as the expression of a picture frame, the uneven surface of a painting, or the screen of a PC).[35]

---

[34] One particularly interesting question is found in the exploration of the reciprocal influences that each has on the other.

[35] A shorter German version of this chapter in: Knape 2005e.

12 On a Theory of the Rhetoric of Feature Films

The experience of watching and listening to a film is like sitting in a moving train and looking out different windows to the outside world. For the passenger in the train, it seems that the outside world is flying by at high speeds and his view is constantly changing depending on which window he looks out of: whether it's his own window, the window across the aisle from him, or the view out of the window in the door looking out the back of the train. Out each of these windows, the passenger sees a different part of the world zipping by. Despite the fact that each window only gives our passenger a small glimpse of the ever changing landscape, he knows that they are all connected together in one continual reality.

The rhetorical question in watching a film is whether and how one can influence the thoughts of the viewer by changing the sights and sounds that he experiences. Through the constantly changing images and sounds on the screen, the observer gets a series of 'glimpses through the window' at a virtual, medialized, and artificial world. Historically speaking, the archetypical form of this type of artificially induced viewing experience has been found in theatrical staging. The philosopher Aristotle, the archeget of rhetorical theory, wrote as early as Greek antiquity about the issues involved in designing and implementing such viewer experiences.

1 Difficulties Associated with Rhetoric in Modern Film Studies

At the outset of the 21st century, a theory of film rhetoric that appropriately focuses on the rhetorical question remains underdeveloped. Works that suitably approach the topic are few and far between.[1] Some of the most recent contributions on this topic, published in 2008, reinforce this skepticism: an essay by Helmut Schanze, 'The Rhetoric of Cinematography' ultimately leads nowhere, and the title of Gesche Joost's published dissertation 'Picture-Language (Bildsprache)' makes it clear that there is little in the way of categorical clarity involved in her work.[2] Joost's dissertation does not actually deal with "picture-language" as such, but rather the aesthetic structures of feature films. Thus, it is no surprise to the informed reader that the book's treatment of

---

[1] An example of such work can be found in John Harrington's rhetorical/persuasion theoretical approach; Harrington 1973.
[2] Schanze 2008; Joost 2008.

rhetorical theory (which is implicit in the subtitle 'The audio-visual rhetoric of film') is misleading at best. To be fair, this obvious helplessness in dealing with the problems of feature film rhetoric is found in older works as well: Anke-Marie Lohmeier's article 'The Rhetoric of Film' in the Historical Dictionary of Rhetoric is but one example.[3]

Although Gesche Joost's book offers an extensive survey of modern research in the area of film studies and formulates a structural analysis that is based on different observations, it is, at its intellectual core, unable to deal with the complicated state of relevant theories of rhetoric. The book is marked by a haphazard use of terminology and a deep misunderstanding about the overall rhetorical approach and the question of the rhetorical factor in feature films. It is startling for the rhetorician to see how a host of different categories, which are normally (and quite correctly) classified as belonging to the field of film aesthetics, are mercilessly lumped together under the obviously misunderstood label of *Rhetoric*.[4] It is no wonder then that Joost's book fails to depict the *aesthetics* of feature film as the natural theoretical counterpart to the *rhetoric* of feature film.[5] Due to the lack of a clear conception of the rhetorical factor in feature films, Joost takes refuge in the vague traditional category of "intended effect."[6] With the help of this category, which she obviously claims exclusively for the field of rhetoric, she then proceeds to identify just about everything that happens in a feature film as rhetorical. With these premises as a starting point, Joost's analysis transforms film-aesthetic calculations of effect into rhetorical ones and treats all types of structures under the rubric of classi-

---

3 Lohmeier 1996.

4 Here we see a form of the *aesthetic fallacy* that is often made by laypersons (cf. pp. 25 f. in this book). For various reasons over the course of history, a series of text structures have been codified under the framework of rhetorical theory, in particular the so called 'rhetorical figures'. Such structures, however, are rhetorically non-specific, and can also be integrated into texts based on aesthetic calculations. Thus, the rhetorical figures represent an intersection in the histories of poetics, aesthetics, and rhetoric. This can lead to fallacies in the systematic use of rhetorical terminology. Just because the figure 'metaphor' was described by Aristotle in his 'Rhetoric' as a text structural phenomenon, for instance, doesn't mean that the appearance of a metaphor in a poem has anything to do with rhetoric: it may simply reflect the informational or aesthetic desires of the author.

5 The term aesthetics is used parenthetically only twice in the entire work. In one case, Joost mentions Eisenstein's use of reflecting light, "to aestheticize and elevate the object" (here: a kettle): Joost 2008, p. 182. Her second use of the term is in a quote from Bernd Spillner commenting on audio-visual figures, where he describes the system of rhetorical figures and tropes, "as a system of ready-made argumentative and aesthetic structures." Spillner 1974, p. 102.

6 Joost 2008, pp. 30 f.

cal rhetorical terminology. Under this conception, every film *motive,* for instance, is directly converted to a rhetorical *topos,* etc.

The theoretical weaknesses of this and other works on the topic of feature film rhetoric all stem from ambiguity in the use of two main categories: "feature film" and "rhetoric". Most available literature that seeks to bring the terms "feature film" and "rhetoric" together still suffer from numerous fundamental misunderstandings, an insufficient ability to differentiate between categories, scarce systematic clarity in regard to the field of rhetoric, and a lack of perspective with respect to the specific features of both motion pictures and rhetoric. Such articles still work with an imperialistic conception of rhetoric, within which aspects of film, picture and media theory as well as viewpoints from fields such as semiotics, aesthetics and art history are incorporated, integrated and mixed without hesitation. These articles thus never approach the question of how rhetoric differentiates itself from other disciplines. At the same time, *the film* is treated as speech, often without any further differentiation into genres. Such approval allows an ostensible and offhand analysis of the material at a narrative and speech act theoretical level.[7] We now find ourselves faced with the central questions of this essay: how does communication with feature films work? Is it possible to incorporate the feature film (as an artificial creation) directly into the practical textual category of "speech" without modification? If this is the case, it would allow for a direct transfer of the rhetorical approach to the analysis of the rhetoric of feature films. Finally, how is the genre of "feature film" differentiated from other genres of film (in particular documentary film)?

We shall begin our discussion of these fundamental questions by considering the *movie theater* or *cinema* (German: *Kino*) as the medium of film. The cinema as a medium (that is, a "device used to save and perform texts") is extremely complex at a concrete technical level.[8] In order to fulfill its two theoretically relevant and inseparable leistungen (functions), saving and performance, the cinema requires vast and diverse technical machinery that stretch from the site of production (the film set) at the studio to the movie

---

7 In such cases where the term "speech" is used metaphorically, and thus improperly, the word no longer has the value that it *should* have as a formal scholarly term. On the other hand, if the term "speech" can be given an appropriate place within the framework of formal rhetorical classifications, it would allow researchers to answer the question of whether the communicative activities in film can legitimately be assigned the status of "speech" that purely verbal interaction has within rhetorical theory. For considerations of speech act theory in this context see also: Kanzog 2001. For a discussion of the fundamental problems in applying speech act theory to works of art see: Knape 2008a, pp. 899–905.

8 Knape 2005c, p. 22.

projector in the theater itself.[9] The technical complexity of the media variants television and video is also quite high for them to be easily called 'media' under the strict definition common in contemporary rhetorical theory today.[10] Only through the use of such technical devices is it possible to deliver a product such as film as a text (cf. pp. 198 f. in this volume) to an audience. To put it another way: someone creates a feature film under the specific conditions demanded by the medium 'cinema' and places it in a communicative event (by showing it in a public theater, for instance) such that it becomes an act of communication that other people can do something with. I have specifically chosen this vague mode of expression; it is by no means easy to say how or what, exactly, the people watching a feature film in a movie theater *do* with what they see. For the rhetorician, the question is even more specific: how does the audience deal with the feature film in the *rhetorical* sense? Before we can begin to address this question there are a few points about the result of the film production process that need to be discussed: the communicative status of the film, as such, must be established.

What is a film in communication? As opposed to its medium (the cinema), a film takes the role of the 'text', according to the expanded definition of the term accepted in semiotics.[11] As a text (or texture), film must also be divided into a variety of genres. These genres (today also routinely called "formats") not only determine the production of film but also, to a high degree, its reception (in the form of audience expectations for the genre).

When analyzing feature film in particular, a further category of considerations must be taken into account that has influenced artistic communication since antiquity: the category of the *opus*.[12] An "opus", or "work", is an artifact that has been created according to some kind of aesthetic principles and which has been released into the communicative space as a *text*.[13] It is important that such a text is conceived as an independent entity that can be released from

---

9 This understanding of "medium" is close to the *apparatus*-theory in Heath 1980; and Baudry 1986.

10 Cf. chapter 13.

11 In this sense: a bounded, ordered complex of signs arranged with communicative intention. In modern film making, this is constructed from a variety of different codes and impulses at the levels of general visuality, moving pictures, tonality and sound. For more on the extremely multi-layered semiotic complexity of film texts and a theoretical division of the levels of code, text/texture, medium and media system see: Knape 2005c, pp. 22–28.

12 Knape 2008a, pp. 896 f.

13 In modern theories of poetics and film, the concept of "closure" is important in defining the boundaries of a text, "the notion of closure is connected to the sense of finality with which a piece of music, a poem, a story, or a typical movie concludes. It is the impression that exactly the point where the work does end is just the *right* point." Carroll 2008, p. 134.

the "circumstances of speech" and used in others (we may call it 'de-pragmatization').[14] The question of whether or not said work is "art" does not necessarily play a role here. In Aristotelian theory, such a text has the status of a *poiēma*, that is, an artificially created artifact. Today, the concept of *opus* is used to describe an artifact (for instance a feature film) that has been released into communicative space by a particular author (creator). Such a term is used in order to express certain expectations that the audience should have about the work itself. These expectations are due to the assumption that individual producers create their works with ambitious and intrinsic calculations. Classic feature films force the audience to assume that they are opuses due to their special circumstances of medialization and their separation from normal and direct daily communicative structures of discourse.

In the case of a rhetorical analysis of Fritz Lang's feature film 'M', it is critically important to establish that this work belongs to the genre *feature film* (and in particular to the sub-genre of detective film) and is not, for instance, a documentary or other genre of film. Why is this so important? The genre of feature film is subject to certain aesthetic constraints that underlie the dispositions and modalities of all artistic (and related) kinds of specialized communication.[15] Unlike documentary films, which have the function of presenting facts of the world to audience members, feature films focus on and play with the creation of virtual realities and possible worlds as "cultural creations," in short, on fictionality.[16] The goal of this type of *text* is thus to enable viewers to experience an imaginary and simulated reality. The feature film shows us a fundamentally artificial phenomenon as we know it from theater: that in the moment of performance our perceptions are manipulated such that an illusion of reality is created. To put it another way, in looking through the "train window" of a film, we are tricked into thinking that we are looking at a real and complete world. This theatrical representation traces its roots to the classical literary genre of *drama*, for which Aristotle wisely developed an entire theory as early as Greek antiquity: his 'Poetics'.

2 The Proto-Theory of Drama (and Feature Film)

What can Aristotle's theory offer us today?[17] At its core it is a theory of simulation (mimesis) through the use of texts. It is important to note that his theory

---

14 Cf. Bühler 1934, p. 418.
15 Knape 2008a, pp. 898–906.
16 Eco 1987, p. 164; for more information on possible world theories see also: Knape 2006d.
17 Cf. Hiltunen 2001.

of poetics stands in contrast to a theory of rhetoric; it is no coincidence that Aristotle wrote completely separate works about these two topics. The central question of the 'Poetics' is how to construct texts that focus on the actions (gr. *drāma*[18] or *práxis*) of people. Aristotle's focus arises from his production theoretical definition of tragedy. The creation of tragedy in the production of texts is a simulation,

> of an action that is heroic and complete and of a certain magnitude – by means of language enriched with all kinds of ornament, each used separately in the different parts of the play: it represents men in action and does not use narrative (*apangelía*), and through pity and fear it effects relief to these and similar emotions (*páthēmata*).[19]

This definition contains the following propositions:
1. The fundamental theme of the poetics of drama is the presentation of simulated, illusionary representations (which can be subsumed under term *mímesis*) and *not* narration.
2. The subjects of these simulations are actions, or rather, acting beings. Aristotle's theory of drama does not include the setting itself; thus the extremely realistic simulated environments as we know them from contemporary feature films are excluded here.
3. The simulations should evoke strong emotions in the audience (pity and terror in tragedies and laughter about the ridiculous or ugly in comedies).
4. Evoking such strong emotions should cause a release of tension and psychological relaxation in the audience. This should lead to a general peace of mind and move audience members to quiet and deliberate contemplation; it should create a space for conscious reflection ("Denkraum der Besonnenheit"[20]).

By emphasizing the first aspect of tragedy (simulation), Aristotle made two important and categorical distinctions. In modern terms, his concern was a focus on the aesthetics of fiction, and his work began a foundational tradition in the history of European aesthetics.[21] He thus makes a clear distinction between *narration* (*apangelía* or *dihēgesis*) and *displayed* but *fictional simula-*

---

18 The dramatic works of Sophocles and others were, "called 'dramas,' because they present people as doing (*drōntas*) things." Aristotle: Poetics, 3.4.
19 Aristotle: Poetics, 6.2.
20 Warburg 1920, p. 267.
21 For Aristotle, structural aesthetics (what Gérard Genette, in reference to verbal texts, called "the aesthetics of diction") are subordinate. In the Roman theory of poetics from Horace, on the other hand, structural aesthetics are given top priority. See: Genette 1991; Knape 2006a, pp. 56 and 58.

tion (*mímesis*). This contrast is well described by Henry James as the pair of opposites *telling* and *showing*.[22]

In the case of the theoretical analysis of feature films, a distinction must also be made between two regulative components: the fictional and the structural aesthetics of film. On the one hand, fictional aesthetics demands, for instance, that the plot follow a planned script. On the other, the structural constraints of things like lighting, setting, camerawork, and editing must be taken into account as well. Modern researchers disagree as to what extent modern feature films can be linked to the classical aesthetics of drama and the concomitant exclusion of narrativity. As so often happens in the humanities, however, such disagreement is largely a result of the lack of clear theoretical frameworks and the lax use of discrete analytical terminology. Even the "classical" theorist James Monaco was thus unsure of how to address this issue in his book, 'How to Read a Film'.[23] It is fitting that he repeatedly loses his way terminologically, given the generally superficial way he addresses the issue of the dramatic character of feature films.[24] After due consideration, Monaco dismisses the analogy between the novel and feature film *in principle*, but remains terminologically trapped within the categorical system of narrativity. The reason for this is the lack of a clear and solid theoretical foundation. In the section titled "Film and Theater" Monaco comes to the conclusion that:

> On the surface, theatrical film seems most closely comparable to stage drama. Certainly the roots of the commercial film in the early years of this [the 20th] century lie there. But film differs from stage drama in several significant respects: it has the vivid, precise visual potential of the pictorial arts; and it has much greater narrative capability.[25]

Let us begin our assessment of this statement with the, "great narrative capability" of film as he calls it. With this careless recourse to narratological terminology Monaco throws away a chance to specifically define what he really means. Instead, over the course of his comparison he comes to the conclusion that the 'scene' forms the basic unit of dramatic construction in both film and

---

22 See: Knape 2006a, p. 107.

23 Monaco 1981. It is thought provoking that this book follows the philological dictum that fails to clearly define the semiotic distinctiveness of film textures. The title of the book itself implies that films have something in common with written text, which one can "read" through watching and interpreting the film itself. Klaus Kanzog's work, 'Introduction to the Philology of Film' also demonstrates a similar misunderstanding of the distinction to be drawn between film texts and written texts. See: Kanzog 1991.

24 One example of this is his use of the term "dramatic narration", which is in itself a theoretical *contradictio in adiecto*. Monaco 1981, p. 33.

25 Monaco 1981, p. 33.

theater, and that the core purpose of each scene is to '*show, not tell*' what is outlined in the script. It is important to note that Aristotle also focuses on the role of the script in drama. Both the playwright and the screenplay writer are obligated to sketch 'showing phenomena' and not to prepare elaborate narrations. Aristotle names 6 different analytical categories within drama, and in tragedy in particular:

A. The fictional-aesthetic level of the dramatic text/screenplay: The scenes that are strung together by the dramatic writer are normally required to have some sort of coherency, within which various figures, each with their own character and personality (*ēthos*/image), perform a series of actions that constitute a story (*mýthos*, lat. *fabula*). Theories of drama and narratology meet in poetology at the deep-structural level of *texts*, i.e. at the level of the story or fable.[26]

According to Aristotle, the sequence of actions in both drama and narrative can be condensed into stories.[27] This sentiment has led many modern film theorists to insist that the feature film be considered part of narrative rather than dramatic theory.[28]

The fact remains, however, that feature films, like theatrical performances, display the fiction of virtual realities before our eyes. Thus, these forms of communication are predicated on theatrical *deíxis* (showing) and not *dihēgesis* (telling); it is exactly this factor that differentiates both theater and feature films from narrative prose. The underlying fable establishes a chain of events that the plot itself need not completely depict: "this also happens in [feature] films: two people kiss, a few months fall off a calendar, and we see a child in

---

26 In this respect, it is legitimate for Umberto Eco to refer to, "narrative structures in nonnarrative texts": Eco 1987, p. 132. Eco, following the Russian formalists, distinguishes more specifically between the analytical categories of *fable* and *plot*: "the fable is the foundational schema of [a given narration], the logic of the narration, the syntax of the individual [characters], the chronologically ordered chain of events." The plot, by contrast, is the actual story that is placed in from of our eyes, "exactly as it appears on the surface, with its chronological shifts, jumps, and the fade-ins of past and future events (through foreshadowing or flash-backs)." Eco 1987, p. 128.

27 "Someone once claimed that the fable of *Oedipus the King* [Sophocles' drama] could be summarized with the phrase, 'find the culprit!'." Eco 1987, p. 129.

28 It is often quite clear in modern film studies literature that researchers have no problem with discussing feature films in an un-terminological and metaphorically lax way. Thus we see Harrington refer "figuratively" to a "camera-as-narrator" phenomenon while in the same context asserting that the camera itself is merely a technical device that simply functions as an extension of the director's will, "the camera 'looks' where and in the fashion the director and cameraman cause it to look." Harrington 1973, p. 89.

a crib. What happened in the interim?"[29] In this way, the feature film works with a series of leerstellen (blanks)[30] that for some reason don't actually bother the viewers.[31] To explain this phenomenon, Umberto Eco introduces the concept of the "inferential stroll": using his general knowledge about the world, the viewer of a feature film (like the reader of a novel) can infer the omitted actions in the plot. In filling in these gaps, the viewer takes, "an inferential stroll through the extratextual universe of intertextuality:" he activates his memories of similar situations in other feature films that he has seen, "and waits to see whether the situation depicted by the fable confirms or refutes his predictions."[32]

Aristotle's theory assigns a crucial function to the story in dramatic texts (and screenplays), one which is at the core of every drama. The story should trigger the most important effect of fictional-aesthetic construction: strong sentiments and emotions. Until it is performed on the stage or in the cinema, the written drama (in the case of the feature film, the screenplay) does, in fact, have similarities to pure narrative:

> Fear and pity sometimes result from the spectacle (*ópsis*) and are sometimes aroused by the actual arrangement of the incidents, which is preferable and the mark of the better poet. The plot should be so constructed that even without seeing the play anyone hearing of the incidents happening thrills with fear and pity as a result of what occurs. So would anyone feel who heard the story of Oedipus.[33]

Ideally, the decisive emotional trigger of a dramatic text should be found in the story itself.

How can we describe the method by which psychological states are triggered by dramatic texts? Aristotle's theory is very clear on this point: the emotional effect is caused by an appeal to our aesthetic 'libido', "since the poet must by 'representation' [simulation/*mímesis*] produce the pleasure (*hēdonē*) which comes from feeling pity and fear, obviously this quality must be embodied in the incidents."[34]

We can now turn our attention to another category within Aristotle's theory of drama: the concept of the dramatic figure, with their individual characteristics (*ēthos*/image) and personal constitution. In modern feature film, the dramatic figure has a unique status, which was described by Walter Benjamin in

---

29 Eco 1987, p. 260.
30 Iser 1970, pp. 15 ff.
31 See also: Barth/Gärtner/Neumann-Braun 1997; and Kimmich 2003.
32 Eco 1987, p. 260.
33 Aristotle: Poetics, 14.1.
34 Aristotle: Poetics, 14.5.

his essay, 'The Work of Art in the Age of Mechanical Reproduction'.[35] In section 8 of this essay, Benjamin describes the difference between primary and secondary mediality (as we would call it today) in terms of the experience that the actors themselves have.[36] In introducing the topic, Benjamin wrote, "The artistic leistung (performance) of a stage actor is definitely presented to the public by the actor in person; that of the screen actor, however, is presented by a camera."[37] Modern rhetoric calls this phenomenon 'dimission', that is, communication over a distance of space and time without the physical presence of the communicator. According to Benjamin, the technical reproduction of the acting performance in film, the secondary mediality, has, "a twofold consequence. The camera that presents the performance of the film actor to the public need not respect the performance as an integral whole. Guided by the cameraman, the camera continually changes its position with respect to the performance."[38] Benjamin calls the medial obstacles that every aesthetic communicator and indeed, all orators, have to deal with the "statement" (Stellungnahme) that the camera makes about the original theatrical output (Leistung):

> The sequence of statements which the editor composes from the material supplied him constitutes the completed film. It comprises certain factors of movement which are in reality those of the camera, not to mention special angles, close-ups, etc. Hence, the output of the actor is subjected to a series of optical tests.[39]

The "statement" of cinema as a medium exists as a series of "optical tests", through which each film text is given a new layer of secondary mediality. "This is the first consequence of the fact that the actor's performance (Leistung) is presented by means of a camera."[40] We can attribute the second consequence of such film medialization to the loss of the ability to intervene; as Benjamin says,

---

35 Benjamin 1939. This work is quoted here with a small variance in the translation of terminology.

36 For more on the difference between these two forms of mediality, see: Knape 2000a, p. 100.

37 Benjamin 1939, p. 259. Benjamin speaks here of the "output" or craft (Leistung) which the actor brings to the stage. This makes it clear that he views the actor as an aesthetic communicator whose capacity as an orator has something to do with the artistic work he is representing. From the rhetorical perspective, we could say that the artist acts as a sort of "artistic communicator" within the frame of his art. When he acts within this role as an orator (that is, when he should be persuasive with his art) then his artistic work is the field in which he interacts with his colleagues in an agōn. In this case the artistic output itself, *as art,* should be persuasive.

38 Benjamin 1939, p. 259.

39 Benjamin 1939, p. 259.

40 Benjamin 1939, p. 259.

the film actor lacks the opportunity of the stage actor to adjust [his craft or output] to the audience during his performance, since he does not present his output to the audience in person. This permits the audience to take the position of a critic, without experiencing any personal contact with the actor. The audience's identification with the actor is really identification with the apparatus. Consequently the audience takes the position of the apparatus; the approach is that of testing. This is not the approach to which cultural values may be exposed.[41]

So far so good. The concluding sentence of the above mentioned quote is, however, somewhat confusing. This sentence may allude to a sort of conservative credo that stemmed from Benjamin's well-educated, middle-class background. What is this sentence supposed to mean? Apodictically speaking, the statement is problematic at best. By "cultural values" Benjamin seems to be referring to the classical dramas, which, upon being filmed, are subjected to the effects of dimission in the form of secondary medialization. The section at hand focuses on the specific performance of acting that takes place on the stage, which seems to be central to the concept of "cultural values". Benjamin asserts that the secondary medialization through film harms the "cultural value" status that classical dramas (and the acting within them) have traditionally had. Today, one might reply that while such stage dramas certainly *are* subjected to the effects of double-, or even multi-medialization (through the convergence of media), this merely creates new aesthetic possibilities. Such dramas are first formulated into written texts, are then performed and dramatically medialized on the stage, and subsequently further medialized into various cinematic and electronic media. At every stage of this process, highly organized, multi-coded textures occur, each with their own unique character and place within the aesthetic realm. For us it is clear: the modern viewer "tests" whether the new layer of textuality is consistent with the new medium. Thus it is sometimes the case that first-class stage productions are considered complete failures when technically reproduced in cinema or television (e.g. if the television production of a stage performance is not appropriate for the medial constraints of television).

Benjamin quotes the then recently deceased Italian Nobel prize winner Luigi Pirandello discussing how, in comparison to the stage actor,

The film actor feels as if in exile – exiled not only from the stage, but from himself. With a vague sense of discomfort he feels inexplicable emptiness: his body loses corporeality, it is deprived of reality, life, voice, and the noises caused by his moving about, in order to change into a mute image, flickering an instant on the screen, then vanishing into silence.[42]

---

41 Benjamin 1939, pp. 259 f.
42 Benjamin 1939, p. 260.

For Benjamin, this sentiment captures the loss of an aura, which we understand as an epiphenomenon of the transition from situation to dimission.[43] Benjamin comments,

> for the first time – and this is the effect of film – man has to operate with his whole living person, yet forgoing his aura. For aura is tied to his presence; there can be no replica of it. The aura which, on stage, emanates from Macbeth, cannot be separated for the spectators from that of the actor. However, the singularity of the shot in the studio is that the apparatus is substituted for the public. Consequently, the aura that envelops the actor vanishes, and with it, the aura of the figure he portrays.[44]

In a world of dimissive communication, however, the modern 'cult' of the movie star can create a sort of ersatz aura at the level of meta-communication:

> The film responds to the shriveling of the aura with an artificial build-up of the 'personality' outside of the studio. The cult of the movie star, fostered by the money of the film industry, preserves not the unique aura of a person but the 'spell of personality,' the phony spell of a commodity.[45]

B. The structural-aesthetic level of style: The scenes performed in a drama are not acted out or realized non-verbally, but rather with a specific, aesthetically calculated repertoire of linguistic formulations (*léxis*) and melodics (*melopoiía*), which in film forms the soundtrack. According to Aristotle, "by 'diction' I mean here the metrical arrangement of the words; and 'song-making' I use in the full, obvious sense of the word."[46] With this sentiment we can bridge the linguistic, aural, and visual elements of feature film.

This perspective led commentators to compare film with visual art at an early stage, despite the fact that visuality is the only *tertium comparationis* between still images and moving film. All the same, such comparisons accentuate the specific characteristics of feature film. James Monaco is right when he says that the feature film activates, "the vivid, precise visual potential of the pictorial arts," better than theater, because modern technology has allowed the feature film to move ever farther in the direction of other visual arts.

In this vein, Walter Benjamin wrote about the new conditions of reception created by the cinema experience. According to Benjamin, the aesthetic experience of "immersion", as individually experienced when viewing an auratic

---

43 For more on the difference between these two fundamental settings see: Knape 2005c, pp. 30 f.; cf. p. 15 in this volume.
44 Benjamin 1939, p. 260.
45 Benjamin 1939, p. 261.
46 Aristotle: Poetics, 6.4.

painting, is no longer desirable in 20th century art. Rather, this form of aesthetic experience is considered part of the, "school of antisocial behavior," because during it, the individual isolates themselves from their connection to the social surroundings; they isolate themselves from the democratic public around them. Benjamin contrasts this experience of "immersion" with a modern category of, "distraction as a game of social behavior." This observation shows just how clairvoyant Benjamin was in his analysis of the new circumstances created by film. Marshall McLuhan, writing almost 30 years later, used such a theory in his 1962 book 'The Gutenberg Galaxy'. "Immersion" (also described as "contemplation" or "collection") is seen as a forced method of reception from the age of the sola scriptura. Writing forces its viewers to conscious awareness and contemplative concentration. The new techno-codes, to use Flusser's terminology,[47] set free modern forms of reception. In the Gutenberg Galaxy, such forms of reception were suspect. Benjamin calls such new modalities of experience "distraction" or dispersion. The viewer, sitting in front of a screen displaying a motion picture, can no longer give himself to "contemplation" or "abandon himself to his associations" as he could in front of a still image. Instead, with motion pictures, "no sooner has his eye grasped a scene than it has already changed," which interrupts his mental process of association. Benjamin here cites Georges Duhamel's description of the cinema experience in 1930, "I can no longer think what I want to think. My thoughts have been replaced by moving images."[48]

C. The performative level of theatrical/cinematographic 'showing': According to Aristotle's theory, the first qualitative component of dramatic theory is the 'staging' (*ópsis*/appearance or view). He places performance in such a prominent position, "since the representation [simulation] is performed by living persons, it follows at once that one essential part of a tragedy is the spectacular effect".[49] With this statement, Aristotle addresses the performative level of drama and directly links it with the performance of the actors. The audience member experiences a drama first and foremost as a theatrical performance. This is why Aristotle mentions *ópsis* as the first building block of dramas, despite that fact that, overall, he makes it clear that the written text of a drama (or the screenplay of a film) is the most important part.

The main effect of a drama, namely the arousal of emotions (in tragedies pity and terror), *can* be triggered by the staging itself, but, "to produce this effect by means of an appeal to the eye is inartistic and needs adventitious

---

47 Flusser 1996, pp. 158–208; cf. Knape 2000e, pp. 14–17.
48 Benjamin 1939, p. 267.
49 Aristotle: Poetics, 6.5.

aid."[50] It is possible, by means of things like sound effects and theatrical tricks (in feature films this includes all kinds of special effects) to evoke particular emotions, especially when the plot or the characters themselves fail to do so. Aristotle refers here specifically to devices used to evoke horror in the audience, "Aristotle criticizes such wonders that defy the laws of nature as mere 'thrills', which are presented for their own sake alone."[51] Further, "those who by such means produce an effect which is not fearful but merely monstrous have nothing in common with tragedy. For one should not seek from tragedy all kinds of pleasure (*hēdonē*) but that which is peculiar to tragedy".[52]

An inquiry into the performative conditions opens the door for a discussion of a theory of cinema as the medium of film. "Performance is that which a medium does with a text."[53] In light of the complex conditions of medialization associated with film we must speak here of a sort of 'multi'-medialization. Aristotle shows us the way by beginning his analysis with the actor as a corporeal medium. Stage actors, as well as those making a feature film, perform the important parts of the dramatic text by acting their parts on stage, in the studio, or on location in particular settings. Of course, much has changed since antiquity. Ancient theater could by and large be performed without a stage setting. By contrast, modern theater has developed considerably, and the technical capabilities available to makers of modern feature films have led to a qualitative jump in the complexity of the movie theater as a medium by allowing for an extremely realistic simulation of reality in the creation and arrangement of settings. The medium *cinema* as a, "device used to save and perform texts," works on a myriad of different levels due to its technical complexity, and such complexity has a large influence on the final product as introduced into communication.

In the case of the feature film we can differentiate between at least two different production complexes: (1) the theatrical complex of staging, with actors playing out the characters in the plot using both their bodies and their voices as well as the set and stage, and (2) the film-specific technical staging complex, which includes the entire array of camera and sound effects as well as production and finishing techniques. We find the both positive proprium of film and theater, as well as their limits, in the necessity to show and be loud, for ostentation, which is demanded by their respective media. Everything that

---

50 Aristotle: Poetics, 14.3.
51 Manfred Fuhrmann's 1982 commentary on chapter 14 in his German translation of Aristotle's Poetics, p. 119, footnote 2.
52 Aristotle: Poetics, 14.4–5.
53 Knape 2008b, p. 146; see also: Knape 2008c.

is performed in theater and film must be either said or displayed in real time (unless one resorts to displaying some kind of written text). Because of this and the medial constraints of ostentation, the fact is that the 'showing' of feature film is in some ways less flexible than narration. Narrativity, or 'telling', as Monaco believes he needs to discuss, allows a story to make large jumps in time or place and allows extremely subtle connections to be made with just a few words. While such breaks in plot can be incorporated into feature films (or dramatic theater) they require the use of a narrating character or voice that presents itself to the viewer to explain the connections from one scene to another. Despite his occasional terminological confusion, Monaco's discussion of film and narrativity makes one thing clear: every feature film (and this essay concentrates entirely on this genre) is a drama saved on celluloid or electronic storage. The difference between film and drama is film's capability to depict extremely realistic scenes and settings (through the use of on-site film shots for example).

Walter Benjamin characterized the technologically enabled performative capabilities of feature film and their effects on viewers by stating that, "such extraneous accessories as camera equipment, lighting machinery, staff assistants, etc.," deny the viewer a single "viewpoint" of perception in the way that stage theater does ("unless his eye were on a line parallel with the lens"). Film is thus fundamentally "illusionary" and is in reality a product that is, "the result of cutting."[54] Benjamin contrasts painting and film. The image, "of the painter is a total one, that of a cameraman consists of multiple fragments which are assembled under a new law." This is because, "the painter maintains in his work a natural distance from reality, while the cameraman penetrates deeply into its web."[55] Film does not, however, merely explore our perception in a unique way. It also allows for a new 'quasi-scientific' experience of the structures of reality which would otherwise remain hidden from our eyes. In other words, film promotes the realization of the old dream of a reciprocal, "intersection of art and science." A close-up shot "reveals entirely new structural formations of the subject," while slow motion video, "not only presents familiar qualities of movement but reveals them in entirely unknown," ways. In this way, "the camera introduces us to unconscious optics as does psychoanalysis to unconscious impulses."[56] Benjamin draws a far reaching conclusion from this new experience, "To demonstrate the identity of the artistic and

---

54 Benjamin 1939, p. 261.
55 Benjamin 1939. p. 263.
56 Benjamin 1939. p. 266.

scientific uses of photography which heretofore were usually separated will be one of the revolutionary functions of the film."[57]

3 The Rhetorical Factor in Drama and Feature Films

To this point we have yet to specifically address the subject of rhetoric. In fact, Aristotle wrote the 'Poetics' specifically about artifacts that were not primarily intended for the rhetorically pragmatic setting. Rather, such works are constructed such that they can be released from a specific situation, and can exist de-pragmatized as poetry readings or on the stage. In Aristotle's conception of the *polis*, rhetoric (in a terminological sense) is to be found in different communicative settings (the political and legal life-world). These settings demand acts that follow the standard-communicative mode of communication and texts that can be used to meet context oriented goals. Perhaps to emphasize the distinction he sees between the two forms, Aristotle's wrote a completely different theoretical work about this type of practical communication, namely his 'Rhetorics'. In the 'Nicomachean Ethics' he distinguished between two fundamental forms of activity involved in these actions: *poiēsis* (the creation of a work) and *práxis*, by which he meant standard-communicative actions with the assistance of pragmatic text genres.

One of Aristotle's more impressive merits as a philosopher was his tendency to use reality to drive his theories. Thus, upon a practical observation of concrete communicative situations, he came to the realization that even though things may be readily theoretically and scientifically definable, they tend to intermingle and are rarely found alone in the real world. Although dramas, for instance, are written for the special setting of the theater, which is distinct from the normal communicative world, the *writers* of dramas often have other reasons for writing other than to merely stir up emotions. Neo-Aristotelic theory of rhetoric calls these concerns, which are distinct from emotions and activate and challenge the thought and rationality of men, the *message* (Botschaft).[58] He therefore introduced a further analytical level that can be applied to any given de-pragmatized and freely positioned artifact, and thus incorporated works of art into his theory of rhetoric.

D. The rhetorical level of the appeal to the cognitive faculty (the rhetorical factor): Those characters that act in a drama use their speech (both in mono-

---

57 Benjamin 1939. p. 265.
58 For more on the term 'message' as it pertains to rhetorical theory see: Knape 2000a, p. 107.

logues and dialogs) to either depict or judge something. According to Aristotle, this effect is to be understood as a part of conscious action or reasoning, *diánoia*.[59] This activity is one of the foundational building blocks of drama, but represents merely one layer in the complex of the overall work. Aristotle asserts that although rational judgment is found in poetry, such activity belongs firmly within the field of its theoretical neighbor rhetoric.[60]

Aristotle first reminds us of why the activities understood by the term *diánoia* fall under the aegis of rhetorical theory: the thought must be formulated from semiotic material, prepared and evoked with words. Such formulation is supported by argumentation, affects and topoi (represented by the topos of the distinction between large and small, for instance[61]), "under the head of thought come all the effects to be produced by the language. Some of these are proof and refutation, the arousing of feelings (*pathē*) like pity, fear, anger, and so on, and then again exaggeration and depreciation."[62]

Aristotle points to two aspects of such rational formulations: the evocation of specific thoughts through (1) argumentation and (2) affects (emotions). Thus, *diánoia* in drama is represented by the "capability" of the characters to say something that makes sense. The content of such reasoning is normative, because its function is, "the ability to say what is possible and appropriate. It comes in the dialogue and is the function of the statesman's or the rhetorician's art. The old writers made their characters talk like statesmen, the moderns like rhetoricians."[63]

Speech, conversation, and all kinds of other verbal expressions are used in both drama and feature films to express particular opinions and positions. In Fritz Lang's "M", two court-trial scenes at the end of the movie illustrate this phenomenon. The first sequence, set in the vehemic court of the underworld, depicts indictments and defense speeches from both the accused and their attorneys. Each is performed with intense emotion and expression, as Quintilian recommends in chapter 6.2–3 of his *Institutio Oratoria*. The viewer hears these expressions, and can understand them and mentally process them. But the viewpoints expressed by the characters in the film have a special communicative status. They are part of a contract of fictionality between the viewer and the film maker; they have the status of specialized communication. The viewer can listen to the arguments embedded in the text of the film and accept

---

59 Aristotle: Poetics, 6.
60 Aristotle: Poetics, 19.2; cf. p. 192 in this volume.
61 Aristotle: Rhetoric, 2.19.
62 Aristotle: Poetics, 19.4.
63 Aristotle: Poetics, 6.22–23.

them, or they can understand such statements as the opinion of a fictional protagonist and distance themselves from them. This phenomenon is made possible by the fictional aesthetic game that writers and audience members play.

But what of the second aspect mentioned above, namely the affects (emotions)? Dramas and feature films are not pragmatic texts, and are certainly not considered pragmatic 'speech' in the rhetorical sense. Thus, the use of devices to arouse emotions is different than it is in rhetorical situations. In a normal rhetorical setting the orator must generate an emotional response using only the words of his text, otherwise, "what would be the use of a speaker, if the required effect were likely to be felt without the aid of the speeches?"[64] As Aristotle puts it, the drama (and feature film), on the other hand, must *show* or *display* something to us "without an explanation."[65] He asserts that the transfer of the rhetorical factor to drama must be determined by the actions and "incidents" within the drama itself: they must be arranged such that the emotions depicted by the drama spring into the minds of the viewers.

> It is clear that in the case of incidents, too, one should work on the same principles, when effects of pity or terror or exaggeration or probability have to be produced. There is just this difference, that some effects must be clear without explanation, whereas others are produced in the speeches by the speaker and are due to the speeches.[66]

According to this line of thought, the "incidents" of a drama (the events and actions taken) that the audience should emotionally experience can be depicted as (1) pitiful or dreadful, (2) important or (3) probable. Aristotle thus counts on a range of different types of reactions in the audience: (1) modal-emotional, (2) quantitative-measuring, or (3) qualitative reactions that estimate how realistic the incidents are. This third type of reaction is particularly important, because it addresses the question of concernment. The audience members must ask themselves in what way the actions depicted pertain to them: "Should I care because something like that might happen to me?" In other words, is the *tua res agitur* principle active?

---

64 Aristotle: Poetics, 19.6.
65 This does not preclude the creation of practical hybrids. The choir, for instance, often had the function of an on-stage commentator in ancient drama. Narrators and commentators can also be present in modern feature film as well, although such figures are still subject to the overall contract of fictionality between the film maker and the audience.
66 Aristotle: Poetics, 19.5.

4 The Evocation of Insight and Knowledge in Feature Films

The *rhetorical factor* in drama and feature film consists of the evocation of rational insight and knowledge. This can occasionally be induced, and can certainly be reinforced by certain emotions. The use of pathos in rhetoric, "acts to help both the speaker and the listener to interpret what is said; its use enables both proper understanding and the appropriate emotional response."[67] This feature of film is distinct from both the *structural-aesthetic factor* and the *fictional-aesthetic factor* mentioned in points A and B above.[68]

The rhetorical factor in feature films ensures that the viewer is able to take something from the artistic world of the film and transfer it to reality. We call this 'something' the *message* of the film. This message *can* be accepted and applied by the viewer, but may not be. Thus, the discussion here is about an analysis of an offering; i.e. an analysis of the real world insight that a feature film offers its viewers, regardless of whether a given viewer accepts the message or not. This aspect of film analysis falls under the aegis of empirical research on the effects of film.

We have now come to a set of problems that deal with the connection between feature film as the presentation of an illusionary, virtual world and its reception and interpretation by viewers. How can I, as a viewer, gain rational insight from a fictional account of an illusory and phantasmagorical world, whether in drama or feature films?[69] In some of his first works on the topic, Umberto Eco pointed to methods of interpretation based on approaches from hermeneutics and literary and artistic criticism. These methods are based not on a simple "decoding" of individual symbols, but rather gain insight based on the interpretation of larger, meaningful textual units. "Logically speaking this kind of interpretation is more akin to *inference*. Moreover, it is specific to that particular form of inference that Peirce called *abduction* (and at other times *hypothesis*)."[70]

Abduction as "a process of forming an explanatory hypothesis" has a central role in Peirce's concept of an interpretive explanation of the world.[71] Peirce went so far as to claim that, "if we are ever to learn anything or to understand phenomena at all, it must be by abduction that this is brought about."[72]

---

67 Wörner 1981, p. 78.
68 The structural-aesthetic factor focuses on the evocation of disinterested pleasure and the fictional-aesthetic factor deals with the evocation of illusions of reality.
69 As early as Aristophanes' 'Birds' (414 BCE) there has been a theatrical concept of 'fantasy' that transcends the human experience.
70 Eco 1976, p. 131.
71 Peirce: CP, 5.171.
72 Peirce: CP, 5.171.

According to this view, "All ideas of science come to it by way of abduction. Abduction consists in studying facts and devising a theory to explain them."[73] Peirce illustrated this idea with an anecdote:

> I once landed in a seaport in a Turkish province; and, as I was walking up to the house which I was to visit, I met a man upon horseback, surrounded by four horsemen holding a canopy over his head. As the governor of the province was the only personage I could think of who would be so greatly honored, I inferred that this was he. This was a hypothesis.[74]

Peirce described this method of generating hypotheses differently in different contexts. In one instance he called abduction a sort of reconstructive "inference" from a known consequence (for instance, a child has gone missing) to an unknown antecedent (it could have been a murder). In another, abductive reasoning was described as an "intrinsic guess" based on a sort of "sixth sense."[75] "Then, abduction is described as a 'conjecture' (CP, 6.469), as a sudden, divinatory 'act of insight' that comes 'like a lightning bolt' (CP, 5.181), in the form of a creative mental short cut."[76] Umberto Eco also described the difficulty in understanding Peirce's concept of abduction: "At first glance abduction seems to be a free movement of the imagination, more endowed with emotion (more similar to a vague 'intuition') than a normal decoding act."[77]

This remark is confirmed by Uwe Wirth's 1999 book on abduction. In a play on Schiller's definition of the aesthetic game, aesthetic abduction (for instance, in relation to a literary detective story by Edgar Allen Poe) can lead to a contemplative "Musement", to "aesthetic contemplation", to a "speculation concerning its cause", or even just to "pure Play."[78] "The unanalyzed aesthetic experience is transformed through abduction into a judgment."[79] This is the phenomenon that Aristotle references in his work: the connection between cognition and emotion. According to Peirce,

> When our nervous system is excited in a complicated way, there being a relation between the elements of the excitation, the result is a single harmonious disturbance which I call emotion [...]. This emotion is essentially the same thing as an hypothetic inference, and

---

73 Peirce: CP, 5.145.
74 Peirce: CP, 2.625.
75 Wirth 1999, pp. 30 f.
76 Wirth 1999, p. 31.
77 Eco 1976, p. 132.
78 Peirce: CP, 6.458; Wirth 1999, p. 199.
79 Wirth 1999, p. 200.

every hypothetic inference involves the formation of such an emotion. We may say, therefore, that hypothesis produces the sensuous element of thought.[80]

He adds an important note to this process, which leads from sensory experience to hypothesis, "If one's observations and reflection are allowed to specialize themselves too much, the Play will be converted into scientific study."[81]

The practice of drawing a conclusion based on the logic and message of an artifact, on the puzzles of the plot and the ideological constructs behind that which is shown, has long been known as a key to interpretation and the mechanism for rhetorical evocation in both modern and ancient poetics.[82] Since then, such an approach has taken on an important role in the methodology of modern film studies. David Bordwell, for instance, sees the key to interpretation in film studies in methodical inference, which can lead to new scholarly constructions of meaning in the analysis of individual feature films. "The sensory data of the film at hand furnish the materials out of which inferential processes of perception and cognition build meanings. Meanings are not found but made."[83] This thesis (and the critical undertone is contains) also refers to the meta-structural character of scholarly film analysis in general. For our context it is important to note that the process of inference forms the methodological foundation of gaining insight.

Such a process becomes even more important when attempting to reconstruct the process of reception in the average viewer of feature films. We can use Eco's category of the "inferential stroll" from 1979, the practice of mentally wandering from the immediate film to others that the viewer remembers, as a starting point.[84] The recipient of a film (the addressee) automatically takes part in such activities; he continually makes a "connection between the text and the encyclopedia," that is, with his experience in the world and what he has seen in other films. This is the process of intertextual comparison. In referencing the reader of a novel, Eco wrote,

> he draws conclusions: but he looks elsewhere for the most probable premises of his own Enthymeme. In other words, if the fable says 'x takes a certain kind of action,' and the reader notices that, 'every time x does this, y happens,' then the reader will assume (and this is the conclusion), 'that x's action will lead to y.' In order to formulate his hypothesis,

---

80 Peirce: CP, 2.643.
81 Peirce: CP, 6.459.
82 Eco again uses the example of Sophocles' Oedipus the King in describing the different intellectual activities that would take place when comparing someone who knows the story well and a viewer that does not. Eco 1987, pp. 131 f.
83 Bordwell 1991, p. 3.
84 Eco 1987, pp. 148–151.

the reader must recall more general or intertextual scenographies: thoughts such as, 'usually; always when, then; like in other stories; according to my own experience; as psychology has taught us; etc.'. To recall a scenography (especially when such is intertextual) is, in reality, to return to a *topos*. We call such emigrations (by 'text' emigrants, who return loaded rich with textual quarry) *inferential strolls*.[85]

Bordwell's method of, "interpretative activity [as] an inferential process," in the analysis of film also has relevance for the reception of film by the everyday viewer: "(1) the interpreter must construct semantic fields that can be ascribed to the film. (2) The interpreter must also find cues and patterns onto which the semantic fields can be 'mapped'."[86] These semantic fields, which generate meaning and sense in a feature film cannot be reduced to the concept of the "theme". Rather, they capture the entire fictional and structural aesthetic offering of the feature film, from which a viewer can draw conclusions that might lead to a change of from A to B in thought patterns, opinions, judgments, attitudes, or beliefs.

> A semantic field is not identical to what is usually assumed to be a ‚theme'. In literary criticism, the theme is usually assumed to be a ‚governing idea', even a universal concept. A semantic field is, in contrast, a conceptual *structure*; it organizes potential meanings in relation to one another. Such fields may be organized in different ways. As I shall suggest, we can think of a 'theme' as a node in a cluster of associated semantic features.[87]

In this sense, we could say that the interpretation of a feature film can lead a viewer to new ways of thinking, and that these new insights (if the viewer accepts the viewpoint offered by the film) may be won through abstraction. As Bordwell puts it, "interpretation needs some abstraction."[88]

At this point, the rhetorician should be asking the question of what this all means for the theory of dramatic production. To be concise: those who wish to convey a pragmatically effective, 'life-world' message, or plan for viewers to abduce such messages within the confines of a feature film (be they political, philosophical, or psychological) must reflect on the relevant structure of the communicative offering when planning production. The fable and plot (that is, the story that is shown to us in a dramatic feature film) are the most important elements of such calculations. This is in line with Aristotle's thinking, and modern film studies reflect such a view as well. In his chapter on, 'Moving

---

85 Eco 1987, pp. 148 f.
86 Bordwell 1991, p. 105.
87 Bordwell 1991, p. 106.
88 Bordwell 1991, p. 127.

Images – Cinematic Sequences and Narration'[89] in the 2008 work, 'The Philosophy of Motion Pictures,' Noël Carroll emphasizes the fact that scene selection and sequencing in feature films (as in other forms of drama) enable what he calls targeted "attention management" of the viewers. Showing and not-showing are in this sense the central processes of such attention management, "Cinematic sequences are built through variable framing which exploits our natural perceptual dispositions in order to guide our attention to where the motion picture maker wants it to be – usually to whatever is important to the unfolding of the action or argument."[90] This process influences the inferences that viewers make in reconstructing and understanding the fable presented to them in a given feature film. Such inferences are naturally dependent on the viewer's choice to accept the film's communicative offering,

> Variable framing leads the viewer by highlighting the ingredients we need to take into account in order to infer what is going on; but generally it remains up to the viewer herself to assemble these cues by making the desired or proposed inferences. Here we see that although the variable framing makes certain inferences likely – indeed, often virtually unavoidable – it still usually depends upon the viewer to arrive at the hypothesis that completes the thought the filmmaker intends to convey.[91]

Noël Carroll's erotetic or erotematic principle of construction is important for our further analysis, and its application need not be limited to feature film alone.[92] "The basic structure of movie narration [!?] is an instance of what can be called erotetic narration."[93] What does he mean by this? The central idea of this approach is that each feature film offers the viewer a network of questions and answers, "some scenes evoke questions; others answer said questions directly. Still other scenes or sequences *sustain* earlier questions: the failure to apprehend the escaped prisoner leaves us still asking whether he will be caught in a subsequent scene."[94] In analyzing the individual scenes of a film, one can speak of "micro-questions;" in light of the whole work, of "macro-questions."[95] It is also important to judge the feature film as a whole

---

89 Unfortunately, we see here yet another case of the categorical mistake made in so much of modern film analysis: Carroll mistakes *Narration* for *Dramatization*, even though he later speaks of the dramatic *scenes* (a classical category of drama) of feature film.
90 Carroll 2008, pp. 124 f.
91 Carroll 2008, p. 130.
92 In Greek, an *erōtēma* is an 'asked question' (and forms the adjective *erōtēmatikós*/about a question); Carroll's adjective '*erotetic*' is a rather rough derivation of the original term.
93 Carroll 2008, p. 134.
94 Carroll 2008, p. 136.
95 Carroll 2008, p. 137.

beginning at its end, because it is here that concluding inferences can be made based on the entirety of the events in the story,

> Ascertain what questions are being answered at the conclusion of the film, and then work your way backwards to the scenes and sequences where those questions were introduced, partially answered, or otherwise sustained, refined, transformed, mutated, and so forth.[96]

Such an analysis demands that viewers form not merely subjective, "Punctum" interpretations, but rather systematic, "Studium" interpretations in the sense of the French semiotician Roland Barthes.[97]

Another of Carroll's distinctions, the "problem/solutions model" is important for the isolation of the rhetorical factor in feature film.[98] This model enables the interpretation of feature film offerings to be transformed to a more abstract level of analysis. Although a drama may pose questions about events within the story, the motivations of characters, or about unexplained reasons for certain actions or consequences, it does not necessarily directly handle any of the more abstract *problems* and *solutions* which are dealt with within the feature film and determine its thematic structure. Precisely these elements, however, should enable the viewer to draw inferences that could help them gain insight into the larger problems which the filmmaker intends them to consider. Ideally, such insight should even lead the viewer to link the problems addressed in the film with their own personal experience (according to the *tua res agitur* principle). From the perspective of rhetoric, such insight is achieved by gleaning dramatic evidence from the events depicted in the feature film.[99] Of course, and this must be stated clearly, not every feature film emphatically activates the rhetorical factor. As Carroll notes, "not even all movies are full-fledged, erotetic narratives," and that (especially when considering modern, highly aestheticized feature films), "not all our questions have answers."[100]

---

96 Carroll 2008. p. 136.
97 For more on *punctum* and *studium* as methods of interpretation see: Knape 2008a, pp. 907 f.
98 Carroll 2008, p. 138.
99 For more on evidence as a rhetorical category, see: Knape 2000a, p. 19.
100 Carroll 2008, p. 142. Some feature films go so far as to play with the frustration that arises with plot coherency issues, as in Robert Altman's *Nashville*, "its ending coming from nowhere – in order to suggest the utter unintelligibility of America in the 1970s. That is, narrative incompleteness = chaos." Carroll 2008, p. 142. Such aesthetically motivated constructions are highly relevant for rhetorical, noetic inferences (i.e. in reference to the rhetorical textual level of *diánoia*), "that is, where we have grounds to suspect that the erotetic irregularity in the movie is not a mistake, but is intentional, we treat it as a heuristic invitation or prompt to search for some other-than-narrative significance." Carroll 2008, p. 144.

Carroll is correct to conclude that each of his models has a separate and distinct approach and set of concerns,

> The question/answer framework will apply to every case where the problem/solution
> model works, since we can always ask: Will the protagonist solve her problems or not?
> However, there are also cases where the question/answer model fits, but where the prob-
> lem/solution model seems strained. Does it really make sense to regard the question of
> whether two people will fall in love a problem? Certainly their falling in love could involve
> problems – obstacles, like parents and rivals, to overcome, and so on. But it need not.
> Though all problems may be translated into questions, it is not evident that all questions
> can be translated into problems.[101]

In the ideal film rhetorical situation, the offerings and discussions presented in the story of a feature film that are related to larger problems and their possible solutions (or lack thereof) must lead to abstraction and stimulate cognitive transfer in the minds of viewers. In this sense, Fritz Lang's film '*M*' may have dealt with such problems as the surveillance society, the stigmatiza-tion of social groups, sickness or criminality, harm and wrongdoing, sorrow and bad luck, guilt and atonement, etc. Seen rhetorically, the discussion of such themes should also enable a shift of opinion from A to B (persuasion) in the minds of the viewers, as long as they are ready for it.[102] If appropriately structured, the aesthetic instruments available in feature film can also stimu-late such receptive readiness in viewers.

5 The Rhetorical Factor in Fritz Lang's Feature Film '*M*'

In the analysis of feature film, the rhetorician always hopes to find a cinematic 'double calculation', namely aesthetic *and* rhetorically pragmatic calculations. Even if in some cases it becomes clear that the filmmaker never considered activating or utilizing the rhetorical factor in his film, a rhetorician need not abandon hope: almost every feature film can be surveyed for its implicit, in some ways connotatively understood messages, even those that may be unin-tended by the filmmaker.[103] Many viewers automatically look for and silently

---

101 Carroll 2008, p. 138.
102 Knape 2003a, col. 875.
103 This is one reason that, despite an explicitly stated "artistic-"caveat, even feature films are consistently the subject of political or moral suspicions, sometimes with legal ramifi-cations. In such situations the accuser can always claim there to be a rhetorically pragmatic drive behind the creation of a work of art that has, in reality, been de-pragmatized and freed from a concrete situation.

abduce personally relevant messages without considering any kind of calculation in the production of the film (motivated perhaps by the expectation of the *tua res agitur* principle). The rhetorical analyst can take exactly this perspective and apply it to a feature film like Fritz Lang's 1931 '*M*': what kinds of messages can be abduced? What kinds of insight and management of perception (moderations) does the film employ in order to potentially evoke cognitive and emotional movement in viewers?[104]

The following will use two examples from this film to illustrate how the fictional and structural aesthetic calculations embedded in feature films can also lead to rhetorical evocations. The starting point for this discussion is that 'showing' (*deixis*) forms the communicatively relevant foundational mode of theater and film. With this approach, a leerstelle (blank), i.e. 'not-showing', also represent an important method for the stimulation of inferences. In reference to the story or fable, such leerstellen allow the viewer to take his "inferential strolls" (intertextually comparative recollection) and create imaginative "phantom chapters" that he can then use to fill spaces between the depicted events.[105] In the feature film genre of crime thriller, the systematic use of this method functions as a strategy of mystification, since each enigma evokes an *erotema*. This heightens the suspense in the film. The tension arises because not-showing, *negative deixis* (as we could call it), is a first rate stimulant of inference and abduction: by not showing certain events the viewer is forced to think about the plot, and to hypothesize abductively about the plot (about the murderer for instance or, if the murderer is already known, about the events of the story or his personality). He then waits in suspense to see whether his mental hypothesis is confirmed or not.

Such obfuscation and Lang's refusal to show, form important methods of stimulation when considering the rhetorical factor in his film. Those elements that are difficult to see or not revealed at all inevitably lead any serious viewer of the film to invest in a partially emotional, partially rational examination of the problems handled in the film. The two main problems of interest handled in the story of '*M*' are relatively easy for the viewer to recognize: 1. How can and should a society deal with the specific kind of criminality depicted in the film? 2. What kind of person is this murderer? The answers to these questions, however, are much more difficult to find, because the film delivers them indirectly using the rhetorical factor.

---

104 For more on the Moderation-Evocation Nexus in rhetoric see: Knape 2008a, pp. 916–924.
105 Eco 1987, pp. 260 ff.

5.1 The Vehemic Court

The problem of handling aberrant criminal behavior, and the possible ways that society can deal with such problems, form the main topic of the entire film. Fritz Lang shows the hysterical reactions of a terrified public to the actions of a serial sex offender in multiple scenes. In others, he shows the meticulous work of the state apparatus parallel to the ruthless and unrestrained machinations of the organized underworld as both follow their own distinct methods to track down the criminal that they are close to catching. When the criminal underworld successfully captures him, they are able to put what they view as a dangerous "competitor" to trial in front of a secret court in their own parallel world (Figure 13).

Figure 13: Secret Court in Fritz Lang's "M".

In an obviously ironic construction, the world of organized crime rejects the sexual predator Hans Beckert as unacceptable. This allows the film to make the exceptional aspect of this vehemic trial explicit: Beckert belongs neither to normal civil society nor to that of the criminal world. His crimes do not fit within the framework of 'acceptable' crime; even the criminals distance themselves from him. Each participant in the trial delivers arguments from their own perspective; together they illustrate the problem in a completely new way for the viewer, namely argumentatively rather than through the portrayal of specific actions by the protagonists.

The process of cognition in the viewer is guided through the arguments within the pseudo-trial along the four specific lines of questioning (*quaestiones*) codified in the status doctrine of classical rhetoric as important in matters of dispute in front of a court. The model of the four *stases* with which one can determine the fundamentals of a legal dispute are at the foundation of the legal process depicted in '*M*'. The court explicitly discusses questions of, (1) whether a criminal act has occurred (the conjectural status: Is there even a crime here? This fact is accepted by all participants in the trial), (2) what kind of a crime the killing of the child actually was (the definitional status: Was it really a murder, or was it a lesser manslaughter, or perhaps merely an unavoidable evil?), (3) whether there is guilt in the usual sense of justice (the status of quality: Did the act occur with enough legal grounding? Did the killer act freely, or was he perhaps himself the victim of uncontrolled, overpowering urges?), and finally (4) whether this "court" of "popular opinion", as articulated in the criminal underworld, is within its appropriate jurisdiction (the status of translation: Is the process before the court legitimate?)

The viewer is both explicitly and abstractly informed about the details of the problem through the series of extremely emotionally charged, antagonistic arguments as well as through a heavily affective monologue from the murderer Beckert himself. But the film denies the viewer any sort of explicit solutions; before the underworld process is able to reach a judgment, the long arm of the law reaches out and grabs Beckert, the police storm in, and the secret court is disbanded.

In following with the fundamental idea of the dramatic plot, this would have been the ideal moment to symmetrically illustrate the fundamental differences between the vehemic court of the underworld and the formal criminal court of the state. Instead, Lang inserts a leerstelle (blank) in the plot of the film. The trial itself is never shown. In its place is a scene that is all of 25 seconds long: the judges walk into a court room, and the lead judge delivers the verdict with the words, "in the name of the people" (Figure 14). We thus know that a trial has taken place, but the brief scene is over before we hear the final verdict. The rhetorical factor of the film, which enables us to glean abductive insight from the aesthetic constructions of the film, is here on full display: those viewers who expect a verdict must hand it down themselves. To put it another way: by now, if not earlier, the appellative structures of the work evoke considerations of axiomative (what kinds of principles, rules, and order are active?), evaluative (what kinds of value judgments, conclusions, or opinions

Figure 14: "In the Name of the People". Judges in Fritz Lang's "M".

do I have about the topic?) and emotional (with what am I most able to emotionally identify, and why?) aspects of the film.[106]

In depicting the trial of the murderer, all of the relevant facts of the virtual world of 'M' that Lang wanted to show us are shown, and the arguments that deal with the events are laid out. But who is left to formulate the conclusion? In this case the viewer has no choice: if there is to be any closure at all they must decide for themselves. They are forced to take on the role of the jury and form their own conclusions based on the events they have seen and the arguments they have heard. Telling, for instance, are the famous conclusions of Joseph Goebbels, Hitler's later propaganda minister, who wrote in his diary after seeing the movie, "Saw 'M' with Magda tonight. Phenomenal! Against sentimental humanitarianism! For the death penalty!" The final shot of the film, which shows three wailing women, suggests perhaps something different altogether: it makes no final judgment, but makes clear that the only way to approach such criminality is with prevention and care. In these cries of anguish lies an offer of interpretation based on the inevitability of evil (Figure 15).

---

106 For more on each of these aspects of orientation see: Knape 2008a, pp. 920–923.

Figure 15: Three Wailing Women in Fritz Lang's "M".

5.2 The Hedge

The second major *erotema* that confronts the viewer throughout the film is not the question of who the criminal actually is (this is revealed relatively early) but rather, what sort of person he actually is. In order to form a differentiated hypothesis about his personality we would need to see Hans Beckert in his every day routine; the film would have to show us some of the context surrounding his living conditions. This is almost completely denied us: we merely see the living space of an obviously unremarkable subtenant and the daily walks of a man that clearly cares deeply about children.

This puzzle surrounding Beckert's character is symbolically condensed in the scene at "Café Laube". This scene forms the end of a larger sequence (the "sex arrow sequence") that shows us one of Beckert's failed kidnappings. At its core, this scene should visualize the psychological condition of Beckert in the moments before and after as a metamorphosis.[107] In the overall sequence of events in the film, Lang inserts this scene directly at the climax of the search for the murderer by both the police and organized crime. During filming, actor

---

107 Because this sequence merely serves to illustrate Beckert's pathological metamorphosis and doesn't actually move the plot along in any meaningful way, we could speak here of a 'pathos dramative' (Pathosdramativ). See: Knape 2010a.

Peter Lorre was told to try and embody the psychological transformation from a respectable subtenant to a psychotically driven man (a Dr. Jekyll and Mr. Hyde phenomenon). Lang then underlines the man's sexual arousal with a series of rapidly moving graphic symbols in a store front decoration, including an arrow moving up and down rhythmically as a phallic symbol (thus my name for it, the "sex arrow sequence") (Figure 16).

Figure 16: Sex arrow sequence in Fritz Lang's "M".

What does the scene in "Café Laube" show us? After his failed attempt to kidnap a child, Beckert comes across the café and hides himself behind a hedge. Our view of the café is limited from behind the hedge: there is only a small opening between the branches through which we can clearly see the waiter. What the viewer perceives as something blocking his view is, for Beckert, an irrational expression of his uncontrollable urges because he feels he must quickly hide himself. What we do notice is that Beckert needs a drink and a cigarette in order to calm his agitated state and return to the respectable, average subtenant. Lang could have helped us here: he could have used a tracking shot to go behind the hedge and give us an unmolested view of Beckert. Instead, the structural aesthetic calculations of the director demand that we sit through the entire drawn out scene with the hedge as a visual obstacle between us and the protagonist. In this way, Lang negates the 'showing' imperative of film, choosing instead the above mentioned negative *deixis*. Due to the structural aesthetic design of the scene, a camera determines the construction of film reality.[108] Only gradually, and after the viewer's curiosity has been piqued and their need for visual participation has been heightened, does Lang release the tension a little. The camera comes ever closer to the hedge and we can see, as through a key-hole, Beckert's face through the branches (Figure 17). His face, however, is still

Figure 17: Hedge in Fritz Lang's "M".

out of focus; it seems that nothing should be really clear in this scene. Lang thus intensifies our feeling that we will never get clear evidence on the character of this man. Instead, we are forced to rely on vague hypotheses derived from the highly selective sequence of the scenes presented to us over the course of the entire plot.

Still, Lang does offer us some information on Beckert's personality in the form of a series of detailed discussions that take place both within the ranks of the police and within the criminal organization. These discussions lead to two reductionist hypotheses that are explicitly stated in the film: he is either a criminal or he is mentally ill. This leads the viewer to ask questions regarding the lines between the two, and the legitimacy of such strict classifications

---

108 This is, in principle, the exact same thing that happens in theater: we can only see what happens on the stage itself. It is clear, however, that film offers better technical capabilities to create illusions of space, in the cut of optical focus, etc.

without at least some clear answers. If Beckert begins as an obvious criminal, it becomes more and more difficult as the film goes on to make a clear cut judgment. On the one hand we see an honest man that cares about and spoils children, on the other we see a psychologically tortured individual. We never see the actual murders, only their consequences in the wider society. It is only in light of the police files and reports, and in light of other speculations that the film explicitly offers us, that we find out that the other protagonists of the film believe that Beckert fluctuates between criminality and illness.

We see here again that the overall aesthetic construction of the film activates the rhetorical factor: viewers are stimulated to arrive at a series of rational and emotional conclusions about the personality and character of the main character in '*M*'.[109]

---

109 A shorter German version of this chapter in: Knape 2010c.

Media Rhetoric

13 The Concept of *Medium* in Rhetoric

In 2008, a collection of essays was published under the title, 'What is a medium?'[1] Taken as a whole, this work represents evidence of a deep confusion about the term *medium*; in fact many of the authors express discomfort using the word 'medium' at all. In his contribution, media philosopher Lorenz Engell considers the question posed by the title of the work to be unanswerable because, "a medium, a medium on its own, is unthinkable." Fifty years after the trend-setting works of Marshall McLuhan, the founder of modern and explicit media theory, such a remark is startling to read.[2] Does the commonly used term 'medium' merely refer to some obscure phenomena? Decades after the publication of his main works, McLuhan's confusing idea of medium continues to be a source of discussion, and has led the concept of 'medium' to become something of an occupational term for researchers, especially those involved in the study of literature.[3] Philosopher of media Ulrike Ramming expresses her deep discomfort with the general confusion surrounding the term:

> In light of such an expanded definition of *medium*, which now includes technical artifacts in general and, further, cultural and intellectual techniques, one must pose the question of whether the concept of *medium*, through its novelty for the field of philosophy and its specific nature, has expanded to the point that it is lost in the darkness of a terminological night in which all cats are grey and all media are the same.[4]

Media theorist Stefan Rieger, who approaches the topic with the ironically titled essay, 'The frog – A medium?' begins with this sobering remark, "the term *medium* is a passe-partout that apparently fits every lock of modernity."[5] Skepticism and criticism are also rained down upon the study of media in general: cultural theorist Dirk Baecker writes that, "research in this field acts as if it concerns itself with an irrational attitude and position, as if it deals with some sort of spiritual communication."[6] Even the editors of the volume express their discontent in their introduction to the work:

> Is there anything left that hasn't already been called a medium? A few examples: a chair, a wheel, a mirror (McLuhan), a school class, a football, a waiting room (Flusser), the

---

1 Münker/Roesler 2008a.
2 Theories of media before McLuhan existed implicitly in a variety of works.
3 See here: Knape 2005a.
4 Ramming 2008, p. 265.
5 Rieger 2008, p. 285.
6 Baecker 2008, p. 131.

electoral system, a national strike, the street (Baudrillard), a horse, the dromedary, the elephant, gramophone, film, typewriter (Kittler), money, power and influence (Parsons), art, faith and love (Luhmann).

It is little wonder, after this summary, that the use of the term *medium* is connected with, "inscrutable conceptual propositions."[7]

This collection of essays also clearly demonstrates that philological and etymological explanations and historical analyses into word use lead nowhere. The terminological conception that arises from such research always leads back to the original Latin meaning of means or the middle, in the sense of the middle between two things.[8] Even this banal definition of the term is often arbitrarily expanded.

This colloquial, non-specific, and non-terminological understanding of the word 'medium' has led to a phenomenon in the humanities that I would like to call *media imperialism*. If one wants to express that something is somehow being conveyed, it has become standard to use the supposedly attractive word 'medium' instead of talking about 'communication'. With such use, the word medium achieves the status of a, "plastic word," linguist Uwe Pörksen's term for arbitrarily applicable empty expressions. To illustrate this point we need look no further than the following definitions from the 'Luhmann Lexicon', which range from monstrous to just strange: "Medium: a certain possibility of facilitating indefinite, possibilities, a loose complex that can take a form," and,

> The most general medium is sense. The full details of what else can be considered a medium is relatively open: gravity, hearing, sight, language, causality, money, power, justice, truth, love; walking requires the medium of gravity, perception uses sight and hearing, and, stated somewhat diffusely, light and air as a medium.[9]

The source of this "diffusely stated" concept of medium is Marshall McLuhan. According to McLuhan's theory of extension, all human artifacts that allow an expansion of human sense and facilitate human action outside the range of physical reach are considered *media*. His book, 'Understanding Media', thus categorizes light, the light bulb, railroads, gunpowder, streets, money, language and television together as types of medium.[10] In such a definition, we can easily recognize the aforementioned casual use of the original Latin meaning of medium as the means for making a connection. Accordingly, we also

---

7 Münker/Roesler 2008b, p. 11.

8 According to Wolfgang Hagen 2008, p. 13, writing with skepticism in his contribution to Münker/Roesler 2008a.

9 Krause 1999, pp. 151f.

10 McLuhan 1964.

find contributions considering money as a medium, and about spiritual media or the transmission of "spiritual powers" in 'What is a Medium?'[11] Each of these essays deals with phenomena of transmission and "something" that lies "between."[12]

These unsatisfying derivations of the trivial conception of mediality found in both McLuhan and his successors have regularly trapped them in the infamous *tautology of medium*. This has made the development of a different, theoretically clear concept necessary for foundational discussions in the philosophy of media. This necessity is demonstrated by examples such as the aforementioned essay from Dirk Baecker, which passes into both theoretical and terminological vagueness when modifying Fritz Heider's concept of medium as nothingness: "the nothing is the emptiness that continually steps between the singular entity and the multiplicity in order to, time and again, motivate new singularities from the multitude." McLuhan's position that we cannot actually perceive the medium is then described through Heider's words, "a medium is something that is empty to us, a 'nothing' that is, however, 'filled with units of a lower order'."[13] I will leave it to the logicians to explain how a nothing can be filled with units of a lower order.

Considerations of this sort lead to a sort of *media fundamentalism*, which philosopher Sybille Krämer has called "media apriorism". A medium becomes, "an irreducible unit upon which something can be based or can be traced back to. According to this media apriorism there is nothing external to media."[14] This proves to be a far reaching thesis, which can be summed up in the form of the theoretical postulate *extra medium nulla existentia* or even *nihil extra medium*. From a logical perspective, the concept of a medium thus includes the entire physical world (at least that which is based on matter). This implies a *media universalism* that is also found in the writings of media theorist Wolfgang Ernst. For him, media have, "a *fundamentum in re*," and are anchored in the fabric of the physical world. What at first seems an uninteresting statement is then specified further: "between objects and the observer is a gap that must be bridged. Aristotle approaches this 'in-between' in his work, 'About the Soul'. There must always be a medium, because without one there would be only emptiness. Not only would nothing be clear, nothing would be seen at all."[15] For Ernst, this 'in-between' takes on an ontological dimension when he speaks

---

11 Esposito 2008, p. 112; Adamowsky 2008, p. 30; Böhme/Matussek 2008, p. 95.
12 As Esposito characterizes it on p. 113; Esposito 2008.
13 Baecker 2008, pp. 142, 133.
14 Krämer 2008, pp. 66 f.
15 Ernst 2008, p. 176.

of the, "emancipation of a technical medium from physics," and declares, "this creates something that is neither purely natural (physical) or classically cultural, rather is – literally – a third (*medium*)."[16]

This idea of medium stretches normal theoretical conceptions to the breaking point and still leaves us with an undefined result: the ontological status of the "third" remains unclear. On the one hand, Ernst's position represents a return to McLuhan's conception that every worldly artifact is a medium. On the other, it is a recourse to the Kittlerian thesis of the materiality of information and communication. At its core, Ernst's theory tends towards this materialist thesis. At the end of his essay he mentions,

> the challenge that quantum physics presents to this idea of the medium. In the place of classical interference in the channel of transmission (noise), which is normally resolved in information theory through redundancy, such interference is now created by the act of measurement. The quantum mechanical conception of information no longer begins with the sender/receiver model (as in Shannon's theory). Instead, it begins with the eternal entanglement of information transfer. In this model the channel of space-time no longer exists.[17]

Hans Ulrich Gumbrecht has also been heavily influenced by Kittler. In his 2005 essay titled, 'The Materialism of Communication', he warns of the continuation of Cartesian metaphysical dualism of "mind" and "matter" in a clear anti-idealist tone.[18] In general, however, Gumbrecht's short summary of the topic is only slightly critical. He observes that,

> as the promise of becoming a paradigm failed to solidify despite concentrated attempts at theory building, the 'materiality of communication' (in a strict sense) could no longer be expanded and sustained through reception, once its popularity as a buzzword subsided.[19]

There are reasons for the minimal response to this approach. The exclusive concentration on medial conditions and the individual aspects of communication leads to oversimplified models that fail to find acceptance due to their reductionism. The correlated mental hypotheses of effect are often speculative because we lack the required sources of knowledge to confirm or disconfirm them. The main problem, however, is found at the methodological level. The question of "materiality" can only be explained with recourse to the biological and neurological equipment of humans and their interface with the rest of the

---

16 Ernst 2008, pp. 178 ff.
17 Ernst 2008, p. 182.
18 Gumbrecht 2005.
19 Gumbrecht 2005, p. 147.

physical world. The German theories of media advanced by Friedrich Kittler, Stefan Rieger or Wolfgang Ernst deal prominently with technological history and questions of engineering as well as all other types of physical knowledge that can be related to the postulated (but never perceivable) "gap" in the material world. Accordingly, Ernst wrote that media no longer belong, "under the purvey of the social, humanities, and cultural sciences. Media theory is more closely related to the natural and technical disciplines of science."[20] These are, of course, problems for the discipline of media studies that lead us farther and farther away from a rigorous theoretical definition of the term *medium*. Ultimately, the theoretical program that Kittler's and Ernst's materialism postulates is clearly recognizable: mediality coincides with the materiality of the world. Thus, Kittler speaks only of the, "formerly so-called nature," because, "the so-called *Church-Turing hypothesis*," entails, "in its most rigorous, physical form, that nature itself be explained as a universal Turing machine."[21]

Parallels to Kittler's media universalism can be found in modern discussions in the neurological sciences.[22] His position mirrors that of some radical neuro-cognitivists, who deny the possibility of modular differentiation in favor of an immediate and synchronized holism. Such a view can unintentionally lead to a sort of Haeckelian *media monism* (in a 19th century sense of the term *monism*) that denies an essential difference between the natural (of individual bodies, individuals) and the artificial (of sociality).[23] Researchers that specialize in human symbolic systems and work undaunted by culturally based approaches (such as rhetoricians) do, in fact, see boundaries and sensible alternatives in theoretical modeling. In particular, such researchers see the potential of a modular approach to methodically isolate structural, procedural, or functional sub-domains of reality, and to describe and analyze their characteristic attributes and properties.[24] The philosophical conception of media that ends in physicalism can thus be legitimately countered with a culturally oriented, modular, (and thus discipline-specific) media concept. By looking at the defined analytical levels derived from this approach, we can also develop a good working set of termini. I will say more on this subject later.

For now, we can maintain that media deal with diverse and materially composed interactive systems. If we simply consider the multitude and diversity of human languages alone, we see that the power of human cognition

---

20 Ernst 2008, p. 181.
21 Kittler 1993, pp. 375, 369.
22 Marshall 1984, pp. 209–242; Stainton 2006.
23 Kittler 1993; see also: Gumbrecht 2005.
24 Cf. Carruthers 2006, pp. 3–21.

allows us to multi-task. We are able to create the most unbelievable living and communicative systems within 'culture' through the use of rules that demand adherence. When we examine such systems individually, we see that their variety is based not only on our biological makeup, but rather on our species' unique ability to adapt to our environments according to evolutionary epistemological theories. This examination does not require us to refer to a left-wing Hegelian superstructure; the search for a 'materiality of communication' originates from an anti-idealistic impetus. Such concerns, however, should no longer be an issue: the fact that every part of communication, that elements of hardware, software and text, all have the same material 'ontological status' is now so widely accepted as to be banal. Not even Kittler himself can avoid mentioning that computer systems must (for the time being) continue to, "coexist in an environment constructed from everyday language."[25] What he wants to say here is that there *is* a difference between textuality on a monitor (as a surface) and the deeper structure of hardware and software. Sciences that focus on action theory, as rhetoric strives to be, still assume a difference and connection between an operator and his instruments. They concern themselves above all with the question of the interactive and systematic environmental context, of the emotional-cognitive 'system' of individuals and their respective consciousness and feelings.[26]

The dependence of such cognitive and emotive systems on the aggregate conditions and dynamic systems in the wider physical world, as well as their dependence on cultural structures and systems, is also an area of great importance to disciplines concerned with theories of action. The anti-functionalism found in some strains of cognitive science that seek to focus exclusively on the internal phenomena of neural processes have a clear deficit when it comes to theories of action and interaction, and are not able to account for elements of cultural influence. While internal neural processing of all kinds is one side of the equation, the external and autonomously constructed cultural environment (without which no human interaction could take place) is the other. The cultural side of existence can and must be investigated for its unique regularities. The theory held by some connectivist and sub-symbolically focused cognitivists that hardware and software are unified based on a range of physically defined base patterns may well be true.[27] Still, such a theory does not by any means make the modularized study of symbolic models obsolete. Hardware

---

25 Kittler 1993, p. 372.
26 Which, according to a measured form of constructivism, must necessarily involve a relatively high amount of environmentally independent self-reference.
27 McClelland/Rumelhart 1986.

and software do not produce texts by themselves. In the technical interaction among humans, machines, and culture, the hardware and software of machines do not formulaically intervene in devices and texts generated on the cultural surface, even when the conditions of realization are dependent on the structure of the hardware and software. There is simply no empirical evidence for a different conclusion. Even the simplest studies of intercultural differences prove this point. There is a wide gap between physics (as a representative for the materiality of the world) and observable, biologically self-organized entities, individual brains, the networks of interaction among humans, their histories and their artifacts, due to uncountable, self-referential levels of processing. If neurocognitivist theory wanted to derive the way that a video camera functions based on the molecular structure of the human brain, it would also have to be able to explain why Bronze Age humans never built video cameras despite having the exact same biological makeup as we do. Instead, we must retain a compromising viewpoint: systematic modularism, functionalism, and holism are not mutually exclusive, but rather complement each other as theoretical approaches.

In light of the indispensable and necessary functional differentiation discussed above, there are other distinctions that must be made in regards to the theoretical term *medium*. In particular, we must distinguish between the observable unit of the semiotically differentiated *text*, which is highly informationally relevant, and its material, socially distributable platform, the *medium*.[28] Such differentiation draws us closer to a modular, discipline-specific and above all practically useful definition of the term. The newest quantum-physical theory of media is able to explain the material constitution of media and information based on scientific theoretical propositions. The practical analysis of their communicative capacity in human cultural interactions, in which actors utilize media as a vehicle for semiotic processes, requires its own theoretical framework.

The general enthusiasm surrounding the concept of media has led to a flood of theories that seek to establish the concept of media as a new universal category. Ultimately, however, recourse to quantum-physics and the more general problem of materiality in the physical world have deprived us of a discrete definition of medium. Such conceptions of medium either overlap with other, pre-existing categories or are so general as to have lost their explanatory usefulness (because they have been stripped of their *differentia specifica*). Image theorist Lambert Wiesing bemoans this loss of useful distinctions directly in

---

28 See: Knape 2005c, pp. 19–22.

his contribution to the collection of essays discussed above.[29] Many of those in the social sciences that have jumped on the media theory bandwagon have only served to amplify the confusion; their works are often much too superficial, essayist, and rarely approach the topic with sufficient scientific and critically methodical rigor.

The disciplinary conception of *medium* that emerges from most German theories of media, influenced by both philosophy and science, has two significant weaknesses that are internally linked. On the one hand we see medium as a universal category that ultimately dissipates into a conception of matter and leads to a sort of monism. Definitions such as this – as stated above – have too little explanatory power. On the other hand, we regularly encounter the previously criticized media tautology as exemplified in the 1970 edition of *Kursbuch*, in which Hans Magnus Enzensberger ruthlessly criticized Marshall McLuhan.[30] McLuhan, the founder of modern media theory with his world famous books 'The Gutenberg Galaxy' (1962), 'Understanding Media' (1964) and 'The Global Village' (1989; with Bruce R. Powers), certainly understood how to finally catch and focus the attention of social and cultural scientists on the question of media. Unfortunately, he was not a very systematic thinker (to put it lightly): he had good ideas, but was unable to unify them within a consistent and robust master theory. Despite this, contemporary media theorists continue to work both implicitly and explicitly on developing the details of his inspiring theses and ideas.

One of McLuhan's most famous sentences was, "The medium is the message."[31] In his 1970 work, Enzensberger attempted to analyze this statement logically and came to the conclusion that although McLuhan understood the medium and the message as separate entities, the use of the verb *is* in the sentence can only mean that the bearer of the message (the television, for instance) paradoxically becomes the content of the message itself. Commenting on this analysis, Enzensberger wrote,

> despite its provocative idiocy, this sentence reveals more than its author knows. It perfectly unmasks the tautological strain of media mysticism. According to his theory, the only notable aspect of the television is the fact that it functions at all; a thesis that certainly has some appeal in light of American programming.[32]

In reality, Enzensberger himself seems to have misunderstood the fact that McLuhan is not necessarily a logician. The actual tautology arises from a sec-

---

29 Wiesing 2008, p. 235.
30 Enzensberger 1970; see also: Leschke 2007, pp. 246, 254.
31 McLuhan 1964, p. 7.
32 Enzensberger 1970, pp. 177 f.

ond sentence, which can be found at elsewhere in 'Understanding Media' and explains the first. In it, McLuhan explains that individual media always occur doubly, where, "the 'content' of any medium is always another medium."[33] This idea is the origin of the tautology found throughout McLuhan's work. Terminological definitions are tautological when the term itself is used in its definition. Where does a medium come from? From a medium. What constitutes a medium? A medium. What does a medium do? It produces media. And so on and so forth, *ad infinitum*. The tautology that this sentence creates explains why McLuhan has no problem equating medium with message: the content, namely the message of the message (which others might designate with terms like *text, language*, or *meaning*) is itself *medium*. This has led to the incorporation of 'media content research' within social scientific studies of media. The undifferentiated expression *media content* does, however, point in the right conceptual direction. Within this term is the idea that media are a kind of container with a certain kind of content. Logically speaking, we can eliminate the tautology as long as we avoid considering the content identical to the container; when the content is not itself a medium. That would be a starting point towards a usable theory of media.

Under this premise, let us now attempt a modular and disciplinary definition for the term *medium*. The editors of the 2008 collection of essays on this topic asked their contributors a relatively straightforward and clearly formulated question: "What is a medium?" The question itself implies that the term refers – as most substantives do – to the set of all individual elements in of the class *medium*, just as one could ask, "What is a book?" After 50 years of research and study on the question of media, one should think that a clear and systematic answer would have been found. Here, as with other scientifically suitable terms, it should be enough to meet merely average expectations of rationality. What we are looking for is a *terminus technicus*, not a colloquial expression. Termini should normally be specifically defined; the classical model of definition according to *genus proximum* and *differentia specifica* continues to be quite useful for this purpose. Regarding a definition of *medium*, however, the ubiquitous media tautology that has barely subsided since McLuhan gives us little hope for clarity. An arbitrary example comes from Jan Marie Lambert Peters on the vast sum of similar confusion in media studies:

Medium = a type of sign, or a sign system (code). [...]

Medium = every specific utterance (in signs), every formulated message, or – to use a general term – every ‚text'. [...]

---

33 McLuhan 1964, p. 8.

Medium = the (transmission) channel wherein the message (after having been converted into technical signals) is carried through space and time to the receiver. [...]

Medium = the communicating organ, the ‚programming' body, the organisational whole in which the production, distribution and consumption of messages comes about.[34]

Philologists and lexicologists writing dictionaries can legitimately and for all intents and purposes accept such formulations. Peters begins his survey with the comment that the term *medium* can be defined as the "'means' of communication." Still, he notes that the common word medium has four different meanings.[35] Peters seems here to be describing the facts of speech behavior from a philological perspective: he is describing the unstable everyday use of the word. There is, however, one disconcerting element that creeps into his definition: he uses the mathematical equals sign (=), which is normally used to indicate logical identity. This notation clearly indicates that a medium is considered to be four distinct things. Lexicologists doing research on word use would have to indicate the varied meaning and use of the term using different methods. The fact is that Peters is not a lexicologist, but rather a mass media theoretician. In this case, we must bear in mind that theoretical terminology should not be directly derived from the everyday meaning of words, even if they originate from such use. Scientific termini, if they are to be considered such, must be based on and defined within a theoretical framework; they must be systematically derived and situated within a systematic *frame*. It is thus understandable that Dirk Baecker, with a clear sense of discomfort in regards to a conception of the term *medium*, postulates:

If we understand a term as an offer of descriptive order, and we measure it based on the boundaries that it sets, the inclusion of the descriptions, and its relation to the order of the subject itself, then we have every reason to accept a definition of media that begins where the problems of observation and description of the common facts begin.[36]

Similarly, Lambert Wiesing demands that, "the term *medium* not devolve into merely a synonym for other terms." In his opinion, what is missing,

are the differences that make a difference. If we follow McLuhan in naming every tool, every possibility, and follow phenomenologists in naming every transparency a medium, there is a demand for the establishment of criteria with which we can distinguish a screwdriver from a television, art from the telephone, and a window pane from a book.[37]

---

34 Peters 1977, p. 34.
35 Peters 1977, p. 33.
36 Baecker 2008, p. 132.
37 Wiesing 2008, p. 239.

Where do we find the problems of observation and description that demand a definition to which Baecker refers? Historically speaking, the study of *mass media* began in the United States in the 1920s. The field was devoted to applicably investigating the communicative activities of dimissive communication as found in media such as the newspaper, cinema, and radio in relation to politics and advertising. Both the rise of the television and McLuhan's work put such concerns on the epistemological agenda in the 1950s. At the time, there was a need to investigate these vast new and important phenomena in the world of communication. Media were thus categorized within the broader field of communication. If we turn our attention to a discrete definition of *medium* according to classical models, and ask about its *genus proximum*, the related categories and hierarchically related concepts can be more clearly illustrated. We can thereby restrict the domain of inquiry and take up a proposal from Sybille Krämer, who assigns *medium* to the category of "generativism". Under this model, she asserts that the concept of medium, "as opposed to the role of the mean, middle, or mediate," should more appropriately take on the, "perspective of the means, thus favor a more or less sublime instrumentalism."[38] From the rhetorical perspective, Krämer's formulation is a plausible proposal for the *genus proximum* in our attempts at a definition: according to her suggestion, a medium is a communicative instrument. The category of instrumentalism fits well within the rhetorical *organon* theory, which deals with communicative instruments. Accordingly, media can be understood as instruments used in the context of communicative activities.

In order to determine the second component of our definition, the *differentia specifica*, we need to look at the various different characteristics that communicative instruments might have. From the perspective of rhetoric, we see that instruments can be assigned to a variety of operational activities that a communicator may undertake. Each instrument can thus be assigned to an abstract category that is determined by the rhetorical calculations and corresponding operations with which the instrument is correlated. As a theory of text production, rhetoric divides calculations and planning into the following levels:

1. Languages, symbolic systems, codes (addressing questions such as: why should languages be mixed? Should the pictorial code be integrated into the work? The color code as well? Etc.)
2. Text (In some agencies, for instance, there are entire copy departments devoted to the production of advertising texts).[39]

---

38 Krämer 2008, p. 67.
39 See also: Knape 2005c.

3. The level of medium, understood as a device for saving and sending formulated texts (calculations at this level pose the question of whether a text should best be transmitted on a post-it note, on a poster, a billboard, or in a magazine, including considerations of cost and relative technical effort).[40]

4. The level of media systems, which considers (within the framework of operational theory) the social institutions that technically and organizationally distribute media (publishers, broadcasting companies, etc.).

Thus, a modular and discipline-specific definition for the term *medium* within rhetoric can be developed that is operationally and functionally based. The "means of communication" that Peters subsumes under the category of "medium" above must therefore be clearly and categorically differentiated into the following termini: 1. Code, 2. Text, 3. Medium as socially distributable platform, 4. Media system (as organizational institutions). The only element that Peters describes that could be considered a medium within the context of rhetoric is the "channel", though Peters' reduction of the channel is too simplified for our purposes. As Peters correctly notes, in a stricter sense of the term, the channel merely regulates the transmission according to Shannon/Weaver's 1949 mathematical model of communication.[41] Umberto Eco also borrowed from this idea, understanding 'medium' as the channel of transmission.[42] The rhetorical definition is not, however, derived from transmission as Eco understood it. It states, abstractly, that a medium is a communicative and instrumental, "device used to save and send texts." This logically implies that the device cannot be identical to the text itself (otherwise we would again be caught it the media tautology).

This is the definition of *medium* within the theory of rhetoric, and it is assigned to a different level than the theoretically distinct concept of the *text*. Many of the contributions to the collection referenced multiple times in this essay show a tendency towards this position; one can sense the deep unrest that these writers have with the media tautology, even if it is not specifically discussed as such. Sybille Krämer writes extensively about the theory of media as a "messenger theory" and about the "postal principle" of media.[43] With such thoughts she is not far from the rhetorical solution to the problem, even though she is ultimately unable to overcome the media tautology. When Dirk

---

40 Cf. pp. 8, 18 ff., 212, 217 f. in this book.
41 See also: Ernst 2008, p. 174.
42 See: Esposito 2008, p. 112.
43 Krämer 2008, pp. 67 ff.

Baecker attempts to investigate the perceived theoretical difference between *medium* and *text*, he notices with a certain amount of contortion that the answer lies somewhere in McLuhan's, "interplay between the figure and its ground."[44] This is indeed correct in an abstract sense: from the rhetorical perspective we can understand text as "the figure" and its medium (its platform) as the "ground". Media researcher Hartmut Winkler's conception is similarly strained: he calls media "sign machines" and refers to them metaphorically as, "biotopes for semiosis."[45] This account also hints at a rhetorical conception of medium. The semiotic level is here clearly separated from the medium; the medial body is understood as the biotope of its texts. In the end, however, all of these authors leave off where Jan Marie Lambert Peters was in 1977: they cannot rid themselves of the plastic word, the putative passe-partout 'medium'. They are unable to rid themselves of the media tautology with a clear theoretical division or to formulate a discrete definition of the term.

A text always requires a medium, a platform upon which it can be displayed, but the text exists at a semiotic level and thus at the higher level of information.[46] The respective technical conditions of these, 'devices used to save and send texts,' that we call *media* define their concrete communicative capacity: a classic telephone can only convey an acoustically notated text, while a piece of paper can only convey an optically notated text. The medial conditions of the production of written texts have an effect on the texts that can be produced.[47] Some have already noticed this connection in other semiotic fields such as music and painting.[48] Paul Pfister, for instance, has written about the difference between the musical text and the musical instrument as its medium, "if we really want to adequately hear a sonata by Carl Philipp Emanuel Bach, we ask about the instrument. Whether we use an organ, a pianoforte, or an electric keyboard to play the piece makes a huge difference, despite the fact that the score remains the same."[49] In 1763, Denis Diderot wrote emphatically about the mediality (not the textual imagery) of the paintings by Jean-Baptiste Siméon Chardin, the most famous French still-life painter of the 18th century,

---

44 Baecker 2008, p. 131.
45 Winkler 2008, p. 213.
46 Knape 2005c, p. 23; also: Ernst 2008, p. 163: "A medium is something that helps the unexpected, informational perception, thus helping free humans of their own subjectivity: the expansion of his senses in *this* sense. One example is that which we hear – since Fourier we have divided acoustics into tones and sounds; between periodical functions (tones) and non-periodical functions (crackling)."
47 Kittler 1985.
48 Knape 2010b, pp. 86–91.
49 Pfister 1996, p. 12.

this man understands the harmony of colors and reflection. O Chardin! That is not white, red, black paint that you mix on your palette: it is the true substance of objects, of air, and of light that you put on the tip of your brush and bring to the canvas." – "There are thick layers of paint, one on top of the other, whose effects can be seen from top to bottom. Sometimes we want to say that a fine dust has been blown onto the canvas, at others as if a light foam has been sprayed on it." – "If you get closer, everything blurs, flattens, and disappears; if you step away, everything forms and is spawned anew.[50]

We can thus say that the structural determinacy of a medium manifestly determines not only the perception of but also, to an extent, the texts themselves that it saves, performs and sends. The constraints, the specific capacity and the effects that a medium has on communicative interaction deserve more consideration.

What exactly is the capacity of media as an instrument of communication? Stated generally, media enable texts to be inserted into communicative interaction, as when a human body like mine is placed within a group of people in a lecture hall and performs a text that has been saved within it into a *situation*. Media that are external to the body, such as books, cinema, television, etc. are capable of carrying texts through *dimission* (without the presence of the author or communicator of the text) in a form of long distance communication through space and time.

A note on the terms "to save" and "to perform" and "to send": even in antiquity, rhetoric contained a theory of saving a text within the body. This part of rhetorical theory was called *mnemonics* in Greek and simply *memoria* in Latin: the art of committing something to memory. Classical rhetoricians developed series of mnemonic techniques that do not further interest us here. As for performance and sending, modern rhetorical theory calls the method with which texts are conveyed by a medium the "act" or "performance of the text". Ancient rhetorical theory considered this process as the fifth stage of production under the heading *actio*. The conception of the performance refers to the process by which the text is brought by the medium into communicative interaction (adpragmatization). The method by which the process of performance functions is known in rhetoric as *staging*. Performance and staging are thus two sides of the same coin, upon which the medium does something with the text.

What the human body actually does as a medium in the performance of texts, what it should or should not do, has – as said before – been the focus of chapters on *actio* within general rhetorical theory since antiquity. The guidelines set out by these theories can be divided into three systematic areas: *vul-*

---

50 Diderot 1763, pp. 222 f.

tus, vox, and *gestus* (facial expressions, vocal conduct, body language). Upon closer look, a certain problem arises, because the human body is a multi-tasking device and not merely a potential medium. The body simultaneously represents the instance of text production, the medium of the text, and at a higher level, occasionally constitutes a type paratextuality created by body language. Only in those cases where such paratextuality exists can we com-pletely accept Sybille Krämer's conclusion that the instrumentalism of media is closely connected to a medial "impulse of sovereignty." According to Krämer, the criteria of generativism and instrumentalism must be simultaneously applied to media,

> media are not instruments and carriers of a purpose given to them by some external source. Rather, media simultaneously generate or produce that which they transmit. They have both constructivist and generativist, not to mention demiurgic characteristics. Media produce that which they transmit.[51]

The theory of rhetoric, on the other hand, conceives of two separate abstrac-tions; it makes a differentiation between production and mediality. From the rhetorical perspective, we can thus say that only the human body functions simultaneously as both producer and *medium*. All other instruments, by defini-tion, require an external *operator* to fulfill their necessary function. Even if Krämer had spoken of 'automatism' or 'automatons' (which contain the idea of self-direction) instead of instrumentalism, one can still ask the question of whether or not an external *operator* is necessary in the real world. In rhetorical theory, at least, it has been established that instruments cannot construct and operate themselves, that they cannot determine their objectives themselves. Instead, instruments always require some kind of external operator who uses them to meet his own goals. From the perspective of rhetoric, the human body first becomes a medium the moment it is used to send the main linguistic text (and possibly simultaneously a corporeal paratext).[52] The declamatory element of a text designed to praise someone, for instance, can be counteracted by extra-communicative elements created by the body as a medium, such as the use of an ironic gesture.

As always in rhetoric, the operative level of *medium* is to be understood as an object of reflective calculation on the part of an orator. The performance (what a medium can do with a text), should assist the normal communication

---

51 Krämer 2008, p. 67.
52 A corporeal paratext can consist of a series of synchronous expressions made during performance, which can include singular symbols (as in the gesture of pointing a thumb downwards) or paralinguistic phenomena (such as giggling or laughing).

of a text and should never contradict or negate the message. In art and other forms of special communication (especially the opera) it has become common to integrate a second semantic level into the performance, within which we find the remnants of a second story. Such considerations lead us away from rhetoric. Christa M. Heilmann investigated the phenomena of corporeal performance in her 2004 essay titled, 'The Concept of the Body in Rhetoric from a Semiotic Perspective.' In it, she correctly comes to the conclusion that we can only speak of a "language" of the body in an informal sense. If such "body language" is able to support the "original expression" (here she means the verbal text) one can speak of,

> amplification [...] as opposed to contradiction, which constitutes an opposition between the text and that conveyed by body language. The corporeal forms of expression may be able to lightly modify what is primarily meant (modification) or, in extreme cases, to substitute it entirely (which breaks the symbiosis of both levels). All four possibilities within the semantic dimension require a high degree of conventionality in order to make the relationship between the first and second message transparent for processes of understanding. Phenomena of bodily expression take on a syntactic dimension through the segmentation of the speech flow, the connection of smaller units to larger ones, or through the synchronization of different channels.[53]

Ancient rhetorical doctrine, as found in chapters on *actio*, was primarily concerned with the problem of how the corporeal performance could adequately be interpreted such that the performance did not negatively affect the actual text, the speech itself (gr. *lógos*, lat. *oratio*). It is little wonder, then, that one of Cicero's main works on rhetorical theory, 'Orator', for long stretches deals solely with agogic, prosodic, and paralinguistic phenomena such as the creation of sounds and voice with the body.

The rhetorical tradition had only rudimentary conceptions of ways to deal with the performance of media external to the body (such as wax tablets or papyri).[54] This dearth has made this set of problems that much more relevant today. With regard to the text, we have learned to consider the connotative effects involved whether Shakespeare wrote his 18th sonnet on a loose sheet of paper, or read the poem aloud to his paramour in a face-to-face situation, whether it disappears in a text-heavy 1000 page thin-print anthology, is presented at a festival printed on a single sheet of hand-made paper with gold leaf, or spoken by a professor in a lecture hall in London:[55]

---

53 Heilmann 2004, p. 280.
54 Knape 2012a.
55 Shakespeare's Sonnets (1997), no. 18, p. 147.

Shall I compare thee to a summer's day?
Thou art more lovely and more temperate:
Rough winds do shake the darling buds of May,
And summer's lease hath all too short a date:
Sometime too hot the eye of heaven shines,
And often is his gold complexion dimmed;
And every fair from fair sometime declines,
By chance, or nature's changing course, untrimmed:
But thy eternal summer shall not fade,
Nor lose possession of that fair thou ow'st,
Nor shall death brag thou wander'st in his shade
When in eternal lines to time thou grow'st:
   So long as men can breathe or eyes can see,
   So long lives this, and this gives life to thee.

The few ancient records that deal with medialization external to the body from a rhetorical perspective make it clear that the human-corporeal *organon* was seen as the measure of linguistic expression. A prime example here is a critical work by the 4th century BC sophist Alcidamas, titled 'On the Writers of Written Texts'. Alcidamas saw the concept of the book as a technical variant of medialization (including the associated idea of writing as 'text-optification') not only as a compromise, but as an impediment to communication. Indeed, the history of the technical-medial possibilities of 'text-performance' (up to and including the invention of modern real-time media) is a history of the fight against unavoidable reductionism: against a sort of performance pauperism on the optical-but-mute page that is in constant competition with the fullness of performance found in the acoustically rich spoken event. A rhetoric that concerned itself with this problem would not begin with problem of adequacy in the relationship between texts and medium (which was never the focus anyway). Instead, it would have to concentrate directly on the implementation of compensation strategies: compensation for the loss of information contained in the text caused by the medium.

These considerations lead us to the question of the systematic place of writing (and scripturality in general) in rhetorical theory, once heavily criticized in Plato's 'Phaedrus' and raised to the level of the leading component of performance in the 'Gutenberg Galaxy'. In order to establish a clear position, we must first make note that as a notational code of speech, writing can only have the status of a medial epiphenomenon. Media are "social platforms used to distribute verbal or non-verbal texts"[56] and as such – as stated earlier – are

---

56 Knape 2000a, p. 62.

devices for saving, performing, and sending texts. Such is the specific capacity of media. How such devices are "technically" designed is not the subject of a definition, but rather a question of the concrete conditions in which they are used. The writings of various human cultures belong to the larger complex of such concrete technical conditions.

According to rhetorical theory, performance begins the moment a *text* begins to be saved on a *medium*, e.g. the moment that the pen is put to paper, and ends with the sending of the text. If someone wants to put a spoken word text to a sheet of paper (the actual *medium*) then they have to write it. This requires the notation-code of *script* which is technically applied to the paper using the appropriate devices (a pen, the ink, etc.). All of these technical components of a given media determine its character as a, "device for saving, performing, and sending texts".

Any trans-medialization that takes place (for instance, the transfer of a complex acoustic act of speaking to the purely optical media of writing on paper) necessarily involves a form of performative reduction. The process of writing a text on a piece of paper that had hitherto been cognitively anchored and vocally performed entails modifying the form of its performance (in which the text is conveyed to addressees). In cultures in which written forms of media enjoy the highest esteem or serve important social functions, special text genres have even been created that are completely dependent on written correspondence. Such cases have led to the creation of so-called *literary languages*. This term refers to the pool of structural and stylistic text variants cultivated by a language community with reference to the conditions of dimissive communication.[57] These stylistic phenomena (so-called "literary styles" or "writing styles", as Gottsched called them in the 18th century) are thus the results, discharge, or consequences of certain performative conditions. Writing in general (as a medial component of performance) must be situated at a different theoretical level than styles of writing (as semiotic components of *text*).

In practice, authors have continually attempted to compensate for the communicative limitations that arise from the restrictive conditions of performance, such as occur when choosing to write a book. This has yielded a field of creative possibilities when it comes to staging a text within the medium 'book'. On the one hand we see book-layouts becoming the playground of book artists as stage managers who, through the use of optically aesthetic stimuli, seek to recapture some of what has been lost acoustically based on the structure of the medium. On the other hand, rhetorically educated authors have repeatedly

---

[57] For more on the difference between the situative and dimissive communicative settings see: Knape 2005c, pp. 30 f.

integrated performance compensating strategies into the formulation of their texts in order to evoke the imagination of the pure literary and reading culture. In such cases, the imaginative potential of a text, or an easy going play on words, is meant to cover up the 'performance poverty' of the book, its endless pages covered in words.[58] It is not rare for the language games used by authors as compensation strategies to be criticized as mannerisms of speech.

Naturally, there is a countermovement to this perspective in the 'Gutenberg Galaxy'. Some writers construct texts that directly utilize the performative reduction of their chosen medium as a principle of staging. As semiotic components of the communicative act, such written texts can thus sometimes be so Spartan as to be confusing. Written texts are persistent, and allow long contemplation of their content on the part of the reader. This contrasts with the ephemeral spoken text, which can only come alive in the situation *hic et nunc*; it must do its job in the moment. Important in spoken situations is the physical corporeal performance, such as the vocal support of the text. Authors can anticipate the need for such elements and plan their text accordingly. Consequently, the author of a book designed to be read by speakers and heard by listeners can write in a different way than one who is consciously writing for readers who are content to sit and read quietly by themselves.

Nihil sine causa

---

58 Interesting observations of this phenomenon as used in the 18th century can be found in Schneider's 2004 doctoral dissertation.

Bibliography

Adamowsky, Natascha (2008): Eine Natur unbegrenzter Geschmeidigkeit. Medientheoretische Überlegungen zum Zusammenhang von Aisthesis, Performativität und Ereignishaftigkeit am Beispiel des Anormalen. In: Stefan Münker / Alexander Roesler (ed.): Was ist ein Medium? Frankfurt a. M., pp. 30–64.

Adamzik, Kirsten (1984): Sprachliches Handeln und sozialer Kontakt. Zur Integration der Kategorie ‚Beziehungsaspekt' in eine sprechakttheoretische Beschreibung des Deutschen. Tübingen (= Tübinger Beiträge zur Linguistik 213).

Adamzik, Kirsten (1994): Beziehungsgestaltung in Dialogen. In: Gerd Fritz / Franz Hundsnurscher (ed.): Handbuch der Dialoganalyse. Tübingen, pp. 357–374.

Adamzik, Kirsten (2001): Aspekte der Gesprächstypologisierung / Aspects of Conversation Typology. In: Klaus Brinker / Gerd Antos / Wolfgang Heinemann / Sven F. Sager (ed.): Text- und Gesprächslinguistik / Linguistics of Text and Conversation. Ein internationales Handbuch zeitgenössischer Forschung / An International Handbook of Contemporary Research. 2. Halbbd. / Vol. 2. Berlin, New York, pp. 1472–1484 (= HSK. Handbücher zur Sprach- und Kommunikationswissenschaft / Handbooks of Linguistics and Communication Science 16. 2).

Albert, Ethel M. (1964): "Rhetoric", "Logic", and "Poetics" in Burundi: Cultural Patterning of Speech Behaviour. In: John J. Gumperz / Dell Hymes (ed.): The Ethnography of Communication = American Anthropologist 66. Number 6, Part 2 (Special Publication), pp. 35–54.

Alcidamas: On Those Who Write Written Speeches or On Sophists. In: Alcidamas: The Works and Fragments. Ed. with Introd., Transl. and Commentary by J. V. Muir. London 2001, pp. 2–21.

Andersen, Øivind (1995): I retorikkens hage. Oslo (German Translation: Im Garten der Rhetorik. Darmstadt 2001).

Appel, Markus (2005): Realität durch Fiktionen. Rezeptionserleben, Medienkompetenz und Überzeugungsänderungen. Berlin.

Aristoteles: Poetik. Hrsg. und übers. von Manfred Fuhrmann. Stuttgart 1982.

Aristoteles: Rhetorik. Übers. und erl. von Christof Rapp. Zwei Halbbände. Berlin 2002 (= Aristoteles. Werke in deutscher Übersetzung 4. 1–2).

Aristotle: On Sophistical Refutations. In: Aristotle: On Sophistical Refutations. On Coming-to-Be and Passing-Away. By E. S. Forster. On the Cosmos. By D. J. Furley. Reprinted. Cambridge, MA, London 1978, pp. 10–155 (= Aristotle in Twenty-Three Volumes 3; The Loeb Classical Library 400).

Aristotle: The "Art" of Rhetoric. With an Engl. Transl. by John Henry Freese. Reprinted. Cambridge, MA, London 1975 (= Aristotle in Twenty-Three Volumes 22; The Loeb Classical Library 193).

Aristotle: The Poetics. In: Aristotle: The Poetics. "Longinus": On the Sublime. With an Engl. Transl. by W. Hamilton Fyfe. Demetrius: On Style. With an Engl. Transl. by W. Rhys Roberts. Reprinted. Cambridge, MA, London 1973, pp. 4–118 (= Aristotle in Twenty-Three Volumes 23; The Loeb Classical Library 199).

Aristotle: Topica. In: Aristotle: Posterior Analytics. By Hugh Tredennick. Topica. By E. S. Forster. Reprinted. Cambridge, MA, London 1976, pp. 272–739 (= Aristotle in Twenty-Three Volumes 2; The Loeb Classical Library 391).

Auerochs, Bernd (2007): Parabel. In: Metzler Lexikon Literatur. 3rd ed., pp. 567 f.

Austin, John L. (1962): How to Do Things with Words. The William James Lectures delivered at Harvard University in 1955. Oxford.

Baecker, Dirk (2008): Medienforschung. In: Stefan Münker / Alexander Roesler (ed.): Was ist ein Medium? Frankfurt a. M., pp. 131–143.

Bar-Lev, Zev (1986): Discourse Theory and "Contrastive Rhetoric". In: Discourse Processes 9, pp. 235–246.

Barclay, Alexander: The Ship of Fools. Ed. by T. H. Jamieson. 2 Vols. Edinburgh 1874.

Barth, Michael / Gärtner, Christel / Neumann-Braun, Klaus (1997): Spielräume der Faszination oder die Zuschauerirritation als dramaturgisches Prinzip in modernen Filmen. Betrachtungen zur Funktion von binären Oppositionen, narrativen Lücken und intertextuellen Referenzen am Beispiel des Kinofilms „Angel Heart". In: Michael Charlton / Silvia Schneider (ed.): Rezeptionsforschung. Theorien und Untersuchungen zum Umgang mit Massenmedien. Opladen, pp. 170–194.

Barthes, Roland (1967): The Death of the Author. In: Roland Barthes: Image-Music-Text. Transl. by Steven Heath. New York 1977, pp. 142–148 (Original in: Aspen Magazine 5/6, 1967).

Barthes, Roland (1970): The Old Rhetoric. In: Roland Barthes: The semiotic challenge. Transl. by Richard Howard. Berkley, CA, 1994. pp. 11–93. (French Original: L'ancienne rhétorique. Aide-mémoire. In: Communications 16, 1970, pp. 172–229).

Barthes, Roland (1978): Leçon: Leçon inaugurale de la chaire de sémiologie littéraire du Collège de France prononcée le 7 janvier 1977. Paris.

Baudry, Jean-Louis (1986): The Apparatus: Metapsychological Approaches to the Impression of Reality in Cinema. In: Philip Rosen (ed.): Narrative, Apparatus, Ideology. A Film Theory Reader. New York, pp. 299–318.

Bauer, Gerhard (1969): Zur Poetik des Dialogs. Leistung und Formen der Gesprächsführung in der neueren deutschen Literatur. Darmstadt (= Impulse der Forschung 1).

Bauer, Matthias / Knape, Joachim / Koch, Peter / Winkler, Susanne (2010): Dimensionen der Ambiguität. In: Wolfgang Klein / Susanne Winkler (ed.): Ambiguität = Zeitschrift für Literaturwissenschaft und Linguistik 40 (no. 158), pp. 7–75.

Bausch, Karl-Heinz / Grosse, Siegfried (1985) (ed.): Praktische Rhetorik. Beiträge zu ihrer Funktion in der Aus- und Fortbildung. Auswahlbibliographie. Mannheim.

Becher, Tony / Kogan, Maurice (1992): Process and Structure in Higher Education. 2nd ed. London.

Becker-Mrotzek, Michael / Brünner, Gisela (2009) (ed.): Analyse und Vermittlung von Gesprächskompetenz. 2nd ed. Frankfurt a. M. (= forum ANGEWANDTE LINGUISTIK 43).

Beißwenger, Michael (2003): Sprachhandlungskoordination im Chat. In: Zeitschrift für germanistische Linguistik 31, pp. 198–231.

Benjamin, Walter (1939): The Work of Art in the Age of Reproducibility. 3rd version. In: Walter Benjamin: Selected Writings Vol. 4. Ed. by Howard Eiland / Michael W. Jennings. Transl. by Rodney Livingstone. London, Cambridge, MA, 2003, pp. 251–283.

Bentele, Günter (1992): Images und Medien-Images. In: Werner Faulstich (ed.): Image – Imageanalyse – Imagegestaltung. 2. Lüneburger Kolloquium zur Medienwissenschaft. Bardowick, pp. 152–176 (= IfAM-Arbeitsberichte 7).

Bergler, Reinhold (1991): Standort als Imagefaktor. In: Deutsche Public Relations Gesellschaft e. V. (DPRG) (ed.): Führung und Kommunikation. Erfolg durch Partnerschaft. Standort als Imagefaktor. DPRG-Jahrestagung 9.–11. 5. 1991 in Essen. Bonn, pp. 47–64.

Bergmann, Regina (1999): Rhetorikratgeberliteratur aus linguistischer Sicht. In: Gisela Brünner / Reinhard Fiehler / Walther Kindt (ed.): Angewandte Diskursforschung. Vol. 2: Methoden und Anwendungsbereiche. Wiesbaden, pp. 226–246.

Bergsdorf, Wolfgang (2009): Rhetorik und Stilistik in der Politologie / Rhetoric and Stylistics in Political Science. In: Ulla Fix / Andreas Gardt / Joachim Knape (ed.): Rhetorik und Stilistik / Rhetoric and Stylistics. Ein internationales Handbuch historischer und systematischer Forschung / An International Handbook of Historical and Systematic Research. 2. Halbbd. / Vol. 2. Berlin, New York, pp. 1842–1856 (= HSK. Handbücher zur Sprach- und Kommunikationswissenschaft / Handbooks of Linguistics and Communication Science 31. 2).

Bernhard, Thomas (1974): Die Jagdgesellschaft. Frankfurt a. M.

Bernhard, Thomas (1975): An Indication of the Cause. In: Thomas Bernhard: Gathering Evidence. Transl. by David McLintock. New York 1985, pp. 75–142. (German Original: Die Ursache. Eine Andeutung. Salzburg 1975).

Bernhard, Thomas (1978): The Voice Imitator. Transl. by Kenneth J. Northcott. Chicago, 1997 (German Original: Der Stimmenimitator. Frankfurt a. M. 1978).

Best, Otto F. (1985): Der Dialog. In: Klaus Weissenberger (ed.): Prosakunst ohne Erzählen. Die Gattungen der nicht-fiktionalen Kunstprosa. Tübingen, pp. 89–104 (= Konzepte der Sprach- und Literaturwissenschaft 34).

Birnbacher, Dieter / Krohn, Dieter (2002) (ed.): Das sokratische Gespräch. Stuttgart.

Bittner, Johannes (2003): Digitalität, Sprache, Kommunikation. Eine Untersuchung zur Medialität von digitalen Kommunikationsformen und Textsorten und deren varietätenlinguistischer Modellierung. Berlin.

Bliese, John R. E. (1974): Medieval Rhetoric. Its Study and Practice in Northern Europe from 1050 to 1250. Unpublished Ph.D.-Thesis: University of Kansas.

Bloomfield, Leonard (1933): Language. New York.

Blumenberg, Hans (1981): Anthropologische Annäherung an die Rhetorik. In: Hans Blumenberg: Wirklichkeiten in denen wir leben. Aufsätze und eine Rede. Stuttgart, pp. 104–136.

Böhme, Hartmut / Matussek, Peter (2008): Die Natur der Medien und die Medien der Natur. In: Stefan Münker / Alexander Roesler (ed.): Was ist ein Medium? Frankfurt a. M., pp. 91–111.

Booth, Wayne C. (1961): The Rhetoric of Fiction. Chicago.

Bordwell, David (1991): Making Meaning. Inference and Rhetoric in the Interpretation of Cinema. Cambridge, MA (= Harvard Film Studies).

Borgstedt, Silke (2008): Der Musik-Star. Vergleichende Imageanalysen von Alfred Brendel, Stefanie Hertel und Robbie Williams. Bielefeld (= Studien zur Popularmusik).

Bornscheuer, Lothar (1976): Topik. Zur Struktur der gesellschaftlichen Einbildungskraft. Frankfurt a. M.

Boskoff, Priscilla S. (1952): Quintilian in the Late Middle Ages. In: Speculum 27, pp. 71–78.

Boulding, Kenneth E. (1956): The Image. Knowledge in Life and Society. Ann Arbor, MI.

Brant, Sebastian: Das Narrenschiff. Transl. by Hermann A. Junghans. Leipzig 1877.

Brant, Sebastian: Das Narrenschiff. Facsimile of the first edition by Franz Schultz. Strassburg 1912. Reprint ed. by Dieter Wuttke. Baden-Baden 1994 (= SAECVLA SPIRITALIA 6).

Brant, Sebastian: Das Narrenschiff. Ed. by Joachim Knape. Stuttgart 2005.

Braungart, Georg (1988): Hofberedsamkeit. Studien zur Praxis höfisch-politischer Rede im deutschen Territorialabsolutismus. Tübingen. (= Studien zur deutschen Literatur 96).

Brenzikofer, Barbara (2002): Reputation von Professoren. Implikationen für das Human Recource Management von Universitäten. Munich, Mering (= Personalwirtschaftliche Schriften 19).

Bressa, Birgit (2003): Plastik. In: Historisches Wörterbuch der Rhetorik 6, col. 1239–1268.

Brinker, Klaus / Antos, Gerd / Heinemann, Wolfgang / Sager, Sven F. (2000–2001) (ed.):
Text- und Gesprächslinguistik / Linguistics of Text and Conversation. Ein internationales
Handbuch zeitgenössischer Forschung / An International Handbook of Contemporary
Research. 2 Halbbde. / 2 Vols. Berlin, New York (= HSK. Handbücher zur Sprach- und
Kommunikationswissenschaft / Handbooks of Linguistics and Communication
Science 16. 1–2).

Brown, Penelope / Levinson, Stephen (1987): Politeness. Some Universals in Language
Usage. Cambridge (= Studies in Interactional Sociolinguistics 4).

Brünner, Gisela (2000): Wirtschaftskommunikation. Linguistische Analyse ihrer mündlichen
Formen. Tübingen (= Germanistische Linguistik 213).

Bühler, Karl (1934): Theory of Language: The Representational Function of Language. Transl.
by Donald Fraser Goodwin. Amsterdam 1990 (German Original: Sprachtheorie. Die
Darstellungsfunktion der Sprache. Jena 1934).

Burgoon, Judee K. / Hale, Jerold L. (1984): The Fundamental Topoi of Relational
Communication. In: Communication Monographs 51, pp. 193–214.

Burgoon, Judee K. / Humpherys, Sean / Moffitt, Kevin (2008): Nonverbal Communication:
Research Areas and Approaches / Nonverbale Kommunikation: Forschungsfelder und
-ansätze. In: Ulla Fix / Andreas Gardt / Joachim Knape (ed.): Rhetorik und Stilistik /
Rhetoric and Stylistics. Ein internationales Handbuch historischer und systematischer
Forschung / An International Handbook of Historical and Systematic Research.
1. Halbbd. / Vol. 1. Berlin, New York, pp. 787–812 (= HSK. Handbücher zur Sprach- und
Kommunikationswissenschaft / Handbooks of Linguistics and Communication
Science 31. 1).

Burke, Kenneth (1931): Counter-Statement. 3rd ed. London 1968.

Burke, Kenneth (1939): The Rhetoric of Hitler's 'Battle'. In: The Philosophy of Literary Form:
Studies in Symbolic Action. 3rd ed. Berkeley 1974, pp. 191–220.

Burke, Kenneth (1941): The Philosophy of Literary Form. Studies in Symbolic Action. 5th ed.
New York 1973.

Burke, Kenneth (1945): A Grammar of Motives. California edition. Los Angeles 1969.

Burke, Kenneth (1950): 'Administrative' Rhetoric in Machiavelli. In: A Rhetoric of Motives.
3rd ed. Berkeley 2000, pp. 158–166.

Burke, Kenneth (1966): Language as Symbolic Action. Essays on Life, Literature, and Method.
Berkeley, CA.

Buttenwieser, Hilda (1930): The Distribution of the Manuscripts of the Latin Classical Authors
in the Middle Ages. Unpublished Ph.D.-Thesis: University of Chicago.

Carawan, Edwin (2007) (ed.): Oxford Readings in the Attic Orators. Oxford (= Oxford
Readings in Classical Studies).

Carroll III, William Myles (2011): The Logic of Poetic Language. Explaining the Power of
Poetry to Transform Our Understanding of the World. With a Foreword by Ed Block.
Lewiston, NY, Queenston, ON, Lampeter.

Carroll, Noël (2008): The Philosophy of Motion Pictures. Malden, MA.

Carruthers, Peter (2006): The Case for Massively Modular Models of Mind. In: Robert J.
Stainton (ed.): Contemporary Debates in Cognitive Science. Malden, MA., pp. 3–21.

Chase, Stuart (1938): The Tyranny of Words. New York.

Chomsky, Noam (1957): Syntactic Structures. Berlin 2002.

Chronicle of the Emperors = Die Kaiserchronik eines Regensburger Geistlichen. Ed. by
Edward Schröder. Hannover 1892 (= Monvmenta Germaniae Historica / Deutsche
Chroniken und andere Geschichtsbücher des Mittelalters I. 1).

Cicero, Marcus Tullius: De Oratore. Books I, II: With an Engl. Transl. by E. W. Sutton. Completed, with an Introd. by H. Rackham. Reprinted. London, Cambridge, MA, 1967. Book III (together with De Fato, Paradoxa Stoicorum, De Partitione Oratoria): With an Engl. Transl. by H. Rackham. Reprinted. London, Cambridge, MA, 1968 (= Cicero in Twenty-Eight Volumes 3–4; The Loeb Classical Library 348–349).

Cicero, Marcus Tullius: Orator. In: Marcus Tullius Cicero: Brutus. With an Engl. Transl. by G. L. Hendrickson. Orator. With an Engl. Transl. by H. M. Hubbell. Revised and Reprinted. London, Cambridge, MA, 1962, pp. 306–509 (= Cicero in Twenty-Eight Volumes 5; The Loeb Classical Library 342).

Clark, Toby (1997) (ed.): Art and Propaganda in the Twentieth Century. The Political Image in the Age of Mass Culture. London.

Connor, Ulla (1996): Contrastive Rhetoric: Cross-Cultural Aspects of Second-Language Writing. Cambridge, MA, New York (= Cambridge Applied Linguistics).

Copeland, Rita (1991): Rhetoric, Hermeneutics, and Translation in the Middle Ages. Academic Traditions and Vernacular Texts. Cambridge (= Cambridge Studies in Medieval Literature 11).

Corbett, Edward P. J. (1963): The Usefulness of Classical Rhetoric. In: College Composition and Communication 14, pp. 162–164.

Corbett, Edward P. J. (1965): Classical Rhetoric for the Modern Student. 4th ed (with Robert J. Connors). Oxford 1999.

Crain, Stephen / Lillo-Martin, Diane (1999): An Introduction to Linguistic Theory and Language Acquisition. Malden, MA (= Blackwell Textbooks in Linguistics 15).

Dahinden, Urs (2006): Framing. Eine integrative Theorie der Massenkommunikation. Konstanz (= Forschungsfeld Kommunikation 22).

de Lairesse, Gerard (1707): Groot Schilderboek. Amsterdam.

de Man, Paul (1971): The Rhetoric of Blindness: Jacque Derrida's reading of Rousseau. In: Paul de Man: Blindness and Insight. Essays in the Rhetoric of Contemporary Criticism. 2nd ed. Minneapolis, MN, 1983, pp. 102–141 (= Theory and History of Literature 7).

de Man, Paul (1979): Allegories of Reading: Figural Language in Rousseau, Nietzsche, Rilke, and Proust. New Haven.

de Man, Paul (1984): Aesthetic Formalization: Kleist's Über das Marionettentheater. In: Paul de Man: The Rhetoric of Romanticism. New York, pp. 263–290.

de Saussure, Ferdinand (1916): Course in General Linguistics. Ed. by Charles Bally and Albert Sechehaye, Transl. by Wade Baskin. New York 1966. (French Original: Cours de linguistique générale. Lausanne, Paris 1916).

Deciu Ritivoi, Andreea / Graff, Richard (2008): Rhetorik und neuere Literaturtheorie / Rhetoric and Modern Literary Theory. In: Ulla Fix / Andreas Gardt / Joachim Knape (ed.): Rhetorik und Stilistik / Rhetoric and Stylistics. Ein internationales Handbuch historischer und systematischer Forschung / An International Handbook of Historical and Systematic Research. 1. Halbbd. / Vol. 1. Berlin, New York, pp. 944–959 (= HSK. Handbücher zur Sprach- und Kommunikationswissenschaft / Handbooks of Linguistics and Communication Science 31. 1).

Deppermann, Arnulf (1997): Glaubwürdigkeit im Konflikt. Rhetorische Techniken in Streitgesprächen. Prozeßanalysen von Schlichtungsgesprächen. Frankfurt a. M. (= European University Studies 21: Linguistics 184).

Deppermann, Arnulf (1998): Argumentieren über Aufrichtigkeit: Zur rhetorischen Funktion einer „Kommunikationsvoraussetzung". In: Alexander Brock / Martin Hartung (ed.):

Neuere Entwicklungen in der Gesprächsforschung: Vorträge der 3. Arbeitstagung des Pragmatischen Kolloquiums Freiburg. Tübingen, pp. 85–105 (= ScriptOralia 108).

Deppermann, Arnulf (2003): Desiderata einer gesprächsanalytischen Argumentationsforschung. In: Arnulf Deppermann / Martin Hartung (ed.): Argumentieren in Gesprächen: Gesprächsanalytische Studien. Tübingen, pp. 10–26 (= Stauffenburg-Linguistik 28).

Diderot, Dennis (1763): Salons. Vol. 1. Ed. by Jean Seznec / Jean Adhémar. Oxford 1957.

Dittmar, Jens (1993) (ed.): Sehr gescherte Reaktion. Leserbrief-Schlachten um Thomas Bernhard. Vienna.

Dolinina, Inga B. / Cecchetto, Vittorina (1998): Facework and Rhetorical Strategies in Intercultural Argumentative Discourse. In: Argumentation 12, pp. 167–181.

Drever, James (1973): A Dictionary of Psychology. Rev. by Henry Wallerstein. Reprinted. Harmondsworth.

Eagleton, Terry (1996): Literary Criticism. An Introduction. 2nd ed. Cambridge, MA.

Eco, Umberto (1976): A Theory of Semiotics. Bloomington, IN, London (= Advances in Semiotics).

Eco, Umberto (1983): Horns, Hooves, Insteps: Some Hypotheses on Three Types of Abduction. In: Umberto Eco / Thomas A. Sebeok (ed.): The Sign of Three: Dupin, Holmes, Peirce. Bloomington, IN, Indianapolis, IN, pp. 198–220 (= Advances in Semiotics).

Eco, Umberto (1987): Lector in Fabula. Die Mitarbeit der Interpretation in erzählenden Texten. Munich (= Edition Akzente).

Eisenegger, Mark (2004): Reputationskonstitution, Issues Monitoring und Issues Management in der Mediengesellschaft. Eine theoretische und empirische Untersuchung mit besonderer Berücksichtigung ökonomischer Organisationen. Zurich.

Enzensberger, Hans Magnus (1970): Baukasten zu einer Theorie der Medien. In: Kursbuch 20, pp. 159–186.

Ernst, Wolfgang (2008): „Merely the Medium"? Die operative Verschränkung von Logik und Materie. In: Stefan Münker / Alexander Roesler (ed.): Was ist ein Medium? Frankfurt a. M., pp. 158–184.

Esposito, Elena (2008): Die normale Unwahrscheinlichkeit der Medien: der Fall des Geldes. In: Stefan Münker / Alexander Roesler (ed.): Was ist ein Medium? Frankfurt a. M., pp. 112–130.

Eyckeler, Franz (1995): Reflexionspoesie. Sprachskepsis, Rhetorik und Poetik in der Prosa Thomas Bernhards. Berlin (= Philologische Studien und Quellen 133).

Fahnestock, Jeanne (1999): Rhetorical Figures in Science. New York.

Faulstich, Werner (2000): Das Image-Konzept. In: Werner Faulstich: Grundwissen Öffentlichkeitsarbeit. Munich, pp. 124–129.

Fiehler, Reinhard (1990): Kommunikation und Emotion. Theoretische und empirische Untersuchungen zur Rolle von Emotionen in der verbalen Interaktion. Berlin, New York (= Grundlagen der Kommunikation und Kognition).

Fiehler, Reinhard (1999): Kann man Kommunikation lernen? Zur Veränderbarkeit von Kommunikationsverhalten durch Kommunikationstrainings. In: Gisela Brünner / Reinhard Fiehler / Walther Kindt (ed.): Angewandte Diskursforschung. Vol. 2: Methoden und Anwendungsbereiche. Wiesbaden, pp. 18–35.

Fiehler, Reinhard (2001a): Emotionalität im Gespräch / Emotionality in Conversation. In: Klaus Brinker / Gerd Antos / Wolfgang Heinemann / Sven F. Sager (ed.): Text- und Gesprächslinguistik / Linguistics of Text and Conversation. Ein internationales

Handbuch zeitgenössischer Forschung / An International Handbook of Contemporary
Research. 2. Halbbd. / Vol. 2. Berlin, New York, pp. 1425–1438 (= HSK. Handbücher zur
Sprach- und Kommunikationswissenschaft / Handbooks of Linguistics and
Communication Science 16. 2).

Fiehler, Reinhard (2001b): Gesprächsanalyse und Kommunikationstraining / Conversation
Linguistics and Communication Training. In: Klaus Brinker / Gerd Antos / Wolfgang
Heinemann / Sven F. Sager (ed.): Text- und Gesprächslinguistik / Linguistics of Text and
Conversation. Ein internationales Handbuch zeitgenössischer Forschung / An
International Handbook of Contemporary Research. 2. Halbbd. / Vol. 2. Berlin, New
York, pp. 1697–1710 (= HSK. Handbücher zur Sprach- und
Kommunikationswissenschaft / Handbooks of Linguistics and Communication
Science 16. 2).

Fiehler, Reinhard (2008): Emotionale Kommunikation / Emotional Communication. In: Ulla
Fix / Andreas Gardt / Joachim Knape (ed.): Rhetorik und Stilistik / Rhetoric and
Stylistics. Ein internationales Handbuch historischer und systematischer Forschung / An
International Handbook of Historical and Systematic Research. 1. Halbbd. / Vol. 1.
Berlin, New York, pp. 757–772 (= HSK. Handbücher zur Sprach- und
Kommunikationswissenschaft / Handbooks of Linguistics and Communication
Science 31. 1).

Fiehler, Reinhard / Schmitt, Reinhold (2011): Gesprächstraining. In: Karlfried Knapp, et. al.
(ed.): Angewandte Linguistik. Ein Lehrbuch. 3rd ed. Tübingen, Basel, pp. 355–375.

Fix, Ulla / Gardt, Andreas / Knape, Joachim (2008–2009) (ed.): Rhetorik und Stilistik /
Rhetoric and Stylistics. Ein internationales Handbuch historischer und systematischer
Forschung / An International Handbook of Historical and Systematic Research.
2 Halbbde. / 2 Vols. Berlin, New York (= HSK. Handbücher zur Sprach- und
Kommunikationswissenschaft / Handbooks of Linguistics and Communication
Science 31. 1–2).

Flusser, Vilém (1996): Kommunikologie. Mannheim (= Vilém Flusser. Schriften 4).

Fohrmann, Jürgen (1993): Misreadings revisited. Eine Kritik des Konzepts von Paul de Man.
In: Karl Heinz Bohrer (ed.): Ästhetik and Rhetorik. Lektüren zu Paul de Man. Frankfurt
a. M., pp. 79–97 (= Aesthetica).

Fortenbaugh, William W. (1992): Aristotle on Persuasion Through Character. In: Rhetorica.
A Journal of the History of Rhetoric 10, pp. 207–244.

Foss, Sonja K. (2005): Theory of Visual Rhetoric. In: Ken Smith / Sandra Moriarty / Gretchen
Barbatsis / Keith Kenney (ed.): Handbook of Visual Communication. Theory, Methods,
and Media. Mahwah, NJ, pp. 141–152 (= LEA's Communication Series).

Foucault, Michel (1961): Madness and Civilization: A History of Insanity in the Age of Reason.
London 1999 (French Original: Histoire de la Folie à l'Age Classique: Folie et Déraison.
Paris 1961).

Fredal, James (2006): Rhetorical Action in Ancient Athens: Persuasive Artistry from Solon to
Demosthenes. Carbondale.

Fromkin, Victoria A. (2000): Linguistics: An Introduction to Linguistic Theory. Malden, MA.

Gaier, Ulrich (1966): Studien zu Sebastian Brants Narrenschiff. Tübingen.

Gansel, Christina (2009): Rhetorik und Stilistik in Text- und Gesprächslinguistik / Rhetoric
and Stylistics in Linguistics of Text and Conversation. In: Ulla Fix / Andreas Gardt /
Joachim Knape (ed.): Rhetorik und Stilistik / Rhetoric and Stylistics. Ein internationales
Handbuch historischer und systematischer Forschung / An International Handbook of
Historical and Systematic Research. 2. Halbbd. / Vol. 2. Berlin, New York, pp. 1907–1921

(= HSK. Handbücher zur Sprach- und Kommunikationswissenschaft / Handbooks of Linguistics and Communication Science 31. 2).

Gardner, Burleigh B. / Rainwater, Lee (1955): The Mass Image of Big Business. In: Harvard Business Review 33 (Issue 6), pp. 61–66.

Garrett, Mary (1998): Short Review: George Kennedy, Comparative Rhetoric: An Historical and Cross-cultural Introduction (New York: Oxford University Press, 1998). In: Rhetorica 16, pp. 431–433.

Geißner, Hellmut (1996): Gesprächsrhetorik. In: Historisches Wörterbuch der Rhetorik 3, col. 953–964.

Genette, Gérard (1972a): Figures III. Paris.

Genette, Gérard (1972b): Rhetoric Restrained. In: Gérard Genette: Figures of Literary Discourse. Transl. by Alan Sheridan. New York 1982, pp. 103–126 (French Original: La rhétorique restreinte. In: Gérard Genette: Figures III. Paris 1972, pp. 21–40).

Genette, Gérard (1987): Paratexts: Thresholds of Interpretation. Transl. by Jane E. Lewin. Cambridge, MA, 1997 (= Literature, Culture, Theory 20) (French Original: Seuils. Paris 1987 = Poétique).

Genette, Gérard (1991): Fiction and Diction. Transl. by Catherine Porter. Ithaca, NY, 1993 (French Original: Fiction et diction. Paris 1991).

Geoffrey of Vinsauf: The Poetria Nova. In: Ernest Gallo (ed.): The Poetria Nova and its Sources in Early Rhetorical Doctrine. The Hague, Paris 1971, pp. 14–123.

Goffman, Erving (1967): Interaction Ritual. Essays on Face-to-Face Behavior. Garden City, NY.

Goffman, Erving (1974): Frame Analysis. An Essay on the Organization of Experience. New York.

Goldschmidt, Harry (1971): Vers und Strophe in Beethovens Instrumentalmusik. In: Erich Schenk (ed.): Beethoven-Symposion Wien 1970. Bericht. Wien, Köln, Graz, pp. 97–120 (= Österreichische Akademie der Wissenschaften: Sitzungsberichte. Philosophisch-Historische Klasse 271).

Goodman, Nelson (1969): Languages of Art. An Approach to a Theory of Symbols. London.

Grabe, William / Kaplan, Robert B. (1996): Theory and Practice of Writing. An Applied Linguistic Perspective. London (= Applied Linguistics and Language Study).

Graff, Richard (2008): Topics/Topoi / Topik/Topoi. In: Ulla Fix / Andreas Gardt and Joachim Knape (ed.): Rhetorik und Stilistik / Rhetoric and Stylistics. Ein internationales Handbuch historischer und systematischer Forschung / An International Handbook of Historical and Systematic Research. 1. Halbbd. / Vol. 1. Berlin, New York, pp. 717–728 (= HSK. Handbücher zur Sprach- und Kommunikationswissenschaft / Handbooks of Linguistics and Communication Science 31. 1).

Greene, Ronald Walter (2008): Rhetoric in Cultural Studies / Rhetorik in den Cultural Studies. In: Ulla Fix / Andreas Gardt / Joachim Knape (ed.): Rhetorik und Stilistik / Rhetoric and Stylistics. Ein internationales Handbuch historischer und systematischer Forschung / An International Handbook of Historical and Systematic Research. 1. Halbbd. / Vol. 1. Berlin, New York, pp. 959–970 (= HSK. Handbücher zur Sprach- und Kommunikationswissenschaft / Handbooks of Linguistics and Communication Science 31. 1).

Grice, Herbert P. (1967): Logic and Conversation. In: Herbert P. Grice: Studies in the Way of Words. Cambridge, MA, London 1989, pp. 22–40. First edition in: Peter Cole / Jerry L. Morgan (ed.): Speech Acts. New York 1975, pp. 41–58 (= Syntax and Semantics 3); the same as the original William James Lectures Typoscript. Cambridge, MA, 1967.

Guhr, Dagny (2008): Argumentation in Courtshipkommunikation. Zu den persuasiven Strategien im Gespräch. Berlin (= neue rhetorik 3).

Gumbrecht, Hans Ulrich (2005): Materialität der Kommunikation. In: Alexander Roesler / Bernd Stiegler (ed.): Grundbegriffe der Medientheorie. Paderborn, pp. 144–149.

Gumperz, John J. (1982): Discourse Strategies. Cambridge (= Studies in Interactional Sociolinguistics 1).

Gürtler, Arno (1948): Volkstümliches Zeichenbuch. Leipzig.

Gusfield, Joseph (1976): The Literary Rhetoric of Science. Comedy and Pathos in Drinking Driver Research. In: American Sociological Review 41, pp. 16–34.

Gutenberg, Norbert (2000): Mündlich realisierte schriftkonstituierte Textsorten / Texts Constituted in a Written Form Yet Realised in a Spoken Form. In: Klaus Brinker / Gerd Antos / Wolfgang Heinemann / Sven F. Sager (ed.): Text- und Gesprächslinguistik / Linguistics of Text and Conversation. Ein internationales Handbuch zeitgenössischer Forschung / An International Handbook of Contemporary Research. 1. Halbbd. / Vol. 1. Berlin, New York, pp. 574–587 (= HSK. Handbücher zur Sprach- und Kommunikationswissenschaft / Handbooks of Linguistics and Communication Science 16. 1).

Habermas, Jürgen (1981): The Theory of Communicative Action. Vol. 1: Reason and the Rationalization of Society. Transl. by Thomas McCarthy. Boston, MA, 1984. (German Original: Theorie des kommunikativen Handelns. Bd. 1: Handlungsrationalität und gesellschaftliche Rationalisierung. Frankfurt a. M. 1981).

Habermas, Jürgen (1984): On the Pragmatics of Social Interaction: Preliminary Studies in the Theory of Communicative Action. Transl. by Barbara Fultner. Cambridge, MA, 2001 (= Studies in Contemporary German Social Thought) (German Original: Vorstudien und Ergänzungen zur Theorie des kommunikativen Handelns. Frankfurt a. M. 1984).

Habermas, Jürgen (1985): The Philosophical Discourse of Modernity. Twelve Lectures. Translated by Frederick Lawrence. Cambridge, MA, 1987 (German Original: Der philosophische Diskurs der Moderne. Zwölf Vorlesungen. Frankfurt a. M. 1985).

Hagen, Wolfgang (2008): Metaxy. Eine historiosemantische Fußnote zum Medienbegriff. In: Stefan Münker / Alexander Roesler (ed.): Was ist ein Medium? Frankfurt a. M., pp. 13–29.

Han, Sang-pil / Shavitt, Sharon (1994): Persuasion and Culture: Advertising Appeals in Individualistic and Collectivistic Societies. In: Journal of Experimental Social Psychology 30, pp. 326–350.

Harrington, John (1973): The Rhetoric of Film. New York.

Hausendorf, Heiko (1992): Gespräch als System. Linguistische Aspekte einer Soziologie der Interaktion. Opladen.

Heath, Stephen (1980): The Cinematic Apparatus: Technology as Historical and Cultural Form. In: Teresa de Lauretis / Stephen Heath (ed.): The Cinematic Apparatus. New York, pp. 1–13.

Heesacker, Martin / Petty, Richard E. / Cacioppo, John T. (1983): Field Dependence and Attitude Change: Source Credibility Can Alter Persuasion by Affecting Message-Relevant Thinking. In: Journal of Personality 51, pp. 653–666.

Heidegger, Martin: Basic Concepts of Aristotelian Philosophy. Transl. by Robert D. Metcalf and Mark B. Tanzer. Bloomington, IN, 2009 (= Studies in Continental Thought) (German Original: Martin Heidegger: Grundbegriffe der aristotelischen Philosophie. Ed. by Mark Michalski. Frankfurt a. M. 2002 = Martin Heidegger: Gesamtausgabe. II. Abteilung: Vorlesungen 1919–1944, Vol. 18).

Heilmann, Christa M. (2004): Das Konzept Körper in der Rhetorik aus semiotischer Sicht. In: Fohrmann, Jürgen (ed.): Rhetorik. Figuration und Performanz. Stuttgart, Weimar, pp. 267–282.

Heinemann, Wolfgang (2000): Textsorte – Textmuster – Texttyp / Text Type – Text Pattern. In: Klaus Brinker / Gerd Antos / Wolfgang Heinemann / Sven F. Sager (ed.): Text- und Gesprächslinguistik / Linguistics of Text and Conversation. Ein internationales Handbuch zeitgenössischer Forschung / An International Handbook of Contemporary Research. 1. Halbbd. / Vol. 1. Berlin, New York, pp. 507–523 (= HSK. Handbücher zur Sprach- und Kommunikationswissenschaft / Handbooks of Linguistics and Communication Science 16. 1).

Heinrichs, Johannes (1972): Dialog. In: Historisches Wörterbuch der Philosophie 2, col. 226–229.

Herder, Johann Gottfried (1785): Briefe, das Studium der Theologie betreffend. Nach der 2. verbesserten Ausgabe 1785. Parts 3 and 4. Ed. by Johann Georg Mueller. Stuttgart, Tübingen 1829. (= Johann Gottfried von Herder's sämmtliche Werke: Zur Religion und Theologie 14).

Heringer, Hans Jürgen (1990): „Ich gebe Ihnen mein Ehrenwort". Politik – Sprache – Moral. Munich.

Hess-Lüttich, Ernest W. B. (1991): Effektive Gesprächsführung. Evaluationskriterien in der Angewandten Rhetorik. In: Gert Ueding (ed.): Rhetorik zwischen den Wissenschaften. Geschichte, System, Praxis als Probleme des Historischen Wörterbuchs der Rhetorik. Tübingen, pp. 35–51 (= Rhetorik-Forschungen 1).

Hess-Lüttich, Ernest W. B. (1994): Dialog. In: Historisches Wörterbuch der Rhetorik 2, col. 606–621.

Hess-Lüttich, Ernest W. B. (1996): Gespräch. In: Historisches Wörterbuch der Rhetorik 3, col. 929–947.

Hess-Lüttich, Ernest W. B. (2001): Gesprächsformen in der Literatur / Forms of Conversation in Literature. In: Klaus Brinker / Gerd Antos / Wolfgang Heinemann / Sven F. Sager (ed.): Text- und Gesprächslinguistik / Linguistics of Text and Conversation. Ein internationales Handbuch zeitgenössischer Forschung / An International Handbook of Contemporary Research. 2. Halbbd. / Vol. 2. Berlin, New York, pp. 1619–1632 (= HSK. Handbücher zur Sprach- und Kommunikationswissenschaft / Handbooks of Linguistics and Communication Science 16. 2).

Hesse, Mary B. (1963): Models and Analogies in Science. London.

Hiltunen, Ari (2001): Aristotle in Hollywood. Visual Stories That Work. Bristol.

Hinkel, Eli (2009): Contrastive Rhetoric / Kontrastive Rhetorik. In: Ulla Fix / Andreas Gardt / Joachim Knape (ed.): Rhetorik und Stilistik / Rhetoric and Stylistics. Ein internationales Handbuch historischer und systematischer Forschung / An International Handbook of Historical and Systematic Research. 2. Halbbd. / Vol. 2. Berlin, New York, pp. 2014–2026 (= HSK. Handbücher zur Sprach- und Kommunikationswissenschaft / Handbooks of Linguistics and Communication Science 31. 2).

Hinnenkamp, Volker (1998): Mißverständnisse in Gesprächen. Eine empirische Untersuchung im Rahmen der interpretativen Soziolinguistik. Opladen, Wiesbaden.

Hoffmann, Harriet (1996): Thema und thematische Entwicklung in Gesprächen. Ein konversationsanalytischer Ansatz. Dissertation: Freie Universität Berlin (Mikrofiche).

Hoffmann, Ludger (2000): Thema, Themenentfaltung, Makrostruktur / Topic, Topic Development, Macro-Structure. In: Klaus Brinker / Gerd Antos / Wolfgang Heinemann / Sven F. Sager (ed.): Text- und Gesprächslinguistik / Linguistics of Text and

Conversation. Ein internationales Handbuch zeitgenössischer Forschung / An International Handbook of Contemporary Research. 1. Halbbd. / Vol. 1. Berlin, New York, pp. 344–356 (= HSK. Handbücher zur Sprach- und Kommunikationswissenschaft / Handbooks of Linguistics and Communication Science 16. 1).

Holly, Werner (1979): Imagearbeit in Gesprächen. Zur linguistischen Beschreibung des Beziehungsaspekts. Tübingen (= Germanistische Linguistik 18).

Holly, Werner (2001): Beziehungsmanagement und Imagearbeit / The Management of Relations and Face-Work. In: Klaus Brinker / Gerd Antos / Wolfgang Heinemann / Sven F. Sager (ed.): Text- und Gesprächslinguistik / Linguistics of Text and Conversation. Ein internationales Handbuch zeitgenössischer Forschung / An International Handbook of Contemporary Research. 2. Halbbd. / Vol. 2. Berlin, New York, pp. 1382–1393 (= HSK. Handbücher zur Sprach- und Kommunikationswissenschaft / Handbooks of Linguistics and Communication Science 16. 2).

Hoppmann, Michael (2008): Pragmatische Aspekte der Kommunikation: Höflichkeit und Ritualisierung / Pragmatic Aspects of Communication: Politeness and Ritualization. In: Ulla Fix / Andreas Gardt / Joachim Knape (ed.): Rhetorik und Stilistik / Rhetoric and Stylistics. Ein internationales Handbuch historischer und systematischer Forschung / An International Handbook of Historical and Systematic Research. 1. Halbbd. / Vol. 1. Berlin, New York, pp. 826–836 (= HSK. Handbücher zur Sprach- und Kommunikationswissenschaft / Handbooks of Linguistics and Communication Science 31. 1).

Hörr, Sara (2009): Musik-Rhetorik: Melodiestruktur und Persuasion. Berlin (= neue rhetorik 8).

Hosman, Lawrence A. (2008): Style and Persuasion / Stil und Persuasion. In: Ulla Fix / Andreas Gardt / Joachim Knape (ed.): Rhetorik und Stilistik / Rhetoric and Stylistics. Ein internationales Handbuch historischer und systematischer Forschung / An International Handbook of Historical and Systematic Research. 1. Halbbd. / Vol. 1. Berlin, New York, pp. 1119–1129 (= HSK. Handbücher zur Sprach- und Kommunikationswissenschaft / Handbooks of Linguistics and Communication Science 31. 1).

Huber, Martin (1987): „Romanfigur klagt den Autor". Zur Rezeption von Thomas Bernhards „Die Ursache. Eine Andeutung". In: Wendelin Schmidt-Dengler / Martin Huber (ed.): Statt Bernhard. Über Misanthropie im Werk Thomas Bernhards. Vienna, pp. 59–110.

Hundsnurscher, Franz (1994): Dialog-Typologie. In: Gerd Fritz / Franz Hundsnurscher (ed.): Handbuch der Dialoganalyse. Tübingen, pp. 203–238.

Husserl, Edmund (1954): The Crisis of European Sciences and Transcendental Phenomenology. Translated with an Introduction by David Carr. Evanston 1970 (German Original: Die Krisis der europäischen Wissenschaften und die transzendentale Phänomenologie: eine Einleitung in die phänomenologische Philosophie. Dordrecht 1954).

Hymes, Dell (1962): The Ethnography of Speaking. In: Thomas Gladwin / William C. Sturtevant (ed.): Anthropology and Human Behavior. Washington, D. C., pp. 13–53.

Hymes, Dell (1964): Introduction: Toward Ethnographies of Communication. In: John J. Gumperz / Dell Hymes (ed.): The Ethnography of Communication = American Anthropologist 66. Number 6, Part 2 (Special Publication), pp. 1–34.

Iser, Wolfgang (1970): Die Appellstruktur der Texte. Unbestimmtheit als Wirkungsbedingung literarischer Prosa. Konstanz (= Konstanzer Universitätsreden 28).

Jacobs, Scott (2002): Language and Interpersonal Communication. In: Mark L. Knapp / Gerald R. Miller (ed.): Handbook of Interpersonal Communication. 3rd ed. Thousand Oaks, CA, pp. 213–239.

Jakobson, Roman (1960): Linguistics and Poetics. In: Thomas A. Sebeok (ed.): Style in Language. New York, pp. 350–377.

Jasinski, James (2008): Rhetorical Criticism in the USA / Rhetorical Criticism in den USA. In: Ulla Fix / Andreas Gardt / Joachim Knape (ed.): Rhetorik und Stilistik / Rhetoric and Stylistics. Ein internationales Handbuch historischer und systematischer Forschung / An International Handbook of Historical and Systematic Research. 1. Halbbd. / Vol. 1. Berlin, New York, pp. 928–943 (= HSK. Handbücher zur Sprach- und Kommunikationswissenschaft / Handbooks of Linguistics and Communication Science 31. 1).

Jens, Walter (1965): Von deutscher Rede. In: Walter Jens: Von deutscher Rede. 4th ed. Munich, Zurich 1985, pp. 24–53.

Jensen, J. Vernon (1992): Values and Practices in Asian Argumentation. In: Argumentation and Advocacy 28, pp. 153–166.

Johnstone, Henry W. (1963): Some Reflections on Argumentation. In: Logique et Analyse 6, pp. 30–39.

Jones, Lee W. / Sinclair, Robert C. / Courneya, Kerry S. (2003): The Effects of Source Credibility and Message Framing on Exercise Intentions, Behaviors, and Attitudes: An Integration of the Elaboration Likelihood Model and Prospect Theory. In: Journal of Applied Social Psychology 33, pp. 179–196.

Joost, Gesche (2008): Bild-Sprache. Die audio-visuelle Rhetorik des Films. Bielefeld (= Film).

Kahneman, Daniel / Tversky, Amos (1979): Prospect Theory. An Analysis of Decision und Risk. In: Econometria 47, pp. 263–291.

Kallmeyer, Werner (1996a) (ed.): Gesprächsrhetorik. Rhetorische Verfahren im Gesprächsprozeß. Tübingen (= Studien zur deutschen Sprache 4).

Kallmeyer, Werner (1996b): Einleitung. Was ist Gesprächsrhetorik? In: Werner Kallmeyer (ed.): Gesprächsrhetorik. Rhetorische Verfahren im Gesprächsprozeß. Tübingen, pp. 7–18 (= Studien zur deutschen Sprache 4).

Kallmeyer, Werner (2007): Theorie verbaler Interaktion – Grundannahmen (http://gais.ids-mannheim.de/information/glossar/theorie.pdf. rev: 09.03.2009).

Kallmeyer, Werner / Schmitt, Reinhold (1996): Forcieren oder: Die verschärfte Gangart. Zur Analyse von Kooperationsformen im Gespräch. In: Werner Kallmeyer (ed.): Gesprächsrhetorik. Rhetorische Verfahren im Gesprächsprozeß. Tübingen, pp. 19–118 (= Studien zur deutschen Sprache 4).

Kamel, Salwa A. (2000): Categories of Comprehension in Argumentative Discourse. A Cross-Linguistic-Study. In: Zeinab M. Ibrahim / Sabiha T. Aydelott / Nagwa Kassabgy (ed.): Diversity in Language: Contrastive Studies in English and Arabic Theoretical Applied Linguistics. Cairo, New York, pp. 193–235.

Kant, Immanuel (1795): To Perpetual Peace: a Philosophical Sketch. Transl. by Ted Humphrey. Indianapolis, IN, 2003 (German Original: Zum Ewigen Frieden. Königsberg 1795).

Kanzog, Klaus (1991): Einführung in die Filmphilologie. Munich (= diskurs film 4).

Kanzog, Klaus (2001): Grundkurs Filmrhetorik. Munich (= diskurs film 9).

Kaplan, Robert B. (1966): Cultural Thought Patterns in Inter-Cultural Education. In: Language Learning 16, pp. 1–20.

Karickam, M. Y. Abraham (1999): Rhetoric Figures. Indian and Western Tradition. Kerala, India (= Comparative Literature Research & Study Centre = CLRSC Series 1).

Kasten, Ingrid (1992): 'Narrheit' und 'Wahnsinn'. Michel Foucaults Rezeption von Sebastian Brants 'Narrenschiff'. In: Johannes Janota et al. (ed.): Festschrift für Walter Haug und Burghart Wachinger. Vol. 1. Tübingen, pp. 233–254.

Kennedy, George A. (1998): Comparative Rhetoric: An Historical and Cross-Cultural Introduction. New York.

Kennedy, George A. (1999): Classical Rhetoric and Its Christian and Secular Tradition From Ancient to Modern Times. 2nd ed. Chapel Hill, NC.

Kilian, Jörg (2002): Lehrgespräch und Sprachgeschichte. Untersuchungen zur historischen Dialogforschung. Tübingen (= Germanistische Linguistik 233).

Kilian, Jörg (2005): Historische Dialogforschung. Eine Einführung. Tübingen (= Germanistische Arbeitshefte 41).

Kimmich, Dorothee (2003): Die Bildlichkeit der Leerstelle. Bemerkungen zur Leerstellenkonzeption in der frühen Filmtheorie. In: Wolfgang Adam / Holger Dainat / Gunter Schandera (ed.): Wissenschaft und Systemveränderung. Rezeptionsforschung in Ost und West – eine konvergente Entwicklung? Heidelberg, pp. 319–339 (= Euphorion: Beihefte 44).

Kittler, Friedrich A. (1985): Discourse Networks 1800/1900. Transl. by Michael Metteer / Chris Cullens. Stanford, CA, 1990. (German Original: Aufschreibesysteme 1800, 1900. Munich 1985).

Kittler, Friedrich A. (1993): Es gibt keine Software. In: Hans Ulrich Gumbrecht / K. Ludwig Pfeiffer (ed.): Schrift. Munich, pp. 367–378 (= Materialität der Zeichen. Reihe A 12).

Kjørup, Søren (1996): Humanities. Geisteswissenschaften. Sciences humaines. Eine Einführung. Stuttgart, Weimar 2001 (Danish Original: Menneskevidenskaberne. Problemer og traditioner i humanioras videnskabsteori. Frederiksberg 1996.)

Klopsch, Paul (1980): Einführung in die Dichtungslehren des lateinischen Mittelalters. Darmstadt (= Das lateinische Mittelalter).

Klotz, Fabian (2008): Der Orator / The Orator. In: Ulla Fix / Andreas Gardt / Joachim Knape (ed.): Rhetorik und Stilistik / Rhetoric and Stylistics. Ein internationales Handbuch historischer und systematischer Forschung / An International Handbook of Historical and Systematic Research. 1. Halbbd. / Vol. 1. Berlin, New York, pp. 587–597 (= HSK. Handbücher zur Sprach- und Kommunikationswissenschaft / Handbooks of Linguistics and Communication Science 31. 1).

Knape, Joachim (1994a): Elocutio. In: Historisches Wörterbuch der Rhetorik 2, col. 1022–1083.

Knape, Joachim (1994b): Rhetorizität und Semiotik. Kategorientransfer zwischen Rhetorik und Kunsttheorie in der Frühen Neuzeit. In: Wilhelm Kühlmann / Wolfgang Neuber (ed.): Intertextualität in der frühen Neuzeit. Studien zu ihren theoretischen und praktischen Perspektiven. Frankfurt a. M., pp. 507–532 (= Frühneuzeit-Studien 2).

Knape, Joachim (1996): Figurenlehre. In: Historisches Wörterbuch der Rhetorik 3, col. 289–432.

Knape, Joachim (1997a) (ed.): 500 Jahre Tübinger Rhetorik. 30 Jahre Rhetorisches Seminar. Katalog zur Ausstellung im Bonatzbau der Universitätsbibliothek Tübingen vom 12. Mai bis 31. Juli 1997. Tübingen.

Knape, Joachim (1997b): Fiktionalität und Faktizität als Erkenntnisproblem am Beispiel spätmittelalterlicher Reiseerzählungen. In: Holger Krapp / Thomas Wägenbaur (ed.): Künstliche Paradiese. Virtuelle Realitäten. Künstliche Räume in Literatur-, Sozial- und Naturwissenschaften. Munich, pp. 47–62.

Knape, Joachim (1998): Zwangloser Zwang. Der Persuasions-Prozeß als Grundlage sozialer Bindung. In: Gert Ueding / Thomas Vogel (ed.): Von der Kunst der Rede und Beredsamkeit. Tübingen, pp. 54–69.

Knape, Joachim (2000a): Was ist Rhetorik? Stuttgart.

Knape, Joachim (2000b): Allgemeine Rhetorik. Stationen der Theoriegeschichte. Stuttgart.

Knape, Joachim (2000c): Die zwei texttheoretischen Betrachtungsweisen der Topik. In: Thomas Schirren / Gert Ueding (ed.): Topik und Rhetorik. Tübingen, pp. 747–766.

Knape, Joachim (2000d): Historia, Textuality and Episteme in the Middle Ages. In: Tuomas M. S. Lehtonen / Päivi Mehtonen (ed.): Historia. The Concept and Genres in the Middle Ages. Helsinki, pp. 11–27 (= Commentationes Humanarum Litterarum 116).

Knape, Joachim (2000e): Die kodierte Welt. Bild, Schrift und Technobild bei Vilém Flusser. In: Joachim Knape / Hermann-Arndt Riethmüller (ed.): Perspektiven der Buch- und Kommunikationskultur. Tübingen, pp. 1–18.

Knape, Joachim (2000f): New Rhetoric und Rhetorik der Dekonstruktion. Von Kenneth Burke zu Paul de Man. In: Sabine Doering / Waltraud Maierhofer / Peter Philipp Riedl (ed.): Resonanzen. Festschrift für Hans Joachim Kreutzer zum 65. Geburtstag. Würzburg, pp. 483–497.

Knape, Joachim (2003a): Persuasion. In: Historisches Wörterbuch der Rhetorik 6, col. 874–907.

Knape, Joachim (2003b): Rede$_2$. In: Reallexikon der deutschen Literaturwissenschaft 3, pp. 233 ff.

Knape, Joachim (2005a) (ed.): Medienrhetorik. Tübingen.

Knape, Joachim (2005b): Medienrhetorik. Einleitung zu den Beiträgen. In: Joachim Knape (ed.): Medienrhetorik. Tübingen, pp. 1–15.

Knape, Joachim (2005c): *The Medium is the Massage?* Medientheoretische Anfragen und Antworten der Rhetorik. In: Joachim Knape (ed.): Medienrhetorik. Tübingen, pp. 17–39.

Knape, Joachim (2005d): Rhetorik und neue Medien. In: Michael Jäckel / Frank Haase (ed.): In medias res. Herausforderung Informationsgesellschaft. Munich, pp. 133–151.

Knape, Joachim (2005e): Rhetorik. In: Klaus Sachs-Hombach (ed.): Bildwissenschaft. Disziplinen, Themen, Methoden. Frankfurt a. M., pp. 134–148.

Knape, Joachim (2006a): Poetik und Rhetorik in Deutschland 1300–1700. Wiesbaden (= Gratia 44).

Knape, Joachim (2006b): Machiavelli und die Rhetorik. In: Rita Franceschini / Rainer Stillers / Maria Moog-Grünewald / Franz Penzenstadler / Norbert Becker / Hannelore Martin (ed.): Retorica: Ordnungen und Brüche. Beiträge des Tübinger Italianistentags. Tübingen, pp. 183–201.

Knape, Joachim (2006c): Gewalt, Sprache und Rhetorik. In: Julia Dietrich / Uta Müller-Koch (ed.): Ethik und Ästhetik der Gewalt. Paderborn, pp. 57–78.

Knape, Joachim (2006d): Virtualität und VIVA-Video World. In: Christoph Jacke / Eva Kimminich / Siegfried J. Schmidt (ed.): Kulturschutt. Über das Recycling von Theorien und Kulturen. Bielefeld, pp. 207–222 (= Cultural Studies 16).

Knape, Joachim (2007a) (ed.): Bildrhetorik. Baden-Baden (= Saecvla Spiritalia 45).

Knape, Joachim (2007b): Bildrhetorik. Einführung in die Beiträge des Bandes. In: Joachim Knape (ed.): Bildrhetorik. Baden-Baden, pp. 9–34 (= Saecvla Spiritalia 45).

Knape, Joachim (2007c): Kann der Orator tolerant sein? Zur Toleranzfrage aus rhetoriktheoretischer Sicht. In: Friedrich Schweitzer / Christoph Schwöbel (ed.): Religion – Toleranz – Bildung. Neukirchen-Vluyn, pp. 39–56 (= Theologie interdisziplinär 3).

Knape, Joachim (2007d): Powerpoint in rhetoriktheoretischer Sicht. In: Bernt Schnettler / Herbert Knoblauch (ed.): Powerpoint-Präsentationen. Neue Formen der gesellschaftlichen Kommunikation von Wissen. Konstanz, pp. 53–66.

Knape, Joachim (2008a): Rhetorik der Künste / Rhetoric and the Arts. In: Ulla Fix / Andreas
    Gardt / Joachim Knape (ed.): Rhetorik und Stilistik / Rhetoric and Stylistics. Ein
    internationales Handbuch historischer und systematischer Forschung / An International
    Handbook of Historical and Systematic Research. 1. Halbbd. / Vol. 1. Berlin, New York,
    pp. 894–927 (= HSK. Handbücher zur Sprach- und Kommunikationswissenschaft /
    Handbooks of Linguistics and Communication Science 31. 1).
Knape, Joachim (2008b): Performanz in rhetoriktheoretischer Sicht. In: Heidrun Kämper /
    Ludwig M. Eichinger (ed.): Sprache – Kognition – Kultur. Sprache zwischen mentaler
    Struktur und kultureller Prägung. Berlin, New York, pp. 135–150 (= Institut für deutsche
    Sprache. Jahrbuch 2007).
Knape, Joachim (2008c): Rhetorik, Medien, Performanz. Eröffnungsvortrag der 4. Salzburger
    Rhetorikgespräche 2007. In: Günther Kreuzbauer / Norbert Gratzl / Ewald Hiebl (ed.):
    Rhetorische Wissenschaft. Rede und Argumentation in Theorie und Praxis. Vienna,
    Berlin, pp. 7–20 (= Salzburger Beiträge zu Rhetorik und Argumentationstheorie 4).
Knape, Joachim (2008d): Ein rhetorischer Regieansatz nach Heinrich von Kleist. In:
    Deutscher Bühnenverein Landesverband Ost, Ulrich Katzer / Kleist-Museum Frankfurt
    (Oder), Wolfgang de Bruyn / Messe und Veranstaltungs GmbH Frankfurt (Oder), Markus
    Wieners (ed.): Kleist oder Die Ordnung der Welt. Berlin, pp. 42–49 (= Theater der Zeit.
    Recherchen 57).
Knape, Joachim (2008e): Gibt es Pathosformeln? Überlegungen zu einem Konzept von Aby
    M. Warburg. In: Wolfgang Dickhut / Stefan Manns / Norbert Winkler (ed.): Muster im
    Wandel. Zur Dynamik topischer Wissensordnungen in Spätmittelalter und Früher
    Neuzeit. Göttingen, pp. 115–137 (= Berliner Mittelalter- und Frühneuzeitforschung 5).
Knape, Joachim (2008f): Rhetorik zwischen Historismus und moderner Wissenschaft. In:
    Seminar für Allgemeine Rhetorik, Tübingen, unter Federführung von Joachim Knape /
    Olaf Kramer / Peter Weit (ed.): „Und es trieb die Rede mich an …“. Festschrift zum
    65. Geburtstag von Gert Ueding. Tübingen, pp. 327–340.
Knape, Joachim (2009): Rhetorik des Gesprächs. In: Joachim Knape (ed.): Rhetorik im
    Gespräch. Ergänzt um Beiträge zum Tübinger Courtshiprhetorik-Projekt. Berlin, pp. 13–
    52 (= neue rhetorik 4).
Knape, Joachim (2010a): Rhetorischer Pathosbegriff und literarische Pathosnarrative. In:
    Cornelia Zumbusch (ed.): Pathos. Zur Geschichte einer problematischen Kategorie.
    Berlin, pp. 25–44.
Knape, Joachim (2010b): Werk, Bildtext und Medium in agonaler Kunstrhetorik. In: Sabine
    Heiser / Christiane Holm (ed.): Gedächtnisparagone – Intermermediale Konstellationen.
    Göttingen, pp. 79–91 (= Formen der Erinnerung 42).
Knape, Joachim (2010c): Zur Theorie der Spielfilmrhetorik mit Blick auf Fritz Langs „M“. In:
    Christoph Bareither / Urs Büttner (ed.): Fritz Lang: „M – Eine Stadt sucht einen
    Mörder“. Texte und Kontexte. Würzburg, pp. 15–32 (= Film – Medium – Diskurs 28).
Knape, Joachim (2011): Zur Problematik literarischer Rhetorik am Beispiel Thomas Bernhards.
    In: Joachim Knape / Olaf Kramer (ed.): Rhetorik und Sprachkunst bei Thomas Bernhard.
    Würzburg, pp. 5–24.
Knape, Joachim (2012a): Duale Performanz in Rom. In: Felix Mundt (ed.):
    Kommunikationsräume im kaiserzeitlichen Rom. Berlin, New York, pp. 123–141 (= Topoi
    6).
Knape, Joachim (2012b): Image, Prestige, Reputation und das Ethos in der aristotelischen
    Rhetorik. In: Birgit Christiansen / Ulrich Thaler (ed.): Ansehenssache. Formen von
    Prestige in Kulturen des Altertums. München, pp. 105–128.

Knape, Joachim (2012c) (ed.): Kunstgespräche. Zur diskursiven Konstitution von Kunst. Baden-Baden (= SAECVLA SPIRITALIA 47).

Knape, Joachim / Becker, Nils / Böhme, Katie (2009): Strategie. In: Historisches Wörterbuch der Rhetorik 9, col. 152–172.

Knape, Joachim / Schirren, Thomas (2005a) (ed.): Aristotelische Rhetoriktradition. Akten der 5. Tagung der Karl und Gertrud Abel-Stiftung vom 5.–6. Oktober 2001 in Tübingen. Stuttgart (= Philosophie der Antike 18).

Knape, Joachim / Schirren, Thomas (2005b): Martin Heidegger liest die Rhetorik des Aristoteles. In: Joachim Knape / Thomas Schirren (ed.): Aristotelische Rhetoriktradition. Akten der 5. Tagung der Karl und Gertrud Abel-Stiftung vom 5. – 6. Oktober 2001 in Tübingen. Stuttgart, pp. 310–327 (= Philosophie der Antike 18).

Krämer, Sybille (2008): Medien, Boten, Spuren. Wenig mehr als ein Literaturbericht. In: Stefan Münker / Alexander Roesler (ed.): Was ist ein Medium? Frankfurt a. M., pp. 65–90.

Krause, Detlef (1999): Luhmann-Lexikon. Eine Einführung in das Gesamtwerk von Niklas Luhmann. 2nd ed. Stuttgart.

Krieger, Leonard (1977): Ranke. The Meaning of History. Chicago, London.

Kripke, Saul A. (1980): Naming and Necessity. Cambridge, MA.

Krones, Hartmut (2009): Rhetorik und Stilistik in der Musikwissenschaft / Rhetoric and Stylistics in Musicology. In: Ulla Fix / Andreas Gardt / Joachim Knape (ed.): Rhetorik und Stilistik / Rhetoric and Stylistics. Ein internationales Handbuch historischer und systematischer Forschung / An International Handbook of Historical and Systematic Research. 2. Halbbd. / Vol. 2. Berlin, New York, pp. 1932–1949 (= HSK. Handbücher zur Sprach- und Kommunikationswissenschaft / Handbooks of Linguistics and Communication Science 31. 2).

Lakoff, George / Johnson, Mark (1980): Metaphors We Live By. Chicago.

Langelier, Carol A. (2001a): Mood Management Leader's Manual. A Cognitive-Behavioral Skills-Building Program for Adolescents. Thousand Oaks, CA.

Langelier, Carol A. (2001b): Mood Management. A Cognitive-Behavioral Skills-Building Program for Adolescents. Skills Workbook. Thousand Oaks, CA.

Lausberg, Heinrich (1960): Handbook of Literary Rhetoric: A Foundation for Literary Study. Foreword by George A. Kennedy. Transl. by Matthew T. Bliss / Annemiek Jansen / David E. Orton. Ed. by David E. Orton / R. Dean Anderson. Leiden, Boston, Köln 1998 (German Original: Handbuch der literarischen Rhetorik. Eine Grundlegung der Literaturwissenschaft. Munich 1960).

Lehmann, Marco / Kopiez, Reinhard (2011): Der Einfluss der Bühnenshow auf die Bewertung der Performanz von Rockgitarristen. In: Rolf F. Nohr / Herbert Schwaab (ed.): Metal Matters: Heavy Metal als Kultur und Welt. Münster, pp. 195–206 (= Medien'Welten. Braunschweiger Schriften zur Medienkultur 16).

Leschke, Rainer (2007): Einführung in die Medientheorie. Munich.

Lévi-Strauss, Claude (1964): The Raw and the Cooked: Introduction to a Science of Mythology. Transl. by John and Doreen Weightman. London 1970. (French Original: Le cru et le cuit. Paris 1964 = Mythologiques).

Lloyd, Keith (2007): Rethinking Rhetoric from an Indian Perspective: Implications in the Nyaya Sutra. In: Rhetoric Review 26, pp. 365–384.

Locher, Jakob: Stultifera Navis. In: Die 'Stultifera Navis'. Jakob Lochers Übertragung von Sebastian Brants 'Narrenschiff'. Vol. 1.2. Ed. and transl. by Nina Hartl. Münster etc. 2001 (= Studien und Texte zum Mittelalter und zur frühen Neuzeit 1).

Locke, John (1690): An Essay Concerning Human Understanding. Ed. by Peter H. Nidditch. Oxford 1975.

Lohmeier, Anke-Marie (1996): Filmrhetorik. In: Historisches Wörterbuch der Rhetorik 3, col. 347–364.

Lorenz, Kuno (1980): Dialog. In: Enzyklopädie Philosophie und Wissenschaftstheorie 1, pp. 471f.

Low, Patrick Kim Cheng (2010): Successfully Negotiating in Asia. Berlin, Heidelberg.

Lu, Xing (1998): Rhetoric in Ancient China, Fifth to Third Century B. C. E.: A Comparison with Classical Greek Rhetoric. Columbia, SC (= Studies in Rhetoric/Communication).

Lyons, John (1982): Language and Linguistics: An Introduction. Cambridge.

Mailloux, Steven (1998): Reception Histories. Rhetoric, Pragmatism, and American Cultural Politics. Ithaca, NY.

Mao, LuMing (2003): Reflective Encounters: Illustrating Comparative Rhetoric. In: Style 37, pp. 401–425.

Marshall, J. C. (1984): Multiple Perspectives on Modularity. In: Cognition 17, pp. 209–242.

Massmann, Hans Ferdinand (1854) (ed.): Der keiser und der kunige buoch oder die sogenannte Kaiserchronik, gedicht des zwölften Jahrhunderts. Vol. III. Quedlinburg, Leipzig (= Bibliothek der gesamten deutschen National-Literatur von der ältesten bis auf die neuere Zeit I. 4).

Matsuda, Paul Kei (2001): On the Origin of Contrastive Rhetoric: A Response to H. G. Ying. In: International Journal of Applied Linguistics 11, pp. 257–260.

Matthew of Vendôme: Mathei Vindocinensis Opera: Ars Versificatoria. Ed. by Franco Munari. Rome 1988.

McClelland, James L. / Rumelhart, David E. (1986) (ed.): Parallel Distributed Processing: Explorations in the Microstructure of Cognition. Vol. 2: Psychological and Biological Models. Cambridge, MA.

McCord Adams, Marilyn (1995): Ockham's razor. In: The Cambridge Dictionary of Philosophy, pp. 545.

McLuhan, Marshall (1962): The Gutenberg Galaxy. The Making of Typographic Man. London.

McLuhan, Marshall (1964): Understanding Media: The Extensions of Man. London 1996.

McLuhan, Marshall / Fiore, Quentin (1967): The Medium is the Massage. An Inventory of Effects. Corte Madera, CA, 1996.

McLuhan, Marshall / Powers, Bruce R. (1989): The Global Village. Transformations in World Life and Media in the 21st Century. New York, Oxford.

Meyer, Christian (2009): Rhetoric and Stylistics in Social/Cultural Anthropology / Rhetorik und Stilistik in der Ethnologie. In: Ulla Fix / Andreas Gardt / Joachim Knape (ed.): Rhetorik und Stilistik / Rhetoric and Stylistics. Ein internationales Handbuch historischer und systematischer Forschung / An International Handbook of Historical and Systematic Research. 2. Halbbd. / Vol. 2. Berlin, New York, pp. 1871–1885 (= HSK. Handbücher zur Sprach- und Kommunikationswissenschaft / Handbooks of Linguistics and Communication Science 31. 2).

Millar, Frank E. / Rogers, L. Edna (1976): Relational Approach to Interpersonal Communication. In: Gerald R. Miller (ed.): Explorations in Interpersonal Communication. London, pp. 87–103 (= Sage Annual Reviews of Communication Research 5).

Mollard, Auguste (1934): L'Imitation de Quintilien dans Guibert de Nogent. In: Le Moyen Âge 44, pp. 81–87.

Mollard, Auguste (1934/1935): La Diffusion de l'Institution Oratoire au XIIe siècle. In: Le Moyen Âge 44, pp. 161–175, and in: Le Moyen Âge 45, pp. 1–9.

Monaco, James (1981): How to Read a Film. The Art, Technology, Language, History and Theory of Film and Media. New York.

Mönnich, Annette (2011): Von der antiken Rhetorik zur Rhetorik der Gegenwart. In: Marita Pabst-Weinschenk (ed.): Grundlagen der Sprechwissenschaft und Sprecherziehung. 2nd ed. Munich, Basel, pp. 105–114.

Morel, Mary-Annick (1983): Vers une rhétorique de la conversation. In: DRLAV. Revue de linguistique 29, pp. 29–68.

Morris, Charles William (1938): Foundations of the Theory of Signs. Chicago (= International Encyclopedia of Unified Science I. 2).

Morrison, John L. (1972): The Absence of a Rhetorical Tradition in Japanese Culture. In: Western Speech 36, pp. 89–102.

Mukařovský, Jan (1948): Kapitel aus der Poetik. Transl. into German by Walter Schamschula. Frankfurt a. M. 1967 (Czech Original: Kapitoly z české poetiky. Prague 1948).

Mummendey, Hans Dieter (1995): Psychologie der Selbstdarstellung. 2nd ed. Göttingen.

Mummendey, Hans Dieter (2000): Psychologie der Selbstschädigung. Göttingen.

Mummendey, Hans Dieter / Bolten, Heinz-Gert (1985): Die Impression-Management-Theorie. In: Dieter Frey / Martin Irle (ed.): Theorien der Sozialpsychologie. Vol. III: Motivations- und Informationsverarbeitungstheorien. Bern, pp. 57–77.

Münker, Stefan / Roesler, Alexander (2008a) (ed.): Was ist ein Medium? Frankfurt a. M.

Münker, Stefan / Roesler, Alexander (2008b): Vorwort. In: Stefan Münker / Alexander Roesler (ed.): Was ist ein Medium? Frankfurt a. M., pp. 7–12.

Murphy, James J. (1974): Rhetoric in the Middle Ages. A History of Rhetorical Theory from Saint Augustine to the Renaissance. 6th ed. Berkeley, Los Angeles, London 1990.

Murphy, James J. / Katula, Richard A. (2003): A Synoptic History of Classical Rhetoric. 3rd ed. London.

Niemöller, Klaus Wolfgang (1980): Der sprachhafte Charakter der Musik. Opladen (= Rheinisch-Westfälische Akademie der Wissenschaften: Vorträge / Geisteswissenschaften 244).

Nietzsche, Friedrich (1872): On Truth and Lies in a Nonmoral Sense. In: Keith Ansell-Pearson / Duncan Large (ed.): The Nietzsche Reader. Oxford, 2006, pp. 114–123 (German Original: Über Wahrheit und Lüge im außermoralischen Sinn; 1873).

Nöth, Winfried (1990): Handbook of Semiotics. Bloomington, IN, Indianapolis, IN (= Advances in Semiotics).

Nothdurft, Werner (2007): Kommunikation. In: Jürgen Straub / Arne Weidemann / Doris Weidemann (ed.): Handbuch interkulturelle Kommunikation und Kompetenz. Grundbegriffe – Theorien – Anwendungsfelder. Stuttgart, Weimar, pp. 24–35.

Oesterreich, Peter L. (2008): Anthropologische Rhetorik / Anthropological Rhetoric. In: Ulla Fix / Andreas Gardt / Joachim Knape (ed.): Rhetorik und Stilistik / Rhetoric and Stylistics. Ein internationales Handbuch historischer und systematischer Forschung / An International Handbook of Historical and Systematic Research. 1. Halbbd. / Vol. 1. Berlin, New York, pp. 869–880 (= HSK. Handbücher zur Sprach- und Kommunikationswissenschaft / Handbooks of Linguistics and Communication Science 31. 1).

Offenhäuser, Stefan (2006): Reputation – der Wert der Emotion. In: Alexander Krylov (ed.): Zur Frage der Reputation. Dokumentation zur Internationalen Wissenschaftlichen Konferenz „Der Faktor Reputation in der internationalen Unternehmensführung". Bremen, pp. 95–99.

Oliver, Robert T. (1971): Communication and Culture in Ancient India and China. Syracuse, NY.

Olmsted, Wendy (2006): Rhetoric. An Historical Introduction. Malden, MA.

Ortak, Nuri (2004): Persuasion. Zur textlinguistischen Beschreibung eines dialogischen Strategiemusters. Tübingen (= Beiträge zur Dialogforschung 26).

Otto von Freising / Otto Episcopus Frisingensis: Chronica sive historia de duabus civitatibus / Chronik oder die Geschichte der zwei Staaten. Ed. by Walther Lammers. Transl. into German by Adolf Schmidt. 4th ed. Darmstadt 1980 (= Ausgewählte Quellen zur deutschen Geschichte des Mittelalters 16).

Pawlowski, Tatjana (2004): Wie kommt das Neue ins Gespräch? Über Bedingungen und Mittel kreativer Kommunikation. Aachen (= Essener Studien zur Semiotik und Kommunikationsforschung 10).

Peirce, Charles Sanders: Collected Papers of Charles Sanders Peirce. Vol. 1–6: Ed. by Charles Hartshorne / Paul Weiss. Two Volumes in One. 2nd printing. Cambridge, MA, 1960. Vol. 7–8: Ed. by Arthur W. Burks. Cambridge, MA, 1958.

Perelman, Chaïm (1977): L'empire rhétorique. Rhétorique et argumentation. Paris.

Perelman, Chaïm / Olbrechts-Tyteca, Lucie (1958): The New Rhetoric. A Treatise on Argumentation. Notre Dame, IN, 1969 (French Original: Traité de l'argumentation. La nouvelle rhétorique. Paris 1958).

Perloff, Richard. M. (2002): The Dynamics of Persuasion: Communication and Attitudes in the 21st Century. 2nd ed. Mahwah, NJ.

Peters, Jan Marie Lambert (1977): Pictorial Communication. Capetown.

Petty, Richard E. / Cacioppo, John T. (1986): The Elaboration Likelihood Model of Persuasion. In: Advances in Experimental Social Psychology 19, pp. 123–205.

Petty, Richard E. / Wegener, Duane T. (1999): The Elaboration Likelihood Model: Current Status and Controversies. In: Shelly Chaiken / Yaacov Trope (ed.): Dual-Process Theories in Social Psychology. New York, pp. 41–72.

Pfister, Paul (1996): Die Bedeutung der Gemäldeoberfläche. In: Paul Pfister (ed.): Von Claude Lorrain bis Giovanni Segantini. Gemäldeoberfläche und Bildwirkung. Katalog zur Ausstellung 24. Oktober 1996–13. Februar 1997. Zurich (= Sammlungsheft 21).

Plato: Gorgias. In: Plato: Lysis. Symposium. Gorgias. With an Engl. Transl. by W. R. M. Lamb. Reprinted. London, Cambridge, MA, 1967, pp. 258–533 (= Plato in Twelve Volumes 3; The Loeb Classical Library 166).

Plato: Phaedrus. In: Plato: Euthyphro. Apology. Crito. Phaedo. Phaedrus. With an Engl. Transl. by Harold North Fowler and an Introd. by W. R. M. Lamb. Reprinted. London, Cambridge, MA, 1966, pp. 412–579 (= Plato in Twelve Volumes 1; The Loeb Classical Library 36).

Plett, Heinrich F. (2004): Rhetoric and Renaissance Culture. Berlin, New York.

Pompen, Fr. Aurelius (1925): The English Versions of the "Ship of Fools." A Contribution to the History of the Early French Renaissance in England. London.

Porter, Katherine Anne (1962): Ship of Fools. Boston, Toronto.

Porter, Katherine Anne (1963): Das Narrenschiff. Reinbek bei Hamburg (Original: The Ship of Fools. Boston, Toronto 1962).

Pratt, Mary L. (1977): Toward a Speech Act Theory of Literary Discourse. Bloomington, IN.

Price Dillard, James / Miraldi, Lori B. (2008): Persuasion: Research Areas and Approaches / Persuasion: Forschungsfelder und -ansätze. In: Ulla Fix / Andreas Gardt / Joachim Knape (ed.): Rhetorik und Stilistik / Rhetoric and Stylistics. Ein internationales Handbuch historischer und systematischer Forschung / An International Handbook of Historical and Systematic Research. 1. Halbbd. / Vol. 1. Berlin, New York, pp. 689–702

(= HSK. Handbücher zur Sprach- und Kommunikationswissenschaft / Handbooks of Linguistics and Communication Science 31. 1).

Püschel, Ulrich (2008): Kommunikativ-pragmatische Stilauffassungen / Communicative-Pragmatic Conceptions of Style. In: Ulla Fix / Andreas Gardt / Joachim Knape (ed.): Rhetorik und Stilistik / Rhetoric and Stylistics. Ein internationales Handbuch historischer und systematischer Forschung / An International Handbook of Historical and Systematic Research. 1. Halbbd. / Vol. 1. Berlin, New York, pp. 1023–1037 (= HSK. Handbücher zur Sprach- und Kommunikationswissenschaft / Handbooks of Linguistics and Communication Science 31. 1).

Quadlbauer, Franz (1962): Die antike Theorie der genera dicendi im lateinischen Mittelalter. Vienna (= Österreichische Akademie der Wissenschaften: Sitzungsberichte. Philosophisch-Historische Klasse 241. 2).

Quine, Willard van Orman (1960): Word and Object. Cambridge, MA (= Studies in Communication).

Quintilian, Marcus Fabius: Institutio Oratoria. In Four Volumes. With an Engl. Transl. by H. E. Butler. Reprinted. Cambridge, MA, London, 1963/1966/1966/1961 (= The Loeb Classical Library 124–127).

Rademacher, Lars (2006): Die Universalität des Reputationsbegriffs. Zur anthropologischen Grundlegung der Reputationskommunikation. In: Alexander Krylov (ed.): Zur Frage der Reputation. Dokumentation zur Internationalen Wissenschaftlichen Konferenz „Der Faktor Reputation in der internationalen Unternehmensführung". Bremen, pp. 43–48.

Ramming, Ulrike (2008): Der Ausdruck „Medium" an der Schnittstelle von Medien-, Wissenschafts- und Technikphilosophie. In: Stefan Münker / Alexander Roesler (ed.): Was ist ein Medium? Frankfurt a. M., pp. 249–271.

Ranke, Leopold (1824): Fürsten und Völker: Geschichten der romanischen und germanischen Völker von 1494–1514. Die Osmanen und die spanische Monarchie im 16. und 17. Jahrhundert. Ed. by Willy Andreas. Wiesbaden 1957.

Rath, Rainer (2001): Gesprächsschritt und Höreraktivitäten / Turns and Hearer Signals. In: Klaus Brinker / Gerd Antos / Wolfgang Heinemann / Sven F. Sager (ed.): Text- und Gesprächslinguistik / Linguistics of Text and Conversation. Ein internationales Handbuch zeitgenössischer Forschung / An International Handbook of Contemporary Research. 2. Halbbd. / Vol. 2. Berlin, New York, pp. 1213–1226 (= HSK. Handbücher zur Sprach- und Kommunikationswissenschaft / Handbooks of Linguistics and Communication Science 16. 2).

Richards, Ivor A. (1936): The Philosophy of Rhetoric. New York, Oxford 1965 (= The Mary Flexner Lectures on the Humanities 3; Galaxy Books 131) (Original: London, Oxford 1936).

Rieger, Stefan (2008): Der Frosch – ein Medium? In: Stefan Münker / Alexander Roesler (ed.): Was ist ein Medium? Frankfurt a. M., pp. 285–303.

Rolf, Eckard (1993): Die Funktionen der Gebrauchstextsorten. Berlin, New York (= Grundlagen der Kommunikation und Kognition / Foundations of Communication and Cognition).

Rüsen, Jörn (1982): Geschichtsschreibung als Theorieproblem der Geschichtswissenschaft. Skizze zum historischen Hintergrund der gegenwärtigen Diskussion. In: Reinhart Koselleck / Heinrich Lutz / Jörn Rüsen (ed.): Formen der Geschichtsschreibung. Munich, pp. 14–35 (= Beiträge zur Historik 4).

Sachs-Hombach, Klaus / Masuch, Maie (2007): Können Bilder uns überzeugen? In: Joachim Knape (ed.): Bildrhetorik. Baden-Baden, pp. 49–70 (= Saecvla Spiritalia 45).

Sacks, Harvey / Schegloff, Emanuel A. / Jefferson, Gail (1974): A Simplest Systematics for the Organisation of Turn-Taking for Conversation. In: Language 50, pp. 696–735.

Sager, Sven F. (1981): Sprache und Beziehung: Linguistische Untersuchungen zum Zusammenhang von sprachlicher Kommunikation und zwischenmenschlicher Beziehung. Tübingen (= Germanistische Linguistik 36).

Sager, Sven F. (2001): Gesprächssorte – Gesprächstyp – Gesprächsmuster – Gesprächsakt / Conversation Type – Conversation Pattern – Conversation Act. In: Klaus Brinker / Gerd Antos / Wolfgang Heinemann / Sven F. Sager (ed.): Text- und Gesprächslinguistik / Linguistics of Text and Conversation. Ein internationales Handbuch zeitgenössischer Forschung / An International Handbook of Contemporary Research. 2. Halbbd. / Vol. 2. Berlin, New York, pp. 1464–1471 (= HSK. Handbücher zur Sprach- und Kommunikationswissenschaft / Handbooks of Linguistics and Communication Science 16. 2).

Sandig, Barbara / Selting, Margret (1997): Discourse Styles. In: Teun A. van Dijk (ed.): Discourse as Structure and Process. London, pp. 138–156 (= Discourse Studies. A Multidisciplinary Introduction 1).

Schank, Gerd (1981): Untersuchungen zum Ablauf natürlicher Dialoge. Munich (= Heutiges Deutsch. Reihe 1: Linguistische Grundlagen 14).

Schank, Gerd / Schwitalla, Johannes (1987) (ed.): Konflikte in Gesprächen. Tübingen (= Tübinger Beiträge zur Linguistik 296).

Schanze, Helmut (2008): Rhetorik und Kinematographie. In: Renate Lachmann / Riccardo Nicolosi / Susanne Strätling (ed.): Rhetorik als kulturelle Praxis. Munich, pp. 241–253 (= Figuren 11).

Schiappa, Edward / Hamm, Jim (2007): Rhetorical Questions. In: Ian Worthington (ed.): A Companion to Greek Rhetoric. Malden, MA, pp. 3–15 (= Blackwell Companions to the Ancient World. Literature and Culture).

Schmitt, Reinhold (2003): Inszenieren: Struktur und Funktion eines gesprächsrhetorischen Verfahrens. In: Gesprächsforschung – Online-Zeitschrift zur verbalen Interaktion 4, pp. 186–250.

Schmitz, H. Walter (2000): „Hören Sie?" – Der Hörer als Gesprächskonstrukteur. In: Hans Rudi Fischer / Siegfried J. Schmidt (ed.): Wirklichkeit und Welterzeugung. In memoriam Nelson Goodman. Heidelberg, pp. 317–324.

Schneider, Johannes Nikolaus (2004): Ins Ohr geschrieben. Lyrik als akustische Kunst zwischen 1750 und 1800. Göttingen (= Das achtzehnte Jahrhundert. Supplementa 9).

Schopenhauer, Arthur (1851): Parerga and Paralipomena. Short Philosophical Essays. Vol. 2. Transl. by E. F. J. Payne. Oxford 2000 (German Original: Parerga und Paralipomena. Berlin 1851).

Schorno, Christian (2004): Autokommunikation. Selbstanrede als Abweichungs- bzw. Parallelphänomen der Kommunikation. Tübingen (= Rhetorik-Forschungen 15).

Schwarz-Friesel, Monika (2007): Sprache und Emotion. Tübingen, Basel.

Schwitalla, Johannes (1996): Beziehungsdynamik. Kategorien für die Beschreibung der Beziehungsgestaltung sowie der Selbst- und Fremddarstellung in einem Streit- und Schlichtungsgespräch. In: Werner Kallmeyer (ed.): Gesprächsrhetorik. Rhetorische Verfahren im Gesprächsprozeß. Tübingen, pp. 279–349 (= Studien zur deutschen Sprache 4).

Schwitalla, Johannes (2001): Konflikte und Verfahren ihrer Bearbeitung / Conflicts and Conflict Management. In: Klaus Brinker / Gerd Antos / Wolfgang Heinemann / Sven F. Sager (ed.): Text- und Gesprächslinguistik / Linguistics of Text and Conversation. Ein internationales Handbuch zeitgenössischer Forschung / An International Handbook of

Contemporary Research. 2. Halbbd. / Vol. 2. Berlin, New York, pp. 1374–1382 (= HSK. Handbücher zur Sprach- und Kommunikationswissenschaft / Handbooks of Linguistics and Communication Science 16. 2).

Schwitalla, Johannes (2008): Gesprächsstile / Conversational Styles. In: Ulla Fix / Andreas Gardt / Joachim Knape (ed.): Rhetorik und Stilistik / Rhetoric and Stylistics. Ein internationales Handbuch historischer und systematischer Forschung / An International Handbook of Historical and Systematic Research. 1. Halbbd. / Vol. 1. Berlin, New York, pp. 1054–1075 (= HSK. Handbücher zur Sprach- und Kommunikationswissenschaft / Handbooks of Linguistics and Communication Science 31. 1).

Seiter, John S. / Gass, Robert H. (2008): Compliance-Gaining Research: A Canonical Review / Streben nach Zustimmung: Forschungsfelder und -ansätze. In: Ulla Fix / Andreas Gardt / Joachim Knape (ed.): Rhetorik und Stilistik / Rhetoric and Stylistics. Ein internationales Handbuch historischer und systematischer Forschung / An International Handbook of Historical and Systematic Research. 1. Halbbd. / Vol. 1. Berlin, New York, pp. 812–825 (= HSK. Handbücher zur Sprach- und Kommunikationswissenschaft / Handbooks of Linguistics and Communication Science 31. 1).

Selting, Margret (2008): Interactional Stylistics and Style as a Contextualization Cue / Handlungsstilistik und Stil als Kontextualisierungssignal. In: Ulla Fix / Andreas Gardt / Joachim Knape (ed.): Rhetorik und Stilistik / Rhetoric and Stylistics. Ein internationales Handbuch historischer und systematischer Forschung / An International Handbook of Historical and Systematic Research. 1. Halbbd. / Vol. 1. Berlin, New York, pp. 1038–1053 (= HSK. Handbücher zur Sprach- und Kommunikationswissenschaft / Handbooks of Linguistics and Communication Science 31. 1).

Shakespeare's Sonnets (1997). Ed. by Katherine Duncan-Jones. Walton-on-Thames (= The Arden Shakespeare).

Shannon, Claude E. / Weaver, Warren (1949): The Mathematical Theory of Communication. Urbana, IL.

Shenkar, Oded / Yuchtman-Yaar, Ephraim (1997): Reputation, Image, Prestige, and Goodwill: An Interdisciplinary Approach to Organizational Standing. In: Human Relations 50, pp. 1361–1381.

Sinclair, Robert C. / Mark, Melvin M. / Clore, Gerald L. (1994): Mood-Related Persuasion Depends on (Mis)Attributions. In: Social Cognition 12, pp. 309–326.

Sornig, Karl (1986): Bemerkungen zu persuasiven Sprachstrategien. In: Franz Hundsnurscher / Edda Weigand (ed.): Dialoganalyse. Referate der 1. Arbeitstagung Münster 1986. Tübingen, pp. 249–263 (= Dialoganalyse 1; Linguistische Arbeiten 176).

Spiegel, Carmen / Spranz-Fogasy, Thomas (2001): Aufbau und Abfolge von Gesprächsphasen / The Construction and Ordering of Conversation Phases. In: Klaus Brinker / Gerd Antos / Wolfgang Heinemann / Sven F. Sager (ed.): Text- und Gesprächslinguistik / Linguistics of Text and Conversation. Ein internationales Handbuch zeitgenössischer Forschung / An International Handbook of Contemporary Research. 2. Halbbd. / Vol. 2. Berlin, New York, pp. 1241–1251 (= HSK. Handbücher zur Sprach- und Kommunikationswissenschaft / Handbooks of Linguistics and Communication Science 16. 2).

Spillner, Bernd (1974): Linguistik und Literaturwissenschaft. Stilforschung, Rhetorik, Textlinguistik. Stuttgart.

Spranz-Fogasy, Thomas (2003): Alles Argumentieren, oder was? Zur Konstitution von Argumentation in Gesprächen. In: Arnulf Deppermann / Martin Hartung (ed.):

Argumentieren in Gesprächen: Gesprächsanalytische Studien. Tübingen, pp. 27–39 (= Stauffenburg-Linguistik 28).

Stainton, Robert J. (2006) (ed.): Contemporary Debates in Cognitive Science. Malden, MA (= Contemporary Debates in Philosophy 7).

Stöckl, Hartmut (2001): Texts with a View – Windows onto the World. Notes on the Textuality of Pictures. In: Wolfgang Thiele / Albrecht Neubert / Christian Todenhagen (ed.): Text – Varieties – Translation. Tübingen, pp. 81–107 (= ZAA Studies 5).

Tannen, Deborah (1984): Conversational Style. Analyzing Talk Among Friends. Norwood, NJ (= Language and Learning for Human Service Professions).

Tiittula, Liisa (2001): Formen der Gesprächssteuerung / Forms of Conversation Management. In: Klaus Brinker / Gerd Antos / Wolfgang Heinemann / Sven F. Sager (ed.): Text- und Gesprächslinguistik / Linguistics of Text and Conversation. Ein internationales Handbuch zeitgenössischer Forschung / An International Handbook of Contemporary Research. 2. Halbbd. / Vol. 2. Berlin, New York, pp. 1361–1374 (= HSK. Handbücher zur Sprach- und Kommunikationswissenschaft / Handbooks of Linguistics and Communication Science 16. 2).

Toulmin, Stephen E. (1958): The Uses of Argument. Reprint. Cambridge 1974.

Trabant, Jürgen (2003): Mithridates im Paradies. Kleine Geschichte des Sprachdenkens. Munich.

Tyler, Stephen A. (1987): The Unspeakable: Discourse, Dialogue, and Rhetoric in the Postmodern World. Madison, WI (= Rhetoric of the Human Sciences).

van Dijk, Teun A. (1978): Textwissenschaft. Eine interdiziplinäre Einführung. Tübingen 1980 (Dutch Original: Tekstwetenschap. Een interdisciplinaire inleiding. Utrecht 1978).

van Eemeren, Frans H. / Grootendorst, Rob (2004): A Systematic Theory of Argumentation. The Pragma-Dialectical Approach. Cambridge.

van Eemeren, Frans H. / Houtlosser, Peter (2006): Strategic Maneuvering: A Synthetic Recapitulation. In: Argumentation 20, pp. 381–392.

van Eemeren, Frans H. / Houtlosser, Peter / Snoeck Henkemans, A. Francisca (2007): Argumentative Indicators. A Pragma-Dialectical Study. Dordrecht (= Argumentation Library 12).

Vickers, Brian (1984): Figures of rhetoric/Figures of music? In: Rhetorica. A Journal of the History of Rhetoric 2, pp. 1–44.

von Humboldt, Wilhelm (1836): On Language: The Diversity of Human Language-Structure and its Influence on the Mental Development of Mankind. Transl. by Peter Heath. New York 1988. (German Original: Über die Verschiedenheit des menschlichen Sprachbaues und ihren Einfluss auf die geistige Entwicklung des Menschengeschlechts. Berlin 1836)

Voswinkel, Stephan (2001): Anerkennung und Reputation. Die Dramaturgie industrieller Beziehungen. Mit einer Fallstudie zum „Bündnis für Arbeit". Konstanz (= Analyse und Forschung 24)

Wagner, Johannes / Petersen, Uwe Helm (1993): Zur Definition von Verhandeln. Unter besonderer Berücksichtigung von Gesprächsverhandlungen. In: Bernd-Dietrich Müller (ed.): Interkulturelle Wirtschaftskommunikation. 2nd ed. Munich, pp. 261–275 (= Studium Deutsch als Fremdsprache – Sprachdidaktik 9).

Wagner, Klaus R. (1978): Sprechplanung: Empirie, Theorie und Didaktik der Sprecherstrategien. Frankfurt a. M.

Wang, Bo (2004): A Survey of Research in Asian Rhetoric. In: Rhetoric Review 23, p. 171–181.

Warburg, Aby (1920): Heidnisch-antike Weissagung in Wort und Bild zu Luthers Zeiten. Heidelberg (= Sitzungsberichte der Heidelberger Akademie der Wissenschaften. Stiftung

Heinrich Lanz. Philosophisch-historische Klasse. Jahrgang 1919, 26. Abhandlung). In: Aby M. Warburg: Ausgewählte Schriften und Würdigungen. Ed. by Dieter Wuttke. 3rd ed. Baden-Baden 1992, pp. 199–304 (= SAECVLA SPIRITALIA 1).

Ward, John O. (1972): Artificiosa Eloquentia in the Middle Ages. Unpublished Ph.D.-Thesis: University of Toronto.

Watzlawick, Paul / Beavin, Janet H. / Jackson, Don D. (1967): Pragmatics of Human Communication. A Study of Interactional Patterns, Pathologies, and Paradoxes. New York.

Weber, Volker (1993): Anekdote. Die andere Geschichte. Erscheinungsformen der Anekdote in der deutschen Literatur, Geschichtsschreibung und Philosophie. Tübingen (= Stauffenburg-Colloquium 26).

Wegener, Bernd (1985): Gibt es Sozialprestige? In: Zeitschrift für Soziologie 14, pp. 209–235.

Weigand, Edda (1986): Dialogisches Grundprinzip und Textklassifikation. In: Franz Hundsnurscher / Edda Weigand (ed.): Dialoganalyse. Referate der 1. Arbeitstagung Münster 1986. Tübingen, pp. 115–125 (= Linguistische Arbeiten 176).

Weigand, Edda (2008) (ed.): Dialogue and Rhetoric. Amsterdam (= Dialogue Studies = DS 2).

Weisler, Steven E. / Milekic, Slavko (2000): Theory of Language. Cambridge, MA.

Welch, Kathleen E. (1987): A Critique of Classical Rhetoric: The Contemporary Appropriation of Ancient Discourse. In: Rhetoric Review 6, pp. 79–86.

White, Hayden (1978a): Tropics of Discourse. Essays in Cultural Criticism. Baltimore.

White, Hayden (1978b): The Historical Text as Literary Artefact. In: Hayden White: Tropics of Discourse. Baltimore, pp. 81–101.

Whitney, William Dwight (1875): The Life and Growth of Language. London.

Whorf, Benjamin Lee (1956): Language, Thought, and Reality: Selected Writings of Benjamin Lee Whorf. Ed. and with an Introd. by John B. Carroll. New York (= Technology Press Books in the Social Sciences).

Wiesing, Lambert (2008): Was sind Medien? In: Stefan Münker / Alexander Roesler (ed.): Was ist ein Medium? Frankfurt a. M., pp. 235–248.

Wilson, Blake / Buelow, George J. / Hoyt, Peter A. (2001): Rhetoric and Music. In: The New Grove Dictionary of Music and Musicians 21 (2nd ed.), pp. 260–275.

Winkler, Hartmut (2008): Zeichenmaschinen. Oder warum die semiotische Dimension für eine Definition der Medien unerlässlich ist. In: Stefan Münker / Alexander Roesler (ed.): Was ist ein Medium? Frankfurt a. M., pp. 211–221.

Winko, Simone / Jannidis, Fotis / Lauer, Gerhard (2009) (ed.): Grenzen der Literatur. Berlin, New York (= Revisionen – Grundbegriffe der Literaturtheorie 2).

Wirth, Uwe (1999): Diskursive Dummheit. Abduktion und Komik als Grenzphänomene des Verstehens. Heidelberg (= Frankfurter Beiträge zur Germanistik 33).

Wittgenstein, Ludwig (1921): Tractatus Logico-Philosophicus. The German Text of Ludwig Wittgenstein's Logisch-philosophische Abhandlung with a New Transl. by D. F. Pears and B. F. McGuinness and with the Introd. by Bertrand Russell. 2nd ed. London, New York 1963 (= International Library of Philosophy and Scientific Method). (German Original: Logisch-Philosophische Abhandlung. In: Annalen der Naturphilosophie 14. Issue 3/4, 1921, pp. 185–262).

Wittgenstein, Ludwig (1953): Philosophical Investigations. Transl. by G. E. M. Anscombe. 3rd ed. Reprint. Malden, MA, 1994 (German Original: Philosophische Untersuchungen. Oxford 1953).

Wolf, Ricarda (1999): Soziale Positionierung im Gespräch. In: Deutsche Sprache 27, pp. 69–94.

Wörner, Markus H. (1981): ‚Pathos' als Überzeugungsmittel in der Rhetorik des Aristoteles. In: Ingrid Craemer-Ruegenberg (ed.): Pathos, Affekt, Gefühl. Philosophische Beiträge. Freiburg, pp. 53–78.

Wörner, Markus H. (1984): Selbstrepräsentation im „Ethos des Redners". Ein Beitrag der aristotelischen Rhetorik zur Untersuchung der Grundlagen sprachlichen Handelns. In: Zeitschrift für Sprachwissenschaft 3, pp. 43–64.

Worthington, Ian (2007) (ed.): A Companion to Greek Rhetoric. Malden, MA.

Wu, Hui (2009): Lost and Found in Transnation: Modern Conceptualization of Chinese Rhetoric. In: Rhetoric Review 28, pp. 148–166.

Wünsch, Marianne (1999): Narrative und rhetorische Strukturen im Bild. Das Beispiel der Werbung. In: Horst Brunner / Claudia Händl / Ernst Hellgardt / Monika Schulz (ed.): helle döne schöne. Versammelte Arbeiten zur älteren und neueren deutschen Literatur. Festschrift für Wolfgang Walliczek. Göppingen, pp. 323–359 (= Göppinger Arbeiten zur Germanistik 668).

Wuthenow, Asa-Bettina (2009): Rhetoric in Japan / Rhetorik in Japan. In: Barbara Mittler / Asa-Bettina Wuthenow: Rhetoric and Stylistics in East Asia / Rhetorik und Stilistik in Ostasien. In: Ulla Fix / Andreas Gardt / Joachim Knape (ed.): Rhetorik und Stilistik / Rhetoric and Stylistics. Ein internationales Handbuch historischer und systematischer Forschung / An International Handbook of Historical and Systematic Research. 2. Halbbd. / Vol. 2. Berlin, New York, pp. 2027–2039, here: pp. 2032–2037 (= HSK. Handbücher zur Sprach- und Kommunikationswissenschaft / Handbooks of Linguistics and Communication Science 31. 2).

Ying, H. G. (2000): The Origin of Contrastive Rhetoric Revisited. In: International Journal of Applied Linguistics 10, pp. 259–268.

Ying, H. G. (2001): On the Origins of Contrastive Rhetoric: A Reply to Matsuda. In: International Journal of Applied Linguistics 11, pp. 261–266.

Index